A 52-Week Bible Journey

ROUTE 52

Explore
Bible People

52 Bible Lessons for Ages 4–6

Kathy Downs

Standard
PUBLISHING

Cincinnati, Ohio

▾ About the Author ▴

Kathy Downs, the wife of a minister and the mother of three children, has worked with children for more than thirty years. She has taught in public and Christian schools, written curriculum and children's books, and is currently teaching first grade in a Christian school in Arizona. She feels that all children learn best when they are actively involved in the learning process. Thus active learning was the foundation for creating this curriculum.

▾ Dedication ▴

To my special friend and prayer partner, Jennie Porter, for praying with me and for me during the writing of this book, and for the many hours she spent proofreading and encouraging me.

This book is a revision of *The Bible Teaches Me* (42034).

Permission is granted to reproduce the indicated material from this book for ministry purposes only.

Scripture taken from the *International Children's Bible*®. Copyright © 1986, 1988, 1999 by Thomas Nelson, Inc. Used by permission. All rights reserved.

Editors: Karen Brewer, Theresa Hayes
Cover Designer: Malwitz Design
Interior Illustrator: Daniel A. Grossmann
Template Designer: Andrew Quach

Published by Standard Publishing, Cincinnati, Ohio
www.standardpub.com

Copyright © 2003 by Standard Publishing.
All rights reserved. #45204. Manufactured in Benton Harbor, MI, USA, December 2012.
Printed in the United States of America.

17 16 15 14 13 12   10 11 12 13 14 15 16 17 18

ISBN-13: 978-0-7847-1323-5
ISBN-10: 0-7847-1323-5

Introduction

There are many things in this world influencing children (and adults). The most influential are people. Many young children want to grow up to be just like daddy, mommy, a certain community helper, a special teacher, a movie star, or a sports hero. Some of these people might be good influences, but many are not. Where can a child go to find a hero worth modeling? The Bible. Its pages are filled with people who encountered the same struggles children are facing, or will face as they mature. Through the lives of Bible heroes, children can see God's goodness, love, and guidance.

In a generation that is struggling to find some purpose in life, only God's Word can provide direction. David said, "Your word is like a lamp for my feet and a light for my way" (Psalm 119:105). Only God shines the true light for us to follow. Many people in the Bible found this to be true and followed His light. These are the people who should be the role models and heroes for children (and adults).

Each unit in this curriculum features ordinary people empowered by God to do extraordinary things. Half of the units are from the Old Testament and half are from the New Testament, with special lessons for Christmas and Easter.

What's Unique About *Explore Bible People*?

It is designed to actively involve children in the learning process.

Preschool children use all five senses to explore and discover information. Children at this age are wiggly, noisy, touchy, feely, animated beings. You teach them according to the way God made them. You provide wiggle and noisy times. You give them objects to touch, feel, and even taste. All activities must be lively and fun. These small people have a huge desire for adventure. The goal of each lesson is to direct the children's five senses to that teachable moment when their minds say, "We understand!"

There are no worksheets in this book. Instead you will find lots of suggested movement, things to create, games to play, songs to sing, and fun foods to taste.

The lesson plans are perforated so they can be removed from the book and photocopied.

Everything you need is printed on pull-out pages. Make enough copies for each leader to have a set. A brief planning session is all you need for team teaching. Each leader then plans and prepares his or her own section. All leaders help the assigned leader. Even if you teach alone, the four-step lesson plan will help you stay on track. There will be times when you will need extra hands. Consider involving parents whenever possible.

Reproducible pages follow the lesson plans.

Visuals, crafts, and games are printed on reproducible pages. No extra purchases are required. Photocopy a few or many. Use year after year.

The materials are non-consumable, so originals can be filed and reused.

Set up a filing system. Use thirteen folders for filing the units, or make a file for each lesson. As you prepare, store any reproduced material in the appropriate folder. After a lesson is taught, drop the lesson plans and any leftover materials in the folder.

You will be asked to make overhead projector transparencies for Units 2, 4, 6, 7, 8, 10, and 11. The transparencies will be used to provide background scenery for dramas, shadow stories, and a mural. Two of them are for teaching sign language. Be sure to save these transparencies for future use.

How is *Explore Bible People* Organized?

Each unit deals with an aspect of everyday life. The goals are expressed in three aims—Know (knowledge), Feel (attitudes and feelings), and Do (action). Knowledge is direction for the mind. New attitudes and feelings develop and mature in the heart. The end result is to take action directed by the mind and the heart.

Each lesson involves the children in activities that accomplish the unit and lesson goals. The amount of time needed to complete each activity will vary according to the age of the children in the class and the number of children doing the activity at one time.

Step 1, "What is this story about?" provides foundational activities on which to build the lesson's theme. Sometimes these activities impart knowledge and other times they explore attitudes. These activities may sometimes be used as centers, operating at the same time, allowing children choices.

Step 2, "What does the Bible say?" examines a person who was empowered by God to think and act in extraordinary ways. Directions for visuals are given at the beginning of each story. It will be important to provide these. Four-, five-, and six-year-olds need visual help to enhance auditory input. This step also includes a story review activity and a Bible memory activity.

Step 3, "What does this mean to me?" will help the children make a direct connection between the Bible person's response to God's will and their own possible responses.

Step 4, "What can I do to please God?" provides an opportunity for each child to respond to the lesson. This step may also include wrap-up activities to clean the room and sum up.

Each unit contains a song written especially for that unit's theme and goals. The tunes are familiar children's songs. The words are simple and easy to memorize. Use these songs to put the message from the Bible into the hearts of children. When it is in their hearts, they can deliver it to friends and family.

▼ Table of Contents ▲

Learning from New Testament People

Learning About Christmas and Easter

	Unit Title	Scripture	Application	Memory Verse
Unit 1	Learning That I Am Special	**Genesis 37** (*Joseph's dreams*) **Genesis 37** (*Joseph's brothers*) **Genesis 39–41** (*Joseph's special job*) **Genesis 41–43** (*Joseph's family comes*)	Praise God for creating us special; show love to others and be a good worker.	**Psalm 139:14** "I praise you because you made me in an amazing and wonderful way."
Unit 2	Learning to Trust God	**Judges 6** (*God chooses Gideon*) **Judges 6** (*Gideon learns to trust*) **Judges 7** (*Gideon obeys God*) **Judges 7** (*trusting God to win*)	Trust in God when afraid; worship God with songs and prayers.	**Proverbs 3:5** "Trust the Lord with all your heart."
Unit 3	Learning to Do What Is Right	**Nehemiah 1, 2** (*asking God for help*) **Nehemiah 2** (*asking others to help*) **Nehemiah 3, 4, 6** (*doing right*) **Nehemiah 8** (*thanking God*)	Pray before making decisions; ask God for help to do right.	**Deuteronomy 6:18** "Do what the Lord says is good and right. Then things will go well for you."
Unit 4	Learning to Be Brave	**Esther 2** (*Esther becomes queen*) **Esther 3, 4** (*in danger*) **Esther 5, 7** (*Esther is brave*) **Esther 8** (*saving God's people*) **Esther 9** (*celebrate Purim*)	Choose to be brave when afraid.	**Genesis 28:15** "I am with you, and I will protect you everywhere you go."
Unit 5	Learning to Pray Always	**Daniel 1** (*refuses king's food*) **Daniel 6** (*Daniel prays*) **Daniel 6** (*in danger*) **Daniel 6** (*Daniel saved*)	Choose to pray anytime and anywhere.	**Psalm 17:6** "I call to you, God, and you answer me."
Unit 6	Learning to Obey God	**Jonah 1** (*disobeyed*) **Jonah 1, 2** (*listened*) **Jonah 3** (*to Nineveh*) **Jonah 4** (*taught to love*)	Choose to listen to and obey God.	**Jeremiah 26:13** "You must start doing good things. You must obey the Lord your God."
Unit 7	Learning to Love	**Matthew 19; Mark 10; Luke 18** (*Jesus loves the children*) **John 11** (*Mary, Martha, Lazarus*) **John 12** (*Mary loves Jesus*) **John 13** (*Jesus loves his friends*)	Choose to show love for Jesus and others.	**1 John 3:18** "We should show . .-.-love by what we do."

	Unit Title	Scripture	Application	Memory Verse
Unit 8	**Learning to Be Happy**	**Luke 15; Psalm 23** (happy shepherd) **Luke 15** (happy woman) **Luke 15** (happy father) **John 14; Revelation 1, 2, 4, 5, 21, 22** (happy forever)	Tell others about the happiness God gives.	**James 5:13** "If one of you is having troubles, he should pray. If one of you is happy, he should sing praises."
Unit 9	**Learning to Be Thankful**	**Luke 2** (Simeon and Anna thank God) **Matthew 6; Psalm 136** (thanks for food, clothes) **Acts 3, 4** (thanks for healthy bodies) **Luke 17** (man with leprosy thanks)	Say thank-you to God.	**Psalm 136:1** "Give thanks to the Lord because he is good. His love continues forever."
Unit 10	**Learning to Share**	**Matthew 14; John 6** (a boy shares) **Luke 20, 21** (a woman shares) **Matthew 28; Acts 1, 2, 4** (the church shares) **Acts 18; Romans 16** (Aquila and Priscilla share)	Share joyfully with others.	**Hebrews 13:16** "Do not forget to do good to others. And share with them what you have."
Unit 11	**Learning to Help Others**	**Mark 5** (Jesus heals a girl) **Mark 2** (four friends help) **Mark 4** (Jesus helps his friends) **Luke 10** (a Samaritan helps) **Acts 9** (Dorcas helps others)	Be helpful to family, friends, and others.	**Luke 6:31** "Do for other people what you want them to do for you."
Unit 12	**Learning to Follow Jesus**	**Luke 19** (Zacchaeus gives) **Luke 22; John 21** (Peter is sorry) **Acts 16** (Philippian jailer) **Philemon** (Onesimus)	Make right choices.	**1 Peter 2:21** "Christ . . . gave you an example to follow. So you should do as he did."
Unit 13	**Learning to Worship Jesus**	**Genesis 3; Luke 2; Matthew 2** (Jesus is born) **Matthew 28; Mark 16** (Jesus is alive)	Tell others about Jesus, choose to worship Jesus.	**John 3:16** "For God loved the world so much that he gave his only Son."

Learning That I Am Special

Unit Bible Words

"I praise you because you made me [in an amazing and wonderful way]" (Psalm 139:14).

(Note: This verse has been divided into two parts. If you are teaching four-year-olds, use only the first part. If you are teaching older children, also include the part of the verse in brackets.)

Bible Character
Joseph

1   Joseph Dreams That He Is Special

Genesis 37:1-11—Jealousy and anger are kindled in the hearts of Joseph's brothers as God begins to reveal His special plan for Joseph. The children will begin learning about how uniquely they were created.

2   Joseph's Brothers Are Jealous

Genesis 37:4, 8, 11-36—God's plan for Joseph begins to unfold when his jealous brothers finally succeed in getting rid of him. The children will learn the importance of working together as a family.

3   Joseph Is Given a Special Job

Genesis 39–41—Everywhere Joseph goes, God's blessing is upon the household or the situation. Joseph is a good worker, and God takes care of him. The children will learn God is always with them, helping them to do their best.

4   Joseph Is Special

Genesis 41:56, 57; 42; 43—Finally God reveals to Joseph and his brothers that indeed he is special. He had been given the job of saving his entire family and the nation of Egypt from starving to death. The children will learn the importance of having a loving heart.

By the end of this unit, the children and leaders will

Know: A Bible person whom God chose for a very special job.
Feel: That God made people in a special way and has a plan for their lives.
Do: Praise God for creating people special by showing love to others and being good workers.

Why Teach This Unit to Four- to Six-Year-Olds?

All people have a basic need to feel good about themselves. Children develop their sense of self-worth based on the way others see them and treat them. Unfortunately, adults sometimes treat children with disrespect, and other children can be extremely cruel. You can help the children in your classroom to understand that they are created by God, and are pleasing to Him. Didn't God use the words "very good" to describe how He felt at the end of the sixth day when He created man and woman?

Four-, five-, and six-year-olds are beginning to have experiences outside the home. They are interacting with peers and adults. They need positive experiences that will help them form positive opinions of themselves, so that they will behave in a positive manner toward others. Negative experiences will only cause them to build defensive walls.

Use this unit to create an environment where the basic needs of children are met. In this environment, affirm each child as a special creation of God. Remind them they are loved and valued by God, by their families, and by you. Encourage them to try new things such as meeting new friends, eating new foods, and participating in new activities. Listen to their stories. Laugh at their jokes. Praise them sincerely and love them dearly.

Meet Joseph

Joseph was second to the youngest of Jacob's twelve sons. Even though his birth order position in the family was low, he was his father's favorite son. Jacob honored Joseph by presenting him with a beautiful coat, the kind men of high position wore. From then on his brothers' hearts were filled with jealousy toward him.

Joseph was also a person who was special in the eyes of his heavenly Father. While Joseph was still a teen-ager, God began preparing him for a very important job. Joseph eventually saved an entire nation and his own family from starvation, but he had to endure his jealous brothers, deep pits, slavery, betrayal, and prison before he achieved that position of power. Through it all Joseph believed he was special. God repeatedly showed him how unique he was.

When children hear the story of Joseph, they will learn about a powerful God who loves and cares for each person He has created. They will learn they are very special—just the way they are!

Unit Songs

The Lord Made Me
(Tune: "This Is the Day")

Verse 1
These are my arms, these are my arms
that the Lord has made, that the Lord has made.
I'll praise the Lord, I'll praise the Lord
for my arms that wave, for my arms that wave.
These are my arms that the Lord has made;
I'll praise the Lord for my arms that wave.
These are my arms, these are my arms
that the Lord has made.

Use these phrases for additional verses, or make up
    your own:

These are my legs that the Lord has made.
I'll praise the Lord for my legs that run.
*(Use "bend" for children with disabilities, or sing about
    other attributes.)*

These are my eyes . . .
. . . for my eyes that see.

These are my ears . . .
. . . for my ears that hear.

This is my tongue . . .
. . . for a tongue that tastes.

This Is My Job
(Tune: "This Is the Day")

Verse 1
This is my job, this is my job,
I can pick up toys, I can pick up toys.
This is my job, this is my job,
I can do it well, I can do it well.
This is my job, I can pick up toys;
This is my job, I can do it well.
This is my job, this is my job,
I can do it well.

For other verses use these jobs:
I can sweep the floor.
I can wipe and dust.
I can wash the car.
I can rake the yard.
I can take out trash.
I can feed the dog.
I can make my bed.

Joseph Dreams That He Is Special

Genesis 37:1-11

▼ 1. What Is This Story About? ▲

Families Count

You will need pink and blue chenille wires for every child.

Help each child make a wire figure for each person (parents and children) in his family. (Make some figures ahead of time if your class is mostly four-year-olds.) Make blue figures for boys and pink for girls.

Gather all the blue figures in a pile and count them. Do the same for the pink ones. Ask, **Are there more girls or more boys? From the blue pile, pick out the correct number of boys in your family, including your father. From the pink pile, pick out the correct number of girls in your family, including your mother. Whose family has the most boys? The most girls? Now let's each make a pile for the number of children in your family who are old enough to go to school. Let's count them.** If you have time, continue to name special groups and count them. As you play, talk about families. **I am glad that God gave each of us a family. Let's pray for our families and thank God for them.** Lead the children in prayer.

Joseph and Me

You will need the words to "The Lord Made Me" from p. 10, two copies of the jointed figure from p. 25 for each child, scissors, crayons and markers, thirteen paper fasteners per child, glue, and scraps of cloth.

Cut out the pieces for the jointed figures before the session. *Note: save this art for use again in Unit 9.*

Have the children join the arms and legs of the two cutouts with paper fasteners. Then have them draw their own face on one figure and the face of Joseph on the other figure. Scraps of cloth can be glued on the figures for clothing. Join one hand of the Joseph figure to the hand of the child's figure with a paper fastener.

God made your body and Joseph's body in an amazing way. He had a special plan for Joseph when he grew up and He has a special plan for you.

Sing "The Lord Made Me," using the figures to demonstrate the waving and running actions.

▼ 2. What Does the Bible Say? ▲

Bible Story: Joseph the Dreamer

You will need a sample of the jointed figure of Joseph from p. 25 (see the activity "Joseph and Me," above), a coat for Joseph made of construction paper or cloth, and four plain white paper plates.

On the first plate, draw twelve faces. On the second plate, draw a colorful long-sleeved coat. On the third plate, draw a bundle of wheat standing up. On the fourth plate, draw a stick person in the center and place eleven stars, the sun and the moon circling the figure.

Say, **Jacob was the father of a big family. He had twelve sons.** (*Show the*

Know: A Bible person whom God chose for a very special job.
Feel: That God made people in a special way and has a plan for their lives.
Do: Praise God for creating people special by showing love to others and being good workers.

Children will accomplish the goals when they

- Tell about their families.
- Describe Joseph's dreams and tell how his family felt about them.
- Begin to memorize Psalm 139:14.
- Name ways they are special to God.
- Praise God for creating them.

first paper plate. Ask the children to count the number of faces.) **One son named Joseph was born when Jacob was very old. Jacob loved all of his sons, but Joseph was very special to his old father. To show Joseph how much he loved him, Jacob gave him a beautiful coat.** *(Show the second plate.)* **This coat was a special gift to Joseph.**

Do you think the other sons were happy that Joseph had been given such a pretty coat? No, they were mad! They grumbled, "That is not fair!" The brothers said many unkind things about their younger brother, Joseph.

One night Joseph had a dream. *(Show third plate.)* **In his dream Joseph and his brothers were in a field tying up bundles of wheat. Joseph's bundle of wheat stood in the center and the brothers' bundles gathered around. The brothers' bundles did an unusual thing. They bowed down to Joseph's bundle.**

The next morning Joseph told his brothers about the dream. He said, "Your bundles of wheat bowed down to my bundle of wheat." When the brothers heard this, they angrily said, "Do you think you are going to be a king and be in charge of us?"

Joseph had another dream. *(Show fourth plate.)* **In this dream eleven stars, the sun, and the moon bowed down to him. Joseph again told his family about this dream. Even his father scolded him saying, "Do you think your mother, your brothers, and I will bow down to you?"**

(Show third and fourth plates.) **These dreams made the brothers more jealous. But Jacob, his father, tried to figure out what they meant.**

The dreams were part of God's special plan for Joseph. We will find out later what that plan was.

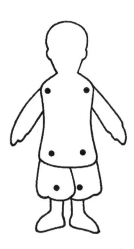

Story Review: Stars and More Stars

You will need star-shaped cereal or graham crackers, and wheat crackers. (If star-shaped cereal or graham crackers are not available, use a star cookie cutter to cut wheat bread and spread with margarine.)

Explain to the children that the snacks remind us of Joseph's dream: the stars in the sky and the bundles of wheat.

Offer a prayer for the snack. As the children eat the star-shaped snack and the wheat crackers, review the Bible story. Use the following questions:

How many sons did Jacob have?
What was the name of Jacob's favorite son?
What kind of gift did Jacob give Joseph?
What happened in Joseph's first dream?
What happened in his second dream?
What did his family think about his dreams?

Bible Words

"I praise you because you made me [in an amazing and wonderful way]" (Psalm 139:14).

(Note: This verse has been divided into two parts. If you are teaching four-year-olds, use only the first part. If you are teaching older children, also include the part of the verse in brackets.)

Bible Memory: Amazing Rhythm

Have the children sit on the floor in pairs, facing each other. Teach the rhythm in the right-hand column on p. 10 using the Bible words for this unit. Use the actions to pat your knees, clap your hands, and slap ("high five") your partner's hands.

We know that God made us because the Bible tells us He did. When God made Joseph, He had a special plan for him. When God made you, He had a special plan, too. As you grow, God will show you what His special plan is.

▼ 3. What Does This Mean to Me? ▲

God Has a Special Plan for You

God has a special plan for you. Part of His plan is for your body to grow bigger and stronger, and for you to learn to do more and more things. Ever since the day you were born, your body has been following God's plan. You do not remember learning to crawl and walk, but you have seen babies learning to crawl and walk. Ask a couple of children to demonstrate how babies crawl and learn to walk. As you continue the discussion, ask children to demonstrate their abilities. **Now you can walk, jump, and run. You can also talk very well, but when you were younger you could not talk very well. When you were one and two years old, you learned to say and understand new words every day. What were some of the first words you learned to say?**

Do you remember learning to ride a tricycle? Who helped you learn to ride a tricycle?

I'm going to act out some things that you can do now that you could not do before your last birthday. (Pantomime riding a bike, buttoning your shirt, tying your shoe. Ask the children to guess what you are doing.) **Who would like to act out something that you could not do when you were little, but that you can do now? The rest of us will try to guess what you are doing!** (Let the children demonstrate such activities as riding a bike or swimming. You might want to whisper some suggestions to willing volunteers.)

God's plan is for you to continue to grow. You will learn to do many things. What would you like to be able to do by the time you are eight? Twelve? Sixteen? What would you like to be when you grow up?

God will always be with you and help you do the things in His plan.

"I	(pat)
praise	(clap)
you	(slap)
because	(pat)
you	(clap)
made	(slap)
me	(pat)
[in	(clap)
an	(slap)
amazing	(pat)
and	(clap)
wonderful	(slap)
way]"	(pat)
(Psalm	(clap)
139:	(clap)
14).	(clap)

The Lord Made Me

You will need the words to the unit song, "The Lord Made Me," p. 10.

Gather the children together as you sing "The Lord Made Me." Say, **Every day is made by the Lord God and is special. Today is special. The day you were born was special, too. Let's find out when everyone's birthday is. If you were born in January, stand up.** Continue naming every month. Many children at this age may not know their birth date. Try to get birth dates when parents bring their children to class. Make comments about children born in the same month, on the same day, and on holidays. **God made you. Your birthday is even more special because God made you. When He made you, He gave you arms, legs, eyes, ears, and even a tongue. Here are new words for the song, "This Is the Day." The words praise God for making you.** Teach the unit song, "The Lord Made Me."

▼ 4. What Can I Do to Please God? ▲

Thank You God for Making Me

You will need the words to "The Lord Made Me," left.

Have the children demonstrate how strong their bodies are by helping you clean up the classroom. Make comments about how "amazing" and "wonderful" their arms, fingers, hands, and legs are.

Gather the children in a circle to sing "The Lord Made Me." Ask the children to add new words that tell other things their bodies can do.

Before the children leave, have a special prayer time so the children can thank God for one of the amazing things their bodies can do. Encourage each child to pray. Give help as needed.

▼ Bonus Activity ▲

Extra Action! Take a Bow

You will need a wide playing area. Mark off two parallel lines fifteen to twenty feet apart.

To play this tag game, divide the children into two groups. One group will be the "stars" and the other "wheat." Select one child to be "Joseph," the tagger. The stars and wheat stand side by side on the same line. Joseph will stand in the middle of the playing area. Joseph calls, "Stars, stars take a bow!" When the tagger says "bow," the stars bow and then run across the playing area to the other line. Joseph tags as many stars as he can. The tagged stars join Joseph as taggers. Joseph calls, "Wheat, wheat take a bow!" Each wheat bows and runs to the other line. The game continues until everyone has been tagged. A new Joseph is chosen and the game starts over.

To help the children calm down and review the story, ask, **Joseph had two dreams. In one dream, eleven bundles of wheat bowed down to him. In another dream the sun, moon, and eleven stars bowed down to him. Why did this anger his brothers?**

Joseph's Brothers Are Jealous

Genesis 37:4, 8, 11-36

▼ 1. What Is This Story About? ▲

Made by God

You will need play dough (purchased or made with the recipe on page 16) a strip of butcher paper, a dark marker, and the words to "The Lord Made Me" from p. 14.

Ask each child to make a play dough figure that looks like him or her. As they are working, sing "The Lord Made Me" and discuss how God made their arms, hands, and fingers in just the right way so that they can shape the play dough. Then tell the children, **Now put one hand behind your back and continue working on your figure.** (*Wait for someone to complain.*) **What? It's too hard? Yes, it is hard to work with only one hand. God knew you would need two arms and two hands. God had a special plan when He made your body. He made every part that you would need to work and play.** Be sensitive to children while doing this activity. Praise each child for his effort. Lead the children in praising God for the wonderful way He created their bodies.

Display the completed figures on a strip of butcher paper and print the children's names by their figures. (Optional: Let them dry and paint them.)

▼ 2. What Does the Bible Say? ▲

Bible Story: The Brothers Sell Joseph

You will need the jointed figure of Joseph made for Lesson 1 Bible Story and a sample of "Joseph in the Pit" that children will make during the Story Review activity for this lesson. Use these as you tell the story.

Joseph had eleven brothers. His father, Jacob, was old when Joseph was born. Jacob loved Joseph very much. This made his brothers jealous. (*Show the jointed figure from Lesson 1.*)

The brothers were even more jealous after Joseph told them about his two dreams. In the dreams Joseph's family bowed down to him as though he were a king.

Jacob owned many sheep. He sent ten of his sons to take care of his large flock of sheep. Jacob worried about their being so far from home. He sent Joseph to check on them.

Joseph had to walk a long way to find his brothers. The brothers were not happy to see their younger brother. They made fun of him and called him "The Dreamer."

The brothers decided to get rid of Joseph. (*Illustrate with the "Joseph in the Pit."*) **First, they put him into a deep hole in the ground. Then, when some travelers came by, the brothers sold Joseph to them, to be a slave.**

The brothers knew that their father, Jacob, would want to know where Joseph was, so they made up a big lie. They killed a goat and put the goat's blood on Joseph's beautiful coat. Then they took the coat home and showed it to their father. "Oh no!" Jacob cried, "He must have been killed by a wild animal!" Jacob tore his clothes to show how very sad he was, and no one could comfort him.

Know: A Bible person whom God chose for a very special job.

Feel: That God made people in a special way and has a plan for their lives.

Do: Praise God for creating people special by showing love to others and being good workers.

Children will accomplish the goals when they

- Describe how families work together.
- Tell about the problem Joseph had with his brothers.
- Memorize Psalm 139:14.
- Name ways God takes care of them and their families.
- Praise God for creating their bodies.

Note: If you have a child with a physical disability in your classroom, talk to his or her parents about this lesson before you present it. Find out from them how best to handle this lesson. Some children who have disabilities are willing to talk about why they are the way they are; others are not. The child with a disability may be eager to show his friends how he copes, or he may not. Be prepared for the other children to ask you why God didn't give their friend hands or legs that work. For more information on this subject, see Jim Pierson's book, *Exceptional Teaching* (03769).

In Egypt, the travelers sold Joseph to a very important man. God had a special job for Joseph and living in Egypt was part of His plan. God was taking care of Joseph.

Story Review: Joseph in the Pit

For each child you will need a plain 8 oz. Styrofoam cup, a craft stick, glue, crayons, and a figure of Joseph from p. 25.

Have the children color the cup and Joseph. Then glue Joseph to the craft stick. Make a slit in the bottom of the cup for the craft stick. Hide Joseph in the pit (cup). Let the children tell the story about Joseph's being put in the pit. Explain the word "pit." Talk about how Joseph got out of the pit. As you work, talk about the story. **Even when Joseph was put in the pit, God was taking care of him. What happened when the brothers saw a group of travelers on their way to Egypt?**

Bible Memory: It's Amazing!

Have the children stand so that they can move without bumping into each other.

The Bible tells us God made our bodies in an amazing way. Exercising helps us take good care of our bodies. It helps our muscles to grow stronger. Learning God's Word is good for us, too. The Bible tells us that praising God is good for us. We are happiest when we are praising God. Let's exercise and praise God for making us. Follow me and I will lead you in some exercises that we can do while we learn Psalm 139:14.

Do simple exercises as you say the Bible words. Let the children take turns leading an exercise and saying the Bible words from memory.

▼ 3. What Does This Mean to Me? ▲

Ways God Cares

You will need a tray and ten small items that represent a way that God cares for us, such as a raw vegetable, a sock, a toy car, an empty medicine bottle, a leaf, a flower, a small container of water, a picture of a family, a plastic egg, a toy house, or anything else.

When Joseph was in the deep hole in the ground, God took care of him. When the travelers took Joseph to Egypt and sold him, God was with him. God is always with us. Even when bad things happen to us, God knows, and He cares. Knowing that God loves us can help us get through the bad times. Look at the things on this tray. Point to something on the tray and tell us how it shows that God cares for you. Discuss all the ways these items show that God cares.

Now remove the tray full of items from view. Secretly take one thing off the tray. Let the children see the tray again. Ask, **What is missing from the tray?** When the children guess the missing item, review how that item shows a way God cares for them. Then remove another item. Play as long as the children remain interested.

Who Can Help?

You will need two copies of the game pieces from pp. 26 and 27 for each game. Mount these pieces on poster board with rubber cement. Cut out the game pieces. Make one game for every three or four children.

This game is played like the game of "Memory" or "Concentration." Mix up the pieces, spread them out, and turn them facedown. Have the children take turns turning over two pieces at a time. They are looking for two pieces that show the same job. On one piece a parent is doing the job (raking) and on the other piece

---

Bible Words

"I praise you because you made me [in an amazing and wonderful way]" (Psalm 139:14).

(Note: This verse has been divided into two parts. If you are teaching four-year-olds, use only the first part. If you are teaching older children, also include the part of the verse in brackets.)

Play Dough
1 cup flour
1 cup water
1/2 cup salt
1 tablespoon cooking oil
2 teaspoons cream of tartar
(Do not omit.)
Food coloring (optional)

Cook, stirring for three minutes or until mixture pulls away from the pan. Knead as soon as it is cool enough to handle. Store in an airtight container. This makes enough for six children.

the child is doing the same job (raking). When the two pieces match, the child keeps them. If the pieces do not match, they are returned to the playing area and turned over. While the game is played, make comments about the parent and child working together. Ask if any of the children help their parents or other caregivers with these jobs, too.

When families work together, they show love to one another. The next time someone in your family asks you to help, do it with a big smile. You will see how happy that makes them. Remember Joseph and his dreams? His family worked together to take care of large flocks of sheep. They did not always work well together. That caused Joseph a big problem.

▼ 4. What Can I Do to Please God? ▲

Thank God for Me

Sing "The Lord Made Me" as you and the children straighten the classroom. Remind the children that one of the ways they can use their wonderful bodies that God made is by doing things to help others.

To close this time, gather the children in a circle. Sing "The Lord Made Me" as a group. Ask each child to praise God for creating his or her wonderful body. Model a praise sentence something like this: **I praise You, God, for making me special. Only You made my legs to run.** Encourage each child to say a praise sentence.

▼ Bonus Activities ▲

Snack Attack! Traveling Food

You will need ingredients for making a trail mix, such as raisins and other dried fruit, nuts, pretzels, small crackers, cereals, and sunflower seeds. You will also need a large mixing bowl, a spoon, and plastic sandwich bags. (You will need five cups of ingredients for every ten children.)

You and the children wash your hands. Let the children help in adding and mixing the ingredients. Give each child a sandwich bag and let them dip 1/2 cup of the mix into the bag. Sit in a circle and pretend you are around a campfire. Let the children talk about their camping experiences. Ask, **Have you ever been camping? Joseph's brothers camped when they were taking care of the flocks of sheep. When you camp, you have to have food that is easy to fix. Trail mix is a good food to take camping. What do you think Joseph ate while he was traveling to Egypt?** Let the children share their ideas about Joseph and his brothers. (Since many of these foods are a choking hazard, remind the children to finish chewing before they begin to speak.)

Extra Action! Rescued From the Pit

This game is played the same as the game of "Duck, Duck, Goose." One child is selected to be the tagger. Have the rest of the children stand in a circle facing the center. The tagger walks around the outside of the circle tapping the children on their shoulders saying, "Joseph's in the pit, in the pit, in the pit." When the tagger taps a child and says "in the pit," that child sits down. The tagger continues and taps one child saying, "Joseph's going to Egypt." On this signal the tapped child chases the tagger around the circle trying to tag the runner before he gets back to the vacant spot. Play until everyone has had a turn "going to Egypt."

God had a special plan for Joseph in Egypt. I am sure Joseph did not like being so far from his family, but God was taking care of him.

The Lord Made Me
(Tune: "This Is the Day")

Verse 1
These are my arms, these
    are my arms
that the Lord has made,
that the Lord has made.
I'll praise the Lord, I'll praise
    the Lord
for my arms that wave,
for my arms that wave,
These are my arms that the
    Lord has made;
I'll praise the Lord for my
    arms that wave.
These are my arms, these
    are my arms
that the Lord has made.

Use these phrases for additional verses, or make up your own.

These are my legs.
For my legs that run.
(Use "bend" for children with disabilities.)

These are my eyes.
For my eyes that see.

These are my ears.
For my ears that hear.

This is my tongue.
For a tongue that tastes.

Joseph Is Given a Special Job

Genesis 39–41

Know: A Bible person whom God chose for a very special job.

Feel: That God made people in a special way and has a plan for their lives.

Do: Praise God for creating people special by showing love to others and being good workers.

Children will accomplish the goals when they

- Sing a song about being a good worker.
- Tell how Joseph helped others.
- Recite Psalm 139:14 and tell what it means.
- Demonstrate how they can be good workers.
- Praise God for being able to help others.

How to Say It
Potiphar: POT-ih-far

▼ 1. What Is This Story About? ▲

This Is My Job

You will need the words to "This Is My Job" from p. 20 and the actual items (or something that represents the jobs) mentioned in the song.

As you teach this song, hold up the item mentioned. Ask a child to demonstrate how it is used.

God has special jobs for each of us to do. One of my special jobs is to be your teacher. I have other jobs, too. Describe your other jobs for the children. **Your parents have special jobs, too.** Let the children share the kind of jobs their parents have. **In our Bible Stories we have been learning about Joseph. We know that God had a special plan for Joseph. In today's story we will hear about three special jobs Joseph had. Whatever our job is, God will help us do it well. Let's ask Him to help us do our jobs well.** Lead in prayer.

▼ 2. What Does the Bible Say? ▲

Bible Story: Joseph's Special Job

You will need to use the Joseph glued to a craft stick, from the Story Review activity "Joseph in the Pit," p. 16. You will also need to decorate two Styrofoam cups. Draw black stripes on one for the jail. Glue fancy trim to the other cup for the palace. Cut a slit in the bottom of both cups.

The travelers who bought Joseph from his brothers took him to Egypt. They sold him to an important man named Potiphar. God was with Joseph and helped him to be the best slave Potiphar had. Do you know what a slave is? A slave is a person sold to another person to work without getting paid.

Joseph was put in charge of Potiphar's house and land. God blessed everything Joseph did and Potiphar was very pleased with Joseph's work.

One day, Potiphar's wife became angry with Joseph. She told her husband a lie about Joseph. Potiphar put Joseph in jail. (*Show Joseph in the black striped cup.*)

Even in jail, God was still helping Joseph. Joseph was such a good worker that he was put in charge of all the prisoners.

One night, two of the prisoners had dreams. The next morning the two men said to Joseph, "No one can tell us what our dreams mean."

Joseph listened to their dreams. God helped him understand what the dreams meant, and Joseph explained the dreams to the men.

The man who used to serve wine to the king dreamed that he would work for the king again some day. Joseph said, "When you get out of jail, will you please tell the king about me so I can get out of jail, too?"

The man said he would, but when he went to work for the king, he forgot about Joseph.

Two years later, the king had two very strange dreams. The king wanted to know what his dreams meant, but no one could tell him what they meant. Then, the man who served wine to the king remembered Joseph. He

told the king that when he was in jail, Joseph had told him what his dream meant. The king sent for Joseph right away. (*Show Joseph in the fancy cup.*)

Joseph listened to the king's dreams. God helped Joseph again to understand what the dreams meant.

In the first dream, seven ugly and skinny cows ate seven healthy and fat cows. In the second dream, seven thin and shriveled heads of grain ate seven full and good heads of grain.

Joseph said to the king, "God is telling you there will be seven years when there will be plenty to eat and lots of crops. Then there will be seven years when crops will not grow. People everywhere will be hungry. This will happen soon. Choose someone to be in charge of saving grain to feed the people. Then, when the crops do not grow, there will be enough saved food for everyone."

The king was so happy with Joseph that he put Joseph in charge. Joseph became the second most important man in Egypt. God helped Joseph to do his job well.

Story Review: Help Wanted!

You will need a copy of the cube from p. 28. If your class is large, divide it into smaller groups and make a cube for each group. You may want to make one for each child. Color the cube, if desired. Then cut out the cube and glue or tape it together. *Note: Save p. 28 art for use in Lesson 4.*

Ask a child to roll the cube and act out one way he can help in the place pictured on top of the cube. If Joseph lands on top, ask the child to tell one thing he remembers about that part of the story. Take turns rolling the cube.

Who helped Joseph do his jobs well? Who helps you do your jobs well? When we ask God for help, He always hears and helps us.

Bible Memory: Drop the Dust Cloth

You will need a dust cloth.

This game is similar to the game of "Drop the Handkerchief." Review the Bible words with the children before playing "Drop the Dust Cloth."

Have the children form a circle. Select one child to carry the dust cloth around the circle and drop it behind another child's back. Have that child pick up the cloth and say the Bible words from Psalm 139:14. If he can say the Bible words, he then gets to go around the circle and drop the cloth. If the child cannot remember the verse, the dropper takes the cloth and continues around the circle. After a child has successfully said the verse and had a turn at being the dropper, she will go to the center of the circle. (If a child does not remember the verse, be sure that he gets another opportunity to try.) Play until everyone has said the verse from memory.

Bible Words
"I praise you because you made me [in an amazing and wonderful way]" (Psalm 139:14).

(Note: This verse has been divided into two parts. If you are teaching four-year-olds, use only the first part. If you are teaching older children, also include the part of the verse in brackets.)

▼ 3. What Does This Mean to Me? ▲

Job Box

You will need a half of a cereal box for each child, construction paper, one set of the pictures of jobs from pp. 26 and 27 for each child, glue, stickers, crayons or markers, and copies of the letter to parents from p. 29.

Help the children cover their box halves with construction paper. Print "(Child's Name)'s Job Box" on the box. Let the children decorate their boxes with stickers. Give each child a complete set of the pictures from the memory game that shows a child doing a job. After the children color the pictures, cut them out and put them in the child's job box, along with a letter to his or her parents found on p. 29. Explain to the children that part of being a family is doing jobs that help the family function. Talk about the jobs that the children do at home. Ask them how they help to keep their rooms clean and what other special jobs they have.

You get to take these Job Boxes home with you today, to help you remember to be a good helper. Joseph did all of his jobs well because God helped him. God will help you do all of your jobs well, too. He has given you a body that is healthy and strong. Your body can do lots of jobs. *(Be aware and sensitive to any children who have disabilities.)*

What's My Job?

You will need the words to "This Is My Job" from the left-hand column.

Have the children form a circle. Select one child to stand in the center. Sing the song "This Is My Job." When you come to the line, "I can . . . ," stop and let the child in the center pantomime a job she can do. The second time a job is mentioned in the song, let another child pantomime the actions. Make sure to give every child a turn.

You have shown us many jobs that children can do. This week, you can help your family by doing the jobs in your job box. I'm sure your family will be happy that you can do so many jobs and you can do them well. Remember that God will always help you.

▼ 4. What Can I Do to Please God? ▲

Here's a Job for You

Make a Classroom Job Box like the ones the children made to use at home. Find or draw pictures of jobs the children can do in the classroom to clean up at the end of each session. Put enough jobs in the box for every child to have one. Some jobs can be done by several children at the same time, so put in several pictures of that job.

Show the Classroom Job Box. Let each child reach in and pick out a job to do. Give help as needed, and give lots of compliments for effort.

When the room is straightened, gather the children for a closing song and prayer. Pass out their individual Job Boxes and the letters to the parents. Remind them to be good helpers at home. Sing "This Is My Job." Then close with prayer, praising God for being able to help others. Encourage each child to praise God in prayer.

▼ Bonus Activity ▲

Snack Attack! Body-Building Food

You will need an assortment of raw fruits and vegetables, a bottle of dressing for dipping, and individual dipping cups for each child. (Miniature paper cups, or paper nut cups, are good.) Cut the fruits and vegetable into pieces.

You and the children should wash your hands. Ask the children to thank God for the healthy snack. As you eat, talk about the value of healthy food.

God made many different kinds of fruits and vegetables for us to eat. They help our bodies grow and become strong. What is your favorite fruit? What is your favorite vegetable? Is there one that you do not like? If that food is part of our snack today, you may want to try a small bite. Who knows? Today you may like it! Learning to eat new foods is a part of growing up. Do you think Joseph might have learned to like different foods while he was living in Egypt?

Joseph Is Special

Genesis 41:56, 57; 42; 43

▼ 1. What Is This Story About? ▲

Helping Hearts

You will need the words to "This Is My Job" from p. 20, copies of the "Helping Heart" card from p. 29, crayons or markers, copies of the pictures of the children doing jobs from pp. 26 and 27, copies of the house, church, and school (cut into squares) from p. 28; one paper fastener per child, glue, and scissors for the adults.

Discuss with the children the importance of helping others. Pass out "Helping Heart" cards, which they will complete and give to someone they would like to help. The person may be a parent, Sunday schoolteacher, public schoolteacher, a neighbor, or anyone else. Let the children decide to whom they will give their cards.

Give each child the appropriate picture of the place where he wants to help. Glue the picture on the front of the card. Inside, glue the pictures showing how the child will help. Let the child color his card and help him print his name.

When we do a job for someone, we should do it with a cheerful heart. Today during our Bible story we will learn how Joseph showed love to his family through the special job God gave him to do. What do you think your parents or your teachers will say when you give them your card? They will be happy you have a helping and cheerful heart. God will also be pleased. Let's thank God for giving us helping hearts. After praying, sing "This Is My Job."

Spin and Tell

You will need one or more copies of the spinner game from p. 30. Follow the directions for assembling it. If your group is large, make several game boards and play the game in small groups.

Give each child a turn to spin the spinner. When the paper clip stops, have the child tell how she uses that sense to know she is loved. If the spinner lands on "eyes," the child will tell a way that she "sees" love from someone in her family. The child's answer might be, "I see a smile from my dad," or "I see my mom wave at me when I leave for school." At first you may have to give a lot of help, but the children will quickly catch on to the idea. (Other examples are hearing kind words, tasting a favorite food, hugging grandma, and smelling clean clothes from the dryer.) **God wants all families to show love to one another. You have told us many good ways to see, hear, taste, smell, and feel love. Let's ask God to help us always show love to our families.**

▼ 2. What Does the Bible Say? ▲

Bible Story: Joseph's Dreams Come True

You will need paper plates with smiling faces on one side and sad faces on the other. Make one for you and each child.

Distribute the paper plates. Tell the children that their smiling faces/sad faces will play the part of Joseph's brothers, and your smiling face/sad face will play the

---

Know: A Bible person whom God chose for a very special job.

Feel: That God made people in a special way and has a plan for their lives.

Do: Praise God for creating people special by showing love to others and being good workers.

Children will accomplish the goals when they

- Describe how families show love to one another.
- Tell how Joseph showed love to his family.
- Recite Psalm 139:14 and praise God for a classmate He made.
- Name ways God helps them show love.
- Praise God for giving them a heart to help others.

part of Joseph. Tell the children that you will let them know when to hold up the smiling face or sad face as you tell the story.

(Teacher, hold up your smiling face.) **Joseph was the second most important man in Egypt. Joseph stored extra grain for seven years while the crops grew well. Then, when the crops didn't grow, everyone bought this grain from Joseph.**

(Students, now make your smiling faces bow down to this smiling face that represents Joseph.) **One day some men from Canaan bowed before Joseph. They said, "We have no more grain to eat in our country. May we buy grain from you?" Joseph knew they were his brothers, but they didn't know he was Joseph. As they bowed, Joseph remembered the dreams he had when he was younger. He had dreamed that his brothers would bow to him as if he were a king.**

(Teacher, show your sad face.) **Joseph pretended not to know his brothers. Joseph had his brothers put in jail.** *(Students, show your sad faces.)* **Joseph said that he would keep one brother, Simeon, in jail while the others returned home with grain. He would let Simeon go only if the brothers came back to Egypt with their littlest brother, Benjamin.**

Joseph secretly put the money his brothers had paid for the grain back into their bags. *(Hold up your sad faces.)* **On the way home, the brothers found the money in their sacks of grain. They were afraid. They did not want anyone to think they had taken the grain without paying.**

(Show your sad faces.) **Your sad faces now represent Jacob. The brothers told their father, Jacob, what had happened in Egypt and that the man who sold the grain wanted them to bring Benjamin to Egypt. Jacob was very sad and said, "No! You can't take Benjamin to Egypt."**

Later, when all the grain was gone, Jacob changed his mind. *(Show your sad faces.)* **He was still afraid that something might happen to his youngest son, but the family needed more food to eat. Jacob sent the brothers back to Egypt with Benjamin and gifts for the man who sold the grain.** *(All, show your smiling faces.)* **Joseph was very happy to see his brothers, but he still didn't tell them he was Joseph.**

Joseph invited his brothers to eat at his house. At the dinner, the brothers bowed before Joseph and gave him the gifts. *(Make your smiling faces bow before my smiling plate—my plate represents Joseph.)* **When Joseph saw Benjamin, his little brother, Joseph had to leave the room to cry.** *(Take away your plate.)* **He loved his little brother very much and had missed him.**

(Teacher, show your smiling face again.) **The next morning, Joseph told his servants to fill his brothers' bags with grain. Again, he put their money back into their bags. This time he also put his silver drinking cup into Benjamin's bag.**

The brothers hadn't gone very far when one of Joseph's servants stopped them. The servant was looking for Joseph's silver cup. He found the cup in Benjamin's bag.

(Students, show your sad faces.) **The brothers were all afraid as they went back to the man who sold the grain.** *(Make all of your sad faces bow before my sad face, which represents Joseph.)* **This time when the brothers bowed before Joseph, he told them, "I am your brother." The brothers were frightened because they thought Joseph would be angry about what they had done to him. But Joseph said, "Don't worry. I'm not angry, God sent me here. See all the grain I have stored? I was part of God's plan to save you and your families from starving."** *(Let's all show our smiling faces!)*

The happy brothers went back to Canaan and told their father the good news. "Joseph is alive! He is the man who sold us the grain. He wants you to come and live in Egypt."

(Gather all your smiling faces around Joseph's smiling face.) **Joseph and his family were together again, just as God had planned.**

How to Say It

Canaan: KAY-nun
Simeon: SIM-ee-un

Story Review: Hearts Galore!

You will need several sheets each of six different colors of construction paper. Cut as many 2" hearts as possible. (A heart-shaped paper punch from your local craft store will make this an easy job!)

In a separate room, scatter all of the hearts. They do not need to be hidden from view. Line the children up at the door. Send the children into the room to collect all of the hearts. When all of the hearts are collected, ask the children to sit on the floor and separate their hearts by color. Look over the collections. Use all the adult helpers to help count and determine who collected the most of each color and the least of each color. As you identify the child with the fewest pink hearts (for example), ask him a review question from this unit on Joseph.

Ask several children to

Name something that happened to Joseph that made him happy.

Name something that happened to Joseph that made him sad.

Name something that happened in the story that made Joseph's brothers happy.

Name something that happened in the story that made Joseph's brothers sad.

Name a way Joseph showed love to his family.

Collect the hearts and repeat the activity if time permits, using the questions listed to the right.

Bible Memory: Musical Hearts

You will need an 8" yellow circle with a happy face drawn on it for every child except one. You will also need one 8" red paper heart. Tape the circles and the heart to the floor making one large circle. You will also need live or taped music.

Have each child stand on a circle or the heart. Start the music. Lead the children in walking the same direction around the circle. Stop the music. Have the children point to the child standing on the heart and say, "I thank You, God, because You made (insert the child's name) [in an amazing and wonderful way]." Start the music and continue until every child has stood on the heart.

▼ 3. What Does This Mean to Me? ▲

You're One of a Kind

You will need white construction paper, several colors of tempera paint (either in squeeze bottles, or use bowls with teaspoons), paint shirts for the children to wear, newspaper to cover the tables, scissors, and markers for the teachers.

Cut a large heart out of white construction paper for each child. Fold the heart in half.

Have the children print their names lightly (pencil is good) somewhere on the edge of the heart. (Front or back doesn't matter.) Have the children lay their hearts out flat, or fold their hearts so that only half of the heart is showing. (Either way you fold the heart, the other side can be folded over it after the paint is in place.) Let the children drop various colors of paint *on one side of the heart only.* Instruct them to make delicate patterns–the less paint, the better. Have them open their hearts and gently fold the other half over the wet paint. Have them smooth their hands over the top to make sure the paint gets on the other side. Open the hearts and see the special designs they made.

Look at the special designs you made. Each one is beautiful and each one is different. When God made you, He made you in an amazing and wonderful way. Each of you is special and each of you is different. I am

Additional questions

Which parts of your amazing body did you use to play this game?

Could you pick up hearts if you couldn't bend at the waist?

Could you pick up hearts if you didn't have fingers?

Could you find the hearts if you didn't have eyes?

Could you count the hearts if you didn't have a brain?

Bible Words

"I praise you because you made me [in an amazing and wonderful way]" (Psalm 139:14).

(Note: This verse has been divided into two parts. If you are teaching four-year-olds, use only the first part. If you are teaching older children, also include the part of the verse in brackets.)

glad God made you just the way you are. He has a special plan for you, and if you ask Him, He will help you every day.

When the paint dries, print the Bible words on each heart.

Loving Cup

You will need a small, round, bathroom size wastebasket, or a round, one-gallon ice cream container, or something of a similar size covered with aluminum foil (to represent the silver cup), twelve 4" red construction paper hearts, twelve 18" lengths of ribbon or yarn, and tape.

Attach the ribbon to the hearts. On three hearts print the capital letter H. On the next three hearts, print the capital letter C, then three hearts with S, and three with J. Put the twelve hearts in the "silver cup" so the ribbons hang over the outside of the cup.

Show the silver cup to the children. Ask, **What kind of cup did Joseph put in Benjamin's grain sack? Yes, it was a silver cup. Here is a large silver cup. Jacob had twelve sons. There are twelve ribbons hanging over the sides of this silver cup. Attached to each ribbon is a heart.** Pull on one of the ribbons until the heart appears. **On each heart is a letter. The letter H stands for Home. The letter C stands for Church. The letter S stands for School. The letter J stands for Joseph. You will each get to pull out one heart from the cup. If you pull out H, C, or S, you will tell how you can show love to the people in those places. If you pull out the letter J, you will tell something you learned about Joseph from the Bible story.**

Wrap up the game by saying, **God gave Joseph a loving heart. Joseph was able to forgive his brothers for selling him into slavery. He was able to forgive them even after he spent years in prison. When Joseph told his brothers that he was Joseph, their brother, he was not angry with them. He did not try to pay them back for how mean they had been. Do you think we should try to be like Joseph? Does God want us to forgive people for the mean things they do and say? Do you think it was easy for Joseph to forgive his brothers? Is it easy for you to forgive someone who has hurt you? Who can help you forgive others?**

(Optional: Use the game as a review of this unit by writing a question on each heart.)

▼ 4. What Can I Do to Please God? ▲

Let's Praise the Lord

You will need the Classroom Job Box made in Lesson 3, the words to "The Lord Made Me" from p. 17, and several familiar worship songs.

Use the Classroom Job Box to help the children clean up the classroom. Then gather everyone in a circle and sit on the floor. Lead in a worship time.

Sing "This Is the Day," "The Lord Made Me," and several worship songs the children know. Ask each child to name a way he or she can show love to someone this week. Use these sentences to encourage each child to praise God: **I praise You, God, for giving me a heart to help others. I can show love this week by _____.**

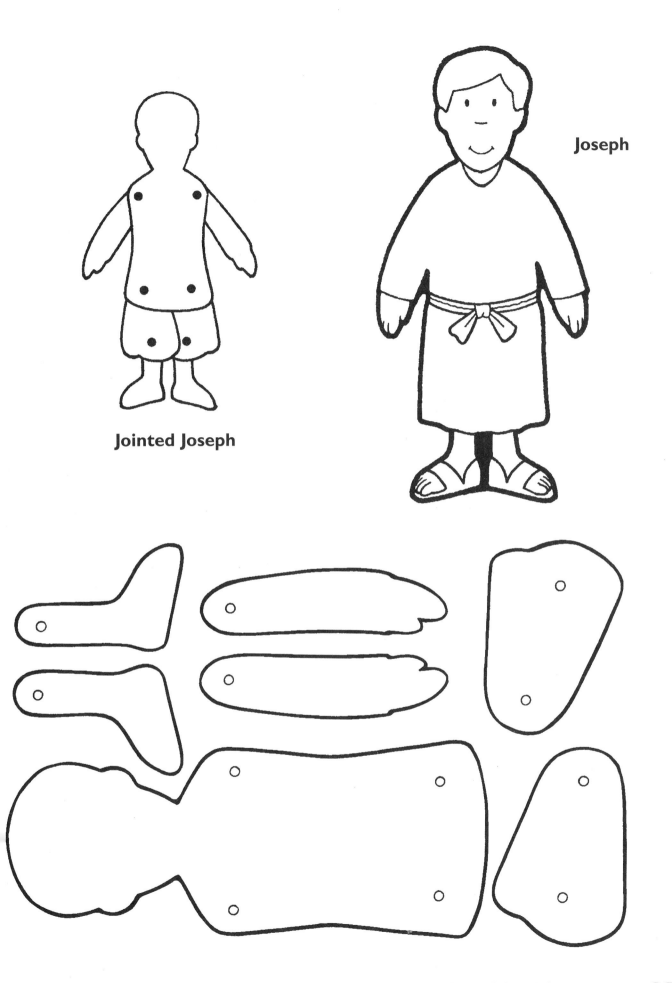

Jointed Joseph

Joseph

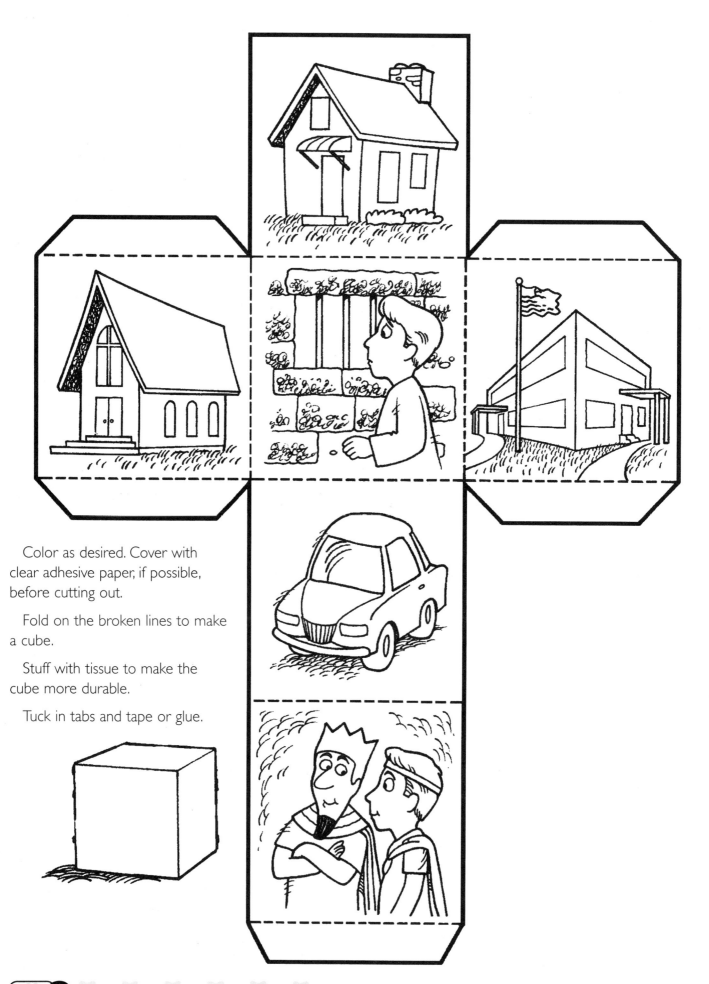

Color as desired. Cover with clear adhesive paper, if possible, before cutting out.

Fold on the broken lines to make a cube.

Stuff with tissue to make the cube more durable.

Tuck in tabs and tape or glue.

Dear Parent,

Today your child learned about a special job God gave to Joseph. Joseph was given the second most important job in Egypt. God had told him a time was coming when no grain would grow in Egypt. Joseph's job was to save grain for all of Egypt to eat during this time.

Joseph was a good worker. Your child wants to be a good worker too. Today each child made his or her own Job Box. Inside the box are pictures of jobs your child can do. Please encourage your child to be a good helper like Joseph. Allow him or her to reach in the box throughout the coming week and select a job to do at home. Good helpers are always a blessing!

Sincerely,

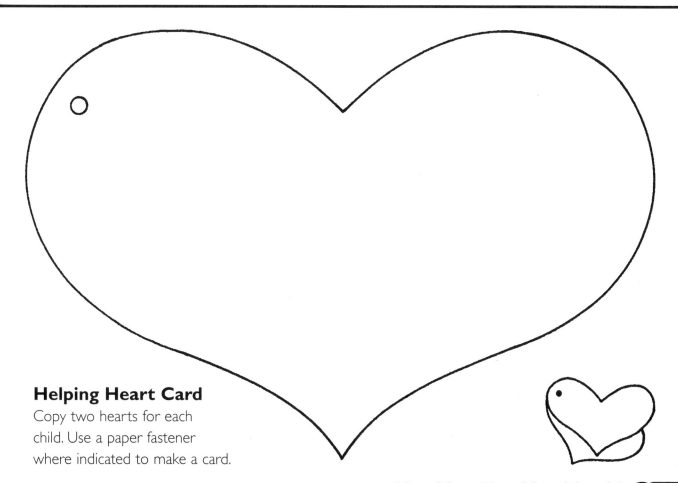

Helping Heart Card

Copy two hearts for each
child. Use a paper fastener
where indicated to make a card.

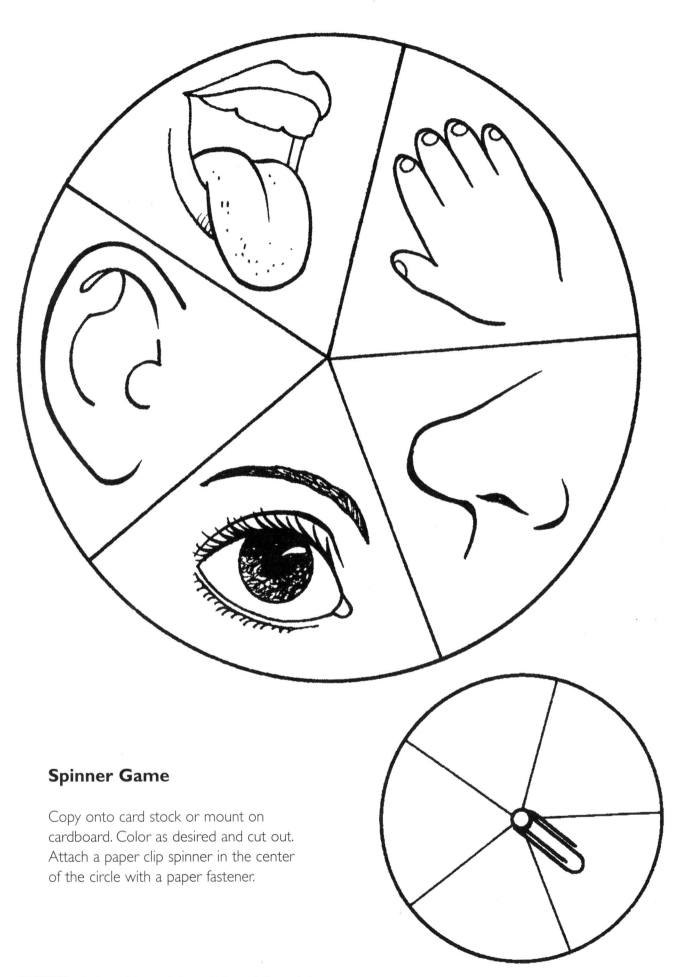

Spinner Game

Copy onto card stock or mount on
cardboard. Color as desired and cut out.
Attach a paper clip spinner in the center
of the circle with a paper fastener.

Unit Bible Words
"Trust the Lord with all your heart" (Proverbs 3:5).

Bible Character
Gideon

5 God Chooses Gideon to Do a Big Job

Judges 6:1-3, 7, 10-24—The Midianites had invaded Canaan. They were cruel and powerful. The Israelites asked God for help. God chose Gideon to lead the Israelite army into battle against the enemy. Gideon was surprised to be chosen for such a big job. He thought he was a nobody!

6 Gideon Learns to Trust God's Power

Judges 6:33-40—Gideon was afraid of the Midianites. The requests that he made of God had a two-fold benefit: Gideon saw God's power, and he learned that God was willing to respond to his requests. Gideon wanted dew to collect only on a piece of wool and not on the ground. God did what Gideon asked. Gideon asked for one more miracle. When God showed His power, and showed that He was listening to Gideon, Gideon put his trust in Him.

7 God Helps Gideon Choose an Army

Judges 7:1-8—Gideon gathered a huge army. God did not want the Israelites to brag about their strength. God told Gideon to send most of the men home. God chose only three hundred men to be in the army.

8 Gideon and His Army Trust God

Judges 7:16-22—God transformed Gideon into a brave commander. Gideon learned to trust God, even though he had only three hundred men. Following God's plan, they surprised the Midianites and caused them to run away from Canaan.

By the end of this unit, the children and leaders will

Know: A Bible person who learned to trust God.
Feel: That God is powerful and worthy of trust.
Do: Put trust in God when afraid, and worship God with songs and prayers.

Why Teach This Unit to Four- to Six-Year-Olds?

Have you ever jokingly said to someone, "Trust me"? You and that person probably both laughed, knowing that you had just warned that person to be skeptical! In reality, trust is not a joking matter. Webster uses the words "hope, belief, confidence, faith, and obligation" to define trust. It is this kind of trust in God that people need and desire.

For children, trust comes easily. Anything a parent or teacher does or says is presumed to be trustworthy. This is why a child's trust places an obligation on the one being trusted. Adults can cause great pain by taking advantage of a child's innocence.

All children need to know there is a living God who is worthy of their trust. He is also worthy of their worship, adoration, and praise. God has the power to help when they are fearful and need protection. His power is available when they need healing or self-control. They need to know that when God says, "Trust Me," they can do so without reservation. There is never a need to view God with skepticism.

Use this unit to create a worshipful environment. Help your students express their trust in God through praise and worship.

Meet Gideon

The Israelites were living in Canaan, the promised land, which would later be known as Israel. Having forgotten all that God had done for them, they worshiped idols. As a result, God no longer protected them from their strong and numerous enemies. Through the years, many nations invaded Canaan and occupied the land. Finally, the oppressed Israelites returned to God for help. God forgave them and sent an angel to recruit Gideon as commanding general of the Israelite army. The angel promised that Gideon would have all he needed—God!

Gideon's family was from one of the weakest tribes of Israel. He considered himself young and unimportant. However, God knew his potential.

The angel of the Lord found Gideon hiding from the Midianites, the current enemies of Canaan. The angel greeted Gideon saying, "The Lord is with you, mighty warrior." What a strange title for a man oppressed with fear! "Who, me?" must have been the expression on Gideon's face. Nevertheless, the angel delivered God's message and Gideon was transformed into the Lord's mighty warrior.

In the story of Gideon, the power of God changed people and events. Gideon was transformed from a fearful man to the bravest of the brave. He tore down the altar to an idol and built an altar to worship the living God. No longer did he fear for his life, instead he trusted God. Only God can provide that kind of courage and peace!

Unit Visuals: A Lively Mural

You will need a transparency made from p. 48, an overhead projector, a roll of white paper at least four feet wide (bulletin board size), markers, paints, scissors, and tape.

Attach the mural paper to a wall with tape. Project the transparency onto the paper. The figures are labeled with a letter. Each lesson indicates the figures needed. Look at the illustration for each lesson and position one figure at a time onto the paper. (For Lesson 5, you will need figures A and B, and object C. For Lesson 6, you will need figure D, etc.) Make the figures correspond in size to the chil-dren you are teaching, and don't put the figures so high from the ground that the children can't reach the holes.

Trace the figures and color them. Then cut out the holes indicated for the heads and arms. The children will insert their heads and arms through the holes to make the mural come alive. Reinforce the holes with wide clear tape.

You can either place all the figures for the unit on the mural at one time, or add them week by week. Having all the figures in place at the beginning may create anticipation among the children.

The objects to be used with the mural (wheat, jar, torch) should be enlarged to a size corresponding with the figures. Trace the objects on separate pieces of paper or card stock and cut them out. You may want to reinforce them by gluing them to cardboard.

Tape the finished mural between two ladders or tall stools. (If these are not available, tape a yard stick to each end of the mural and have two adults hold it tightly.) Make sure to leave space behind the mural for the live actors.

Give your teaching assistant a copy of each Bible story. Have her stand behind the mural with the actors and prompt them on what they are to do and say.

Unit Song

Praise, Praise, Praise the Lord
(Tune: "Row, Row, Row Your Boat")

Verse 1
Praise, praise, praise the Lord.
Worship Him today.
Trust the Lord with all your heart.
Worship Him and pray.

Verse 2
Trust, trust, trust the Lord.
Now's the time to start.
He is good and He is wise;
Trust Him with your heart.

God Chooses Gideon to Do a Big Job  LESSON 5

Judges 6:1-3, 7, 10-24

▼ 1. What Is This Story About? ▲

Our Own Worship Center

You will need a small table, a Bible, a picture of Jesus, some fresh or artificial flowers. Have all of these supplies in a box. You will also need finger paint paper, several salt shakers filled with colored gelatin, water, and paint shirts.

Prepare an area of your classroom to become a worship center. Let the children help arrange the area and the things you have collected. Ask the children to make special finger-paint pictures to decorate the new worship center.

To finger paint with gelatin, wet the glossy side of finger-paint paper. Let the children sprinkle the gelatin and spread it with their fingers. The colors can be mixed to make new colors. Allow the papers to dry and then hang the pictures on the walls around the worship center.

As the children paint, talk about why we worship and what worship is. Then say, **We worship God because He is wonderful. We also worship His Son, Jesus. Every week we will visit our new worship center. We will worship by praying, singing, and praising God.**

During today's Bible story, you will hear about a time when God's people stopped worshiping Him. It was a very sad time. We should always worship God. He is the only true and living God.

Give Praise to the Lord

You will need the words to "Praise, Praise, Praise the Lord" from p. 35.

Teach verse one of "Praise, "Praise, "Praise the Lord." As the children learn the words, encourage them to share ways they can worship the Lord. Be sure to include praying, singing, reading the Bible, giving offerings, being obedient, and serving others in your list of ways to worship God.

Our new song tells us to worship God by loving Him. It pleases God when we say we love Him while we are worshiping. God is glad when we want to worship Him.

▼ 2. What Does the Bible Say? ▲

Bible Story: A Big Job for Gideon

You will need to make "A Lively Mural" for this activity. (See p. 32 for directions.) You will need figures A (angel), B (Gideon standing), and C (bundle of wheat) from p. 48.

A long time before Jesus was born, God's people, the Israelites, had a big problem. The Israelites were living in Canaan, the land God had given them. But some people who lived near them, the Midianites, had come to live in Canaan and had taken over the country. The Midianites were powerful and mean. They took everything that belonged to the Israelites. It was not even safe for the Israelites to plant crops. The enemies would attack them while they were in the fields. The Israelites had very little to eat,

---

> **Know:** A Bible person who learned to trust God.
> **Feel:** That God is powerful and worthy of trust.
> **Do:** Put trust in God when afraid, and worship God with songs and prayers.
>
> **Children will accomplish the goals when they**
> - Help set up a classroom worship center.
> - Tell why Gideon was hiding and why God visited him.
> - Begin to memorize Proverbs 3:5.
> - Sing about worshiping God.
> - Choose to worship God.

> **How to Say It**
> Canaan: KAY-nun
> Gideon: GID-e-un
> Israelite: IZ-ray-el-ite
> Midianite: MID-ee-un-ite

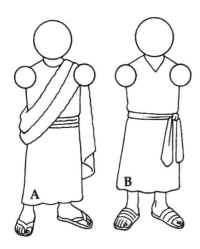

no sheep, no cattle, and no donkeys. They were very poor. Many were so afraid that they lived in caves.

Why did God's people have such a terrible problem? They had stopped worshiping and obeying God. Instead, they worshiped idols. Idols were statues made of stone, wood, or metal. The Israelites worshiped them as if they had power. Do you think that was the wrong thing to do? (Yes.)

The Israelites worshiped idols and God stopped helping them. He let other people come and take over the land that He had given them.

Finally, the Israelites asked God for help. (Have two children bring the figures of Gideon and the angel to life by putting their heads and arms in the appropriate holes on the mural. Give Gideon the wheat to hold.) God sent an angel to visit a man named Gideon. The angel found Gideon hiding wheat from the Midianites. (Have Gideon pretend to be afraid.) He was afraid the enemy would steal his wheat.

The angel spoke to Gideon and said, "The Lord is with you, mighty warrior!" (Have the angel point to Gideon and/or say these words.)

Do you think that was a strange thing to say to a man who was afraid and hiding? Yes! Gideon thought so, too. Gideon told the angel that God was no longer helping them. The Midianites had taken away their land.

(Have the angel point to Gideon.) Again the angel said to Gideon, "You are strong. Go and save the people of Israel from the Midianites."

Gideon answered, "How can I save Israel? I am not an important person." The angel said, "God will be with you."

Gideon was surprised that God had chosen him for such a big job. (Take wheat from Gideon.) In the place where God's angel visited him, he built a special place just to worship God. (Gideon pretends to be building and then stops and prays.)

Story Review: Find Gideon

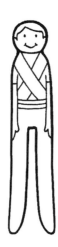

You will need markers to draw a man's face and clothing on a clothespin. This will be "Gideon." To play this game, take the children outside of the classroom while an adult attaches Gideon somewhere in the room. He can be attached to chairs, table legs, curtains, and so on. Keep him in sight. Bring the children back into the room. Tell the children **Gideon is hiding from the Midianites and must be found.** Let the child who finds Gideon answer a review question and then hide Gideon (with help as needed) while the other children are out of the classroom again. Play as long as time allows.

What was Gideon doing when the angel visited him?
Why was Gideon hiding? Why were the Israelites hiding?
Where was he hiding?
Who sent the angel?
What was the angel's job?
What job did God have for Gideon to do?
Was Gideon a brave man?
What did Gideon do after the angel of the Lord left?
What did the Israelites worship instead of God?

Bible Memory: A Trusting Heart

You will need the heart puzzle from p. 52. Before class time, copy and cut out one puzzle for yourself and one for each child. If you have time, mount the puzzle on stiff paper and cover with clear adhesive paper for durability. Cut the puzzle pieces apart. Provide envelopes for the children's puzzles. Put each child's name on an envelope.

Introduce the memory verse by showing only your puzzle. Save the individual puzzles for later in this activity.

Here are some pieces to a puzzle. Help me put it together. *(Stop and let the children help.)* **There are some words on this puzzle. Let me read them to you.** *(Read Proverbs 3:5.)* **Do you know what it means to trust someone?** *(Let the children respond.)* **It means that you believe someone is able to do what he says he can do. It means that you believe whatever he says is true. This verse tells us to trust the Lord.**

How does this verse tell us to trust the Lord? Yes, it says *with your heart.* It also says with *all* your heart. *(Hold up one piece of the puzzle.)* **Does God want us to trust Him with part of our heart? No, we are to trust Him with all of our heart. That means we are to trust Him all the time. Let's say these words together.**

Repeat the verse several times. Then pass out the envelopes with a puzzle in each. Let the children put the puzzles together. Instruct the children to store their puzzle pieces in the envelopes.

▼ 3. What Does This Mean to Me? ▲

Let's Worship!

You will need the "Worship God" banner and the four pictures from p. 49. Enlarge the banner and pictures if possible. Then color them and cut them out. Provide pushpins or tape for posting the banner and pictures.

Gather the children at the worship center. Say, **Gideon knew it was important to worship God instead of idols. That is why he made a special place to worship God. We also have made a place where we can worship.** *(Point to the banner.)* **These words say "Worship God." Do you know how to worship God?**

Encourage the children to give their ideas. As they name ways to worship that correspond with the pictures you have prepared, post those pictures. Discuss why the actions of the children in the pictures are pleasing to God. Show any remaining pictures and ask them to tell what the children in the pictures are doing. Explain why these children are also worshiping. Post all the pictures.

Every week we will come to our worship center and praise God for His greatness.

Bible Words

"Trust the Lord with all your heart" (Proverbs 3:5).

Do you know what the word "trust" means? It means that we believe in someone's ability. When we trust God, we are believing that He can do whatever He says He will do. If I say, "I will trust God to help me when I am afraid," I am saying, "I believe God will help me."

Praise, Praise, Praise the Lord
(Tune: "Row, Row, Row Your Boat")

Verse I
Praise, praise, praise the Lord.
Worship Him today.
Trust the Lord with all your heart.
Worship Him and pray.

Verse 2
Trust, trust, trust the Lord.
Now's the time to start.
He is good and He is wise;
Trust Him with your heart.

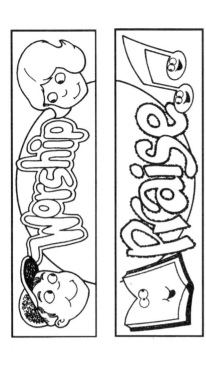

Praise Bookmarks

You will need copies of the bookmarks from p. 54. Do not cut them out before class. It will be easier for the children to color them before they are cut. You will also need a variety of stickers, crayons and/or markers, clear adhesive paper, and scissors (for the adults).

Give each child two bookmarks to color and decorate with stickers. The stickers can be placed on the blank side of each bookmark after an adult has cut it out. When the bookmark is finished, cover both sides with clear adhesive paper and trim the edges.

Tell the children that the words on the bookmarks say "Worship" and "Praise." They can keep one for their own Bible and give one away. Review the meaning of the words "worship" and "praise." A simple definition of worship is telling and showing God how special He is.

▼ 4. What Can I Do to Please God? ▲

What's Your Favorite Way to Worship?

You will need to provide the words to "Praise, Praise, Praise the Lord" from p. 35, any additional praise songs familiar to the children, and an *International Children's Bible* or another children's version.

Lead the children in a time of worship. Sing verse one of the unit song "Praise, Praise, Praise the Lord." Sing other praise songs the children know. Read Psalm 150. Discuss how music helps us praise the Lord. If you collect an offering as the children arrive, place it on the table. Pray with the children, worshiping God with your words and attitude. Use worship sentences that are simple enough for the children to understand and repeat: **God, You are special. I know You are always with me. I worship You, God, because You are good.**

If you need to clean up, say, **Our room looks like the Midianites have been here. Let's be brave and clean it up.** Send the children to different areas to clean up and straighten the room. Compliment them on their bravery!

▼ Bonus Activity ▲

Snack Attack! Gideon's Wheat

You will need to provide round wheat crackers, creamy peanut butter or cream cheese, raisins, jumbo craft sticks (for spreading), and paper towels. (Check for peanut allergies among your students.)

Wash hands. Let each child spread peanut butter or cream cheese on several crackers. Show how to add raisins to made the face of Gideon.

As the children eat, review the story of Gideon using the same questions you used in the Story Review activity, p. 34.

Gideon Learns to Trust God's Power

Judges 6:33-40

▼ 1. What Is This Story About? ▲

Make Dew!

You will need two one-pound tin coffee cans without lids, one cup of rock salt, four cups of crushed ice, and a spoon for stirring.

About thirty minutes before this activity begins, place two cups of crushed ice and one-half cup of rock salt in one of the coffee cans. Stir and let sit. In about thirty minutes "dew" should begin to form on the sides of the can. As the can cools, the moisture in the air condenses on the surface of the cool can. The can will continue to become cooler and the "dew" on the can will freeze and become "frost."

Have you ever walked on grass early in the morning? What did you feel on your feet or shoes? (*Allow children to respond.*) **That water is called "dew."**

Every night when the sun goes down, the grass starts to cool off. The air is warmer than the grass. The air has water in it, and when it touches the cool grass, the water sticks to the grass. This water is called "dew."

Show the can that you prepared ahead of time. Let the children feel the surface of the can. Direct them in setting up the second can so they can see how you did the experiment. Involve as many children as possible. Let everyone stir the salt and ice. Set both cans aside for use during "Praise God's Power."

Do you know who made the dew form on the can? It wasn't me. I just put the ice and salt in the can. God made the dew. God created everything in our world. He created the grass and the air. He created the dew. We have a powerful God. Everywhere we look we see God's power.

Let's praise Him for His power. (*Lead the children in a prayer of praise.*)

Trust the Lord

You will need the words to "Praise, Praise, Praise the Lord" from p. 35. Review verse one and teach the words to verse two.

Do you know what the word "trust" means? It means to believe in someone's ability. When we trust God, we are believing that He can do whatever He says He will do. If I say, "I will trust God to help me when I am afraid," I am saying, "I believe God will help me." Let's sing a song about trusting God. (Do so.)

▼ 2. What Does the Bible Say? ▲

Bible Story: Proof for Gideon

You will need the mural used in Lesson 5, with figures added for this lesson. (See p. 32 for directions on how to create this visual.) Use figure D (Gideon kneeling) from p. 48. You will need a bowl of water and two "wool" cloths (any rough fabric will do; place mats are a good size).

Use the portion of the mural from Lesson 5 to help review the story. Have two children bring the figures to life.

The Israelites stopped worshiping God. Now they had many problems.

Know ... Bible person who learned to trust God.
Feel: That God is powerful and worthy of trust.
Do: Put trust in God when afraid, and worship God with songs and prayers.

Children will accomplish the goals when they
• Observe God's power in nature.
• Tell how Gideon learned to trust God.
• Memorize Proverbs 3:5.
• Sing about trusting God.
• Praise God for showing His power in nature.

Canaan was taken over by the mean Midianites. Finally the Israelites asked God for help. God chose Gideon to save His people.

Gideon was not chosen because he was brave. When God chose Gideon, he was hiding wheat from the Midianites. God had an important lesson to teach Gideon. It was a lesson about trust. This is how God taught this lesson to Gideon.

After God told Gideon he was to save Israel, Gideon built a special place to pray and worship God. God's spirit came to live in him. Gideon began gathering an army to fight the Midianites. He blew a loud trumpet and sent messengers to gather the men of Israel from all over Canaan. Thousands of men came to join Gideon's army.

Remember how afraid Gideon was of the Midianites? Well, Gideon wanted to make sure God was going to help him. He wanted to see God's power, so he asked for a miracle. A miracle is something that only God can do, because God has power that no one else has. Sometimes God helps people to do miracles, too.

(Have a child be the kneeling Gideon, holding the wool cloth.) **Gideon put a piece of wool on the ground and said to God, "In the morning, make this wool wet with dew. Make the ground around it dry."**

Do you think God could do such a miracle?

(Have Gideon dip the cloth in the bowl of water.) **The next morning the wool was wet and the ground was dry! The wool was so wet that when Gideon squeezed it, the water filled a bowl.** *(Have Gideon squeeze the cloth.)*

Was that a miracle? Yes! Was Gideon ready to fight the Midianites? Not yet! He was still afraid.

Gideon said, "God, do not be angry with me. Please do one more miracle."

This time Gideon asked God to make the ground wet with the dew during the night, but keep the wool dry.

Guess what? It happened! The next morning the ground was wet and the wool was dry. *(Have Gideon feel the ground and pretend it is wet. Let him pass the dry cloth around.)* **God gave Gideon another miracle. Was Gideon now ready to fight the Midianites and save God's people? Yes, he was!**

These miracles were just the beginning of many lessons Gideon would learn about trusting God.

Story Review: Praise God's Power

You will need the coffee cans from the first activity (the dew on the first one should be turning to frost by now).

Show the coffee cans. **Remember the can that showed how dew is formed? Now the dew has frozen. This is what happens to the dew on very cold nights. This is called "frost." Then we mixed ice and salt in this can. Look at what has happened on the outside of this can. What is this called?** (Dew.)

Pass the cans around. Let all the children feel the dew and frost. **Our God made this happen. He has great power. Remember how God showed Gideon His power by using dew? When Gideon found dew only on the wool and not the ground, he saw God's power. Next, God showed His power when the dew was only on the ground and not on the wool. When Gideon saw the greatness of God's power, and he learned that God was willing to respond to his requests, he knew he could trust God to help him fight the Midianites. We can trust God to help us every day, too.**

Bible Memory: Real Power

You will need a ball of wool yarn and a spray bottle of water. Just before playing the game, spray the ball of yarn with water. Play the following game like the game of "Hot Potato."

Have the children sit in a circle. Review the memory verse several times. Remind the children that to trust God means to believe in His ability.

Gideon saw God's power make the wool wet and the ground dry. Then he saw God's power make the wool dry and the ground wet. When he saw these things, he put his trust in God. God wanted Gideon to trust Him. God wants us to trust Him, too.

Here is a wet ball of wool. Let's pretend it is wet with dew. Because it is wet, I do not want to hold on to it. I want to hold it only long enough to say one word of the Bible verse. Then I will toss it quickly to the next person. When that person catches the wool, he will say the next word in the verse and quickly toss it again. Demonstrate.

Play until everyone can say the verse from memory.

▼ 3. What Does This Mean to Me? ▲

Praise Visors

You will need heavy white paper, scissors, a hole punch, a black permanent marker, yarn, colored markers or water paints, paint shirts, and the visor pattern on p. 52.

Prepare visors ahead of time. Trace the visor pattern onto folded heavy paper. Cut out and punch holes where indicated. Print "Praise the Lord" across the front of each visor. Print each child's name on the underside of a visor.

During class time, let the children decorate their visors with colored markers or water paints. Fit the visors to the children's heads and tie them with pieces of yarn threaded through the holes.

As you work, talk about the sun and what it does for us. **Who created the sun? Yes, God did. What does the sun give us?** (Light, heat, daytime, energy for plants.) **A sunny day shows the power of God. When you wear this Praise Visor, remember to praise the Lord for the bright sun He made. We can trust God to give us light every day.**

Give Me Some Wool

You will need a blindfold.

Have the children stand in a circle. Choose one child to be blindfolded. Have the child sit in the center of the circle. Instruct the standing children ("sheep") to walk slowly around the blindfolded child until you say stop. Tell the blindfolded child to point toward the children and say, "Please give me some wool." The child closest to where the blindfolded child is pointing must respond by saying "Baa" like a sheep, three times. Give the blindfolded child three chances to guess the baa-ing sheep's name. If the blindfolded child is correct, he trades places with the one who baaaed. Before the blindfold is put on the next child, ask him to tell about something in nature that shows the power of God, or some way that he trusts God.

▼ 4. What Can I Do to Please God? ▲

Praise for Your Power

You will need the words to "Praise, Praise, Praise the Lord" from p. 35.

Have the children help clean up the classroom and then have them gather at the worship center.

Review the four pictures displayed under the worship banner and talk about what it means to worship God.

Gideon learned to trust God when he saw God's power and when he saw that God had answered his prayers. We can see God's power everywhere we look, and our trust in God grows stronger when we learn that He answers our prayers. Let's name some things that show God's power, and tell about times when He answered our prayers. Help the children look around the classroom for things from nature. You may find some living plants, animals, bugs, rocks, flowers, and so on. **What about your friends here in the classroom? Are they examples of God's power? Look at your hands. Are your hands and eyes examples of God's power?**

Who can tell us about a time when God answered your prayer? I'll start by telling you about an answered prayer in my life. Do so. Encourage the children to share.

Let's praise God for the things we have seen that show His power. Let's praise God for the way He helped Gideon and for the ways He helps us. Encourage each child to say a sentence prayer of praise. Give help as needed.

Sing both verses of the unit song. Review what it means to trust God. As the children leave, remind them to look for examples of God's power.

▼ Bonus Activity ▲

Snack Attack! Frozen Sunshine Snack

You will need orange juice, small paper cups, and small plastic spoons or jumbo craft sticks. Before class, prepare and freeze orange juice Popsicles. To make the Popsicles, put a spoon or stick in each cup, fill with juice, and freeze. Remove the cups from the freezer when ready to serve. (If you let the juice partially freeze before adding the sticks, the sticks will stay upright.)

Wash hands. Pray with the children before they eat their snack. Thank God for His power to make oranges and water. While the children are eating, review the Bible story. Also discuss how water is frozen. Ask them to tell about other frozen foods they like to eat. Also, ask them if they have ever walked or skated on frozen water. Allow time for discussion.

God Helps Gideon Choose an Army

Judges 7:1-8

▼ 1. What Is This Story About? ▲

God Sends Helpers

You will need to make a poster board collage before class or cover a bulletin board with pictures of people who help us. Magazines are a great source of pictures. Use teachers, doctors, nurses, parents, farmers, grocers, manufacturers, truck drivers, pilots, police officers, fire fighters, and any other helpers you can find. (Some figures are on p. 54.)

Talk to the children about how many different kinds of people help them. Ask the children to point to helpers on the board as they answer these questions: **Where do you get your food? Who pays for it? Who fixes it? Where do your clothes come from? Who helps you when you are sick? Who teaches you important things? Who makes your toothpaste? If your house caught on fire, could you put the fire out by yourself? Who would help you if you got lost?** Help the children understand that God sends many, many helpers into their lives. **Let's thank God for the helpers He gives us, and let's thank God for loving us.**

God Helps Me

You will need a variety of items that represent the ways God provides for us. For example, fresh fruit or vegetables, an article of clothing, a picture of a family, an empty medicine bottle, a small picture of Jesus, a small toy house or a picture of a real house, and a picture of your church building. Put these items on a tray and cover with a towel.

Remove the towel to show the items to the children. Ask questions about how and why God provides these things to help them. Cover the tray with the towel. **The things under this towel show ways that God helps you. How many can you remember?** (Allow responses.) **You can trust God to always help you. Let's pray and tell God we trust Him to always help us.**

▼ 2. What Does the Bible Say? ▲

Bible Story: God Chooses a Small Army

You will need the murals used in Lessons 5 and 6 and you will need to add a section for this lesson. (See p. 32 for directions on how to create this visual.) Use figures E (Gideon standing), F (soldier standing, use two copies), and G (soldier kneeling) from p. 48.

Use the murals from Lessons 5 and 6 to review. Have the children bring the figures to life.

God's people, the Israelites, needed help. The Midianites had taken the Israelites' land from them. God chose Gideon to gather an army to fight this powerful enemy, but Gideon was afraid. God showed Gideon that He would help by doing two miracles. Who remembers what the two miracles were? (*Give help as needed.*) **When Gideon saw these miracles, he knew he could trust God to help him fight the Midianites.**

Know: A Bible person who learned to trust God.
Feel: That God is powerful and worthy of trust.
Do: Put trust in God when afraid, and worship God with songs and prayers.

Children will accomplish the goals when they
- Remember how God helps them.
- Tell how God helped Gideon.
- Recite Proverbs 3:5 and tell what it means.
- Praise God for His help every day.

How to Say It
Gideon: GID-e-un
Israelite: IZ-ray-el-ite
Midianite: MID-ee-un-ite

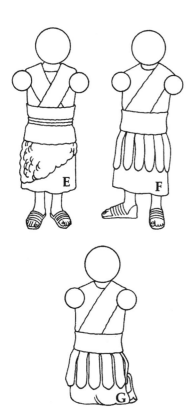

Gideon gathered his army at the top of a hill. Thousands and thousands of men came to join Gideon's army. The big army was ready to fight. In the valley below was the campsite of the Midianite army.

(Using the new section of the mural, have a child bring the figures of Gideon to life with a smile.) Gideon was probably happy that so many men came to fight the Midianites. But God had a different plan for the battle against this powerful enemy. God knew that if a huge army fought the Midianites, the soldiers would brag about how they had saved the country.

God said to Gideon, "You have too many men. Tell all of the men who are afraid to go home." *(Tell Gideon to look sad.)*

Many men went home. Still many, many men were left.

Again God said to Gideon, "You still have too many men. Take them to get a drink of water. While they drink I will tell you who to send home and who to keep.

(Have three children bring the standing soldiers and the kneeling soldier to life. Ask the soldiers who are standing to pretend to be drinking water out of their hands and to be looking around watching for the enemy. The child kneeling should have his head down and pretend to be drinking.) Gideon watched the men drink the water from the stream. God told him to send home the ones who got down on their knees to drink the water. *(The kneeling child leaves.)* Gideon was told to keep the ones who stood and used their hands to bring the water up to their mouths. Those men would be good soldiers.

Gideon had taken ten thousand men to the stream. That's a lot. Now only three hundred of them were left. That's not very many.

But God said, "This is the army you will use to fight the Midianites."

Did Gideon learn another lesson about trust? Yes, he did! He obeyed God and did what God told him to do. He trusted God to help him and to have a good plan.

Story Review: God Helped Gideon

You will need a story circle and wheel from pp. 50 and 51 for each child. Cut out all of the circles and wheels before class time. You will also need crayons and/or markers and paper fasteners.

Give each child a story circle to color. Then have them attach the wheel to the circle with a paper fastener.

As the children turn the wheel, use the picture that shows through the opening to review the Bible story.

Gideon called the men of Israel together to form an army. Did a lot of men come? (Look at the first picture.) Were there a lot of soldiers, or just a few? (Allow responses.) Yes! There were a lot of men—in fact, there were 32,000. What did God say about that big army? (Allow responses.) Who did God say should go home? (Look at the second picture.) Yes, God said all the men who were afraid to fight should go home. Gideon still had 10,000 men in his army. What did God say about that? (Allow responses.) Yes, God said that was still too many men. What did God tell Gideon to do to find out whether or not the men would be good soldiers? (Look at the next picture. Allow responses.) Only 300 men brought the water up to their mouths! All the rest got down on their knees to drink! What happened to all those men who got down on their knees? Yes, Gideon sent them home. (Look at the next picture.) Now, did Gideon have a big army or a small army? (Allow responses.) Is this going to be enough soldiers to fight the Midianites? We will find out next week!

Look at your last picture. What is it? What does a heart remind you of? Did Gideon trust God with all his heart? Let's say our Bible words together, "Trust the Lord with all your heart (Proverbs 3:5)."

Bible Words
"Trust the Lord with all your heart" (Proverbs 3:5).

Bible Memory: Praise Partners

Divide the children into pairs. Have each pair stand and face each other. Teach the rhythm in the narrow column using the Bible words for this unit and these actions: slap your thighs, clap your hands, slap your partner's hands, and put your hands on your heart.

Have the partners say the verse and do the rhythm several times. Then have the children stop and tell each other what the word "trust" means. Change partners, do the rhythm memory words again, and ask the partner to tell each other one reason why they trust God. Then change partners, do the rhythm memory words again, and ask the children to tell each other one thing that they trust God to do. Continue as long as interest remains.

"Trust	(thighs)
the	(clap)
Lord	(slap)
with	(thighs)
all	(clap)
your	(slap)
heart"	(heart)
(Proverbs	(thighs)
3:	(clap)
5).	(slap)

▼ 3. What Does This Mean to Me? ▲

Worship a Helping God

You will need the worship center as set up in Lessons 5 and 6, an *International Children's Bible* or another children's version, additional praise songs, the words to "Praise, Praise, Praise the Lord" from p. 35, the collage of helpers, and the items and tray from the activity "God Helps Me," p. 41.

Gather the children at the worship center. Lead them in a review of how to worship God. Spend time singing some praise songs, including the unit song. Select verses from Psalm 86 to read. Explain how the children's offering is used. Have a prayer time in which each child can praise God for helping him. Use the helpers collage and the tray of items to give the children ideas for prayer.

God helped Gideon choose the men for his army. Gideon listened to what God told him. He followed God's directions because he knew God is powerful. He trusted God. Let's put our trust in God, too. God will also help us.

▼ 4. What Can I Do to Please God? ▲

God Is My Helper

You will need the words to "Have You Ever Heard Me Praise God?" printed on the right.

Line up all the children like soldiers and march them around the room looking for things to clean up. When you come to a messy area, send some of your "soldiers" to clean that area. Continue until you have used all of your soldiers and the room is clean.

Gather the children in a line again and march to the worship center. Sing "Have You Ever Heard Me Praise God?" Fill in the name of one child in your class each time you sing the verse. You can alternate the words between boys and girls, or between short names and long names. After each verse, stop and let that child tell one thing she praises God for, or one thing he thanks God for. Encourage the children to praise God because He is our helper.

Have You Ever Heard Me Praise God?
(Tune: "Did You Ever See a Lassie?")

Have you ever heard
   Samantha
Samantha, Samantha?
Have you ever heard
   Samantha
Praise God for His gifts?

She praises and praises,
She praises His good works.
Have you ever heard
   Samantha
Praise God for His gifts?

Have you ever heard Tyler
Heard Tyler, heard Tyler?
Have you ever heard Tyler
Thank God for His care?

He thanks God and thanks
   God
For all of His good care.
Have you ever heard Tyler
Thank God for His care?

Gideon and His Army Trust God

Judges 7:16-22

Know: A Bible person who learned to trust God.
Feel: That God is powerful and worthy of trust.
Do: Put trust in God when afraid, and worship God with songs and prayers.

Children will accomplish the goals when they
- Choose to trust God.
- Tell others to put their trust in God.
- Tell how Gideon and his army trusted God.
- Recite Proverbs 3:5 and tell how they will trust God.
- Praise God for being trustworthy.

▼ 1. What Is This Story About? ▲

Trust God Day and Night

You will need a large yellow paper circle. This will be the sun.

Have the children stand in a circle. Instead of facing the center of the circle, have them turn around and face outward. Choose one child to walk slowly around the outside of the circle carrying the paper sun. As the sun passes, the children who can see the sun will pretend to do a normal daytime activity, such as running (in place). Those who can not see the sun should pretend to be sleeping because for them, it is nighttime. As the sun walks around, the children will wake up and run in place or stop running and go to sleep. It may take the sun several trips around the circle for everyone to catch on.

When everyone understands what to do, let the children choose their own daytime activity. Each one can do something different, such as pretending to be eating, riding a bike, swimming, skating, reading, singing, and so on. Let the children take turns carrying the sun. Before going to another activity, have the children sit down. Ask, **Can you trust God to help you in the daytime? What kind of things will God help you do? Can you trust God to take care of you during the night? What kind of things are scary in the night? How did Gideon learn to trust God?**

Trust God Doorknob Hangers

You will need the doorknob hanger pattern from p. 53, heavy white paper, and an X-Acto knife. Copy the doorknob hanger onto heavy white paper or card stock. Cut out one for each child and use the knife to make the slits. Print the words "to" and "from" on the back of each hanger. Provide crayons or markers.

Instruct the children to color and decorate the hangers. Review the Bible words. **Our Bible words say, "Trust in God." What can you tell your family about trusting God? Why should they trust God? How does God help the adults who take care of you?**

What can you tell your friends about trusting God? Why should they trust God? How does God help children? God wants us to tell others to trust Him. What do you think Gideon told his army about God?

Ask each child to think of someone to whom he would like to give his doorknob hanger. Fill in the blanks on the back of the hanger.

▼ 2. What Does the Bible Say? ▲

How to Say It
Gideon: GID-e-un
Israelite: IZ-ray-el-ite
Midianite: MID-ee-un-ite

Bible Story: God Can Be Trusted

You will need "A Lively Mural" used in Lesson 7. Use two standing soldiers and Gideon for this lesson. From p. 48, trace H (jar) and I (torch) onto cardboard. Make two of each item. Cut them out and color each one. Tape a jar and a torch back to back. You will also need three trumpets from the Story Review activity, "Trumpets for Gideon's Army." See p. 45.

Gideon was often afraid. When God called him to save the Israelites, he was hiding from the Midianites. After God told him to gather an army, he asked God for a miracle. When God gave him a miracle, Gideon asked for another one. Finally, Gideon was ready to trust God, and to help save His people.

(Have three children bring Gideon and the standing soldiers to life.) **God gave Gideon an army of three hundred men to fight the powerful Midianites. Then God told Gideon how to win without even fighting.**

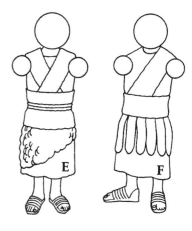

This was the plan. Each man carried a trumpet and a clay jar, and inside the jar was a flaming torch. *(Hand each of the soldiers a trumpet and a jar/torch. Show the children both sides of the jar/torch. Then have the soldiers hold up the jar sides.)* **Gideon and his army waited until the very middle of the night, when the Midianites were sound asleep. Gideon said, "Watch me and do what I do."** *(Ask Gideon to repeat this sentence.)* **Some of Gideon's men surrounded the campsite of the Midianites. Others went with Gideon to the edge of the campsite. When Gideon blew his trumpet,** *(have Gideon make trumpet noises),* **every man smashed his clay jar on the ground and blew his trumpet! Suddenly the Midianites were surrounded by terrifying noise and flaming torches!** *(Tell the soldier/children to make loud trumpet noises and wave their torches.)* **The soldiers waved their torches and shouted, "For the Lord and for Gideon!"** *(Have the soldier/children shout, "For the Lord and for Gideon." Then have the entire class shout, "For the Lord and for Gideon.")*

What do you think happened to the sleeping Midianites? If you think they were scared, you are right. They jumped up from their beds, scared and confused. In the middle of the night, the three hundred flaming torches made them think that a huge army was surrounding them. Someone probably shouted, "The enemy is here!"

Gideon and his army stood still and watched. The Midianites were so frightened and mixed up they fought each other and ran away. Gideon and his army did not even have to fight. They won the battle without fighting!

Now, do you think Gideon and his army trusted God? Yes, they did.

Story Review: Trumpets for Gideon's Army

You will need the horn pattern from p. 53, heavy white paper, a white cardboard toilet paper tube (or paper towel tubes cut into thirds) for each trumpet, crayons or markers, and glue or tape.

Before class time, trace the horn onto heavy paper and cut out. Provide one for each child.

Give each child a horn and a cardboard tube to color and decorate. Have them put their names on their trumpets. Glue or tape the tube and the horn together as illustrated on p. 53.

Show the children how to make trumpet sounds. Use the trumpets for reviewing the story of Gideon. Ask questions that can be answered with only yes or no. If the answer is yes, the children are to make a high sound with their trumpets. If the answer is no, the children are to make a low sound. Here are some sample questions:

Were the Midianites mean to God's people?

When the angel visited Gideon, was he sleeping?

Was Gideon chosen to save God's people because he was brave and important?

Use the questions and Story Review activities on pages 34, 38, and 42 to make up more yes and no questions. Ask as many review questions as time will allow.

Bible Memory: Campfire Time

You will need a tent (made by spreading a sheet over a table), a pretend campfire (made by attaching red and yellow tissue paper to brown paper towel tubes stacked like logs), several flashlights (a couple in the campfire would be good), and words to several camping songs.

Gather the children around the campfire. If possible, turn out the classroom lights. Let the children take turns holding the flashlights. Sing several camping songs. Ask the children to say Proverbs 3:5 in unison. Go around the campfire and ask each teacher to tell how he or she will trust God this week. Go around the campfire again and ask the children to share how they will trust God this week. Close with a prayer asking for help to trust Him.

▼ 3. What Does This Mean to Me? ▲

Let's Trust God

You will need the worship center set up as in Lessons 5-7, an *International Children's Bible* or another children's version, and the words to "Praise, Praise, Praise the Lord" from p. 35.

Gather the children at the worship center. This will be the last time to use this center unless you want to keep it as a regular part of each class. Review the words "Worship God" and the pictures of children worshiping. Sing the unit song. Then read Proverbs 3:1, 5, 6.

These Bible words tell us it is important for children to remember to trust the Lord. If you trust the Lord, He will help you. Let's say together the part we have memorized.

Lead the children in saying Proverbs 3:5. If you have collected an offering, remind the children that giving an offering is one way to show God their love. Close the worship time with prayer. Thank God for being trustworthy.

Gideon Says!

Play "Gideon Says" similar to the way you play the game of "Simon Says."

When Gideon was telling his army God's plan for fighting the Midianites, he said, "Watch me! Do what I do!" Let's play a game about following Gideon. If I say, "Gideon says, 'Trust the Lord,'" then you must jump three times. If I only say, "Trust the Lord," you must not jump because I did not say, "Gideon says." Demonstrate and then give only positive directions when you say "Gideon says." For example:

(Gideon says)	(Say nothing)
Don't be afraid!	Be selfish!
Ask God for help!	Fight with your friends!
Praise the Lord!	Don't obey your parents!
Thank God for His help!	Complain about your food!

▼ 4. What Can I Do to Please God? ▲

Trusting Hearts

You will need copies of the "Gideon Award" from p. 54. Prepare an award for each child by filling in the appropriate information. You will also need the words to "Praise, Praise, Praise the Lord" from p. 35.

Gather the children in the center of the classroom. Tell them to pretend they are Gideon's army surrounding the Midianites. Say, **Before we can surprise the Midianites, we must clean up the room. Follow me silently on your tiptoes around the classroom and I will point to certain soldiers to clean up or pick up a messy area. You must watch me carefully so you will know what to do.**

After our room is clean, tiptoe quietly back to worship center. Then we will surprise the Midianites. As the children arrive in the worship center, hand them their trumpets. Remind them that they must be very, very quiet. When all the children are gathered, whisper **As soon as I blow my trumpet, you may blow your trumpets and shout, "For the Lord and for Gideon!"** Let the children make a lot of noise, then sing both verses of "Praise, Praise, Praise the Lord."

This is our last lesson about Gideon. You have learned a lot about trusting God. Remember that your doorknob hanger says, "Trust in God." When you take your hanger to your friend, tell your friend what you have learned about trusting God.

You have also learned how to worship. I know God is pleased. I have a "Gideon Award" for each of you. Gideon learned to trust God and God helped his army win the battle with the Midianites without fighting. You have learned how important it is to trust God with all of your heart.

Present the awards and close with prayer.

▼ Bonus Activity ▲

Snack Attack! S'mores

You will need jumbo craft sticks (for spreaders); graham crackers, a jar of marshmallow creme, and chocolate bars to make S'mores; and the pretend campfire from the Bible Memory activity, "Campfire Time."

Wash hands. Let the children make their own S'mores. Each child will need two graham cracker halves, one section of a chocolate bar, and a craft stick for spreading the marshmallow creme. Show the children how to spread the marshmallow creme on one cracker half. Then place a piece of chocolate on top of the creme. Finally place the other cracker on top. Give help as needed.

Gather the children around the pretend campfire. Offer a prayer for the snack. As the children eat, ask them to share their camping experiences.

A
angel

B
Gideon

F
soldier

E
Gideon

D
Gideon

I

G
soldier

Story Circle

Cut out the story circle and the story wheel (p. 51).
Color the story circle as desired.
Lay the story wheel on top of the story circle and
attach in the center with a paper fastener.

Story Wheel

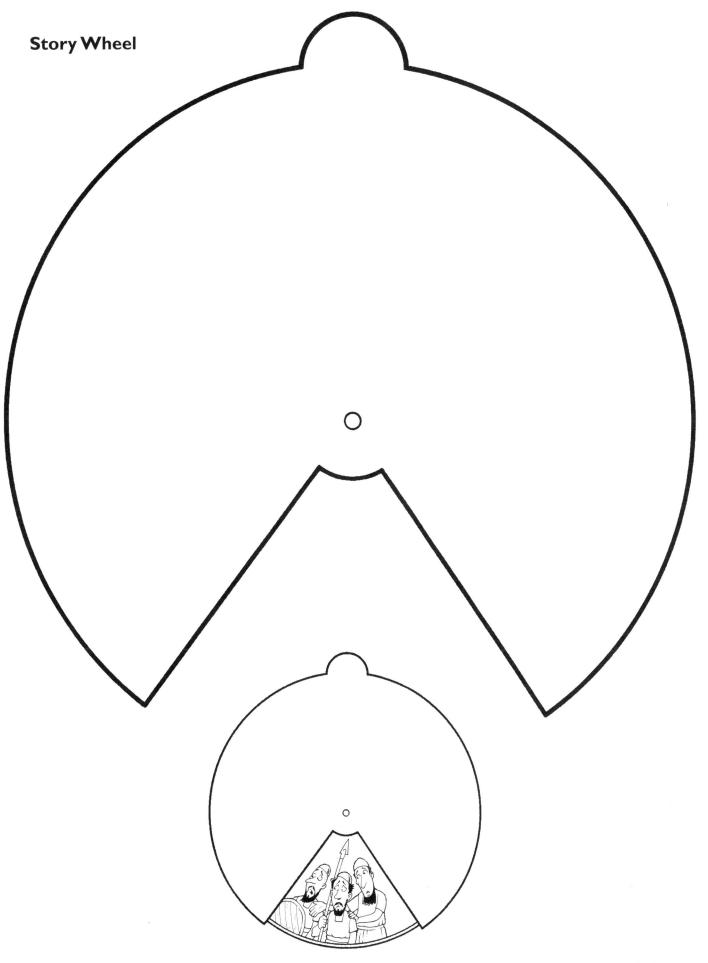

Heart Puzzle

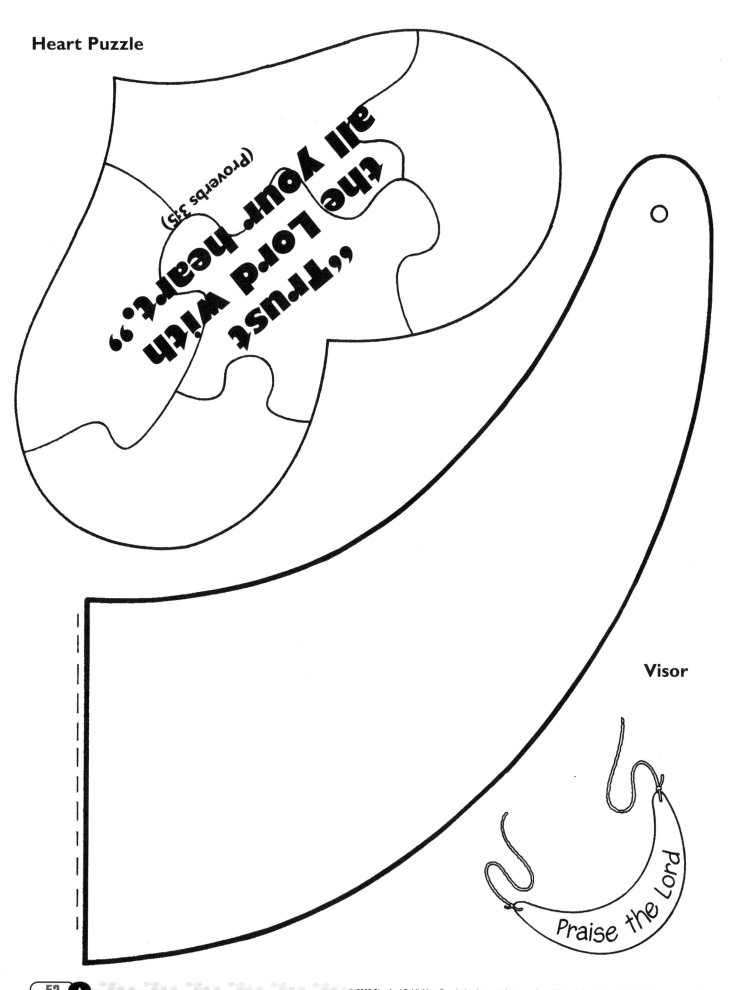

"Trust in the Lord with all your heart." (Proverbs 3:5)

Visor

Praise the Lord

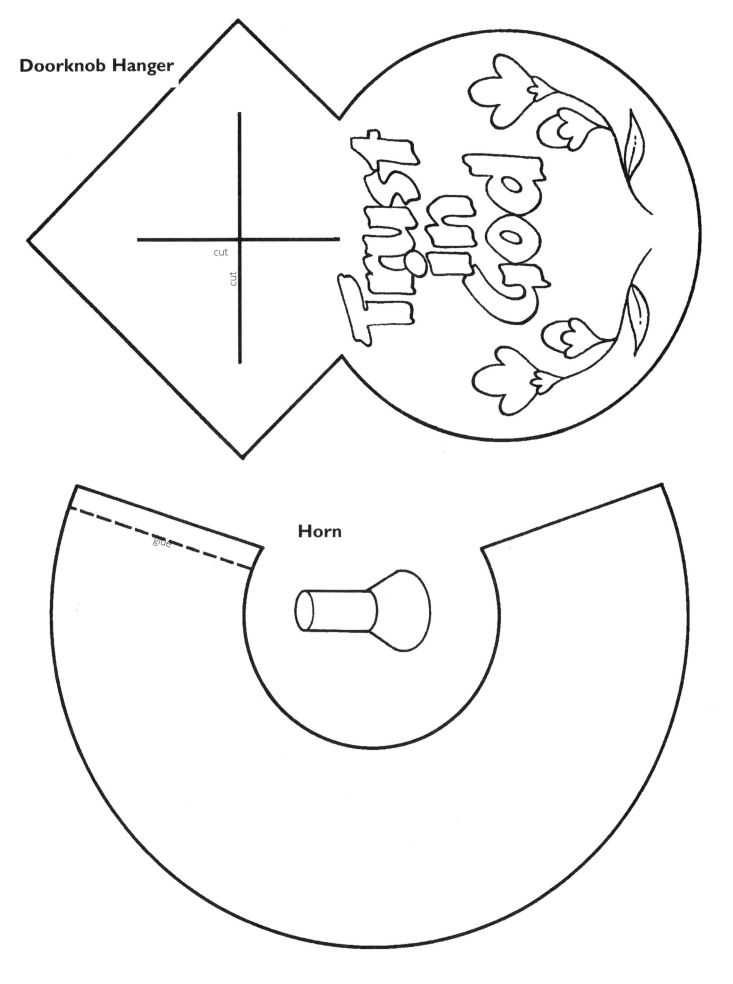

Doorknob Hanger

cut

cut

Trust in God

Horn

glue

Bookmarks

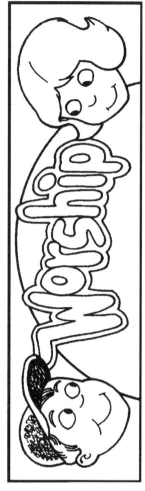

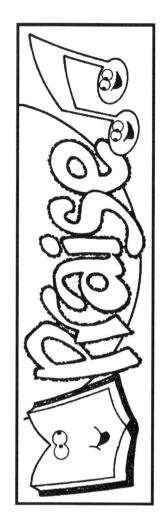

Gideon Award

Congratulations to

_____

for learning to trust God with all your heart.

Presented by _____

on _____

Helpers

UNIT 3

Learning to Do What Is Right

Lessons 9-12

Unit Bible Words
"Do what the Lord says is good and right. [Then things will go well for you]" (Deuteronomy 6:18).

(Note: This verse has been divided into two parts. If you are teaching four-year-olds, use the first part only. If you are teaching older children, include the words in brackets.)

Bible Character
Nehemiah

9 Nehemiah Wants to Do What Is Right
Nehemiah 1:1–2:6—Nehemiah, a cupbearer for a Persian king, prays that God will help him return to Jerusalem to rebuild the city's gates and wall, a task that had been neglected.

10 Nehemiah Asks Others to Help Him
Nehemiah 2:11-20—Nehemiah returns to Jerusalem. During a night inspection of the gates and wall, he determines what needs to be done. Nehemiah approaches the people and asks for their help. The people respond by saying, "Let's get started."

11 God's People Do What Is Right
Nehemiah 3; 4; 6:15, 16—Nehemiah and the people work hard to rebuild the wall and gates. When some enemies try to cause trouble, Nehemiah prays for God's help. With God's help, Nehemiah maintains peace and keeps all the people working. The wall is rebuilt in just fifty-two days!

12 God's People Thank God
Nehemiah 8:1-12—When the wall is finished, the people gather to thank God. Ezra, the temple priest, reads from the Book of the Teachings of Moses. The people listen and are sad because they have not obeyed God. Nehemiah tells them to celebrate because the joy of the Lord will make them strong.

By the end of this unit, the children and leaders will
Know: A Bible person who chose to do what was right.
Feel: That God will help them do right.
Do: Pray before making decisions and ask God to help them do right.

Why Teach This Unit to Four- to Six-Year-Olds?
One way children learn is by observing others. This unit provides an opportunity for children to be actively involved in role plays and to observe others acting out right and wrong behaviors. Through role playing they will experience and observe the consequences of these behaviors. Consequences, either natural or structured, have a powerful effect in training a child. Use this unit to provide an environment in which children can learn valuable lessons about the choices they make.

In this unit the children will meet Nehemiah and will observe his efforts that rebuilt the wall around Jerusalem. They will also learn that the key to Nehemiah's success was his faith in God. Nehemiah trusted God to hear and answer his prayers. Children will learn from Nehemiah the importance of doing what is right. They will also learn that God is always there to help them.

Meet Nehemiah
Nehemiah was a Jew living in exile. He had a very responsible job as the cupbearer for the Persian king, Artaxerxes. The king placed great trust in Nehemiah.

When Nehemiah heard that the wall around Jerusalem had not been rebuilt even though many Jews had returned from exile, he was very upset. He prayed to

God to help him do what was right. God heard his prayer. The answer gave Nehemiah the enormous task of gathering the workers and the supplies to rebuild the gates and the wall around Jerusalem.

At every obstacle Nehemiah turned to God in prayer for help and guidance. In record-breaking time, just fifty-two days, the wall was completed and Jerusalem was safe from her enemies. With God's help, Nehemiah and his crew of workers had accomplished a task so enormous that even their enemies had to admit their God had helped them.

Nehemiah is a role model who put total faith in God to help him do what was right. As a man of prayer, Nehemiah will show children the importance of being guided by God in every thing they do.

Unit Visuals: A Living Drama

Use adults or teenagers to play the parts of the Bible characters. Keep costuming simple, such as bathrobes and oversized colored T-shirts tied with fabric belts. Special props required are described at the beginning of each story.

Unit Song

Do What Is Right

(Tune: "The Wise Man Built His House Upon the Rock")

Verse 1
Pray for help to do what is right. *(Fold hands in prayer.)*
(Repeat two more times.)
And God will hear your prayer. *(Cup hands to your ears.)*

Verse 2
God will help you do what is right. *(Point upward.)*
(Repeat two more times.)
And He will answer your prayer. *(Clap! Clap!)*

Verse 3
Come, let's rebuild Jerusalem's wall. *(Motion others to come.)*
(Repeat two more times.)
Let's all work and do what is right. *(Put one fist on top of the other—building motions.)*

Verse 4
Nehemiah prayed as the wall was rebuilt.
(Fold hands in prayer and then put one fist on top of the other.)
(Repeat two more times.)
And Jerusalem was made safe. *(Clasp hands together.)*

Verse 5
The people rejoiced and praised the Lord. *(Clap hands as you sing the words.)*
(Repeat two more times.)
For helping them rebuild the wall. *(Put one fist on top of the other.)*

Nehemiah Wants to Do What Is Right

LESSON 9

Nehemiah 1:1–2:6

▼ 1. What Is This Story About? ▲

Right or Wrong?

You will need two clear plastic cups. On one cup draw a sad face and on the other cup draw a happy face. You will also need the story strips from p. 71. Cut the story strips apart.

Draw the faces on the cups so that all the children can see them. Read the strips one at a time. Discuss the behavior of the child in the story. If the child did what was right, put the strip in the happy face cup. If the child did what was wrong, put the strip in the sad face cup.

When you do what is wrong, how do you feel inside? How does doing what is right make you feel? Today you will meet a Bible man named Nehemiah. Some people did a very bad thing, and it made Nehemiah cry. He wanted to do what was right. He prayed and asked God to help him. God will help you and me do what is right, too. Let's pray and ask God for His help.

Do What Is Right

You will need the words to verses one and two of "Do What Is Right" from p. 56.

We all want to do what is right, but we need help. Today we will meet a Bible man named Nehemiah. He knew the only way to do right was to ask God for His help.

Prayer is the way we ask God for help. Here is a song that will help us remember to pray.

Teach the words to "Do What Is Right." Ask the children to tell you about a time when they needed God's help to do what was right. Pray with the children, asking God to help them do what is right today during class time.

▼ 2. What Does the Bible Say? ▲

Bible Story: Nehemiah Prays for Help

You will need a male storyteller to play the part of Nehemiah dressed in a Bible costume. If this is not possible, use a puppet dressed as Nehemiah. You will also need to provide a goblet and several large rocks.

Hello, boys and girls. My name is Nehemiah. I lived back in Bible times before Jesus was born. I want to tell you how God helped me to do what was right.

First, do you know the difference between right and wrong behavior? (*Let the children respond. If you did not use the activity, "Right or Wrong?," discuss briefly.*) **I am glad you know so much about doing what is right.**

God helped me to do what was right when I was the cupbearer for a powerful king. (*Show the goblet.*) **A cupbearer's job is very important. He serves the king whatever he wants to drink. Part of the cupbearer's job**

Know: A Bible person who chose to do what was right.

Feel: That God will help them do right.

Do: Pray before making decisions and ask God to help them do right.

Children will accomplish the goals when they

- Discuss the difference between right and wrong behavior.
- Tell why Nehemiah wanted to build a new wall around Jerusalem.
- Begin to memorize Deuteronomy 6:18.
- Sing a song about doing right.
- Ask God to help them do what is right.

How to Say It
Nehemiah: Nee-huh-MY-uh
Judah: JOO-duh

is to make sure that no enemy puts anything bad in the king's drink. Only someone the king trusts to protect him can be a cupbearer. I was given this important job even though I was not from Persia, the same country as the king.

I am a Jew. My family came from Judah, the land that belonged to God's chosen people. Long ago, Jerusalem, the city where God was worshiped, was attacked by enemy kings and their armies. Many Jews were taken away to live in other places. The beautiful city of Jerusalem was torn down and burned. The wall that went all the way around the city was just a pile of rocks. (*Stack rocks. Knock them over.*) The wooden gates were burned down. I was taken from Jerusalem to live in Persia. The king learned that he could trust me, and that's when I became his cupbearer.

While I was living in Persia, my brother came to see me. I wanted to hear news about the Jews, and about Jerusalem. My brother said that many had come back to live in Judah, but no one had repaired the walls of Jerusalem, or built new gates. The Jews were in great danger. There were many enemies who did not like God's people. Without a wall around Jerusalem they were not safe.

This news made me very sad. I cried for several days. I could not eat. Do you know what to do when you are sad? The best thing to do is pray, and that is just what I did.

Listen to my prayer. (*Fold your hands. Bow your head.*) God, You are a great God. I am Your servant. I love You! Your people did many things that were not right. You sent them far away. Now they have come back home, but they have not repaired the city. I want to serve You, Lord. I am going to talk to the king about the trouble in Jerusalem. Please let the king be kind to me. Amen.

Soon after that, the king called me to give him something to drink. (*Lift up the goblet.*) When I handed him the cup, he saw the sad look on my face.

"Why do you look so sad?" he asked.

I was afraid, but I told him about my family's city, Jerusalem. I said, "I am sad because no one has repaired the city walls or gates."

The king said, "What do you want me to do?"

Before I answered, I prayed! Then I asked the king to let me go to Jerusalem to rebuild the wall and the gates.

God answered my prayer. The king was kind to me. He said, "Go to Jerusalem and rebuild the wall."

I was glad I could go and do what was right.

Story Review: Builder's Relay

You will need a fairly large number of building blocks, at least two or three for each child in your class. You may borrow these from the toddler room, or collect and cover shoe boxes with brown mailing paper. You will also need to compile a list of questions about Nehemiah (see the questions in the narrow column).

Mark off two boundaries about fifteen feet apart. Divide the class into two teams. Line up the teams behind one of the boundary lines. The leader will stand opposite the teams on the other boundary. Place equal piles of building blocks in front of each team. Tell the children that you are going to call out questions about Nehemiah and the first child to raise his or her hand will get to answer. Tell the children that you are going to have a race to see which team can get its half of the wall built first. Call out a question. Have your assistants help you spot the first hand to go up. (Try to alternate calling on teams.) When a child correctly answers a question, he or she gets to pick up a block and run and place it on the opposite boundary line. Play until every child has had a turn to answer a question, or as long as the children are interested.

What did Nehemiah do for the king?

What was important about being a cupbearer?

In what country did Nehemiah serve this king?

Where did Nehemiah and his family used to live?

What happened to the city of Jerusalem?

What did the walls of Jerusalem look like?

What happened to the wooden gates of the city?

What could happen to the people without a city wall?

Name one thing Nehemiah did when he heard about Jerusalem.

Name another thing Nehemiah did when he heard about Jerusalem.

What did the king let Nehemiah do?

Bible Memory: Please Pass the Cup

You will need a plastic or paper cup, or you can use the goblet you used during the Bible story.

As you begin to teach Deuteronomy 6:18, say the words several times for the children. Have the children sit in a circle on the floor. Pass the cup around the circle as each word is said. Do this in unison. (Optional: as the cup is passed, only the child holding the cup will say the next word in the verse.)

▼ 3. What Does This Mean to Me? ▲

Cup O' Good Deeds

You will need copies of the letter to parents from p. 72. Also provide two 16-ounce plastic cups per child, packing pellets (sometimes called "peanuts"), plastic sandwich bags, stickers, and black permanent markers. Before class, print "Cup O' Good Deeds" on half of the cups. Print each child's name on one of the other (blank) cups.

Give each child two cups. One cup is labeled with his or her name and the other cup is labeled "Cup O' Good Deeds." Let the children decorate both of their cups with stickers and/or markers. Fill a sandwich bag for each child with packing pellets. Place the bags in the "name" cups. Read the parents' letter aloud. Discuss with the children how they will fill their "Cup O' Good Deeds." Review the story strips used in "Right or Wrong?" if necessary.

A Handy Prayer

You will need copies of the label "My Handy Prayer" and a set of stickers from p. 71 for each child. Also provide paper and crayons or markers. Before class time, follow the directions on p. 71 to prepare the label and stickers.

Trace each child's right hand onto a piece of paper. Print the following letters on the thumb and fingers: "T" on thumb; "P" on pointer; "M" on Middle; "R" on ring; "L" on little finger.

Pass out the stickers one at a time, discuss each one, and instruct the children to attach each sticker above the corresponding thumb or finger. (Optional: Let the children color the sticker.)

When Nehemiah wanted to do what was right, he asked God to help him. When he prayed, God listened and helped him. God will help you do what is right, too.

Your hand will help you remember how to pray for God's help. Look at your hand that you traced. The word "thumb" begins with the letter "T" and so does the word "today." Place this sticker of a sun above your thumb on your paper. It will remind you to pray today and every day for God's help in doing what is right.

Look at your pointing finger. "Pointing" begins with the letter "P" and so does "play." Place this sticker of some toys above your pointing finger. Always pray for God's help in doing what is right when you play.

Here is a sticker of some food. This sticker stands for "mealtimes." Put it above your middle finger. "Mealtimes" and "middle" begin with the letter "M." Always remember to thank God for the food He has given you to eat and not fuss about it. You can also thank God for the person who earned the money to buy the food, and the person who fixed it for you.

Look at your ring finger. What letter do you see? Yes, "R" stands for "ring" and "rest." Here is a sticker of a bed. When it is time to take a nap or it is bedtime, you can do what is right by not fussing. When you are resting in your bed is a perfect time to talk to God. You can thank Him for all the

Bible Words
"Do what the Lord says is good and right. [Then things will go well for you]" (Deuteronomy 6:18).

(Note: This verse has been divided into two parts. If you are teaching four-year-olds, use the first part only. If you are teaching older children, include the words in brackets.)

6:18
And thou shalt do that which is right and good in the sight of the Lord; that it ~~might~~ may be well with thee...

many things He has given you, and ask Him for help with the problems in your life.

The last finger is your little finger. "L" stands for "little" and "love." Loving others is always the right thing to do. God wants to help you love others. When you feel angry and feel like yelling at someone, stop and pray, and ask God to help you love that person.

Give each child a "My Handy Prayer" label to add to the paper. **Let's use our "Handy Prayer" and ask God to help us do what is right today!**

▼ 4. What Can I Do to Please God? ▲

Ready to Do What Is Right

You will need the "Handy Prayer" pictures, copies of the parents' letters regarding the "Cup O' Good Deeds," and the words to verses one and two of "Do What Is Right."

Gather the children in a circle. Review what they are to do this week with their "Cup O' Good Deeds." Pass out the parents' explanation letter to be taken home with each child.

Then use the "Handy Prayer." **Let's ask God for help today.** Give the children opportunity to pray silently or aloud. Model a simple prayer sentence for each finger of the "Handy Prayer." Example: **Dear God, help me do what is right today. Help me be kind when I play.**

Doing what is right at church means helping to clean up our classroom. Let's sing our new song as we work together. Compliment the children as you see them put the room back in order.

▼ Bonus Activity ▲

Snack Attack! Fit for a King

You will need to make fruit-flavored gelatin in clear plastic cups. To make it even prettier, mix cubes of different colored gelatin in each cup. Provide plastic spoons.

When you serve the jeweled gelatin to the children, pretend to be a cupbearer. Let the children play the kings and queens. Review why Nehemiah's job was so important and why he prayed that the king would be kind to him.

Nehemiah Asks Others to Help Him   LESSON 10
Nehemiah 2:11-20

▼ 1. What Is This Story About? ▲

Let's Pretend

You will need some adults or teens to role-play the following four situations. Give the situations to the players beforehand so that they are familiar with what they are supposed to do. The leader may narrate the action, but Michael should say his own lines.

• Michael and some other children are playing in the sandbox at school. Playtime is over, so the teacher calls the children to line up. The children in the sandbox are very busy building a road and a tunnel. No one wants to stop. Finally, Michael says, "It's time to go. We can play in the sandbox next time." All the children line up.

• It is Bible story time. The children are sitting on the floor. Joshua is next to Michael. Joshua gets tired of sitting, so he lies down. Michael decides to lie down like Joshua. The teacher says, "Michael and Joshua, please sit up. It is time to be good listeners." Michael sits up, but Joshua doesn't. Michael says to Joshua, "Come on, Joshua, let's be good listeners."

• Michael is riding home from church with Emily and her mother. Michael and Emily are sitting in the back seat with their seat belts on. When they are half way home, Michael and Emily decide to trade seats. They take off their seat belts, trade seats, and forget to put the seat belts on again.

• It is music time. Every child is given a rhythm instrument to play. The teacher asks everyone to watch her for the signal to begin playing the instruments. Hannah doesn't wait for the signal. She begins tapping her sticks. Michael decides to shake his tambourine, too.

After each role play, discuss with the children how Michael helped others do what was right or how he could have helped others do right.

A Friendship Wall

You will need old shirts to cover children's clothing, newspaper, craft sticks, and ingredients for making molding clay. The recipe makes four 3" x 1" x 1" bricks. Multiply the recipe so that you have enough clay for each child in your class to make three or four bricks. You will also need trays or boards to set the bricks on until they are dry. Prepare the molding clay recipe before class. Provide one or more model bricks to show the children the correct size and shape.

This activity will take two lessons to complete. In this lesson, bricks will be made. In the next lesson, the dry bricks will be connected with fresh molding clay used as mortar to form a wall.

Spread newspaper over the work area. Cover the children's clothing with old shirts. Let the children make bricks. Try to keep the bricks the same size. Use a pointed instrument to print each child's initials on the bricks he or she makes.

When Nehemiah went to Jerusalem to rebuild the wall, he needed many people to help him. He needed a lot of rocks and bricks. Everyone had to help and work together. Each person was needed to get the job done. We need each of you to help make our friendship bricks. We must work together to get the job done. Next week, when the bricks are dry, we will cement them together to make our friendship wall.

During the week, bake the bricks at 200° for about an hour.

Know: A Bible person who chose to do what was right.
Feel: That God will help them do right.
Do: Pray before making decisions and ask God to help them do right.

Children will accomplish the goals when they

• Discuss how they can help others do what is right.
• Tell about others who decided to help Nehemiah build the wall.
• Memorize Deuteronomy 6:18.
• Start building a friendship wall.
• Demonstrate how they can choose to do right.

Molding Clay
1 cup sand
1/2 cup cornstarch
1/2 cup boiling water
Mix sand and cornstarch in a saucepan. Pour in boiling water. Stir constantly. Cook until thick. When cool, mold as desired or wrap in plastic until ready to use.

▼ 2. What Does the Bible Say? ▲

Bible Story: Nehemiah Needs Help

You will need a storyteller dressed as Nehemiah in a Bible costume. If this is not possible, use a puppet dressed as Nehemiah. You will also need several large rocks, several pieces of old, charred wood, and the words to verse three of "Do What Is Right" from p. 56.

How to Say It

Nehemiah: Nee-huh-MY-uh

Hello, boys and girls! Do you remember me? My name is Nehemiah. The last time I saw you, I told you I worked for a king. Do you remember what my job was? *(Let the children respond.)* **Yes, I was his cupbearer.**

I also told you something that made me very sad. What was it? *(Let the children respond.)* **That's right! I was sad because God's chosen people were in trouble. The wall around Jerusalem was just a pile of rocks, and the gates had been burned down. Someone needed to do what was right. The wall and gates needed to be repaired.**

What was my prayer? *(Allow children to respond.)* **Yes, I asked God to help the king be kind to me. Then I asked the king to let me go to Jerusalem and rebuild the wall.**

Do you remember what made me happy? Yes, the king said I could go to Jerusalem and repair the wall and make new gates. I could do what was right for Jerusalem and God's people.

Well, I went to Jerusalem. At first I did not tell anyone God had sent me to rebuild the wall. I waited three days. Later, when it was night. I rode an animal around the city. I wanted to look closely at the broken wall. I saw the piles of rock. *(Show rocks.)* **I saw the burned wooden gates.** *(Show pieces of charred wood.)* **In some places there was not room for the animal I was riding to walk. I had to ride down in the valley to look up at the broken wall. It was then that I decided what needed to be done to rebuild the wall and its gates.**

Finally, I said to the people of Jerusalem, "Come, let's build the wall. Let's do what is right." I told the people that God had answered my prayer for the king to be kind to me. The king let me leave my important job as his cupbearer and sent me to rebuild the wall. The people listened and said, "Let's start rebuilding the wall!"

All of God's people worked very hard to do what was right.

Teach verse three of "Do What Is Right."

Story Review: Do Right at Night

You will need copies of the sleeping child on p. 71, one small envelope for each child, fabric scraps, crayons, glue, scissors, and craft sticks.

Before class time, cut out one figure of the sleeping child for each child in your class. Cut a slit in the envelopes as illustrated here; then seal them.

Have each child color the figure of the sleeping child and the pajamas to look like himself. Glue a craft stick to the back of each figure for extra support. Pass out the envelopes and let the children decorate them with fabric to look like their beds.

Review the Bible story using the sleeping child to "act out" answers to questions.

What do you do at nighttime? (Children show the sleeping child.)

What did Nehemiah do when it was nighttime? (Take the sleeping child out of the bed and pretend it is Nehemiah riding.)

How did Nehemiah feel when he saw the broken walls? (Children can make sad faces.)

What did Nehemiah decide to do? (Pretend to ask others for help with sleeping child.)

Bible Memory: Do Right Light

You will need a flashlight.

Hold up the flashlight and say, **Nehemiah did not have a flashlight to take with him as he inspected the wall around Jerusalem at night. I am sure he could have used one. Instead of a flashlight, what might have helped him see the broken wall? Yes, the moon and stars also help people see at night. Yes, perhaps he had a torch.**

Today we are going to use this flashlight to help us remember our Bible words.

Review the Bible words. Then play "Flashlight Tag." Designate the boundaries of your playing area. The children are to move about within this area. (Optional: Turn off the lights. You will want the room darkened, but not totally dark.) Begin the game by telling the children that they may begin moving around the area. Shine the flashlight on the moving feet of an adult assistant. She will say the Bible words. You will then shine the light on the feet of one of the moving children. All the children are to stop moving and listen to the child who was tagged by the light say the Bible words. Be sure every child is tagged.

▼ 3. What Does This Mean to Me? ▲

Do Right Times

You will need the spinner game from p. 72, one paper fastener, and one paper clip. Assemble the spinner game according to the instructions.

Divide the children into groups of no more than ten. Provide a spinner for each group. Let the children take turns spinning the spinner and pantomiming how they can choose to do right during the times of the day pictured. Give ideas as needed.

▼ 4. What Can I Do to Please God? ▲

Want to See Me Do Right?

You will need two adults to demonstrate the actions and words of child A and B.

Have the children sit in a circle. Child A says to child B, "Want to see me do what is right?' Child B says, "Yes! Yes!" Child A demonstrates a good deed, such as picking up toys. Child B says, "That was good!" Child B then turns to child C and says, "Want to see me do what is right?" Child B then demonstrates another type of good deed. The routine is repeated around the circle until Child A is reached.

Help Others Do What Is Right

You will need the words to verses one, two, and three of "Do What Is Right" from p. 56.

Gather the children in the center of the classroom. Select several children to walk around the room inspecting the classroom for things that need to be cleaned, picked up, or put away. Have them report back to the rest of the children what jobs need to be done. Let the children choose what jobs they will do. Then send all of the children to clean up the room.

After the room is straightened, gather the children in a circle. Compliment the children for their efforts. Sing three verses of "Do What Is Right." Close with prayer, asking God to help children and leaders do what is right.

God's People Do What Is Right

Know: A Bible person who chose to do what was right.

Feel: That God will help them do right.

Do: Pray before making decisions and ask God to help them do right.

Children will accomplish the goals when they

- Finish building a friendship wall.
- Tell how Nehemiah and the people built the wall.
- Recite Deuteronomy 6:18.
- Demonstrate what it means to be a peacemaker.
- Do a good deed.

▼ 1. What Is This Story About? ▲

A Friendship Wall

You will need the dry bricks made in Lesson 10 along with fresh molding clay to be used as mortar (see recipe on p. 61), old shirts to cover children's clothing, craft sticks, newspaper, and the words to "Do What Is Right" from p. 56.

Cover the work area with newspaper. Put shirts over the children's clothing. Use a thin layer of fresh molding clay for the mortar to connect all bricks. As the bricks are stacked, place the initialed sides all on the same side of the wall. (Let the children do as much of the work as they can. It is the doing that is important and not the finished product.)

When the people started rebuilding the wall around Jerusalem, they had to work together. Some people hauled stones. Others made bricks. Water needed to be carried. Wood needed to be cut. All of the people worked very hard. We are building a friendship wall. We need to help each other. Some will spread the mortar. All of us will add bricks. Others will clean up. Helping one another is the right thing to do.

As the children work, sing the first three verses of "Do What is Right."

▼ 2. What Does the Bible Say? ▲

Bible Story: How the Wall Was Built

You will need the storyteller dressed as Nehemiah in a Bible costume (preferably the same man you used before) and two men or older boys dressed in biblical costumes to play the parts of Sanballat and Tobiah, or use three puppets as the characters. You will also need several rocks, several pieces of new wood, tools such as a hammer, saw, trowel, and tape measure, and a carpenter's apron for Nehemiah to wear.

Nehemiah: **Hello, boys and girls. Do you remember my name?** (*Allow responses.*) **That's right! I'm Nehemiah. Do you remember what I wanted to do that was right?** (*Allow responses.*) **Good! I wanted to rebuild the wall and gates around Jerusalem. This was the right thing to do because Jerusalem was the city where God's people came to worship Him. Without the wall, God's people were in danger.**

Do you remember what the people of Jerusalem said when I told them my plan? That's right! They said, "Let's build the wall!"

I knew God would help us rebuild the wall. He heard and answered all my prayers to help me do what was right.

There were many workers. People came from all over Judah. Goldsmiths, traders, perfume makers, and fabric weavers helped to rebuild the wall.

There were many different jobs. Stones and bricks had to be put back in place. (*Stack the rocks.*) **New wooden gates had to be made.** (*Show the wood.*) **Water and supplies had to be carried from place to place. Here are tools like the ones we used.** (*Show the carpenter's apron and demonstrate how to use the tools.*)

How to Say It

Judah: JOO-duh
Nehemiah: Nee-huh-MY-uh
Sanballat: San-BAL-ut
Tobiah: Toe-BYE-uh

While some people were working hard, others laughed at us and tried to stir up trouble. Listen to what two men named Sanballat and Tobiah said about our hard work.

(Enter Sanballat and Tobiah laughing.)

Sanballat: **Look! They think they can rebuild the wall in one day. To do that, those stones would have to be alive.** *(Laugh.)*

Tobiah: **That new wall is so weak it would crumble if a fox jumped on it.** *(Laugh. Both mockers exit laughing.)*

Nehemiah: **Sanballat, Tobiah, and others were angry with me. They did not want Jerusalem to have a strong wall. I knew these people wanted to cause trouble. I needed to be a peacemaker. I needed to help the workers not be angry with these troublemakers.**

Who remembers what I did every time I needed God's help? *(Allow responses.)* **You are right! I prayed. I told God these men were making fun of us. God helped me be a peacemaker, and the people kept working.**

When the wall was half done, I prayed to God again. I put guards around the wall during the day and nighttime.

The workers were still afraid. I told them to remember the Lord and think about His greatness. I reminded them that they were doing what was right for God and their families.

Finally, the enemies stopped stirring up trouble. All of the workers went back to their jobs. Half of the people worked on the wall and the other half were guards.

In just fifty-two days the wall was finished! Our enemies were surprised. They knew God helped us do what was right.

Teach the fourth verse to "Do What Is Right." Then sing the first four verses.

Story Review: Pray, Pray, Work!

You will need a playing area, and a list of questions about Nehemiah compiled from the first three lessons.

Play this game the same way "Duck, Duck, Goose" is played. Have the children sit on the floor in a circle. Select one child to walk around the circle, tapping the children on the head and saying, "Pray, pray, work!" If a child is tapped when the word "work" is said, that child jumps up and answers a question. If he answers correctly, he becomes the tapper. If he answers incorrectly, he sits down and the original tapper continues around the circle. When a child answers a question correctly and finishes her turn as tapper, she sits in the center of the circle. This way each child will get a chance to answer a question, and by the end of the game, everyone will be in the middle.

Who did Nehemiah work for?
What was his job?
What news had made Nehemiah cry?
Who was kind to sad Nehemiah?
Why were the people in Jerusalem in danger?
What time of day did Nehemiah inspect the wall?
What did Nehemiah see when he inspected the wall and gate?
What did Nehemiah do when he had problems rebuilding the wall?
What is a peacemaker?
How many days did it take to rebuild the wall?

Bible Memory: Do Right Hands

You will need copies of the memory verse from p. 73, washable tempera paint, paper plates, old shirts, newspaper, and a bucket of water and towels for cleanup (if you don't have a classroom sink).

Before class, make a copy of the Bible words for each child in your class, and print their names on the paper.

Cover the work area with newspaper and cover the children's clothing with old shirts. Put some paint in the center of a paper plate. One at a time let each child press his hands on the paint and then place his handprints on both sides of the memory verse. Let dry. (An assembly line of assistants would be a good idea here: one to get the paint shirts on the children, one to supervise the stamping, one to help children wash their hands.) Help the children wash their hands in the bucket of water or classroom sink.

As the children work on this project, have each one recite the Bible words and talk about what the verse means.

What does our verse say we should do?

What will happen when we do what the Lord says?

▼ 3. What Does This Mean to Me? ▲

Be a Peacemaker

You will need to make a headband 22" to 26" long from a 2" wide strip of paper for each child. Print "Peacemaker" on each headband and draw some smiling faces (or use stickers). Use several paper clips to adjust the size of the headband to the children's heads. You will also need one puzzle, three cookies, and a toy dog.

In today's story, Nehemiah was a peacemaker. A peacemaker is a person who stops others who are fighting or causing trouble. A peacemaker does what is right.

You can be a peacemaker, too. Let's act out some problems that might happen here at church. I will choose someone to be the peacemaker to help solve the problem.

Help the children role-play the following scenes:

1. The children are lining up at the door. Some children argue over wanting to be the first in the line.

2. Give two children a puzzle. They argue over who will play with it first.

3. Give two children three wrapped cookies. They each take one and then argue over who gets to eat the third cookie.

4. Give a group of children a toy dog. They argue over who will hold the puppy first and how long.

5. The children are sitting on the floor for story time. Some children argue over who will sit next to the teacher.

First describe the situation and let the children briefly act it out. Stop the action and place the "Peacemaker" headband on one child. Choose a child who will not be afraid to speak up and play the role of the peacemaker. Resume the action. Ask the peacemaker to help the other child/children do what is right.

If time allows, act out situations that have happened in your classroom.

Memory Tools

You will need some objects that will remind children of their daily activities such as a cereal bowl, a toothbrush, some clothes, a pillow, some toys, a picture of a TV, and so on.

Set the objects on a low table. Have the children gather around. As you point to an object, ask the children if this object reminds them of a time or a way they can do what is right. Go through the objects directing the children to talk about sharing, being a peacemaker, not complaining or fussing, being a helper, and so on.

Finish by asking, **When you see these things at home, what can you remember to do that is right? When it is time to watch TV, what can you remember to do to be a peacemaker?**

▼ 4. What Can I Do to Please God? ▲

Good Deed Workers

You will need a copy of the certificate on p. 72 for each child and the words to verses one and two of "Do What Is Right" from p. 56.

Look around your building or meeting place. Is there something your class can do as a special project? What about picking up litter around the building and parking lot, pulling weeds and watering plants, picking up papers left in the worship area, sweeping floors, emptying wastebaskets, or dusting chairs? Choose a small project you can accomplish with the children during your class time.

When you have selected a project, complete a certificate for each child. Fill in the blank labeled "Good Deed" with the task they will do.

As the children do the good deed, sing verses of "Do What Is Right." When the job is completed, pray with the children, thanking God for helping them do right.

Pass out certificates earned by the children during the class. As each child is called to receive his certificate, compliment him on a specific thing you observed. (When the child is picked up, also make sure to tell the parent about the specific thing you saw the child do. Parents appreciate hearing positive comments!)

▼ Bonus Activities ▲

Snack Attack! Wall Crunchers

You will need graham crackers, creamy peanut butter, large craft sticks, and paper towels. (Check for peanut allergies. Other products, such as jelly, can be used.)

Break the graham crackers into sections. (The pieces will break better if you use a knife on the perforations.) Give each child a paper towel, a jumbo craft stick, several graham cracker sections, and some creamy peanut butter.

Demonstrate how to stack the crackers on top of each other using the peanut butter as the cement to make a "wall." Stack no more than four sections together.

Before eating, have the children say a thank-you prayer for the snack. As the children eat, review today's Bible story. Talk about the jobs the workers did to rebuild the wall.

God's People Thank God

Nehemiah 8:1-12

Know: A Bible person who chose to do what was right.
Feel: That God will help them do right.
Do: Pray before making decisions and ask God to help them do right.

Children will accomplish the goals when they

- Review what the Bible says about doing right.
- Tell how the people of Jerusalem thanked God for helping them do what was right.
- Recite Deuteronomy 6:18 and thank God for helping them.
- Show how it feels to do what is right.
- Praise and thank God for helping them do what is right.

How to Say It
Ezra: EZ-ruh
Nehemiah: Nee-huh-MY-uh

▼ 1. What Is This Story About? ▲

The Bible Says to Do What Is Right

You will need a cloth ball, Nerf ball, or a beanbag.

Gather the children in a circle, sitting on the floor. **God has given us a special book to teach us to do what is right. What is the name of that book?** (Allow responses.) **Yes, it is the Bible. We can trust the Bible to tell us what is right. The Bible says to share.** Roll the ball or toss the beanbag to one of the children in the circle. **Matthew, what do you have at your house that can you share?** Then ask Matthew to roll the ball or toss the beanbag back, or to another child. **Ashley, what do you use in class that you can share? Madison, what is in your car that you can share?** Continue this activity until every child has had a turn.

Use these questions to continue reviewing what the Bible says about doing right:
The Bible says to obey your parents; how do you obey your parents?
The Bible says to love others; how do you show love to your friends?
The Bible says to praise the Lord; how do you praise the Lord?
The Bible says to give cheerfully; what can you give to others?

▼ 2. What Does the Bible Say? ▲

Bible Story: The People Thank God

You will need a storyteller dressed as Nehemiah and someone dressed as Ezra, or use two puppets. You will also need a scroll and may want to use the sample from the Story Review activity "Make a Scroll." You will need the words for "Do What Is Right" from p. 56.

Nehemiah: **Hello, boys and girls! This is my last visit with you. I want to tell you what happened when the wall and gates around Jerusalem were finished.**

How many days did it take to repair the wall and gates? (Allow responses.) **Yes, it took fifty-two days. The workers knew God helped them because the wall was rebuilt so fast. Even our enemies knew God helped us. Without God's help we could not have done the work so quickly.**

On my first visit with you, I told you that enemy kings and their armies took God's people far away to live. After many years the Jews started coming back to their homes. When the wall and the gates were finished, more people returned to live in Jerusalem and the towns around it.

One special day, all of the people gathered near the new gate. The workers had built a tall stage. People came to hear the Book of the Teachings of Moses. God had given these teachings to the people long ago. They were written on a scroll that looked something like this. (Show the scroll.) **On this day a man named Ezra stood on the stage and read the teachings to the people.**

(Enter Ezra.) **I would like for you to meet the man who read the teachings.** (Shake Ezra's hand, welcome him, and introduce him to the children.)

Ezra, please tell these boys and girls what happened when you read the teachings from the scroll to the people.

Ezra: **Well, boys and girls, I read the Teachings of Moses from very early in the morning until noon. While I was reading, some very interesting things happened. All the men, women, and children stood when I opened the scroll. I began praising the Lord. All the people held up their hands and said, "Amen! Amen!" Then they bowed and worshiped God.**

As I read out loud, other men who understood the words well explained them to the people. Everyone listened carefully. As the people listened and understood, they began to cry. They were sad. They had disobeyed God's teachings and they were very sorry.

Nehemiah, my helpers, and I told the people this was a special day. It was not a sad day. They should be happy because their sins had been forgiven. Finally, Nehemiah, you said to them, "The joy of the Lord will make you strong. Go home and celebrate!" The people went home and had a party with good food and sweet drinks. They were thankful that God helped them return home. They were thankful that He helped them rebuild the wall and gates. They wanted to obey God's teachings and do what was right.

Nehemiah: **Thank you Ezra for coming today. Boys and girls, Ezra and I want you to always do what is right. Remember how God helped us. He will help you, too!**

Teach verse five of "Do What Is Right." Then sing all five verses of the unit song.

Story Review: Make a Scroll

You will need a roll of butcher or shelf paper at least 9" wide; paper towel tubes or thick wooden dowel rods at least 2" wider than the paper you are using; glue; crayons or markers; and yarn or ribbon. Also provide Bible story pictures of Nehemiah's story from old Sunday school take-home papers or curriculum. (Ask other teachers or your children's director for pictures if you have none.)

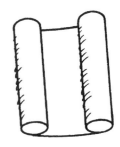

Give each child a 30" strip of paper to make a scroll. Help the children glue the tubes or rods on the narrow ends of the paper. Keep the scroll unrolled by placing objects on the ends to hold it open as the child works on the inside of the scroll. Do this project on the floor so that each child has room to work.

Guide children to glue on the pictures and color their scrolls. Have them print their names on the very edge of the other side of the paper. When the glue is dry, the scrolls should be rolled up and each tied with ribbon or yarn.

Review the Bible story with these questions. **Who read from a scroll? What did he read? What did the people do when they heard God's teachings? What did Nehemiah tell the people to do?**

Bible Memory: Celebrate God's Help

You will need several inflated balloons.

As the children recite the words of Deuteronomy 6:18, have them try, as a group, to keep one balloon in the air by tapping it lightly. *(Demonstrate.)* Remind them that they will need to take turns. The object is for everyone to help keep the balloon up. After the children have recited the verse several times, stop the activity. **We are having a lot of fun keeping the balloon up in the air and saying the Bible words at the same time. This takes a lot of strength! Remember when the people were crying because they had not obeyed God's teachings? Nehemiah told them that the joy of the Lord would make them strong. He told them to celebrate. Let's celebrate by saying the Bible words and keeping these balloons in the air.** Add a balloon, one at a time, until there are several in the air! End with a prayer thanking God for the joy that He gives us when we do what is right.

Bible Words
"Do what the Lord says is good and right. [Then things will go well for you]" (Deuteronomy 6:18).

(Note: This verse has been divided into two parts. If you are teaching four-year-olds, use the first part only. If you are teaching older children, include the words in brackets.)

▼ 3. What Does This Mean to Me? ▲

Joy Flags!

You will need one copy of the pennant and pictures from p. 74 and a 12" dowel rod for each child. Provide crayons or markers, glue, and a selection of songs about joy.

Before class, cut out all the pennants and pictures.

Give each child a pennant and say, **We have been learning about doing what is right. We have done many things that have been right to do. How does that make you feel?** (Allow responses.) **Doing right makes you feel happy. The Bible uses another word for happy and that word is "joy." Joy is happiness that comes from God. Let's make "Joy Flags" to celebrate the joy that God gives us when we do what is right.**

Pass out the pictures, glue, and crayons. Have each child print his name on his pennant. Discuss the pictures. Tell the children to choose pictures that show things that give them joy. They can glue those on their pennants. When the pennants are decorated and colored, tape each pennant to a dowel rod.

While the children work, play songs your class knows that have the word "joy" in them.

▼ 4. What Can I Do to Please God? ▲

Praise Pennants

You will need the words for "Do What Is Right" from p. 56 and the pennants made in the "Joy Flags!" activity.

Ask each child to tell about her pennant and the pictures she chose by completing the statement, **"I praise and thank God for helping me _____."** After each child has had a turn, sing all five verse of "Do What Is Right." Use this time to compliment each child on his or her efforts to do what is right during this unit of study.

Review with these questions:

What Bible person chose to do what was right?

What are some ways that Nehemiah did the right thing?

What did Nehemiah always do that helped him do the right thing?

Who can say our Bible words?

What do our Bible words remind us to do?

Let's thank God and ask Him to help us always do what is right. Pray, giving each child an opportunity to thank and praise God.

Story Strips

Mom told Andrew to pick up the toys in his room. Andrew wanted to play outside with Ryan, so he stuffed all his toys in his closet and under his bed.

Sara was asked to empty the wastebaskets into the garbage can. Her favorite program was starting on TV, so she set the baskets outside the back door instead. The wind knocked over the baskets, blowing trash all over the backyard.

Grandma cooked broccoli for dinner. Elizabeth didn't like broccoli, so she fussed and fussed about not liking broccoli.

At bedtime Kayla's dad read her a story and gave her a drink. She wanted one more story and one more drink and cried to get them.

Anthony's mommy was on the phone. Anthony wanted a glass of milk. He fussed while she was talking. Then he tried to pour his own glass of milk and spilled milk all over the floor.

Alexis and her daddy went to the library and checked out five books. When she got home, Alexis put the books on the top shelf of her bookcase so that her baby brother couldn't tear the pages.

Mr. Porter was telling a Bible story about Jesus. All of the children were listening.

Mother was very busy getting dinner ready. John asked whether he could help. Mother said he could put the silverware next to the dishes. John set out the silverware carefully.

It was time to take a bath and go to bed. Christopher and Brandon were playing with their Legos when Mom called them. They put their Legos away quickly.

Ms. Lane was telling the children about how God made the animals. Daniel wanted to tell about his favorite animal, the elephant. Daniel raised his hand and waited for Ms. Lane to call on him.

Sleeping Child

Stickers

My Handy Prayer

Directions:

You will need white glue, vinegar, peppermint extract (optional), a small paintbrush, and scissors.

Mix two parts white glue and one part vinegar. Add a few drops of peppermint extract, if desired. Lightly "paint" the mixture onto the backs of the uncut stickers and label. Let them dry. Cut out the stickers and "My Handy Prayer" label.

Good Deed Certificate

Presented to

_____
(Child's Name)

on

_____
(Date)

for

_____
(Good Deed)

You did what was right!

Presented by _____

"Do what the Lord says is good and right. Then things will go well for you" (Deuteronomy 6:18)

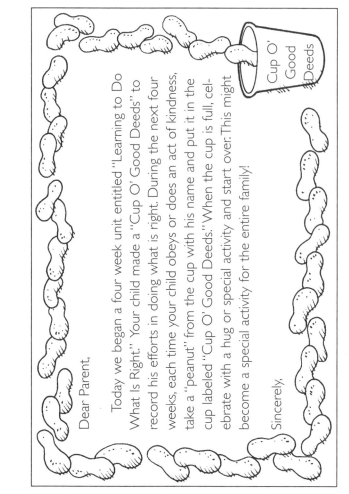

Dear Parent,

Today we began a four week unit entitled "Learning to Do What Is Right." Your child made a "Cup O' Good Deeds" to record his efforts in doing what is right. During the next four weeks, each time your child obeys or does an act of kindness, take a "peanut" from the cup with his name and put it in the cup labeled "Cup O' Good Deeds." When the cup is full, celebrate with a hug or special activity and start over. This might become a special activity for the entire family!

Sincerely,

Cup O' Good Deeds

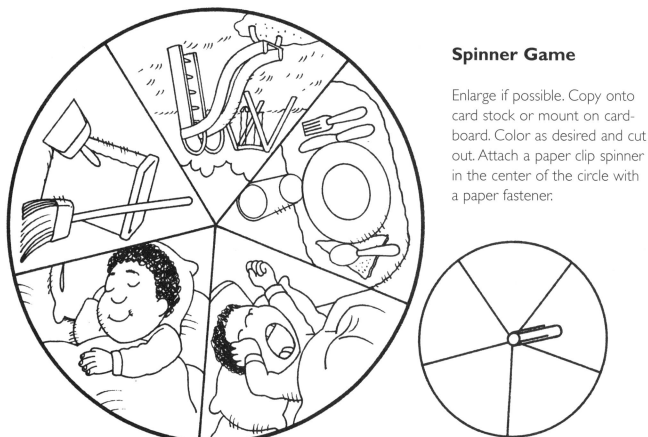

Spinner Game

Enlarge if possible. Copy onto card stock or mount on cardboard. Color as desired and cut out. Attach a paper clip spinner in the center of the circle with a paper fastener.

"Do what
the Lord says
is good and right.
Then
things
will go well
for you"
(Deuteronomy 6:18).

Pennant

Learning to Be Brave

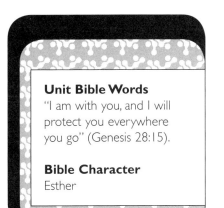

Unit Bible Words
"I am with you, and I will protect you everywhere you go" (Genesis 28:15).

Bible Character
Esther

13 Esther Becomes Queen

Esther 2:2-18—King Xerxes, a powerful king of a very large kingdom, chooses beautiful, young Esther to become his queen. No one in the palace knows Esther is Jewish.

14 Esther's Life Is in Danger

Esther 3, 4—Haman, next in power to King Xerxes, does not like the Jews. He makes a law giving all who live in the kingdom permission to kill the Jews.

15 Esther Is Brave

Esther 5:1-8; 7:1-7—Queen Esther spends three days praying and then does a very brave thing. She goes to see King Xerxes without an invitation. This is dangerous and could result in her death. The king welcomes her. Esther tells the king about Haman's plan to kill the Jews.

16 Esther Saves God's People

Esther 8—Haman is gone, but the law he wrote has not changed. Again Queen Esther's help is needed. She goes back to see the king and asks that a new law be written to protect the Jews.

17 Celebrate Purim

Esther 9:1, 2, 18-32—Every year, two days are set aside to celebrate how God used Queen Esther to save the Jews. This is one of the happiest of all the Jewish holidays. It is a favorite among children.

By the end of this unit, the children and leaders will

Know: A Bible person who was brave.
Feel: God is always with them and helps them be brave.
Do: Choose to be brave when they are afraid.

Why Teach This Unit to Four- to Six-Year-Olds?

How often are young children told, "Be brave!"? Probably every time they are taken to the doctor, left with a new baby-sitter, or even when mom has to pull out a splinter. How does a young child learn to be brave? Many are left to tough it out on their own in the world of hard knocks. Wouldn't it be better to give them a source for strength and help? That source is God! Use this unit to provide opportunities for children to practice calling on God for help to be brave.

In this unit the children will meet Esther and observe how she prayed for help when she faced a life or death situation. Hopefully your students will never face such a crisis. Yet, in the imaginative minds of young children, a twisted shadow in a dark bedroom in the middle of the night can produce the same fear that Esther felt. Esther's example will show them that even someone as important as a queen depended on God for help to be brave.

Meet Esther

Esther was an orphan. An orphan is someone whose parents have died. Esther's parents died and she was raised by her cousin, Mordecai. Esther's family was Jewish. They lived in the capital city of Persia. In those days Persia was an extremely large kingdom and was ruled by the powerful king, Xerxes.

King Xerxes, angered by Queen Vashti's refusal to obey him, decided to choose a new queen. The suggestion that she be young and beautiful pleased the king. Esther met these requirements.

Esther's position as queen provided her with an opportunity to save the lives of all the Jews living in Persia.

Haman, second in power to the king, had decided to rid Persia of all Jews. He did so not knowing that his evil plan would include the queen.

Without an invitation, Esther bravely went to see the king. This could have resulted in her death. Instead the king welcomed her, and she later had the opportunity to tell the king about Haman's plan.

Esther's bravery, which came from her faith in God, saved the Jews. Mordecai and Esther instructed the people to celebrate God's care and protection with a yearly holiday called "Purim."

Unit Visuals: A Living Drama

This unit will be illustrated by using an overhead projector, transparencies made with p. 105, and silhouettes from p. 106. Photocopy the silhouettes onto card stock and cut out, or glue them onto light cardboard and cut out. Make a transparency from p. 105 and cut it into sections 4A and 4B. Color may be added to the transparencies. Use only permanent overhead projector pens. (Hint: Handle transparencies as little as possible. Colored pens will not mark easily over fingerprints.)

If a plain wall is not available for projection, tack a large white sheet to the wall.

In each Bible story you will find a list of the transparencies and silhouettes needed for that lesson. Project the transparency and place the appropriate silhouette(s) on the transparency according to directions throughout the story. Sometimes the silhouettes will be projected alone.

Unit Song

When I'm Afraid
(Tune: "King of Kings")

Verse 1
When I'm afraid and want to cry,
"Help me! O, Lord, I pray."
When I'm afraid and want to cry,
"Help me! O, Lord, I pray."
God will answer quickly,
"I'm here!
Don't be afraid."
God will answer quickly,
"I'm here!
Don't be afraid."

Verse 2
I'll not fear. I will be brave.
Help me! O, Lord, I pray.
I'll not fear. I will be brave.
Help me! O, Lord, I pray.
God is in control.
He's here.
I'm not afraid.
God is in control.
He's here.
I'm not afraid.

Esther Becomes Queen

Esther 2:2-18

▼ 1. What Is This Story About? ▲

Treasure Chest Banks

You will need one copy of the bank from p. 98 for each student; scissors, and an X-Acto knife. If possible, photocopy the pattern onto card stock for added strength. You will also need to provide glue or tape and crayons or markers.

Before class, cut out the banks and cut the coin slots with a knife. Print on the bank the name of the organization that will receive the money. Also, print the date the bank is to be returned.

At the end of our lessons about brave Queen Esther, we are going to celebrate Purim, a special Jewish holiday. Giving to the poor was a special part of this Jewish celebration. So today we are going to make banks that look like a king's treasure chest. Take this bank home and ask your family to help you fill it with coins. In four weeks, when we celebrate Purim, bring the bank back. We will give the money to people who need it. (Choose an organization that helps the poor or homeless.)

Have the children color the banks. Encourage them to keep the crayons off the tabs (so glue will stick to them). Or, decorate the banks with stickers. Give help as needed to fold on the broken lines, making a cube. Tuck in tabs and tape or glue. When the parents arrive to pick up the children, explain the purpose of the banks, or send home a letter of explanation. (See Lesson 17, "Celebrate Purim.")

We'll learn more about Esther in our Bible story today.

▼ 2. What Does the Bible Say? ▲

Bible Story: And the New Queen Is . . .

You will need transparencies made from p. 105 and the following silhouettes from p. 106: 4-a king (standing), 4-b girl Esther, 4-c Mordecai, and 4-d crown. (See p. 76 for directions on how to use these visuals.)

(Project transparency 4A.) **A long time before Jesus was born, King Xerxes was the powerful king of Persia. He lived in a huge palace with many servants.**

Add silhouette 4-a. **One day King Xerxes said, "I am going to choose a new queen. Search the whole kingdom for the most beautiful girls. Bring them to my palace, and I will choose one to be the new queen."** *(Remove transparency 4A and silhouette 4-a.)*

The search for beautiful young girls began. Girls from all over the kingdom were brought to the palace. *(Project silhouette 4-b with no transparency background.)* **One of the chosen girls was Esther.**

Esther was a Jew. She was one of God's special people. *(Place silhouette 4-c next to 4-b.)* **Esther lived with her cousin Mordecai. Esther's mother and father had died, so Mordecai adopted her as his daughter. Esther was very beautiful. Before she left to live in the palace, Mordecai told her not to tell anyone that she was a Jew.** *(Remove both silhouettes.)*

(Project transparency 4B. Add silhouette 4-c.) **Mordecai was one of the king's officers, which meant he sat at the king's gate. Every day he asked about**

Know: A Bible person who was brave.
Feel: God is always with them and helps them be brave.
Do: Choose to be brave when they are afraid.

Children will accomplish the goals when they
• Begin to learn about Purim.
• Tell how Esther was chosen to be queen.
• Begin to memorize Genesis 28:15.
• Tell what a hero does.
• Praise God for always being with them.

How to Say It
Mordecai: MOR-dih-kye
Xerxes: ZERK-seez

Esther. He cared about her and wanted to know if she was OK. *(Remove silhouette 4-c and transparency 4B.)*

(Project transparency 4A. Add silhouette 4-b). **At the palace, all of the girls were treated in a special way. They were given lotions and perfumes for their skin and hair. The man in charge of the girls liked Esther the best. He gave her a special room in which to live, seven servants to take care of her, and special food to eat.**

(Add silhouette 4-a.) **When the girls were ready, they were sent one at a time to see the king. The king liked Esther the best.** *(Add silhouette 4-d to 4-b.)* **He placed a gold crown on her head and said she would be the new queen.**

A special party was given for Queen Esther. All of the important men and royal officers in the kingdom were invited. The king said, "Let's have a holiday and celebrate. I have chosen a new queen." He gave everyone gifts.

How do you think Esther felt about being chosen as the new queen for such an important king? Do you think she was afraid? She might have been, but God had a very important job for her to do. God helped her to be brave. *(Turn off the projector.)*

Story Review: Where's the Queen?

You will need a gold button to represent the Queen, a hand-held cassette or CD player, and a cassette or CD of fun marching music.

Have the children stand in a circle. The leader stands in the center with the music. A gold button is passed around the circle while music is playing. When the music stops, the child holding the button may choose between telling one thing she knows about the story of Esther, or answering a question about the story. Play until each child has had an opportunity to talk. Don't worry if the children repeat facts. Let this be a low-stress game for them.

What was the king's name?
What country did he rule?
Why was Esther chosen to be the new queen?
Esther was one of God's special people. What were they called?
What was the name of Esther's cousin?
What did Mordecai tell Esther not to tell anyone?
What was Mordecai's job?
What special treatment did Esther receive at the palace?
What did the king do to celebrate his new queen?

Bible Memory: You Can't Hide From God

You will need a Bible and a large sheet or blanket.

Divide the children into small groups. The size of the group will depend on the size of the sheet you are using. Gather the children under the sheet.

Let's hide under this sheet. Do you think anyone can see us? The rest of the teachers and children in our classroom cannot see us, but there is someone who can. God can! We cannot hide from Him. We cannot get lost from Him. He is with us wherever we go. Listen to this verse in the Bible. Read Genesis 28:15 from your Bible. **Let's learn these important words. They will help us whenever we are afraid.**

Repeat the words with the children several times. Ask for volunteers to say the verse by themselves.

Bible Words
"I am with you, and I will protect you everywhere you go" (Genesis 28:15).

▼ 3. What Does This Mean to Me? ▲

What Is a Hero?

You will need copies of the booklet from pp. 96 and 97. Provide glue, staples, and crayons or markers. Assemble the booklets according to the directions.

Explain the word *hero*. As the children color the cover of the booklet "My Bible Heroes," ask them if they know a hero and what he or she does. Expect the children to respond with the names of cartoon or fictional heroes. Briefly explain the difference between a real hero and a pretend hero. **In the Bible there are many real heroes. The little book you are making will remind you about four of them.**

Discuss and review the first three heroes with the children. Read the brief description of each person and let the children color the corresponding picture.

These Bible people are the best heroes for us to have. Today we heard a story about Esther. She became a hero by saving God's people, the Jews. Let the children color her picture.

Name some ways all of the Bible heroes are alike. (They all had hard jobs to do, trusted God to help them, were brave.)

How can we be like these Bible heroes?

Are You Ever Afraid?

You will need the words to "When I'm Afraid" from p. 76.

Everyone is afraid at some time. Are you afraid of the dark? Are afraid of big dogs? What do you do when you are afraid?

Let's sing a song that tells us the best thing to do when you are afraid. Teach the song "When I'm Afraid" to the children. Then talk about what it means that God is in control.

Tell about a time you were afraid.

What helped you to be brave?

We can remember this song and our Bible words the next time we are afraid.

▼ 4. What Can I Do to Please God? ▲

A Bag Full of Praises

You will need the pictures from p. 95, a paper lunch sack, scissors, and crayons or markers.

Make a praise bag by decorating a paper lunch sack. Cut apart the pictures from p. 95. Put the pictures in the sack.

Our Bible words remind us that God is always with us. Let's take turns praising God because He is with us everywhere we go.

Let the children take turns reaching into the sack and pulling out a picture. Have the children complete this sentence: **"I praise You, God, for being with me when ____ (I am swimming, I visit my grandma, I am sleeping)."** After everyone has had a turn or the sack is empty, lead the children in saying a prayer to thank God for being with them everywhere they go.

To clean up, designate some children to be queens and kings and some to be servants. The queens and kings walk around the room looking for things that need to be picked up or cleaned. The servants do the picking up or cleaning. After a few minutes, have the children switch roles.

When I'm Afraid
(Tune: "King of Kings")

Verse 1

When I'm afraid and want
  to cry,
"Help me! O, Lord, I pray."
When I'm afraid and want
  to cry,
"Help me! O, Lord, I pray."
God will answer quickly, "I'm
  here!
Don't be afraid."
God will answer quickly, "I'm
  here!
Don't be afraid."

Verse 2

I'll not fear. I will be brave.
Help me! O, Lord, I pray.
I'll not fear. I will be brave.
Help me! O, Lord, I pray.
God is in control. He's here.
I'm not afraid.
God is in control. He's here.
I'm not afraid.

Esther's Life Is in Danger

Esther 3, 4

Know: A Bible person who chose to do what was right.

Feel: That God will help them do right.

Do: Pray before making decisions and ask God to help them do right.

Children will accomplish the goals when they

- Explore what scares people.
- Tell why Esther's life was in danger.
- Memorize Genesis 28:15.
- Name ways to stay safe in dangerous situations.
- Praise God for protecting them.

▼ 1. What Is This Story About? ▲

That Scares Me!

You will need a copy of the pictures from p. 99 (enlarged if possible), scissors, construction paper, two paper plates per child, one craft stick per child, glue, a black permanent marker, and crayons or markers.

Before class, cut the pictures apart and mount them individually on construction paper. Add color as desired. For each child, glue two paper plates back-to-back with one craft stick in between for a handle. Use a black permanent marker to draw a sad face on one side of the paper plate and a happy face on the other.

After the children have colored their paper plates to look like themselves, gather them in a circle holding the handles of their plates. One at a time, show a picture of a common fear. Describe the picture and the situation it represents. Children who have that fear are to show the sad side of their plates. Those who do not have that fear are to show the happy side.

As each fear is mentioned, discuss ways to help the children who have that fear. Give ideas until those children feel they can turn their plates to the happy side.

Today you will hear about a time when Queen Esther was afraid. She prayed for God's help. We can ask God to help us when we are afraid, too.

What's an Enemy?

You will need plain drawing paper and crayons or markers.

Today you will hear how Haman became the enemy of all the Jews living in King Xerxes' kingdom. Do you know what an enemy is? Who can tell us what an enemy does? Encourage children to respond with their ideas. Add the following descriptions if needed. **An enemy is someone who dislikes another person or group of people. An enemy plans to hurt others. Enemies do nasty things. They say unkind words. An enemy tries to make someone cry. Do you think that God wants people to be enemies? On this drawing paper, draw a picture of what you think an enemy looks like.**

Let the children draw and then tell about their drawings. **People who are mean can scare us and make us afraid. We can ask God to help us when we are afraid.**

▼ 2. What Does the Bible Say? ▲

Bible Story: The Jews Have an Enemy

You will need transparencies made from p. 105, and the following silhouettes from p. 106: 4-a king (standing), 4-b girl Esther, 4-c Mordecai, 4-e Queen Esther, 4-f Haman, 4-g bowing man, 4-h king (sitting), and 4-i scepter. (See p. 76 for directions on how to use these visuals.) You will also need a sample of the scepter that will be made by the children in Lesson 15 Story Review activity "A King's Scepter," p. 85.

How to Say It
Haman: HAY-mun
Mordecai: MOR-dih-kye
Xerxes: ZERK-seez

(Project silhouette 4-b without a transparency background.) **Esther, a beautiful young Jewish girl, was chosen to be the new queen of King Xerxes.** *(Remove silhouette 4-b.)*

(Project silhouettes 4-c and 4-e.) **Her cousin, Mordecai, who was one of the king's royal officers, told her not to tell anyone she was a Jew.** *(Remove silhouettes 4-c and 4-e.)*

(Project transparency 4B. Add silhouette 4-f.) **King Xerxes had many royal officers. One was a man named Haman. He was the king's chief officer. In the kingdom of Persia, only the king was more important. Haman was very proud of his important job.** *(Add silhouette 4-g.)* **He was pleased when the other royal officers bowed down as he walked by.**

Every day Haman walked by the royal officers sitting at the king's gate. *(Add silhouette 4-c.)* **Everyone except Mordecai bowed down. Jews do not bow before any man the way they bow before God. This made Haman very angry.** *(Remove the silhouettes and transparency 4B.)*

(Project transparency 4A. Add silhouettes 4-a and 4-f.) **Haman decided to get rid of Mordecai and all the Jews living in Persia. So Haman went to King Xerxes and said, "There are people living in your country who have their own laws and do not obey your laws. They should not live in your kingdom, and I would like your permission to destroy them."**

The king replied, "Do what you want with these people." *(Remove silhouette 4-a.)*

Haman wrote a new law. It said, "On the thirteenth day of the twelfth month, the people of Persia have permission to kill all of the Jews."

Haman stamped the law with the king's special ring. This meant the law was from the king and no one could change it. *(Remove transparency 4A and silhouette 4-f.)*

The new law made the Jews very afraid. *(Project silhouette 4-c with no transparency background.)* **Mordecai took off his soft clothes and put rough cloth against his skin. He also put gray ashes all over his body. This let others know that he was grieving.**

Esther heard that Mordecai was grieving. She sent her servant to find out what was wrong. Mordecai gave the servant a copy of the new law written by their enemy Haman. Mordecai told the servant to tell Esther to go see the king and beg him not to kill the Jews. *(Remove silhouette 4-c.)*

(Project silhouette 4-e with no transparency background.) **Esther knew going to see the king without being invited was dangerous. The king could choose to see the person by holding out his gold scepter.** *(Demonstrate with a sample scepter made by following the instructions for the Story Review activity, "A King's Scepter," Lesson 15, p. 85.)* **If the king did not hold out his scepter, the uninvited visitor could be killed. Esther was afraid. Mordecai sent her another message that said, "Maybe this is why you were chosen to be the queen."**

Esther sent Mordecai another message. It said, "I will go see the king, even if he does not want to see me. Have all the Jews in the city join me in praying for three days. Then I will go see the king. If I die, I die."

Esther was ready to do a very brave thing. She was willing to go see the king without being invited. Before she went, she wanted her people to pray constantly and not even take time to eat. She needed God's help to be brave. *(Turn off the projector.)* **Next time we meet, I will tell you what happened to Esther and her people!**

Story Review: Stamp of Approval

You will need a half of a raw potato and a paint shirt for each child. You will also need tempera paint, paper plates, and blank paper.

Before class, cut a shape in the cut side of each potato half. Trim away the unnecessary pieces to make a raised picture that can be stamped on paper. Cut many different shapes. An easy way to cut shapes is to push a cookie cutter into the potato. Leaving it in place, trim away all the excess potato, then lift out the cookie cutter. (Or, you could borrow rubber stamps from someone.)

Be sure to cut (or borrow) a crown and a ring (can be just a donut shape). Demonstrate how to load the stamp with paint and then stamp the paper. Let the children share the different designs and cover the paper.

Use the following questions to review the Bible story:

Who in today's story wore a crown?
What did King Xerxes give Haman?
Why was the king's ring so special?
What did Haman do with the king's special ring?
Did the king sign a good law or a bad law?
What did Mordecai do?
What did Mordecai want Queen Esther to do?
Why was Esther's life in danger?

Bible Memory: God's Protection

You will need an umbrella, a raincoat, mittens or gloves, several kinds of hats, a sweater, and boots.

Show each item and ask the children what kind of protection it provides. **Our Bible words say that God will protect us everywhere we go. Let's say Genesis 28:15 together.** Repeat the verse several times.

Divide the children into groups of ten or less. Have the children stand in a circle. Pass out the items you collected. You will need one item for each child in the circle. Have the children place the items on the floor next to their feet. Ask a child to pick up his or her item and say the first word of the memory verse and then pass the item to the left. The next child says the second word and passes the item to the next child. Continue passing the item around the circle until all the words in the verse have been said. Repeat the process with each child's item.

Who wants to say the Bible words by himself?
What do our Bible words remind us about God?

<table>
<tr><td>

Bible Words

"I am with you, and I will protect you everywhere you go" (Genesis 28:15).

</td></tr>
</table>

▼ 3. What Does This Mean to Me? ▲

Stop! Look! Listen!

You will need the words to "When I'm Afraid" from p. 76 and the Stop! Look! Listen! pictures from p. 100. Cut the pictures apart. (Optional: Enlarge each picture and add color.)

We've talked about things and people that sometimes scare us. Even Queen Esther was scared to go to the king. Let's look at some pictures of kids who might be in danger.

Show picture 1 (child swimming): **What is this child doing? When is swimming dangerous? Who knows some good rules to remember about playing in or near water?** Discuss safety rules for the pool, lake, ocean, and river.

Show picture 2 (child wearing seat belt): **Where is this child? What is this child wearing? Why is it dangerous not to wear a seat belt?** Discuss safety rules for riding in a car, truck, or van.

Show picture 3 (child standing on the curb of a busy street): **Where is this child? Why are busy streets dangerous? What are the rules for crossing a street safely?** Discuss safety rules for crossing the street.

Show picture 4 (child playing with burning matches): **What is this child doing? Why is it dangerous to play with fire? What should you do if your clothes catch on fire?** Discuss fire prevention and fire safety (stop, drop, and roll).

Show picture 5 (child and a stranger with a candy bar): **What does this man have behind his back? Should the child take a candy bar from someone he** does not know? Why shouldn't you talk to a stranger when you are alone? Discuss stranger danger.

Show picture 6 (child near a stove with a pot of boiling water): **What is on the stove? How do you know it is hot? Why should the child not touch the stove or pot? Why should the child not stand near the stove?** Discuss safety rules for the kitchen.

One of the ways God protects us is by giving us minds that let us learn about how to be safe.

Have you ever been in danger?

What do our Bible words remind us about God?

What can we do when we're in danger or scared?

▼ 4. What Can I Do to Please God? ▲

Praise Hat

You will need a Bible, paper, marker, hat or sack, scissors, pictures from pp. 99 and 100 used earlier in this lesson, and the words for "When I'm Afraid" from p. 76.

Put the pictures (sixteen combined cut-out pictures from previous activities) into a hat or sack. Gather the children in a circle.

We can praise God because He is always with us. When I'm afraid, I can say, "I praise You, God, because You are here with me."

Let's praise God using pictures to help us think of times God is with us. Ask each child to take a turn choosing a picture from the hat, telling about the picture, and praising God in a sentence. Help each child use the sentence you modeled or make up one of her own.

Our Bible words remind us that God is always with us. Let's say them together. Do so, then sing together "When I'm Afraid." Close with a prayer, thanking God for His protection.

▼ Bonus Activity ▲

Snack Attack! Edible Rings

You will need ring-shaped (round and hollow) pretzels or cookies.

As you pass the treat out to the children, they will probably put the rings on their fingers. If not, show them how to do it. As you eat, talk about the special meaning of the king's ring.

What was so special about King Xerxes' ring?

Did Haman use the king's ring for something good or something bad?

What would you do if you had a special ring?

Extra Action! Hide and Seek

You will need a playing area where the children can hide easily.

Play your own version of the game "Hide and Seek." As the seeker finds each child, have the found child name a place he likes to go. Ask the child whether God goes with him there. Then ask everyone to say the Bible words together. Try to give everyone a turn being the seeker.

Esther Is Brave

Esther 5:1-8; 7:1-7

Know: A Bible person who was brave.

Feel: God is always with them and helps them be brave.

Do: Choose to be brave when they are afraid.

Children will accomplish the goals when they

- Explore what kings do.
- Tell about the brave thing Esther did.
- Recite Genesis 28:15 and tell about a time God is with them.
- Demonstrate being brave when they are afraid.
- Praise God for helping them to be brave.

How to Say It
Haman: HAY-mun
Mordecai: MOR-dih-kye
Xerxes: ZERK-seez

▼ 1. What Is This Story About? ▲

A King's Scepter

You will need the following items for each child: a copy of the scepter wrapper from p. 101, paper towel tube, 2" Styrofoam ball, and 10" square of yellow tissue paper. You will also need crayons, assorted foil star stickers, white glue, various colors of curling ribbon, and scissors.

Kings are very special! We're going to make something that only kings can use.

Have the children color the scepter wrappers and add star stickers. Help them glue the wrappers around the paper towel tubes.

Give each child a tissue paper square and a Styrofoam ball. Show the children how to cover the ball with the tissue paper so the four corners of the paper come together in a twisted point. Put glue around one end of the tube. Place the point of the tissue-paper-covered ball in that end. Let dry.

Tie the ribbon around the tube near the ball. Leave long ends of ribbon that can be curled with a pair of scissors.

You have made a king's scepter. What is special about a scepter?

Why do only kings have scepters?

In our story today, Queen Esther is planning to visit the king. We'll find out what he does with his scepter.

▼ 2. What Does the Bible Say? ▲

Bible Story: Queen Esther Is Brave

You will need the scepters the children made, a transparency made from p. 105, and the following silhouettes from p. 106: 4-a king (standing), 4-e Queen Esther, 4-f Haman, 4-h king (sitting), 4-i scepter, and 4-j banquet table. (See p. 76 for directions on how to use these visuals.)

(Project transparency 4A. Add silhouette 4-e.) **Haman's plan to kill the Jews meant that even the beautiful Queen Esther would die. No one in the palace knew the queen was a Jew. Esther's cousin, Mordecai, asked Esther to tell the king about Haman's plan. She was the only one who could ask the king for help.**

After three days of praying and not eating, Esther dressed in her royal clothes and went to see the king. *(Remove silhouette 4-e.)*

(Add silhouette 4-h.) **King Xerxes was sitting on his throne. Esther walked up to the king.** *(Add silhouette 4-e.)* **Would the king welcome her, or send her away to die?** *(Ask the children to hold their scepters down.)* **When the king saw Esther, he smiled and held out his gold scepter.** *(Add silhouette 4-i to 4-h. Ask the children to hold their scepters high.)* **Esther touched it. The king welcomed her visit. She would not die. God had heard her prayers and answered them.** *(Children can put their scepters in their laps.)*

"What do you want? I'll give you up to half of my kingdom," said King Xerxes.

"I would like you and Haman to come today to a special dinner I have prepared," replied Queen Esther. *(Remove silhouettes 4-h and 4-i.)*

(Add silhouettes 4-a, 4-f, and 4-j.) **The king and Haman came to the dinner. While they were eating, the king again asked Queen Esther, "What do you want? I'll give you anything, even half of my kingdom."**

Esther replied, "Please come again tomorrow and I will prepare another dinner for you and Haman. Then I will tell you what I want." *(Remove all the silhouettes.)*

The next day Haman and King Xerxes again came to a special dinner prepared for them by Queen Esther. *(Add silhouettes 4-a, 4-e, 4-f, and 4-j.)*

The king again asked, "Queen Esther, what do you want me to do for you?"

This time the queen replied, "If you are happy with me as your queen, please let me and my people live. A law has been made giving permission to kill every Jew in your kingdom."

King Xerxes was very surprised and asked, "Who would do such a terrible thing to you and your people?"

"Our enemy is wicked Haman," answered the queen. "He made the terrible law."

Haman begged the queen to save his life, but the king said he must die for making such a terrible law. *(Remove silhouette 4-f.)*

Queen Esther helped save God's people. God heard her prayers and the prayers of the Jews. God helped her to be brave. *(Turn off the projector.)*

Story Review: King, May I?

You will need one scepter used during the Bible story.

Play this game using the same rules as the game of "Mother, May I?"

The adult leader of this activity is the "king" and holds a scepter. The rest of the children should stand in a line about fifteen feet away, facing the king. The king calls a child's name and gives a command, such as "Take two king-size steps forward," or "Take three queen-size steps backward." The child named must respond by saying, "King, may I?" The king will then hold out the scepter, and the child follows the command. If the child forgets to say, "King, may I?" the king will not hold out the scepter and the child must return to the starting line.

To review the Bible story, respond to each child by holding out the scepter and saying, "If you can answer this question." Then use one of the following questions:

Why does the king have a scepter? How does he use it? Why was Queen Esther afraid to go see the king? What did she do when she was afraid? How do you know Queen Esther was brave?

Bible Memory: Crown Around

You will need a crown made from the pattern and directions from p. 102. Have the children sit in a circle.

Let's play a game to help us remember our Bible words.

Say the Bible words together, then place the crown on a child's head. Ask the child to say the verse from memory. Give help as needed. Ask the child to tell about a time when God was with him. When the child has finished telling, ask him to crown another child. Be sure every child gets a turn.

Our Bible words remind us that God is with us. Let's all say the words again.

> **Bible Words**
> "I am with you, and I will protect you everywhere you go" (Genesis 28:15).

▼ 3. What Does This Mean to Me? ▲

I'll Not Fear

You will need the words to "When I'm Afraid" from p. 76.

We have been singing a song about what we should do when we are afraid. Let's sing it now. Sing verse one of "When I'm Afraid."

What does this song tell us to do when we are afraid? (Pray.) **Who can think of some times when someone might be afraid?** (Accept all answers.)

Can we ask God to give us courage during a storm? Can we ask God to help us be brave when we go to the doctor?

Let's learn a new verse about being brave, as Queen Esther was. Teach verse two of the song.

I Will Be Brave

You will need the "Stop! Look! Listen!" pictures from p. 100. (These pictures were used in Lesson 14.)

In our Bible story, God helped Queen Esther be brave. Who will help you when you need to be brave? Yes, God is with us and will always help us to be brave.

Ask for a volunteer to pantomime someone being brave. Show the volunteer one of the pictures to act out. Have the rest of the class guess what the child is doing. Repeat with other volunteers and pictures.

Our Bible words remind us that God is always with us. Let's say them together again.

▼ 4. What Can I Do to Please God? ▲

Praises Overflowing

You will need a clear plastic tumbler, water, blue and yellow food coloring, a 9" x 13" pan, a spoon, a black permanent marker, and a small paper cup for each child.

Fill the tumbler half full of water. Add two drops of blue coloring. Stir. Place the tumbler in the center of the pan. Ask, **What color is the water in this glass? Yes, it is blue. When you wake up in the night and you are alone and it is dark, are you sad?** Draw two eyes and a frown on the tumbler. **Let's pretend this glass of blue water is you, feeling sad and lonely in the dark.**

What is the best thing to do when you are afraid? (Allow responses.) **Yes, you should pray and ask God to help you be brave. Add three drops of yellow coloring. Stir. What happened to the blue water? Yes, it changed colors. Now it is green. When you pray, God changes you from being afraid to being brave. Let's change the frown on the glass to a smile.** (Turn the tumbler around. Draw two eyes and a smile.)

Let's praise God for hearing our prayers and helping us to be brave. We'll each thank God for a time He helps us to be brave, and we'll pour our praise water into this glass of brave feelings. (Give each child a small paper cup half full of water.)

Ask each child to complete the following sentence after he pours his cup of water into the tumbler: **I praise God for helping me be brave when** (when I'm afraid of the doctor, when I am left with a new baby-sitter). If the water in the tumbler overflows, say, **Look! We have so many praises that this glass cannot hold them all! God helps us be brave. Let's always praise Him.**

Let's Be Brave

You will need a scepter used earlier in this lesson.

Gather the children in the center of the room. When the circle is formed, lead the children in a prayer by holding the scepter and beginning the prayer with, **Thank You, God, for helping me be brave when-.-.-.-**Hand the scepter to the child next to you. Help the child repeat the sentence, add his own ending, and pass the scepter to the person next to him. When the scepter comes back to you, end the prayer by saying, **in Jesus name, Amen.**

Esther Saves God's People

Esther 8

▼ 1. What Is This Story About? ▲

Story Hats

You will need the patterns and directions from p. 102; one hat for each child, plus extras to provide choice. You will also need material children can use for decorations: ribbon, yarn, glitter, buttons, feathers, jewels, foil paper, markers, crayons.

In our Bible story, both Queen Esther and Mordecai are helpers. We're going to make hats like the ones Esther and Mordecai wore.

Show samples of the hat and crown. Let the children choose what they want to make. Spread out the materials and let the children be creative.

Our story hats remind us of Queen Esther and Mordecai.

How did Esther help others?

How did Mordecai help others?

In our story today, we'll learn more about how Esther and Mordecai helped their people.

The hats and crowns may be worn the rest of the class time. If you are planning to have the Purim Parade, suggested in Lesson 17, keep the hats until next week. After the parade they may be taken home.

> **Know:** A Bible person who was a brave helper.
>
> **Feel:** God is always with them and helps them be helpers.
>
> **Do:** Choose to help others.
>
> **Children will accomplish the goals when they**
>
> - Explore Bible people who helped.
> - Tell how Esther saved God's people.
> - Recite Genesis 28:15 and tell about a time God protected them.
> - Choose ways to be brave helpers.
> - Praise God for using them to help others.

▼ 2. What Does the Bible Say? ▲

Bible Story: God's People Are Saved

You will need to make transparency 4A from p. 105, and use the following silhouettes from p. 106: 4-a king (standing), 4-c Mordecai, 4-e Queen Esther, 4-f Haman, 4-h king (sitting), 4-i scepter, 4-j banquet table, 4-k Queen Esther (bowing), and 4-l horse and rider. (See p. 76 for directions on how to use these visuals.)

(Project transparency 4A. Add silhouettes 4-a, 4-e, 4-f, and 4-j.) **After inviting King Xerxes and Haman to two special dinners, Queen Esther finally asked the king to let her and the Jews live. The king was angry when he heard about Haman's terrible law. Haman was killed that very day.** *(Remove silhouettes 4-f and 4-j.)*

Now Queen Esther could tell the king that Mordecai was her cousin and had adopted her. *(Add silhouette 4-c.)* **The king was happy Mordecai had been so kind to his queen. To show how pleased he was, King Xerxes gave Mordecai his special ring. It was the same ring he had given to Haman— the one Haman had used to stamp the law giving permission to kill the Jews. Now it belonged to Mordecai.** *(Remove all silhouettes.)*

Haman was gone, but the law to kill the Jews still had to be obeyed. *(Add silhouettes 4-h and 4-k.)* **Queen Esther went again to see the king without being invited. She fell down at the king's feet and begged him to stop Haman's terrible plan. Would the king hold out his golden scepter to her again? What do you think he did?** *(Add silhouette 4-i.)* **Yes, again he welcomed the queen.**

(Remove silhouettes 4-i and 4-k. Add silhouette 4-e.) **Queen Esther stood before the king and said, "Please write a new law that protects my people."**

(Add silhouette 4-c.) **The king said Mordecai could write a new law. He was to seal it with the stamp of the king's special ring. Laws stamped with the king's ring cannot be changed.**

So Mordecai wrote a law that gave the Jews permission to fight and protect themselves from their enemies on the day Haman said the Jews could be killed.

King Xerxes agreed with the new law. He ordered it delivered quickly to everyone in his kingdom. *(Remove all silhouettes and transparency 4A. Project silhouette 4-l without a transparency.)* **He even let the messengers ride the fastest horses he owned. When the new law was delivered, all the Jews were happy and joyful. Everyone celebrated and shouted for joy.** *(Turn off the projector.)*

Story Review: Kingly Questions

You will need a crown from the "Story Hats" activity and a copy of all the silhouettes used in this lesson. Cut out each silhouette and fold it into a small shape. Place the folded pictures inside the crown on the floor.

Seat the children in a circle around the crown. Give each child a turn to choose a paper, unfold it, and tell or show what it is. Let the child tell one thing that happened in the story to that person or with that object.

The children may re-fold their papers and hold onto them. If you have more children than pieces of paper, let all the children toss their papers back into the crown after the last paper has been drawn. Make sure every child gets to tell something about the story.

Bible Memory: Tell the Good News

You will need a broom, which will be referred to as the king's horse, and a rolled piece of paper tied with a string, which will be Mordecai's new law.

Divide your students into two groups and line them up opposite each other with a space of about ten feet between them. Give one group the horse and rolled paper. Someone from that group will ride the horse to the other group and hand the new law to another child. As the child hands the new law to another child, he will recite Genesis 28:15. The child with the new law will take the horse and ride back to the other group and recite the memory verse. Continue until everyone has had a turn.

▼ 3. What Does This Mean to Me? ▲

God Protects Me

You will need the "God Protects Me Pictures" from p. 100 and silhouette 4-e Queen Esther from p. 106. Enlarge each one to 8 1/2" x 11" and mount them on poster board. Add color to the pictures. You will also need masking tape and a beanbag. (A sock filled with rice or beans works well for a beanbag.)

Our Bible words remind us that God is always with us. Let's play a game about the places we go.

Tape the pictures in random order to the floor. Line the children up about five feet from the pictures. Give each child a turn to toss the beanbag onto the pictures. Ask each child to tell how God helps him when he is in the place in the picture. When the beanbag lands on the silhouette of Queen Esther, ask all the children to recite Genesis 28:15 together.

Isn't it great that God is always with us? How does that make you feel? Even when we're afraid or we need to help someone, God is with us.

Help! Help!

You will need to provide props for the situations listed below. Use your students, teens, or adults to act out the situations. Encourage them to ad-lib.

1. Someone has fallen and is crying.
2. Mother is cooking dinner, talking on the phone, and trying to set the dinner table.
3. A teacher is arranging classroom chairs to form a circle.
4. Someone is carrying two or three bags of groceries.
5. Someone is sad and lonely with no one to talk or play with him.

We are going to watch some skits. The people in the skits will need help. When you know what kind of help is needed and you would like to help them, raise your hand.

Present the skits. Choose a child to help at the end of each skit. Give suggestions as needed.

Did you like helping these people? How did helping make you feel? Who would like to tell us about a time you helped someone?

We have been learning about a brave queen named Esther. Because she was brave and trusted God to protect her, she helped a lot of people. God wants us to help others, too.

▼ 4. What Can I Do to Please God? ▲

Let's All Help!

You will need to find a job around your church or school building in which all of your students can participate. Provide the necessary equipment, such as dust cloths, trash bags, brooms, and so on.

After the job is completed, gather the children to observe what they have accomplished. **Did you like helping with this project? How did it look before we started? How does it look now? What was your favorite part about helping? Would you like to help again sometime? Let's pray and give praise to God for using us to help others.** Encourage each child to praise God.

A Helper's Chant

You will need copies of the letter to parents from p. 103.

A rhythmic chant is a combination of repetition and rhythm. It is used to tell a story. The leader says a line and the children say a responding line. The responding line is usually the same every time.

Use the following chant as a guide to help you and your students create your own rhythmic chant. Go ahead and give it a try! It is fun and easy to do.

Leader: Who will help me sweep the floor?
Children: I will help! I will help!
Leader: Who will help me dust the shelves?
Children: I will help! I will help!
Leader: Who will help me feed the dog?
Children: I will help! I will help!
Leader: Who will help me rake the leaves?
Children: I will help! I will help!
(Motions: The leader will clap as she says each word. The children will raise their hands every time they say "I.")

Let's praise God for using us to help others. Begin with a praise sentence of your own, then encourage each child to participate. **I praise You, God, because I can help others. What will you say to praise God?** After the children have praised God, close with prayer.

Send home a letter to parents with each child. The letter tells parents about the Purim celebration next class time and asks that children return their treasure chest banks made in Lesson 13.

▼ Bonus Activity ▲

Snack Attack! Haystacks

You will need to provide chow mein noodles, cheese spread, small paper plate, a warmer, and a spoon.

To make a haystack, pile some chow mein noodles on a small paper plate. Heat the cheese spread until it is runny. Dribble a small amount of runny cheese over the noodles. As the cheese cools, it will firm up. Make one haystack for each child.

Lead the children in a thank-you prayer for today's snack. Serve the haystacks. As the children eat, review the Bible story.

What animal in today's story eats hay? What important job was given to the king's horses and riders? Who wrote the new law? What did it say? How did Queen Esther show her bravery?

Celebrate Purim

Esther 9:1, 2, 18-32

▼ 1. What Is This Story About? ▲

Praise Makers

You will need an empty 12-ounce frozen juice can and lid for each child. You will also need copies of the wrapper from p. 104, the words to "When I'm Afraid" from p. 76, crayons or markers, some small pebbles, masking tape, and glue. (Optional: stickers for decorating the wrapper.)

Today we are going to celebrate Purim. It is a special holiday to remember how Queen Esther saved her people. We're going to make Praise Makers to use during the story and in a parade.

Give each child a wrapper to decorate. Then gather the children in small groups around a pile of pebbles and give each child a can. Allow the children to take turns putting pebbles in their cans. When the cans have enough pebbles to make a good sound, give each child a lid. Secure the lids to the cans by crisscrossing the lid several times with masking tape. Help the children glue the wrappers around their cans.

Let's use our Praise Makers while we sing about how God is with us. Use the cans as rhythm instruments to sing both verses of "When I'm Afraid."

Purim Masks

You will need large paper plates, colored paper, crayons or markers, yarn (colors for hair), glue, scissors (for adults), tape, and jumbo craft sticks.

Before class, make a sample mask. Draw eyes, nose, and mouth in the center of the plate. Cut out holes for the eyes. Color in the other features of the face. Glue on yarn for hair and eyebrows.

Today we are going to celebrate a special holiday called Purim. Mordecai and Queen Esther told the people that every year they were to celebrate and remember how God saved the Jews. During Purim the children dress up like people in the story of Queen Esther. Right now we are going to make our masks.

Show your sample mask and distribute the supplies. The boys may want to add beards and mustaches. They can choose to be the king or Mordecai. The girls will be Queen Esther. They can add earrings to their masks by punching holes in the side and attaching loops of yarn. Tape a jumbo craft stick to the back of the mask for holding it up in front of faces.

We can wear our masks in a special Purim parade to celebrate how God cares for His people.

Royal Robes

You will need a large paper grocery sack for each child, some decorating paper (wallpaper scraps are nice) or fabric scraps, crayons or markers, scissors, and glue.

Before class, cut the paper sacks into royal robes as illustrated.

During Purim, the children like to dress up in costumes that make them look like the people in the Bible story.

Let each child decorate a royal robe to go with the mask he or she made.

> **Know:** A Bible person who was brave and did right.
> **Feel:** God is always with them and helps them be brave and do right.
> **Do:** Choose to be brave and do right.
> **Children will accomplish the goals when they**
> • Explore the Purim celebration.
> • Remember the story of brave Queen Esther.
> • Recite Genesis 28:15 and tell what the verse means.
> • Identify good choices they can make.
> • Praise God by sharing with someone.

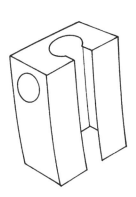

Sometimes the children wear their costumes to act out the story of brave Queen Esther. Sometimes they have a parade. Today we are going to wear our costumes in a special Purim parade.

▼ 2. What Does the Bible Say? ▲

Bible Story: Listen and Celebrate!

You will need the following silhouettes from p. 106: 4-c Mordecai, 4-e Queen Esther, 4-f Haman. (See p. 76 for directions on how to use these visuals.) The children will need the Praise Makers they made in step 1, p. 91.

Purim is a special holiday to remember how brave Queen Esther saved her people. *(Project silhouette 4-e.)* **Once a year (in February or March) Jewish people go to a synagogue to hear the story of Queen Esther read from a special scroll. Everyone listens quietly.** *(Remove silhouette 4-e and add 4-f.)* **When the children hear the name of Haman, they shake their noisemakers. They want to cover up the name of Haman with noise so his name cannot be heard.** *(Demonstrate. Remove silhouette 4-f and add 4-e.)* **When they hear Queen Esther's name, they clap their hands to honor her.** *(Demonstrate. Remove silhouette 4-e.)*

Let's pretend we are in the synagogue listening to the story of Esther being read. When you hear Haman's name, shake your Praise Makers. When you hear "Esther," clap. Let's add something for Mordecai. *(Project silhouette 4-c.)* **When you hear his name, cheer "Hooray! Hooray!"** *(Demonstrate. Remove silhouette 4-c.)* **Listen carefully!**

(Tell the story projecting the silhouettes for Esther, Mordecai, and Haman as their names are mentioned in the story. Remove the previous silhouette as the next one is added.)

A very powerful king wanted a new queen. A beautiful girl named Esther *(clap)* **was chosen. Her cousin, Mordecai** *(hooray),* **told her not to tell anyone her family was Jewish.**

Mean Haman *(noise)* **made a law giving permission for all the Jews to be killed. Haman** *(noise)* **did not know Queen Esther** *(clap)* **was Jewish.**

Mordecai *(hooray)* **told Queen Esther** *(clap)* **to go to the king and ask him to change the law or she would be killed. The king was angry with Haman** *(noise)* **when he heard about Haman's** *(noise)* **bad plan.**

The king could not change the law, but he let Mordecai *(hooray)* **write a new law. The new law said the Jews could fight and protect themselves on the day which Haman** *(noise)* **had said all the Jews could be killed.**

On that day the Jews gathered in groups and protected each other. The fighting lasted two days. There was no one strong enough to win against the Jews.

Mordecai *(hooray)* **wanted the people to remember how brave Queen Esther** *(clap)* **saved her people. Mordecai** *(hooray)* **wrote a letter to all the Jews telling them to celebrate with joy and feasting because their enemies were gone. Mordecai** *(hooray)* **also told them to show their joy by giving food to one another and presents to the poor. This celebration was named Purim.**

The Jews still celebrate Purim today. It is the happiest of all their celebrations. Purim celebrates the happy ending of the story of the mean Haman *(noise),* **smart Mordecai** *(hooray),* **and brave Queen Esther** *(clap). (Turn off projector.)*

How to Say It

Haman: HAY-mun
Mordecai: MOR-dih-kye
Purim: (poo-REEM)

Bible Memory: Musical Crowns

You will need the crown pattern from p. 102, yellow construction paper, a variety of other colors of construction paper, tape, recorded joyful music, and a cassette or CD player. Play this game like the game of "Musical Chairs."

Before class, trace and cut out one crown pattern for each child. Leave the crowns flat. Decorate only one crown with jewels cut from pieces of colored paper. Tape all the crowns to the floor in a circle. If you have more than ten students make several circles. Make sure to have one decorated crown for each circle.

Our Bible words remind us that God is always with us. Let's play a game to help us think about where God is.

Have the children stand on the crowns. Review the memory verse several times. Play some joyful music and have the children march around the circle, stepping on the crowns. Stop the music. Ask the child standing on the decorated crown to say Genesis 28:15 from memory. Always give help as needed. Ask the children standing on both sides of this child to tell how they know God is with them. Start and stop the music until everyone has said the memory verse.

> **Bible Words**
> "I am with you, and I will protect you everywhere you go" (Genesis 28:15).

▼ 3. What Does This Mean to Me? ▲

Hamantaschen

You will need cookies baked according to the recipe for Hamantaschen Cookies from p. 103, copies of the recipe, plastic wrap, curling ribbon, and scissors.

Make enough for your class to eat for a snack and enough for each child to wrap up one or two as a gift.

A fun part of celebrating Purim is eating a special cookie called Hamantaschen. These cookies are shaped like the three-cornered hat that Haman might have worn to show he was an important man in the kingdom.

When Mordecai told the Jews to celebrate Purim, he said they were to eat special food and give gifts to others. Today, we are going to do what Mordecai said.

Thank God for the snack and pass out the Hamantaschen cookies for the children to eat.

When a child is finished eating, give him a piece of plastic wrap, one or two cookies, and a folded recipe. Place the folded paper and cookies on the plastic wrap. Show how to join the four corners of the wrap and twist. Have an adult tie each one with a ribbon and curl it. Save these for the Purim parade.

During the Purim parade, we will give our wrapped cookies away.

> **How to Say It**
> Hamantaschen:
> HAY-mun-TA-shin

I Will Do What Is Right

You will need the Praise Makers made in step 1, p. 71.

The story of Esther is about a queen who chose to be brave and do what was right to save her people. Every day we make choices, too. We can choose to do what is right or we can choose to do wrong. Listen to these choices. If you hear a bad choice, shake your noisemaker. If you hear a good choice, clap your hands as you did when you heard the name "Esther." Read the following choices and give the children time to respond:

I pick up my toys when I am finished playing with them.

When my mom calls me to come inside, I keep playing.

I hide my favorite toy when my friend comes to play.

When my dad is talking to someone, I wait patiently and do not interrupt.

I stand in line behind my teacher without pushing.

When my brother wants to watch TV, I hide the remote.

Discuss each choice made by the children. Add specific examples that are appropriate for your students.

Our Bible words remind us that God is always with us. Does that help you want to make good choices?

What can help us make good choices?

Who made good choices in our Bible story?

▼ 4. What Can I Do to Please God? ▲

Purim Parade

You will need the Praise Makers, Purim Masks, and Royal Robes made today and the Story Hats made during Lesson 16. Also use the wrapped cookies from the "Hamantaschen" activity. You will also need some fun music, and a cassette or CD player.

Today, we are going to have a parade. Dress the children in their royal robes and hats. Pass out the Praise Makers, masks, and wrapped Hamantaschen cookies. Lead the children around to other classrooms where they can give away their cookies. In each classroom, have one child tell the story of Queen Esther. Also, have your students tell about their costumes, gifts, and the reason for the parade.

If you cannot visit another class, play some joyful music as you walk around your classroom. Have the children exchange cookies with each other. Save the cookies to be taken home.

What can you say to praise God for saving Esther and her people?

What can you do to show you love God? (Help others, be brave, share.)

Treasure Gifts

You will need the treasure chests the children brought today from home. You will also need the words to "When I'm Afraid" from p. 76.

After the children have helped clean up the classroom, gather them in a circle sitting on the floor. Pass out the returned treasure chests and the extras (put some money in these) so that everyone has a chest to hold.

Mordecai wanted Purim to be a special holiday for everyone. He wanted the poor to celebrate, too. Mordecai told the people to give presents to the poor during Purim. A few weeks ago we made banks that looked like a treasure chest. We took them home to have our families help us put coins in them. Today we are going to give these banks to (an organization of your choice). **They will use the money to help others.**

Purim is an important celebration. It reminds us God helps us be brave. It also reminds us to do what is right.

Sing "When I'm Afraid" and lead the children in prayer. Give each child a turn to pray, praising or thanking God for being with him.

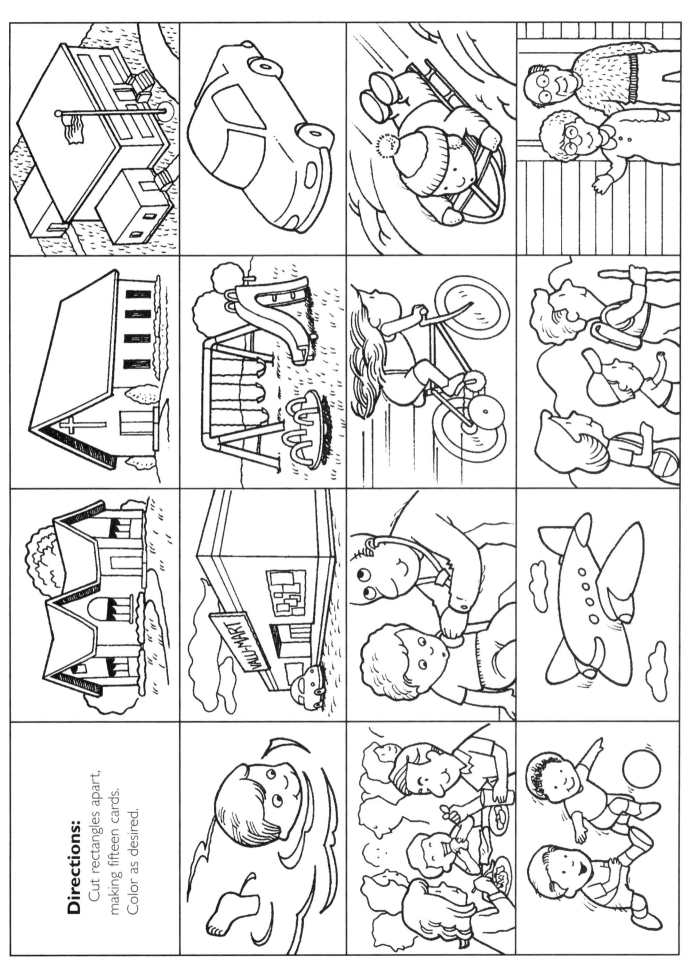

Directions:
Cut rectangles apart, making fifteen cards. Color as desired.

Meet Esther

God's people were in danger. Queen Esther asked the king for help. The king said, "Yes!" God's people were saved. Queen Esther was their hero.

Nehemiah smiles as he looks at the new walls around the city of Jerusalem where God's people come to worship. He remembers how sad he was when there were no walls or strong gates to protect this special city.

Nehemiah and many workers rebuilt the walls and gates. When their enemies tried to cause trouble, Nehemiah prayed and asked God to help them. The wall was finished in only fifty-two days!

My Bible Heroes

Joseph

Booklet Directions:

1. Cut off the direction strips on this page and page 97.

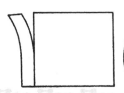

2. Fold the booklet pages in half on the broken lines. Glue the blank sides together.

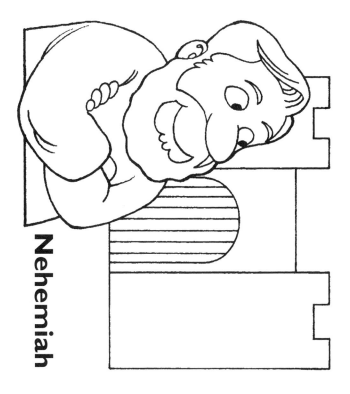

Nehemiah

God chose Gideon to lead a small army in a battle against a very strong army. At first, Gideon was afraid. God promised to help him.

On a dark night Gideon and his men held their torches up high and blew on their trumpets. This scared the enemy. They ran away without fighting. Gideon and his men won!

Joseph's brothers were very mean to him. They sold him to travelers going to Egypt. God was with him. He became an important ruler in Egypt.

Joseph was in charge of storing grain. When his brothers came to Egypt looking for food to feed their hungry families, Joseph gave them grain. He was not angry. Joseph saved his family.

Gideon

3. Fold in half on the dotted lines. Insert one folded booklet into the other so that the pages are in order. Staple on the fold.

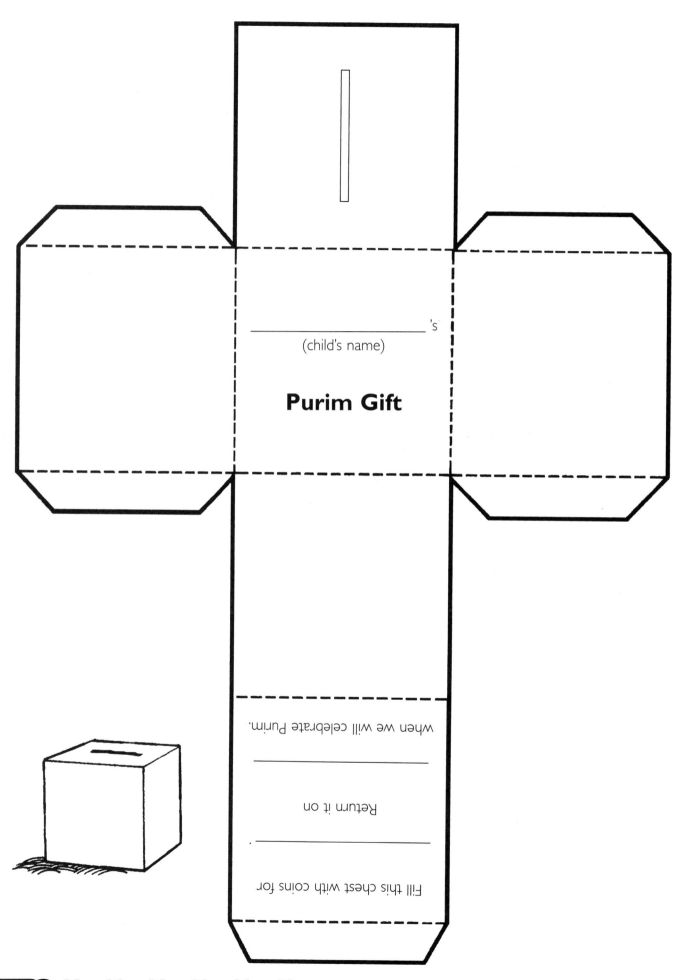

_____'s
(child's name)

Purim Gift

when we will celebrate Purim.

Return it on

Fill this chest with coins for

The Dark

Shadows

Dogs

A New Teacher

Sirens

New People

Moving to a New House

New Food

Bugs

The Doctor

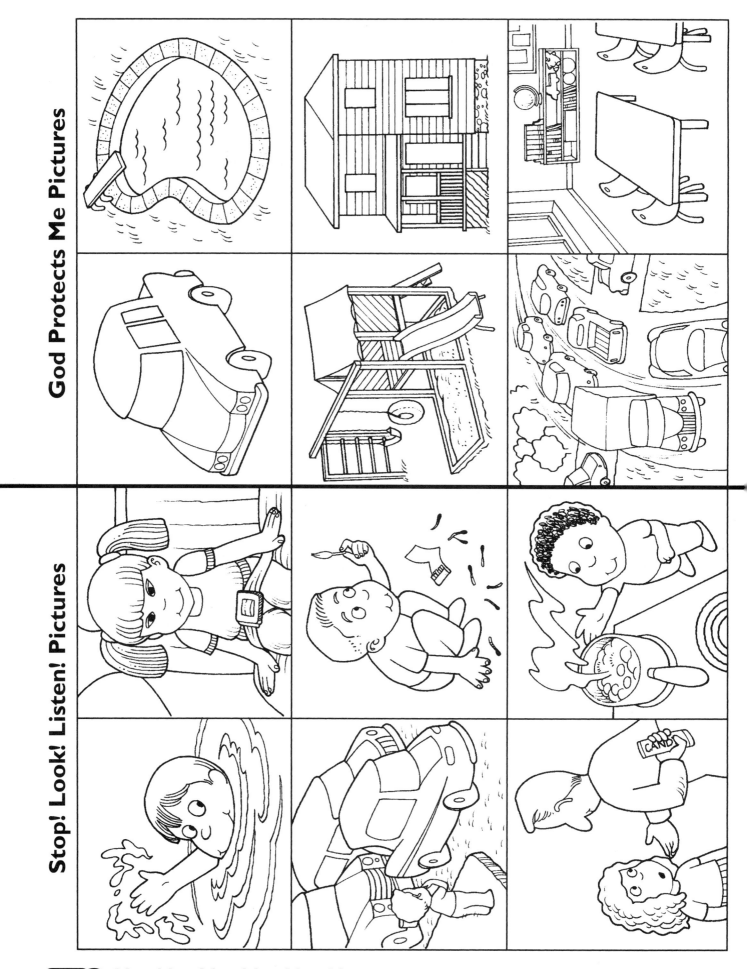

God Protects Me Pictures

Stop! Look! Listen! Pictures

"I am with you."

(Genesis 28:15)

Scepter Wrapper

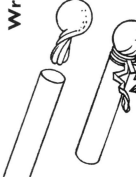

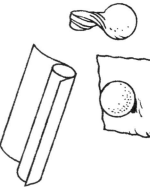

Directions:

1. Glue wrapper around paper towel tube.

2. Twist tissue paper around Styrofoam ball.

3. Stuff the gathered tissue paper into one end of the tube. Glue to the end of the tube.

4. Tie ribbon around the end of the tube near the ball. Curl with scissors.

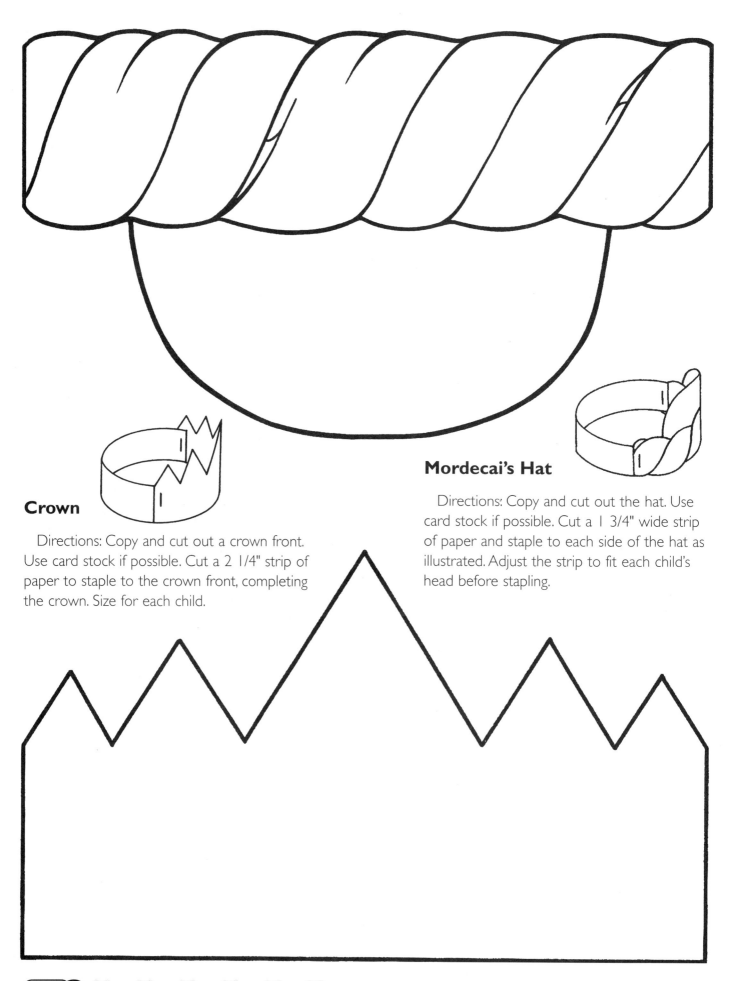

Crown

Directions: Copy and cut out a crown front. Use card stock if possible. Cut a 2 1/4" strip of paper to staple to the crown front, completing the crown. Size for each child.

Mordecai's Hat

Directions: Copy and cut out the hat. Use card stock if possible. Cut a 1 3/4" wide strip of paper and staple to each side of the hat as illustrated. Adjust the strip to fit each child's head before stapling.

Hamantaschen Cookies
(Makes 3 dozen)

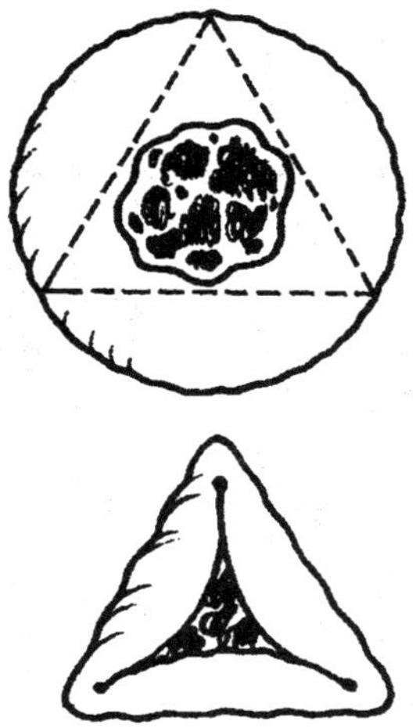

1 cup oil
1 1/2 cup sugar
4 eggs
2 tablespoons vanilla
2 tablespoons baking powder
5 1/2 cups flour
6 ounces of preserves (any flavor)

Preheat oven to 350°. Grease and lightly flour cookie sheets.

Combine the oil, sugar, eggs, vanilla, and baking powder in a large bowl. Mix well. Add flour a little at a time. Blend well.

Roll out the dough 1/4" thick on a floured surface. Cut 2" circles with a cookie cutter or cup. Spoon 1/2 to 1 teaspoon of preserves in the center of each circle. Bring three edges of each circle to the center to form a triangle. Pinch edges together.

Bake for 25 to 30 minutes or until golden brown. Cool before serving.

Purim is a special Jewish holiday. It is a happy time when the story of how Queen Esther saved God's people is read and acted out. Eating these cookies are part of celebrating Purim. Some people say they are the shape of the three-cornered hat worn by Haman. Haman was an evil man who wanted to get rid of all the Jews. When Queen Esther risked her life to tell the king about Haman's plan, the king got rid of Haman instead!

Dear Parent,

We have one more lesson in our unit titled "Learning to Be Brave."

In this unit, we have learned how even someone as important as Queen Esther depended on God for help to be brave.

The story of Esther is an exciting one. She was an orphan who became the beautiful queen of Persia. An evil man, named Haman, plotted to have all the Jews in Persia killed. He didn't know Queen Esther was a Jew. Esther bravely told the king about the evil plan. The king quickly got rid of Haman. The Jews were saved.

Every year Jews celebrate the story of brave Queen Esther with a holiday called Purim. This is one of the happiest of all the Jewish holidays and is a favorite among children. Special food, gifts, and acting out the story of Queen Esther are all part of this holiday.

Next week our class will celebrate Purim. Please have your child bring back his or her treasure chest bank containing some coins. Giving the coins to those in need will be part of our Purim celebration.

Sincerely,

PURIM

Praise Maker Wrapper

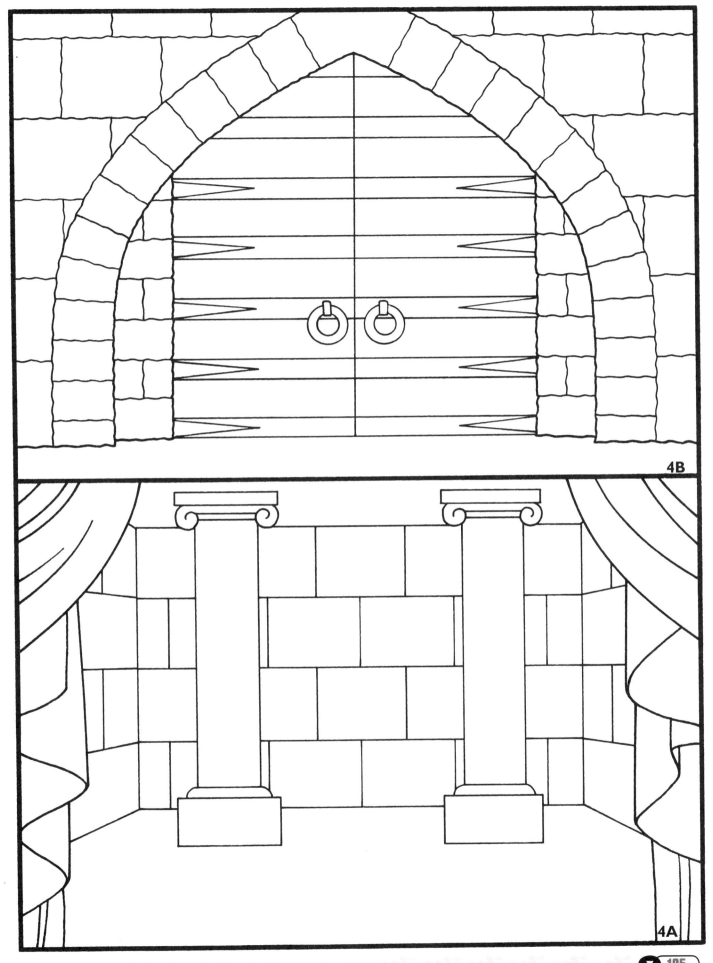

4B

4A

Silhouettes

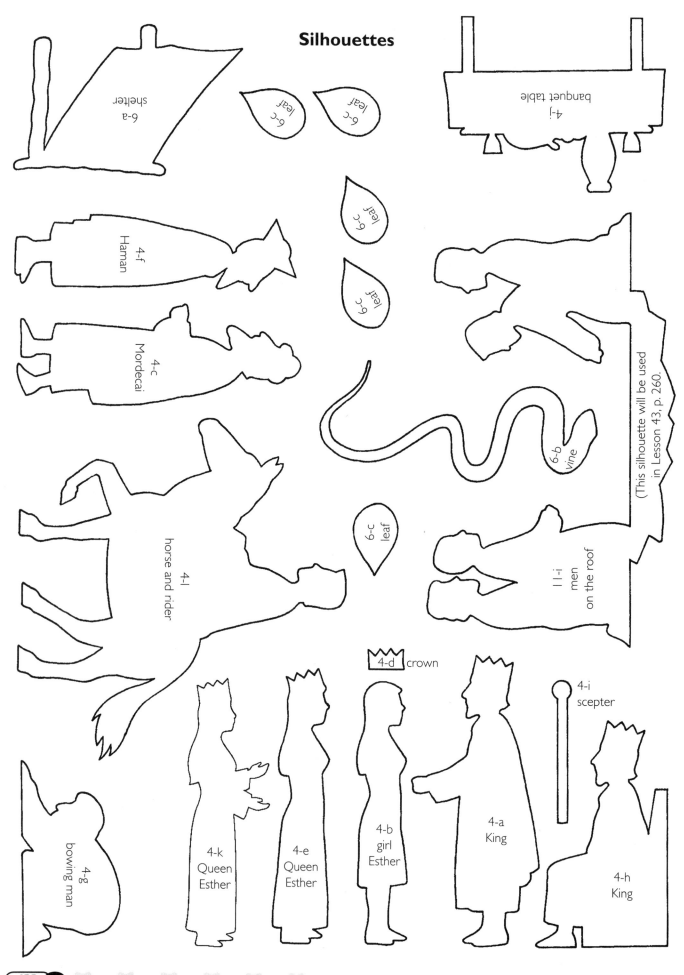

6-a shelter

6-c leaf

6-c leaf

4-j banquet table

4-f Haman

4-c Mordecai

6-c leaf

6-c leaf

6-b vine

(This silhouette will be used in Lesson 43, p. 260.)

6-c leaf

4-l horse and rider

11-i men on the roof

4-d crown

4-i scepter

4-g bowing man

4-k Queen Esther

4-e Queen Esther

4-b girl Esther

4-a King

4-h King

Learning to Pray Always

Unit Bible Words
"I call to you, God, and you answer me" (Psalm 17:6).

Bible Character
Daniel

18 Daniel, a Man Who Obeyed God

Daniel 1—Daniel refuses to eat the king's food. Instead he obeys God's laws. He is rewarded with the best job in the kingdom.

19 Daniel, a Man Who Always Prayed

Daniel 6:1-10—Some men are jealous of Daniel's top position in the kingdom. They trick the king into declaring that all prayers be said to him. The penalty for not praying to the king is to be thrown into a den of lions. Daniel chooses to pray to God.

20 Daniel, a Man Who Was in Danger

Daniel 6:11-18—Daniel trusts God to protect him from the lions. The king, who doesn't want Daniel to die, and doesn't know of God's greatness, worries all night. Trusting in God is the best way to live.

21 Daniel, a Man Protected by God

Daniel 6:19-23, 25-27—God protects Daniel from the lions. The king learns to put his trust in the living God. We can trust God to hear and answer our prayers, too.

By the end of this unit, the children and leaders will

Know: A Bible person who chose to pray during a difficult time.
Feel: That God hears and answers their prayers.
Do: Choose to pray anytime and anywhere.

Why Teach This Unit to Four- to Six-Year-Olds?

Children at this age consider prayer very important. They hear the prayers and observe the prayer lives of parents and teachers. From these adults they learn how to pray and when to pray.

In addition to these influences, Daniel will become a role model during this unit on prayer. Create an environment that will provide an opportunity for these children to experience God's greatness in answering their prayers like those of Daniel. Children at this age expect God to hear and answer their prayers. This unit provides the proof!

Meet Daniel

As a young Hebrew, Daniel put his trust in God. Early in life he found that obedience to God's laws was the best way for a person to live. He obeyed God's dietary laws and was rewarded with robust health. That, and the character he developed by obeying God, landed him the best job in a foreign kingdom.

Daniel provides an example of a person devoted to living every day for God. When Daniel was forced to make a decision concerning to whom he would pray, without hesitation he went to his room, opened his window, and bowed in prayer to the living God. Even when such conduct meant being thrown into a den of lions, Daniel put his trust in God for protection. He knew his prayers for help would be heard and answered. As Daniel was led to the lions' den, there is no record that he went kicking and screaming. He prayed and then trusted God.

Daniel is a role model of unconditional trust in God to hear and answer prayer. Children should be encouraged to imitate Daniel's example.

Unit Songs

Daniel
(Tune: "Did You Ever See a Lassie?")

Verse 1
Daniel prayed to God each day,
        each day, each day.
Daniel prayed to God each day,
        yes, three times a day. *(Clap as you sing each word.)*
He prayed and he prayed. *(Fold hands in prayer.)*
        It was the best way.
Daniel prayed to God each day.
        Yes, three times a day. *(Clap as you sing each word.)*

Verse 2
Jealous men wrote a new law,
        a new law, a new law. *(Pointer finger writes on other palm.)*
Jealous men wrote a new law,
        "You must pray to the king." *(Shake pointer finger.)*
But Daniel said "Oh no, *(Shake head no.)*
        I'll pray to God only."
"Then you'll end up with the lions
        and they'll eat you up!" *(Place palms together horizontally. Keeping wrists together, open and close hands.)*

Verse 3
God saved Daniel from the lions,
        the lions, the lions.
God saved Daniel from the lions.
        He shut their jaws tight. (Clap!)
They growled and they roared (Roar!)
        'til God made them snore. (Snore!)
God saved Daniel from the lions.
        He shut their jaws tight. (Clap!)

Verse 4
Yes, Daniel is alive, *(Clap as you sing* yes.)
        alive, alive.
Yes, Daniel is alive. *(Clap as you sing* yes.)
        God saved him last night.
The king was so sad, *(Rub eyes.)*
        but now he is glad. *(Use pointing fingers to make lips smile.)*
Yes, Daniel is alive. *(Clap as you sing* yes.)
        God saved him last night.

The Best Job
(Tune: "Here We Go 'Round the Mulberry Bush")

The king gave Daniel the very best job,
the very best job, the very best job.
The king gave Daniel the very best job,
because he was strong and healthy.

Daniel, a Man Who Obeyed God

LESSON 18

Daniel 1

▼ 1. What Is This Story About? ▲

A Recipe for Success!

You will need a Bible, copies of "Good for You" from p. 123, crayons, paper plates, and red, yellow, green, and orange colored play dough. Purchase play dough or make your own with the recipe on the right.

In today's story, we are going to meet a young man named Daniel, who chose to eat only the foods that would make him strong and healthy. Let's talk about foods that are good for us to eat.

Give each child a copy of the chart from p. 123 and crayons. Ask the children to color their favorite foods. Then distribute the play dough and ask the children to make their favorite foods. Display their food creations on a plate. Talk about the good food we can eat.

What is your favorite food? Why do you like it?

Why is it important to eat good food?

Eating food that helps us grow strong and healthy is a good choice. In our story today, Daniel makes a good choice about food.

▼ 2. What Does the Bible Say? ▲

Bible Story: Daniel Obeyed God

You will need a Daniel puppet. Make one using the pattern from p. 125.

Jerusalem was a special city in Bible times. God's people came from everywhere to worship Him in the temple in Jerusalem. A long time before Jesus was born, a terrible thing happened to the city of Jerusalem. King Nebuchadnezzar and his army came and tore down the city. The king and his army took some special things from God's temple. They also took many of God's people. God's people were taken far away to a country called Babylon.

In Babylon, the king chose the best young men from Jerusalem to be trained to serve him. A young man named Daniel was one of those young men. (Show puppet and have him bow.)

The king made some rules for Daniel and the other young men. He said, "For the next three years these young men will live in my house. Teach them our alphabet so they can read and speak as we do. Also feed them the same kind of food I eat."

Daniel and the other young men were treated in a very special way. But when Daniel saw the king's food, he knew it was not good for him. (Have the puppet shake his head no.) **Daniel knew that God's rules said to eat food that would make him strong and healthy.**

Daniel said to the man in charge, "My three friends and I would like permission to eat only vegetables and drink water for ten days. After ten days you can decide whether or not we look healthy." (Move the puppet as though he is talking.)

After ten days, Daniel and his three friends looked healthier than all the

---

Know: A Bible person who chose to pray during a difficult time.

Feel: That God hears and answers their prayers.

Do: Choose to pray anytime and anywhere.

Children will accomplish the goals when they

• Talk about good food.
• Tell why it was good for Daniel to obey God.
• Begin to memorize Psalm 17:6.
• Tell what it means to obey God.
• Ask God to help them make good choices.

Play Dough

1 cup flour
1 cup water
1/2 cup salt
1 tablespoon cooking oil
2 teaspoons cream of tartar (do not omit)
food coloring (optional)

Cook, stirring for three minutes or until mixture pulls away from the pan. Knead as soon as you can handle it. Store in an airtight container. This makes enough for six children.

How to Say It

Babylon: BAB-uh-lun
Nebuchadnezzar: Neb-yuh-cud-NEZ-er

other young men. For the next three years the four men were given only vegetables and water.

God was pleased that Daniel had obeyed Him. He helped Daniel and his three friends to become smarter and healthier than all the other young men.

At the end of the three years it was time for the king to test the young men from Jerusalem. The king asked many questions. Daniel and his friends answered the king's questions better than anyone else. The king was very happy with them and gave them the best job in the kingdom. God was also pleased with them because they obeyed Him.

Do you know what it means to obey God? *(Allow the children to give answers.)* Daniel chose to obey God when he ate only healthy food. We obey God when we choose to follow His rules, too.

Story Review: And the Winner Is . . . Daniel!

You will need the words to "The Best Job" from p. 108.

Teach the song "The Best Job." Have the children form a circle around one child who will play the part of Daniel. As the children sing and march around in a circle, "Daniel" can show his muscles. Let the children take turns playing the part of Daniel. After each turn, use the following questions to review the story:

Why was it good that Daniel obeyed God?

What happened to Daniel when he ate healthy food?

What happened when the king saw how healthy Daniel was?

Bible Memory: Hide God's Word in Your Heart

You will need a toy telephone.

Gather the children around you as you hold the toy telephone. **Do you like to talk on the telephone? Who do you like to call on the phone? Praying is the way we talk to God, just as calling on the telephone is the way you talk to your grandparents. I can talk to God anytime. He always hears and answers my prayers. Let's use this telephone to practice saying our Bible words.** Talk into the phone as you say the Bible words, **"I call to you, God, and you answer me."** Give each child a turn to use the phone to say the Bible words. Give help as needed.

Bible Words

"I call to you, God, and you answer me" (Psalm 17:6).

▼ 3. What Does This Mean to Me? ▲

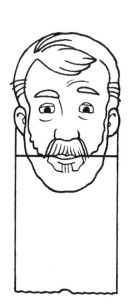

Make a Daniel Puppet

You will need a photocopy of the Daniel puppet from p. 125 for each child, paper lunch sacks, scraps of fabric, construction paper, yarn, glue, and scissors.

Daniel made good choices in our story today. Let's make a Daniel puppet to remind us to make good choices.

Distribute materials and help the children make a Daniel puppet. When the children finish making puppets, let the children use them to talk about good choices.

What good choices did Daniel make when he was chosen to work for the king?

Daniel's good choices showed that he obeyed God. Good choices are good because they are choices God wants us to make. When we make good choices, we are obeying what God says is right.

What good choices can you make when you're playing with your friends?

What good choices can you make when you are riding in a car?

What good choices can you make at the supper table?

Grocery Cart Upset

This game is a version of the game "Fruit Basket Upset." Set chairs in a circle facing each other, one for each child in the class. Explain the game to the children.

Let's pretend our circle of chairs is a grocery cart. Who can name a good food that we could put in our cart?

Encourage the children to choose healthy foods. Select three or four foods from their suggestions to be in the grocery cart. Then go around the circle telling each child what food he will be in the cart. For example, four children will be apples, four others will be potatoes, and four others will be eggs. Continue until all the children are something.

Remove one chair from the circle. The child who was sitting in that chair will be the first caller and will stand in the center. The caller calls the name of one of the foods in the grocery cart. All the children with that food name, plus the caller, must run to a different chair and sit on it. The child left without a chair calls out another food and those children exchange chairs. The caller can also say, "Grocery Cart Upset." Then all of the children must change chairs.

Play the game for several minutes. Then stop the action to talk about rules and what it means to obey God.

It is fun to play when everyone obeys the rules. We have had a good time playing this game. What happens when we don't follow rules?

Do you like it when you are playing a game with someone who won't follow the rules? What would happen on the street if drivers didn't follow the rules?

What are some of the rules at your house? In your school?

Why do we have rules?

Why does God give us rules?

How do we know what God wants us to do?

When we follow God's rules we are obeying God like Daniel did.

▼ 4. What Can I Do to Please God? ▲

Right or Wrong?

Divide your classroom into two parts. Call one side the "right" side and the other side the "wrong" side.

I'm going to say some things that will be right to do and some things that will be wrong to do. If what I say is wrong, run over to the wrong side of the room. If what I say is right, run over to the right side of the room. Listen carefully and make good choices.

Use the following statements and add more of your own:

Eating a lot of candy is good for you.

Drinking milk helps to make your bones strong.

After eating a snack in the car, it is good to throw the trash out the window.

Fruits and vegetables are good for you.

It is important to get your hands dirty before you eat.

You have made many good choices. I'm glad you know the difference between right and wrong things to do. When you make good choices, you are obeying God. Listen carefully to this last sentence. "You can pray anywhere and anytime." Great! Now that we are all standing on the "right" side of the room, let's pray. Lead the children in a prayer asking God's help in making good choices. Give each child a turn to pray. Model a sentence like this: **Dear God, thank You for all the good things You give us. Help me obey You by making good choices this week.**

▼ Bonus Activities ▲

Snack Attack! Food for Thought

You will need a bag of regular pretzels, a bag of pretzel sticks, and napkins.

Before the children begin eating their pretzels, demonstrate how to take bits out of a pretzel to make a letter of the alphabet. Also demonstrate how to form letters using the stick pretzels. Help each child form his name on a napkin.

Daniel learned many new things in Babylon. He even had to learn a new alphabet. Look at our snack. Let the children pick out letters they know. Older children may want to use the letters to spell simple words. **Our snack is food that is good for us. Was the king's food good for Daniel to eat? How did Daniel obey God?**

Snack Attack! Body Fuel

(This activity can also be used with Lesson 19.)

You will need dried fruit, nuts, and seeds. Provide a large bowl and large spoons for the children to help you mix the ingredients.

Wash hands. Gather the children around you.

Daniel knew how important food was for his body. Remember how he chose to eat only good food? He knew his body needed good food to make the energy he needed to be a good worker.

Lead the children in a few simple exercises. They will enjoy jumping jacks, touching their toes, reaching for the sky, and running in place. (If you have children with disabilities in your class, be sure to include exercises that they can do.) Talk about how your body uses food to get the energy to do these exercises.

Daniel also chose to pray every day. Before we eat our snack, let's each thank God for something that our bodies can do. I want to thank God for giving me fingers that can pick up paper. Encourage each child to say a sentence prayer before you eat.

Daniel, a Man Who Always Prayed

Daniel 6:1-10

▼ 1. What Is This Story About? ▲

Moms and Dads Are Good Workers

You will need to invite two or three parents to share briefly about their occupations. Ask them to bring and demonstrate any special equipment they use in their jobs. If they wear uniforms to work, ask them to wear them.

Our guests today are going to tell us about their jobs. Listen quietly, and then we'll have time to ask them questions.

Have each parent tell how he or she learned to do his or her job. Encourage the children to ask questions about the parents' jobs.

Would you like one of these jobs when you grow up? Which one? Each of these jobs needs someone who will be a good worker.

We learned that Daniel was given the best job because he was healthy and he obeyed God. In our story today, Daniel is given the best job in the kingdom. God was pleased with Daniel.

▼ 2. What Does the Bible Say? ▲

Bible Story: Daniel Always Prayed

You will need the Daniel puppet made from the pattern, p. 125. (See Lesson 18.) Also use that pattern to make King Darius (add a crown) and two jealous men. (Vary clothing and hair colors to make each man different.)

Ask four children to work the puppets. Stand behind the puppeteers as you read the dialogue. Place your hand on each child's head as a signal for the puppet to "talk" as you speak. Put masking tape labels on the backs of the children so you will know who is who.

King Darius *(speaking seriously):* **Hum! Hum! Listen to me! I, King Darius, have a very important announcement. Ruling this kingdom is too big of a job for me. I need help. I will choose 120 men to rule over my kingdom. Also I have decided to put Daniel and two other men in charge of these men.**

Teacher: **King Darius began to notice that Daniel was the best worker of all of his men. He planned to put Daniel in charge of everyone in his kingdom. Listen to what happened.**

Man #1: **I've just heard some bad news. King Darius is planning to put Daniel in charge of the whole kingdom. He says Daniel is his best worker.**

Man #2: **That's not fair! I want that job!**

Man #1: **You're right, it's not fair! I want that job, too. Hey, I've got an idea! Let's watch Daniel. As soon as he does something wrong, we'll tell the king.**

Teacher: **Those jealous men watched Daniel every day and every night. This is what they saw. Daniel was a hard worker. He wasn't lazy. He always told the truth. He never did anything wrong. The men also saw Daniel pray three times a day to God. Now listen to what the men decided to do.**

Man #1: **We have a problem. Daniel is the king's best worker. He never does anything wrong. He isn't lazy like we are. We can't find anything bad to tell the king.**

Know: A Bible person who chose to pray during a difficult time.
Feel: That God hears and answers their prayers.
Do: Choose to pray anytime and anywhere.

Children will accomplish the goals when they

- Explore jobs people do.
- Tell about a good choice Daniel made.
- Memorize Psalm 17:6.
- Name times to pray each day.
- Choose to pray.

How to Say It
Darius: Duh-RYE-us

Man #2: **I've got a plan. I watched Daniel pray three times a day to his God. Let's have the king make a law that for the next thirty days no one can pray to any god or man except King Darius.**

Teacher: **All of the jealous rulers went to see King Darius. They asked the king to pass a law that everyone in the land would have to obey. This was the law: For thirty days no one could pray to any god or man except King Darius. Anyone disobeying this law was to be thrown into a den of lions. When King Darius signed the law, not even he could change it. Do you think Daniel stopped praying to God? Let's see what happened.**

Daniel: **I just heard about the king's new law. But I will not pray to the king because I worship the living God. I will pray to God three times a day just as I always do.** (*Daniel bows his head.*)

Teacher: **What good choice did Daniel make?** (*Allow the children to respond.*) **Daniel obeyed God. He knew that talking to God was a good thing to do. God wants us to pray every day, too.**

Story Review: When I Grow Up . . .

Play this version of the game "Charades." Let the children take turns pantomiming the actions of workers they would like to be when they grow up. Have the class guess what kind of worker is being pantomimed.

When the children have guessed the job, ask the pantomimer a review question.

Why did King Darius need help?

Why did he choose Daniel for the best job?

What did some jealous men think when they saw what a good job Daniel did?

What did those men do to hurt Daniel?

What was the king's new law?

When Daniel heard about the new law, did he obey it?

How was Daniel faithful to God?

Did Daniel risk his life by being obedient to God?

Why was God pleased with Daniel?

Bible Memory: Toss and Tell

You will need one beanbag for every two children. If beanbags are not available, put a cup of dried rice or beans in socks and tie knots in the tops.

Who remembers the Bible words that we started learning last week? The words are from Psalms and begin "I call to . . ." Wow! What good memories you have. Let's say the words together a couple of times, and then we are going to say them with a friend.

When the children are ready to work in pairs, pass out the beanbags to half of the children. Direct the children without beanbags to become partners with children holding beanbags. Each child holding a beanbag recites, "I call to you, God," as he tosses the beanbag to this partner. The receiver catches the bag and says, "and you answer me." Together the two children say, "Psalm 17:6." After several turns, mix up the partners. Bring the entire group together to say the verse in unison.

> **Bible Words**
> "I call to you, God, and you answer me" (Psalm 17:6).

▼ 3. What Does This Mean to Me? ▲

Prayer Burst

You will need a jar of liquid bubbles and a wand.

Daniel prayed to God three times each day. Why do you think he prayed three times? When do you like to pray to God? Do you pray when you're sick? When you need help? When you're sad? When you're happy?

We're going to use these bubbles to help us name times we can pray to God. As you blow the bubbles, ask the children to shout out times they can pray to God as they burst the bubbles (morning, mealtime, nighttime). Try to repeat what the children say so they can think of other times to pray. Then ask the children to tell what they pray for (people to get well, food for hungry, thank-you for family). Continue blowing bubbles for the children to burst.

We can even pray to God when we're blowing bubbles. Let's thank God for something each time we burst a bubble. Give children the opportunity to thank God and then close with **In Jesus' name, amen.**

Pray Like Daniel

You will need the words to verse one of "Daniel" from p. 108.

Daniel obeyed God in everything he did. He loved God and talked to him. Three times a day Daniel would get down on his knees and pray. Let's learn a song about Daniel.

Teach the first verse of "Daniel" to the children. Using the motions from the beginning will help the children remember the words. Sing the song several times.

Do you talk to God each day? Where do you like to talk to God?

Is there any place where you cannot talk to God?

We can talk to God anytime and anywhere.

▼ 4. What Can I Do to Please God? ▲

My Job Chart

You will need copies of My Job Chart from p. 124 and Job Pictures from p. 126, scissors, glue, and crayons or markers. Optional: Purchase star stickers for the children to use at home.

Daniel was given the best job because he was the best worker in the kingdom. This pleased God. God wants us to be good workers, too. We're going to make a job chart to help us remember to pray and do our best work.

Pass out the charts and job pictures. Discuss the job that each picture represents. Coloring the chart during class is optional. Help the children cut out the pictures of jobs they can do or would like to do. Glue them in the squares in the left-hand column. Explain that when they complete a job, they can draw a star (or put a sticker) in the box for that job and that day.

What jobs do you do at your home? Give each child a turn to tell about his chart.

Our job charts will help us remember to pray to God this week. God wants us to talk to Him just as Daniel did. When will you pray this week? Give each child a turn to tell when she will pray. Close with prayer, thanking God for hearing us when we pray.

Good Workers in Action

You will need a sticker for each child. Any kind of fun sticker or smiley face will do. You will also need verses one and two of "Daniel" from p. 108.

Let the children demonstrate how good workers can help clean up the classroom. Compliment each child for her efforts. Place a sticker on each child as you comment about her workmanship.

I like the way you have cleaned up our classroom. You remind me of Daniel. He was a good worker, too. Let's sing our new song about Daniel.

Sing verse one, then teach the words for the second verse. Sing the second verse several times so the children can learn the words and motions. Close with prayer, giving each child a turn to pray.

Daniel, a Man Who Was in Danger

Daniel 6:11-18

▼ 1. What Is This Story About? ▲

Building Trust

You will need some wooden or cardboard building blocks for constructing a booster-seat-type chair. If you have only small blocks, find a small piece of plywood to use for the seat of the chair.

Let's build a chair. First we will stack some blocks on top of each other to make the legs of the chair. Now let's lay some long blocks across the top of the legs. Would someone like to try sitting on this chair made of blocks? Check the blocks to be sure they are stable. Keep the legs short. Once a child sits on the chair, others will want to try, too.

When you want to sit down, you find a chair and sit on it. You trust the chair to hold you and not let you fall on the floor. What other things do we trust? Who are some people you trust?

Daniel knew a lot about trust. He knew he could trust God to take care of him. We'll learn more about trusting God in our story today.

Trust Walk

You will need blindfolds for half of your class.

Group the children in pairs. Instruct the children in each pair to take turns wearing the blindfold. The child not wearing the blindfold is to lead his partner carefully around the classroom.

As your partner leads you around the room, you will have to trust him to keep you from bumping into chairs, tables, and other children.

After all the children have had a turn wearing the blindfold, discuss how they felt when they had to trust the other person.

Who did you trust in your walk around the room?

How did you feel when you couldn't see?

What is hard about trusting someone?

When Daniel chose to pray to God and not King Darius, he had to trust God to take care of him. We'll learn more about trusting God in our story today.

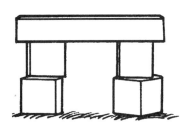

▼ 2. What Does the Bible Say? ▲

Bible Story: Daniel Was in Danger

You will need the puppets from Lesson 19 and four of the lion puppets that the children will make during the Story Review activity. Ask four children to work the people puppets and four children ready to work the lion puppets. Stand behind the puppeteers as you read the dialogue. Place your hand on each child's head as a signal for the puppet to "talk" as you speak.

Daniel *(head bowed):* **Dear God, please help me.**

Man 1: **Look! There's Daniel. It looks like he's praying.**

Man 2: **Shhh! I just heard him say, "Dear God, please help me." He's** broken the king's law.

Man 1: **Let's go tell King Darius.**

Teacher: **The jealous men went to the king and reminded him that he had written a law that said, "No one can pray to any god or man except King Darius." They also reminded him that the law said that any person who disobeys would be thrown into a den of lions. Let's listen to what the king said.**

King Darius: **Yes, I wrote that law, and it cannot be changed.**

Man 1: **Well, Daniel is not obeying your law. He still prays to his God three times a day.**

Teacher: **The news about Daniel made the king really sad. He knew Daniel was a good man who always worked hard. Daniel never did anything wrong. The king could always trust Daniel to tell the truth. The king wondered if he could save Daniel from the lions' den.**

King Darius (*pacing back and forth*): **I must save Daniel. Maybe I can think of a way. I must save Daniel! There must be a way. I must save Daniel!**

Man 1 (*entering and bowing before the king*): **King Darius, do you remember that a law made by a king can't be changed? Well, you can't change your law. Daniel must be put into the lions' den.**

King Darius (*sadly*): **OK, go get Daniel.**

Teacher: (*Hold Daniel puppet and have the four children with lion puppets gather around.*) **Daniel was thrown into the den of lions. Can you make the lions roar? Before a big stone was rolled over the opening, King Darius said to Daniel, "May the God you serve save your life." Then the king went back to his palace.**

King Darius (*pacing back and forth*): **I'm worried about Daniel. He's in a den full of hungry lions. I'm really worried!**

Man 1: **Here is some food to eat. It will make you feel better.**

Man 2: **We'll play some music for you. Music will make you feel better.**

King Darius (*still pacing*): **Nothing will help. I feel terrible! Poor Daniel! He's the best worker I've ever had. I hope his God will save him.**

Teacher: **King Darius stayed awake all night. He couldn't stop worrying about Daniel.**

Story Review: Grrr-eat Choice

You will need a copy of the Lion Sack Puppet from p. 125 and a paper lunch sack for each child, scissors, glue, and crayons. Pieces of brown and gold felt or construction paper, moveable eyes, and yarn for the mane are optional, but would make the puppet more interesting. You will also need the words to verse one and two of "Daniel" from p. 108.

Help the children make the lion puppet. Help the children sign their names on their puppets.

As they work on this project, review the Bible story from Lessons 19 and 20.

Who wanted to get Daniel in trouble with the king?

What did these men trick the king into doing?

What did Daniel do when he heard about King Darius' new law?

How many times a day did Daniel pray? Was that the right choice?

If you had been Daniel, would you have chosen to pray to God?

Whom did Daniel trust to take care of him?

Why was Daniel put in the lions' den?

Why was the king worried about Daniel?

What did King Darius say when Daniel was thrown in the den of lions?

Review the words and motions and sing verses one and two of "Daniel."

Bible Memory: Bold Lions

You will need the puppets made in the Story Review activity.

Have the children sit in a circle holding their lion puppets (no more than six children per circle). Have the children say the Bible words together. Then the "lions" will recite the verse one word at a time, including the book, chapter, and verse. Go around the circle several times, changing directions. Ask whether any "lion" would like to say the verse alone. Compliment each "lion" who does for his boldness!

Our Bible words remind us what prayer is.

Who hears all of your prayers?

Who answers your prayers?

How do you know?

▼ 3. What Does This Mean to Me? ▲

Going on a Lion Hunt

You will need copies of the Lion Sack Puppet picture from p. 125. Before class, hide somewhere in the room one picture for each child in the class.

The lions are loose and must be found. Ask each child to find one of the lion pictures hiding in the room. When all the lions have been found, gather the children around you and talk about the "lions" in their lives.

Lions are wild and loud and scary! These lions can remind us of other things in our lives that are scary. What kinds of things worry you, frighten you, or upset you?

When do you get angry? When are you afraid? When are you sad?

What can we do when we feel like that? Who can help us?

What are some ways that we show we trust God to take care of us? (Praying to God shows we trust Him to answer our prayers; obeying God shows we trust that He knows what is best for us.) Encourage the children to tell times they have trusted God by praying and obeying.

▼ 4. What Can I Do to Please God? ▲

Prayer Reminder Rock

You will need rocks about the size of your fist (smooth ones are best), tempera paints, brushes, paint shirts, newspaper, colored glue, and the words to "Daniel" from p. 108.

We're going to make something right now that can help us to remember to pray to God at all times.

Help the children paint their rocks. When they are dry, use the colored glue to print the word "pray" on each rock. (Optional: Add a praying hands sticker instead of the word.) As the children work, sing verses one and two of "Daniel."

We don't know for sure how many times a day Daniel prayed—he may have gone about his business praying all day! But we do know that three times a day he went to his window that faced Jerusalem, got down on his knees and prayed. This rock will help you remember to trust God and pray every day as Daniel did.

Let's pray right now! We can tell God we love Him and that we want to trust Him always. Pray a simple prayer: **God, I want to trust You every day.** Then give each child a turn to pray.

Roaring Success

You will need copies of the "Grrrrr-eat" coupon from p. 123 and the words to "Daniel" from p. 108.

Ask the children to help clean up the classroom. Then gather everyone on the floor. Hold up a coupon and read the child's name. Ask the other leaders and helpers to give that child a compliment. Write the compliment on the child's coupon and give it to the child. Do the same for each child. (Option: you and the other leaders can write down the good deeds as you notice them.)

Daniel pleased God by being a good worker. God is pleased when we are good workers, too. Our classroom is a happy place to be when all of us are good workers. You all have made this a grrrrr-eat place to be.

Form a circle and sing verses one and two of "Daniel." Close with a prayer: **Dear God, we love You. We want to trust You to always hear our prayers. We want to be good workers for You. In Jesus' name, amen.**

▼ Bonus Activity ▲

Snack Attack! Hungry as a Lion

You will need English muffins (a half for each child), peanut butter, chow mien noodles, raisins, jumbo craft sticks, and napkins. Also provide a drink. (In case of peanut allergies, flavored [brown] cream cheese can used instead.)

Wash hands. Set out the ingredients and utensils. Help the children make "lions." First spread peanut butter on the English muffin. Use raisins for the eyes, nose, and mouth. Use the noodles for the mane.

As the children eat their "lions," discuss what happened to Daniel when he chose to pray to God. **Daniel put his trust in God when he chose not to pray to King Darius. Do you think Daniel was worried about being put in a lions' den? How do you think he felt?**

Daniel, a Man Protected by God

Daniel 6:19-23; 25-27

Know: A Bible person who chose to pray during a difficult time.
Feel: That God hears and answers their prayers.
Do: Choose to pray anytime and anywhere.

Children will accomplish the goals when they
- Name ways God protects them.
- Tell who saved Daniel from the lions.
- Recite Psalm 17:6
- Tell how they know God hears their prayers.
- Choose to trust God to answer their prayers.

▼ 1. What Is This Story About? ▲

You're a VIP

You will need a copy of the VIP badge from p. 126 for each child, masking tape, and markers or crayons.

Show the children the VIP badge. **You are a V-I-P to God! Do you know what these letters mean? They stand for "Very Important Person."**

Give each child a VIP badge to color. As the children color their badges, ask the children questions about how God protects them.

Who has God put in your life to take care of you and protect you?

What have you learned at school, at home, or from television about what to do in an emergency?

Who gave you a brain that helps you learn these important things?

Who made your ears so that you can hear and listen to warnings?

Do you have a warm and safe place to sleep at night? Do you have lots of good food to eat? Do you have a jacket to keep you warm outside? Who gives you these things?

When the children finish coloring their badges, tape them on the children.

Our VIP badges will help us remember that we are very important to God. They will also help us remember all the ways God protects us.

▼ 2. What Does the Bible Say? ▲

How to Say It
Darius: Duh-RYE-us

Bible Story: God Protected Daniel

You will need the puppets Daniel, King Darius, and several lions.

Ask two children to hold the Daniel and King Darius puppets. Stand behind the puppeteers as you read the dialogue. Place your hand on each child's head as a signal for the puppet to "talk" as you speak. Also ask several children to hold the lion puppets.

Teacher: **King Darius made a law that said everyone must pray only to him for thirty days. Anyone who didn't pray to him would be thrown in a den of hungry lions. Daniel, who always prayed to God, would not pray to the king. He was thrown into the lions' den. King Darius wanted to save Daniel, but he couldn't change his own law. The king stayed awake all night worrying. As soon as the sun came up, the king ran to the lions' den to see what had happened to Daniel.**

(Surround Daniel with lions.)

King Darius: **Daniel! Daniel! Did the living God you worship save you from the lions?**

Daniel: **Yes! Yes! My God sent an angel to shut the lions' mouths. He knows I never did anything wrong to you, King Darius.**

King Darius: **I want Daniel taken out of the lions' den right now!**

Teacher: **Some men lifted Daniel out of the lions' den.**

King Darius: **Let me see you, Daniel. Are you okay? I was so-ooo worried about you.**

Daniel: **I'm okay! The lions didn't hurt me. God protected me.**

Teacher: **The king was happy because there wasn't a scratch or bruise or a bite on Daniel. Daniel trusted God, and God protected Daniel.**

King Darius: **Here is a new law! Every person in my kingdom must honor and serve the God of Daniel. His God is the only mighty and living God. Daniel's God saved him from the powerful lions. Only Daniel's God can save and rescue people.**

Story Review: Were the Lions Hungry?

You will need the king puppet used during the Bible story and the words for "Daniel" from p. 108. Optional: clothing props for the children to wear as they act out the song.

Let's sing a song to review the whole story of Daniel.

Review the words and motions to the first two verses, and then teach the words and motions for the last two verses. Sing the whole song together. Then ask for volunteers to act out the story as the rest of the children sing. Assign each verse to different children.

Review the story with these questions:

Why did the king like Daniel?

Why was the king so worried about Daniel?

What made the king begin to trust God?

Bible Memory: God's Phone Is Never Busy

You will need a sample of the telephones that you will make in "Does God Have a Phone Number?" You'll also need a Daniel puppet used during the Bible story.

Our Bible words remind us that we can talk to God and He will always hear us. Let's have some fun saying our Bible words to each other.

Let the children take turns using the phone to recite Psalm 17:6 from memory to the child listening at the other end of the cord. Then talk about what the words mean.

Who can call to God? (Anyone can pray to God.)

What will God do when we call to Him? (He will answer us.)

Does that mean He will always give us what we ask? (He will always hear us and answer us, but it might not be the answer we were expecting.)

How do we know God will answer us? (The Bible tells us He will.)

Can we trust Him to give us the best answer? (Yes!)

> **Bible Words**
> "I call to you, God, and you answer me" (Psalm 17:6).

▼ 3. What Does This Mean to Me? ▲

Does God Have a Phone Number?

You will need two twelve-ounce frozen concentrate juice cans, two copies of the juice can covers from p. 126, and about five feet of nylon string for each child. Also provide glue, scissors, and markers, water paints, or crayons.

Ahead of time, punch a hole in the bottom of each can and connect two cans with a five-foot piece of string. Before inserting the string in the first can, tie a large knot in one end. Then insert the string in the opening of the can and pull it all the way through until the knot stops it. Next, insert the string in the bottom of the second can. Push it through until it comes out the opening. Tie another large knot. This will secure the string so the children can pull it taut.

Cut the juice can covers to fit the cans. Let the children color them with markers, paint, or crayons. Glue the covers on the cans.

Let's talk to each other about praying to God. Find a partner to talk with, and decide whose phone you will use. Talk to each other about the ques-

Help each child find a partner, and then ask the following questions:
Who are the people you pray for?
What are some things you tell God when you pray?
How do you know that God hears your prayers?
What do our Bible words tell us about praying to God?
We know that God hears our prayers because He tells us that in the Bible, and many times we can see God's answers to our prayers.

No Li-on!

You will need a blindfold.
God hears our prayers. Who can tell us about a time God answered a prayer?

Have the children stand in a circle. Choose one child to blindfold and have him sit in the center of the circle. The standing children walk slowly around the blindfolded child until the leader says stop. The blindfolded child points to someone. That child must roar. Give the blindfolded child three chances to guess the name of the "roaring lion." If the blindfolded child is correct, he trades places with the lion. Before the blindfold is put on the next child, ask her to tell something about prayer.

God hears our prayers. Sometimes we must wait for an answer, and sometimes we get an answer we don't like, but God knows what is best. He will always answer our prayers.

How do know God will always answer your prayers? Give the children an opportunity to answer; then emphasize what the Bible words tell us about God.

Our Bible words remind us that God will answer us.

How do you know God can hear you when you pray? Are you sure He is listening even when you can't see Him? Give the children time to answer; then remind them of the Bible words from the stories about Esther.

Our Bible words we learned weeks ago remind us that God is always with us. ("I am with you, and I will protect you everywhere you go" Genesis 28:15.)

What are some other reasons we know God will answer our prayers? (We see prayers answered, our family and friends trust God to hear and answer prayer, the Bible tells us to pray to God.)

▼ 4. What Can I Do to Please God? ▲

Be a Lion Tamer

Have the children sit in a circle. Make small circles of no more than six children. **Who did Daniel trust to answer his prayer? Did God help Daniel? Who can we trust to answer our prayers?** Choose one child to be the angel who shuts the lions' mouths. The rest of the children will be lions. Have the angel walk around the inside of the circle as the lions roar. When the angel stops in front of one of the roaring lions, that child becomes Daniel. The angel pats Daniel's head and asks, **"Who answers your prayers?"** All the lions stop roaring and listen as Daniel says, **"I trust God to answer my prayers."** Daniel then trades places with the angel. Continue until everyone has had a turn playing the part of the angel or Daniel.

Ask the children to share their prayer requests. Respond to each request with a statement about how God can be trusted to give the right answer. **Do you think Daniel prayed during the night he spent in the lions' den? He trusted God to give the right answer to his prayers. We can trust God to answer our prayers, too.**

Lead the children in a time of prayer. Encourage them to pray to thank God for hearing their prayers, to ask God to help them make good choices, or to tell God they trust Him to always answer their prayers.

Bonus Activity

Snack Attack!
Don't Feed the Animals
You will need large round crackers, and squirt cheese in a can.

Wash hands. Let the children make lion faces on the crackers with the cheese.

When you go to the zoo you will see signs that say, "Don't feed the animals." You never see signs that say, "Don't feed the children." So let's make lion crackers and feed them to each other.

As you make a lion cracker, think of a question you can ask about how God saved Daniel. Find a child and ask him or her your question. When the child gives the answer, give him or her your lion cracker.

Make sure each child shares and each receives.

_____

(child's name)

is Grrrrreat because

_____

_____

Good for You

All of these foods are good for you.
Color the foods you like to eat.

Why not try some of the foods that you didn't color?
You might like them, too!

My Job Chart

My Jobs	Sunday	Monday	Tuesday	Wednesday	Thursday	Friday	Saturday

Lion Sack Puppet

Daniel Sack Puppet

Can Cover

Job Pictures

"I call to you, God, and you answer me."

(Psalm 17:6)

Special Helper

_____ is a **VIP** to God!

Learning to Obey God

Unit Bible Words
"Now change your lives and start doing good and obey the LORD your God" (Jeremiah 26:13).

Bible Character
Jonah

22 Jonah Hears, but Disobeys

Jonah 1—The people of Nineveh are enemies of the Jews. God tells Jonah to go there and warn the people to repent of their evil ways. Jonah hears God, but gets on a boat headed in the opposite direction. God causes a storm to almost wreck the boat. Jonah tells the sailors to throw him overboard. A giant fish swallows him.

23 Jonah Listens to God

Jonah 1:17–2:10—Jonah lives for three days and three nights inside the giant fish. He spends this time praying. He is thankful to be alive and promises to obey God. God causes the fish to spit Jonah onto dry land.

24 Nineveh Listens and Obeys

Jonah 3—God again tells Jonah to go to Nineveh and warn the people there. After one day of preaching, the entire city, including the king, repents. God changes His mind and forgives the people for all their evil ways. He does not destroy the city.

25 God Teaches Jonah About Love

Jonah 4—God forgives the city of Nineveh. Now Jonah is angry. He wanted the enemy to be destroyed. Hoping God will still destroy the city, he sits on a hill and waits to see what God is going to do. It is very hot, so God provides a vine for shade. This makes Jonah happy. When God causes the vine to die, He teaches Jonah an important lesson about His love for all people.

By the end of this unit, the children and leaders will

Know: A Bible person who obeyed God.
Feel: Eager to please God and happy when they listen and obey.
Do: Choose to listen to and obey God.

Why Teach This Unit to Four- to Six-Year-Olds?

Obedience is a key word in raising children. Hopefully, the children in your class are learning the importance of obeying their parents and teachers. They should have had some experience with the joy of choosing to do the right thing, and the consequences of disobedience. As they learn about Jonah's disobedience and repentance, your job will be to relate his experiences to theirs.

During this unit, create an environment that gives children opportunities to practice obeying simple directions. Help them to see and understand that following directions makes their lives easier. Help them to see that obeying rules creates a pleasant environment for everyone.

The most important thing a child can do is to obey God. As children mature, they will discover that God's rewards are endless. Joy can be experienced daily. The ultimate reward is eternal life. The value of learning to obey God is measureless.

Listening skills are included in this unit because they are essential in learning to follow directions. It is important for a child to know that the Bible is God's set of directions, which He wants them to obey.

As you take a closer look at Jonah's story, you will find more than just a story about a man who was swallowed by a big fish. You will find valuable lessons about listening, obeying, and loving. These are important for young children to learn.

Meet Jonah

Jonah was a man who had to learn about obedience the hard way. As a prophet, his job was to deliver messages from God to people. This required listening to God and obeying Him. Jonah didn't have any trouble *hearing* God, but he struggled with doing what he was told.

God told Jonah to go to Nineveh and preach. Nineveh was well known for its brutality. The people were wicked and did not honor or worship God. They were enemies of Israel. Yet, God loved these people and wanted them to change.

Jonah didn't want the people of Nineveh to receive the opportunity to change, so he boarded a ship to Tarshish, a city 2,000 miles from Nineveh. Surely God would not bother to find him and bring him back to preach to these wicked people!

Jonah was wrong! No one can run away from God or hide from Him. God caused a violent storm to convince Jonah that he had made a bad choice. In order to save his shipmates, Jonah instructed them to throw him into the sea. Then God rescued Jonah by sending a great fish to swallow him.

For three days and nights Jonah prayed inside the fish. He repented and God gave him a second chance.

This time, Jonah obeyed and went to Nineveh. There he preached God's message and the entire city turned toward God and obeyed.

This pleased God and He decided not to destroy them. Jonah, however, was not happy. He was angry. God again patiently taught him another lesson. This lesson dealt with love, which is fundamental to understanding the heart of God.

Unit Visuals: A Living Drama

You will need to make transparencies of pp. 144 and 145 for use in this unit. Cut each of the two transparencies in half to make sections 6A, 6B, 6C, and 6D. You may color the transparencies with permanent overhead projector pens. (Hint: Handle transparencies as little as possible. Colored pens will not mark easily over fingerprints.)

If a plain wall is not available for projection, tack a large, plain white sheet to the wall. Be sure that one edge of the sheet meets the floor.

These four transparency sections will be used as backdrops to the Bible Time stories. Therefore, project each scene at floor level. When Jonah steps into the light, he will come to life in his surroundings.

The silhouettes (6-a, 6-b, 6-c) found on p. 106 will be used in Lesson 25. Copy the silhouettes onto card stock and cut out, or glue onto light cardboard and cut out.

Unit Song

Where Is Jonah?
(Tune: "Where Is Thumbkin?" or "Are You Sleeping?")

Verse 1
Where is Jonah?
Where is Jonah?
In a boat! In a boat!
What is Jonah doing?
What is Jonah doing?
Running from God.
Running from God.

Verse 2
Where is Jonah?
Where is Jonah?
In a fish! In a fish!
What is Jonah doing?
What is Jonah doing?
Praying to God.
Praying to God.

Verse 3
Where is Jonah?
Where is Jonah?
Nineveh! Nineveh!
What is Jonah doing?
What is Jonah doing?
Preaching for God.
Preaching for God.

Verse 4
Where is Jonah?
Where is Jonah?
On a hill! On a hill!
What is Jonah doing?
What is Jonah doing?
Learning to love.
Learning to love.

Jonah Hears, But Disobeys

Jonah 1

▼ 1. What Is This Story About? ▲

Listen! Listen!

You will need twenty opaque 35 mm film cans. (Most photo shops will give you all you can use for free.) Collect small items, such as jingle bells, rice, coins, popcorn kernels, water, or paper clips, to put in the cans that will make a unique sound. Leave two cans empty. Use each noise-making item twice so that you have nine sets of cans, each set sounding alike.

Let's use our ears to have some fun.

Mix up the cans and place them on the table or floor. Let the children shake the cans and listen to the sounds. Ask the children to match the cans with the same sounds. (It might work best to let one child hold a can and then shake the others to find its match.) Open each pair to see whether they were correctly matched. (Be sensitive to any children with hearing loss.)

Talk about why we need ears.

My Ear Book

You will need copies of "My Ear Book" (p. 146) and pictures (pp. 146 and 151), and materials listed on p. 146. Before class, prepare the books as directed on p. 146. Make the pictures into stickers or provide glue for the children to attach the pictures to their books.

God gave us ears so we can hear all kinds of sounds. Let's make a book to remind us of all the wonderful things we can hear.

Give each child an assembled book and the eight pictures/stickers. Ask the children to color each picture and decide where to put the pictures in their books. Talk about the pictures while the children work.

What sounds do these animals make? Let the children demonstrate the sounds.

What sounds do people make?

What sounds do cars and trucks make?

What sounds do you hear at a playground?

What sounds do fire trucks make? Airplanes?

The music notes help people and instruments make sounds. What is your favorite song?

The picture of the Bible reminds us to say our Bible words. Which Bible words can you remember? Ask for volunteers to say Bible words from previous units.

▼ 2. What Does the Bible Say? ▲

Bible Story: Jonah Runs Away

You will need transparencies 6A, 6B, and 6C, an overhead projector, and someone (child or adult) dressed as Jonah. (See Unit 6 p. 128 for directions on how to use these visuals.)

Know: A Bible person who obeyed God.

Feel: Eager to please God and happy when they listen and obey.

Do: Choose to listen to and obey God.

Children will accomplish the goals when they

- Explore ears and hearing.
- Tell what happened when Jonah chose to disobey God.
- Begin to memorize Jeremiah 26:13.
- Identify what happens when someone chooses to disobey.
- Choose to obey.

How to Say It

Nineveh: NIN-uh-vuh.

A long time before Jesus was born, there was a big city named Nineveh. *(Project transparency 6C.)* **This city was full of people who did not know about God. They did many terrible things. God planned to destroy this city unless the people changed. He chose Jonah to go to Nineveh and tell the people His plan.**

Why did God choose Jonah for this important job? Because Jonah was a prophet. A prophet is someone who tells people messages from God. God needed someone to deliver this special message to the people living in Nineveh. *(Remove transparency 6C.)*

(Jonah stands in the projector's light, with arms folded, shaking his head no.) **Jonah did not like the people of Nineveh. He wanted God to destroy them. Jonah did not want to obey God. He decided to run away.** *(Jonah runs to one edge of the light and then runs in place.)*

Jonah thought that if he went far away from Nineveh, God could not find him. *(Project transparency 6A. Jonah climbs into the boat.)* **So he got on a boat that was going far away. He went down in the bottom of the boat to sleep.** *(Jonah curls up as though he is sleeping.)*

While Jonah was sleeping, God sent a terrible storm. The sailors were very frightened. They thought the boat was going to break in half. Everyone tried to save the boat. They threw boxes into the water hoping to make the boat lighter, but that did not help. The sailors prayed to their own gods, but that did not help either. Nothing they did helped. The boat was still rocking back and forth and up and down all at the same time. *(Move transparency 6A back and forth, keeping Jonah in the boat.)*

Where was Jonah? He was still sleeping! The captain of the boat woke Jonah up.

"Get up and pray," yelled the captain. **"Maybe your god will listen and save us!"** *(Jonah sits up, stretches, and yawns. Then Jonah stands up.)* **Jonah got up and said, "My God made the sky, the land, and the sea. I am running away from Him because I do not want to obey Him. My God made this storm."**

The storm grew worse. The waves grew higher and washed over the boat. *(Rock the boat again.)* **Jonah looked over the side of the boat. "If you throw me into the sea, the storm will stop," said Jonah.**

None of the sailors wanted to hurt Jonah, so they tried to row the boat back to land. Still the storm grew worse. Soon the boat would break in half and they all might die.

Finally, they threw Jonah into the sea. *(As the boat is rocking, Jonah jumps into the water and pretends to sink.)* **The storm stopped! The waves were calm. The boat gently rocked in the water.** *(Remove transparency 6A.)*

What happened to Jonah? God had a plan. As Jonah was falling down to the bottom of the sea, God sent a big fish to swallow him. *(Project transparency 6B. Jonah swims into the fish and sits down.)* **Jonah stayed in the stomach of the big fish for three days and three nights.**

Jonah had listened to what God wanted him to do, but he did not obey. Jonah tried to run away, but God knew exactly where he was! Jonah was right when he said the storm was caused by God. *(Turn off the projector.)*

Story Review: Where Is Jonah?

You will need the words for "Where Is Jonah?" from p. 128.

Let's learn a song that will help us remember the story of Jonah.

Teach the first verse of "Where Is Jonah?" and use the following motions:

Where is Jonah? (Raise arms up and slightly out so that they look like the sides of a *W* for *where*. Use the same motion both times you sing this phrase.)

In a boat! (Lean to the left the first time you sing the phrase and lean to the right the second time—as if you are on a boat that is moving and shifting.)

What is Jonah doing? (Do the *W* motion again for these two phrases.)

Running from God. (Run in place.)

Sing the verse several times. In between each time, ask the following questions:

What did God ask Jonah to do?
What was wrong with Nineveh?
What is a prophet?
Why didn't Jonah obey God?
What did Jonah do instead of going to Nineveh?
What happened while Jonah was sleeping?
What happened when Jonah was thrown into the sea?

Bible Memory: I Hear an Echo!

Our Bible words remind us to obey God.

Ask the children to echo each phrase of the Bible words as you say them. Explain that an echo is no louder than the original sound. As you say the phrases, vary your speaking level from a whisper to a shout. Remind the children to be good listeners and copy what you say and how you say it. Use the following phrases:

Now change your lives
and start doing good
and obey the LORD
your God.
Jeremiah
26:13

Repeat the echo activity several times, varying how you use your voice. Talk about what the Bible words mean.

What good thing did God want Jonah to do?
Did Jonah hear what God wanted him to do? Did he obey God?
How can we know what God wants us to do? (Listen and learn from the Bible, teachers, parents.)

> **Bible Words**
> "Now change your lives and start doing good and obey the LORD your God." (Jeremiah 26:13).

▼ 3. What Does This Mean to Me? ▲

Oh-oh!

You will need the "Choosing to Disobey Pictures" from p. 147. Enlarge, if possible, color, and cut apart.

These pictures show someone disobeying or something that happened because someone disobeyed.

Show the pictures one at a time. (If your students enjoy role-play, most of the pictures can be reenacted in the classroom.) Ask for volunteers to demonstrate and/or tell what might happen to the people who are disobeying in each picture. Ask the children to tell what a parent or teacher might say or do as a result of these acts.

When you disobey your parents or teachers, how do you feel? Do you feel bad? Sad?

Is it sometimes hard to obey? Is it sometimes easy?

What do you think about the job God asked Jonah to do? Was it hard or easy?

Choose and Do

You will need the "Choosing to Disobey Pictures" from p. 147. Enlarge if possible, color and cut out.

These pictures show someone disobeying or something that happened because someone disobeyed.

Place the pictures facedown on a table or the floor. Ask a child to choose one of the pictures and turn it over. The child will then tell how he would obey in that situation. Compliment the children for their good ideas. Repeat the activity until every child has had a turn; then use the following questions:

How do you feel when you disobey? How do you feel when you obey?

Our Bible words remind us that God wants us to obey Him. He knows what is best for us. He knows we are happy when we obey.

▼ 4. What Can I Do to Please God? ▲

Listen and Tell

God has given us good ears for listening. Let's see how well we can listen today.

Play the game "Telephone." Have the children sit in a circle. The teacher starts by whispering a sentence that begins, "I choose to obey . . ." in the ear of the child on her right. For example, "I choose to obey when my mom asks me to help," or "I choose to obey by not fighting with my brother." The child listens carefully and then whispers what he heard to the child on his right. This continues around the circle until the sentence is whispered into the teacher's ear. The teacher repeats what she heard and tells whether or not the sentence is correct. If it is, the children were very good listeners. Ask for volunteers to start a new sentence around the circle. After several sentences, talk about listening to God.

God has given us good ears for listening. We can listen to our parents and obey. We can listen to God's Word and obey it, too. Our Bible words remind us that God wants us to do good things and obey Him. Let's ask God to help us listen and obey.

Model a prayer something like this: **God, I choose to obey You. I will listen to Your Word and obey.** Give each child a turn to pray. Close the prayer time, thanking God for ears that can hear good things to do.

Shipshape!

You will need the words to "Where Is Jonah?" from p. 128.

After Jonah was thrown into the sea, I am sure the sailors on the boat had a big mess to clean up. The storm must have caused many things on the boat to fall and slide around. The captain probably gave lots of directions. When everything on a boat is in the right place, we say it is "shipshape." Our room looks like a boat that has been through a storm. Listen and I will give you directions on how to clean it up. If you obey my directions, our room will soon be "shipshape."

Direct each child to help clean and straighten the room. This will give the children practice in listening and obeying directions. Ask each child who wants to obey to respond with, **"I choose to obey!"** Compliment every effort no matter how small.

Gather the children to sing verse one of "Where Is Jonah?" and pray.

▼ Bonus Activity ▲

Snack Attack! The Deep Blue Sea

You will need blue gelatin (prepared as directed on the box), small paper cups, and spoons. To serve, cut into small pieces and serve in cups. Before the children eat, offer a prayer thanking God for the story of Jonah.

As the children eat, ask them what they've learned about being good listeners.

Jonah Listens to God

Jonah 1:17–2:10

▼ 1. What Is This Story About? ▲

Listen and Do

You will need items for an obstacle course, such as a table, chairs, rope, and Hula-Hoops.

We can have lots of fun when we listen and obey. Let's see who can listen and follow directions through our obstacle course.

Instruct the children individually how to go through the obstacle course. Give short directions, such as, "Crawl under the table," "Jump over the rope," "Sit on the chair," "Go through the Hula-Hoop." Try to vary the directions for different children, asking the most adventurous to climb over the table, and so on. Add variety by changing directions or having two children go through together.

Did you have fun going through the obstacle course?

What did you use in order to follow my directions?

It is important to listen and then obey by doing what we heard. An obstacle course is fun and easy when we listen and obey the directions.

Listen and Find

You will need fish crackers in snack-size plastic bags hidden in the classroom. Hide one bag for each child, and make a list of where each bag is hidden.

When our ears hear something, we can think about what we heard and choose to do something. Let's see how our ears help us follow directions.

One at a time, give each child directions on how to find a bag of crackers. Example: Jacob, please go around the table, pass the coat rack, and look under the table by the window. Also ask each child to hold the crackers in his lap and wait to eat until everyone has a bag. When each person has a snack, eat and discuss listening and obeying.

Were you a good listener? Why? What does a good listener do? Was Jonah a good listener? Why or why not?

▼ 2. What Does the Bible Say? ▲

Bible Story: Jonah Listens

You will need transparencies 6A and 6B, an overhead projector, and a child or adult dressed as Jonah. (See pp. 128 for directions on how to use these visuals.)

Jonah was a prophet. God gave him a message to tell the people living in Nineveh. The message was that God was going to destroy the city because the people did many terrible things. Jonah did not like the people of Nineveh, so he didn't care that God was angry with them. Instead of delivering the warning, Jonah disobeyed God and tried to run away on a boat. (*Project transparency 6A. Jonah steps into the boat and the boat rocks back and forth.*)

God made a terrible storm toss the boat up and down and back and forth. Finally, the sailors threw Jonah into the sea and the storm stopped.

> **Know:** A Bible person who obeyed God.
>
> **Feel:** Eager to please God and happy when they listen and obey.
>
> **Do:** Choose to listen to and obey God.
>
> **Children will accomplish the goals when they**
>
> - Explore listening to and following directions.
> - Tell what Jonah did inside the great fish.
> - Memorize Jeremiah 26:13.
> - Tell about a time when they can choose to listen.
> - Promise to listen to God's Word and obey it.

> **How to Say It**
> Nineveh: NIN-uh-vuh

(Jonah leaps from the boat, falling into the water. The boat stops rocking. Remove transparency 6A.)

(Jonah, holding his nose, flounders in front of the projector's light.) **God did not want Jonah to die. He wanted him to go to Nineveh, so God decided to give Jonah another chance. God sent a big fish to swallow Jonah.** *(Project transparency 6B over Jonah while he curls up on the floor.)*

Jonah lived inside the fish's stomach for three days and three nights. What do you think it was like inside that big fish? If you think it was dark, you are right! If you think it was slippery and slimy, you are right again! If you think it smelled terrible, you are right about that, too!

What was Jonah going to do? Was he still going to try to hide from God? No! Jonah knew he could not run away or hide from God. The best thing for Jonah to do was to pray, and that is just what he did. *(Jonah kneels and folds his hands in prayer.)*

Jonah prayed, "Dear God, I was scared. As I was falling down into the water, I felt the stormy waves all around me. I was sure I was going to die, so I called out to You to save me. Thank You, God, for hearing my prayer. I will always praise You. I will always do what I promise. You are the only God who saves people. Amen."

God heard Jonah pray, and He forgave him for disobeying. God still wanted Jonah to go to Nineveh, so He spoke to the fish and told it to spit Jonah out. *(Remove transparency 6B.)* **Suddenly Jonah was lying on a beach.** *(Jonah lies flat on the floor.)* **God saved his life.**

God again told Jonah to go to Nineveh. What do you think Jonah did this time? Yes! He listened and obeyed God. *(Jonah stands up and walks away. Turn off the projector.)*

Story Review: Where Is Jonah?

You will need the words for "Where Is Jonah?" from p. 128.

Let's learn another verse to the song that will help us remember the story of Jonah.

Teach the second verse of "Where Is Jonah?" and use the following motions:

Where is Jonah? (Use the same motion suggested for this phrase on p. 130.)

In a fish! (Move right hand in wavy motion from right to left in front of your body, like a fish in water, the first time you sing the phrase and move your left hand in a wavy motion from left to right the second time.)

What is Jonah doing? (Do the *W* motion again for these two phrases.)

Praying to God. (Fold hands the first time, and go down on your knees when you repeat the phrase.)

Sing the second verse several times; then add the first verse. In between verses, ask the following questions:

Where did God tell Jonah to go? What was Jonah to tell the people of Nineveh? How did Jonah disobey God? Why was Jonah thrown into the sea? What happened to Jonah in the sea? How long did Jonah live in the big fish? What did he do inside the fish? What did God again tell Jonah to do? What did Jonah do?

Bible Memory: Jonah Toss

You will need a Bible, a small laundry basket, and three beanbags. (If no beanbag is available, fill a sock with dry rice or beans. Tie the opening in a knot.)

Our Bible words remind us that we need to obey God. Let's play a game to learn Jeremiah 26:13.

Say Jeremiah 26:13 several times with the children. Then show the beanbag and tell the children the beanbag is "Jonah." Show the basket. The basket is the big fish's "mouth." Line the children up about six to eight feet from the basket. Ask the first child to say the first sentence of the verse. When the child can correctly say it, give him a Jonah to toss into the fish's mouth. Continue until everyone in the line has said the first sentence. Repeat the same procedure with the second sentence and the reference. Make sure each child says the entire verse and reference before you end the game.

What do our Bible words remind us about good things? About obeying?

▼ 3. What Does This Mean to Me? ▲

Choose to Listen

You will need the "Choosing to Listen Pictures" from p. 147. Color and cut out the pictures, and place them in a sack or hat.

We can choose to be good listeners all day long. Let's look at some pictures to remind us of times that we can be good listeners.

Give each child a turn to choose a picture from the sack or hat. Ask questions about listening for each picture. For example, if the child chooses the picture of the bed, you might ask: When do you use your bed? What does your mother say when it is time for bed? What can you do or say that shows you are a good listener at bedtime? For the pictures of people, you might ask: Whom does this remind you of at your home? When do you need to listen to this person? What can you do or say that shows you are a good listener?

Thank you for choosing to be good listeners.

▼ 4. What Can I Do to Please God? ▲

Hold Your Nose!

You will need the words to "Where Is Jonah?" from p. 128.

What do you think it was like inside the fish? Do you think it was slippery? Do you think it smelled? What do you do when you smell something you do not like? Yes, you hold your nose. Let's pretend our classroom is the inside of Jonah's fish. Let's clean up the inside of this fish! Hold your nose with one hand and help clean up with the other.

When the room is straightened, gather the children around you in a circle as you sing the first two verses of "Where Is Jonah?" with motions.

Then sit down in a circle and pray. Say a prayer like this: **Dear God, I want to listen to Your Word and obey it.** Give each child a turn to pray.

Hear the Word of God and Do It

You will need copies of the fish from p. 144. Make enough copies to form a circle on the floor of your classroom. Color one fish and leave the rest white.

All of our Bible words remind us what God wants us to do. Let's learn a song about doing what God wants.

Have the children stand in a circle just outside the circle of fish. As they sing the song "Do What God Says," the children will walk on or around the circle of fish. After they sing the last line, stop and ask the child on the colored fish to tell something the Bible says to do. Help children remember Bible words and other things God wants: obey parents, sing praise to God, trust God, do good, share, love each other, give, pray, help. Continue until everyone has had a turn to stand on the colored fish.

Sit and pray together. Begin with a prayer like this: **God, thank You for Your Word. I want to listen to it and obey it.** Encourage each child to pray.

Bonus Activity

Jonah in a Bottle

You will need to provide for each child an empty, clear two-liter bottle with lid and two sponge figures as described on p. 151. Also provide water, funnels, cups, blue food coloring, green yarn cut into 4" pieces and glue.

Show the children how to fill the bottles with the water using the funnels and cups. Fill to within 3" of the top. Let each child put several drops of blue coloring in his bottle of water. Put the lid on and shake until all of the water is blue. Remove the lid and help each child stuff a sponge fish and a sponge man into the bottle. Also add several pieces of green yarn for seaweed. Seal the bottle's lid with glue. The children will enjoy rolling the bottle and shaking it.

Do What God Says
(Tune: "Ten Little Indians.")

Hear the Word of God and do it.
Hear the Word of God and do it.
Hear the Word of God and do it.
Do just what God says.

Nineveh Listens and Obeys

Jonah 3

Know: A Bible person who obeyed God.

Feel: Eager to please God and happy when they listen and obey.

Do: Choose to listen to and obey God.

Children will accomplish the goals when they

- Demonstrate how well they can listen.
- Tell what the people of Nineveh did when Jonah preached.
- Recite Jeremiah 26:13 and tell what it means.
- Tell the difference between obeying and disobeying.
- Ask God to help them obey.

▼ 1. What Is This Story About? ▲

What Do You Hear?

You will need several objects that make a noise, such as pan lids, sandpaper, bells, blocks, whistle, toy drum, tambourine, and electronic toys. Place these on a table and cover the items with a sheet so the children cannot see them.

Let's see how well you can listen. I am going to make a noise. You listen carefully. When you think you know what is making the sound, raise your hand.

Have the children sit with their backs to you. Ask them to put their hands over their eyes. (Be sensitive to children who are hearing impaired.)

When the children have guessed all of the sounds, say, **You are good listeners!** Let the children come to the table and make noise with the objects.

Do What I Do

Use your listening ears to play this game. I am going to clap my hands. Listen and count how many times I clap. Then you clap the same number of times. Compliment the children for obeying. Continue varying the number of claps. When the children are successful at clapping, change to jumping, patting your head, slapping your knees, or tapping your feet.

You are good listeners. Listening helped you obey the number of times I clapped, jumped, slapped, or tapped. Let's thank God for giving us ears that hear.

▼ 2. What Does the Bible Say? ▲

Bible Story: Jonah Preaches and Nineveh Listens

You will need transparencies 6A and 6B from p. 144 and 6C from p. 145, an overhead projector, a crown made from p. 102, and someone (child or adult) dressed as Jonah. (See p. 128 for directions on how to use these visuals.)

Jonah did not like the people of Nineveh. When God told Jonah to tell the Ninevites to stop doing wrong, Jonah ran away. He tried to hide from God on a boat. (Project transparency 6A.) **God caused a terrible storm. The boat almost broke into pieces. When the sailors threw Jonah into the water, the sea became calm.** (Remove transparency 6A.)

(Project transparency 6B.) **God sent a big fish to swallow Jonah. While Jonah was inside the fish, he prayed. He promised to obey God. After three days, the fish spit Jonah onto a beach.** (Remove transparency 6B.)

God again told Jonah to go to Nineveh. (Project transparency 6C.) **This time Jonah obeyed and went to Nineveh.** (Jonah stands in front of Nineveh.)

Nineveh was a very large city. Many people lived there. It was so big it took three days to walk from one side to the other. As Jonah walked through the city, he told the people God's message. (Jonah walks back and forth extending his arm up and pointing toward Heaven.)

How to Say It
Nineveh: NIN-uh-vuh

Jonah said, "In forty days, God is going to tear down your city because you have done so many evil things."

No one had ever told the people of Nineveh they were doing horrible things. They did not know what was good. When they heard Jonah's message from God, they were very sorry. *(Invite all the children to come up and play the people of Nineveh. They can stand in a group to the left of Jonah.)* **The people changed. Everyone believed in God. To show how sad they were, they wore clothes made out of very rough cloth. They also stopped eating for a while. All the people did this.**

(Choose one child from the group to play the king. Put a crown on his head and have him stand on the right side of Jonah.) **When the king of Nineveh heard Jonah's message, he took off his beautiful robe and put on rough clothing, too! He said, "Everyone should pray. Stop doing evil things. Ask God to forgive us. Maybe He will change His mind and not tear down our city."** *(Instruct all the children, including the king, to kneel and fold their hands as if they are praying. Jonah keeps standing.)*

God saw how sorry the people were. He saw everyone doing good. This made Him happy, so He decided not to tear down the city. *(Tell everyone except Jonah to cheer.)*

Because Jonah obeyed God, a huge city full of people heard God's message and decided to obey God, too. This pleased God very much! *(Turn off the projector.)*

Story Review: Where Is Jonah?

You will need the words for "Where Is Jonah?" from p. 128.

Let's learn another verse to the song that will help us remember the story of Jonah.

Teach the third verse of "Where Is Jonah?" and use the following motions:

Where is Jonah? (Use the same motion suggested for this phrase in verse one, p. 130.)

Nineveh! (Turn right and march in place three steps the first time you sing the phrase and turn left and march in place three steps the second time. This represents Jonah walking around Nineveh.)

What is Jonah doing? (Do the *W* motion again for these two phrases.)

Preaching for God. (Hold hands like a book/Bible for "preaching," then point up for "God.")

Sing the third verse several times; then add the first two verses. In between verses, ask the following questions:

What happened when Jonah was thrown into the sea?
What did Jonah do inside the fish?
Why was he praying?
Why did God send Jonah to Nineveh?
What did the people of Nineveh do when they heard Jonah?
How did the people show they were sorry?
What did God decide to do?

Bible Memory: Stop and Go!

You will need a copy of the stop sign and the traffic light from p. 151, scissors, craft sticks, and red and green markers. Cut out the stop sign and color it red. Cut out the traffic light and color only the green light. Glue each one onto a craft stick. (These can be made for or by the children if time allows.)

Our Bible words remind us what God wants us to do. Who can say the Bible words for the rest of the class?

Say Jeremiah 26:13 in unison. Use the stop and go signs to indicate when the children are to recite and when they are not to talk. Repeat the verse several times.

Talk about what the words mean.

Bible Words

"Now change your lives and start doing good and obey the LORD your God" (Jeremiah 26:13).

What does it mean to obey God? (Do what He says to do.)

What are some good things God wants us to do? (Share, help, love, pray, praise, thank, and so on.)

▼ 3. What Does This Mean to Me? ▲

Be Wise and Obey

You will need a copy of the "Danger Cube" from p. 148. Follow the directions for making the cube. For extra durability, cover the page with clear adhesive vinyl paper before you fold and tape the cube.

At my house, one of our rules is "No running in the house." What is a rule at your house? (Give children time to respond.) **Let's look at some pictures that remind us of important rules.**

Seat the children in a circle. Ask a volunteer to toss the cube, tell about the picture that lands facing up on the cube, and name a rule that the picture reminds her to obey. For each picture, ask questions to help the children tell the difference between obeying and disobeying.

What rule does this picture remind you of?

What can happen if you disobey the rule? How would that make you feel?

What happens if you obey the rule? How does obeying make you feel?

These rules are made to protect you, so it's important to obey them. God gives us rules in His Word that also help and protect us, and God wants us to obey them.

Red Light, Green Light

You will need the stop and go signs prepared for the Bible Memory activity.

Let's play a game to see how much you know about obeying and disobeying.

Hold the signs in your hands behind your back. Ask a child to choose which hand he wants you to show. If the hand he chooses is holding the stop sign, ask the child to describe someone who is disobeying (not picking up toys, crying when Mom says it is time to go to bed, talking while Dad is on the phone, arguing, fighting). If the hand he chooses is holding the green light, ask the child to describe someone who is obeying (sharing a toy, wearing a seat belt, helping in the garden, praying to God).

After each child has had a turn, help the children tell the difference between obeying and disobeying.

What can happen if you disobey your parents? How does that make you feel?

What happens when you obey parents? How does that make you feel?

Why is it important to obey your parents? Obey God?

▼ 4. What Can I Do to Please God? ▲

Choose to Obey

You will need the six "Choosing to Disobey Pictures" from p. 147 used in Lesson 22 and the eight "Choosing to Listen Pictures" from p. 147 used in Lesson 23. Make enough copies of the pictures for each child to have one picture.

After Jonah disobeyed God, how did he tell God he was sorry? (Prayed in the fish.) **Then what did he do?** (Obeyed God.) **After the people of Nineveh heard Jonah's message, how did they tell God they were sorry?** (Prayed for forgiveness.) **Then what did they do?** (Stopped disobeying, started doing good things.)

Let's look at some pictures to help us remember to stop disobeying, pray to God, and start doing good things.

Divide the children into groups of no more than six. Each group will need an adult leader. Have the leaders take groups to different areas of the room. The leader of the group will give each child a picture and ask the children to take turns describing their pictures. For each picture, use questions to help the children talk about choosing to obey.

Tell what is in your picture.

What can happen when you disobey (like the picture shows, or the person in the picture, or using the object in the picture)?

What can we do after we disobey? (Pray like Jonah and the people of Nineveh, start doing good things.)

Our Bible words remind us what God wants us to do. Ask the children to say the Bible words with you. **Let's pray now to ask God to help us obey and do good things.**

Model a prayer for the children: **Dear God, I want to obey You. Please help me do good things.** Then give each child an opportunity to pray.

Ears a Job for You!

You will need the words to "Where Is Jonah?" from p. 128.

Use your ears to find out what job you will do to help clean up our room. Listen carefully and obey what you hear. If you are wearing a red shirt, pick up paper on the floor and put it in the wastebasket. If you are wearing shoes with shoe strings, push the chairs back under the tables. Continue with these types of directions until the room is clean.

Gather the children and compliment them on using their ears to obey. Sing the first two verses of "Where Is Jonah?" with motions. When the children are on their knees because of the song motions, ask them to stay on their knees for prayer. Model a prayer sentence like this: **Dear God, I want to obey You. Please help me do good things.** Give each child the opportunity to pray. Close by reciting the Bible words together.

▼ Bonus Activities ▲

Snack Attack! Edible Play Dough

You will need an eighteen-ounce jar of creamy peanut butter, six tablespoons of honey, a box of non-fat powdered milk, flour, raisins, and waxed paper. Mix the peanut butter and honey. Add dry milk until the mixture is play-dough consistency. A little flour may be added to make the dough easier to handle.

Wash tables and ask all the children to wash their hands. Praise them for obeying. Give each child a length of waxed paper to work on and a ball of dough. Tell the children to make something from the story of Jonah. Let them decorate with raisins. Have each child tell what he made. Say a prayer for the snack and then let the children eat their creations. Don't use this activity if you have children with peanut allergies in your class.

God Teaches Jonah About Love

Jonah 4

Know: A Bible person who obeyed God.

Feel: Eager to please God and happy when they listen and obey.

Do: Choose to listen to and obey God.

Children will accomplish the goals when they

• Tell how obeying makes them happy.

• Tell how Jonah felt when the people of Nineveh listened and obeyed.

• Recite Jeremiah 26:13 and tell good things they can do.

• Discover what the Bible says about love.

• Choose to love others.

▼ 1. What Is This Story About? ▲

Obeying Collage

You will need a piece of poster board, a colored marker, magazines dedicated to parenting and children, and glue. Print "Obeying Makes Me Happy" at the top of the poster board.

We're going to make a poster to help us remember to obey.

First, instruct the children to look through the magazines to find pictures of smiling children, mothers, and fathers. Have them tear around the faces. Save them for later.

Look for a picture of a toy. When you find one, tear it out. What are some rules your parents give you about your toys? How do you feel when you obey? How do you think your parents feel? Let each child glue a toy on the poster. Also, have them glue a picture of a smiling child and a smiling parent on the poster.

Next, ask the children to look for beds, bedding, or pillows. Ask what their parents tell them to do at bedtime. Follow the same procedure used for the toys. Continue looking for other items that relate to children and obedience, such as soap, food, pets, clothing, books, and cars. Add a smiling face whenever the children talk about obedience.

Obeying does make us happy. Our parents are also happy when we obey. Remember when Jonah was on the boat? Was he obeying or disobeying? That's right! He was disobeying. Do you think he was happy? No, I am sure he wasn't. When do you think Jonah might have been happy? Yes, when God gave Jonah a second chance to obey.

▼ 2. What Does the Bible Say? ▲

Bible Story: Jonah Learns About Love

How to Say It

Nineveh: NIN-uh-vuh

You will need transparencies 6C and 6D and the following silhouettes from p. 106: 6-a shelter, 6-b vine, 6-c leaves. You will also need someone (child or adult) dressed as Jonah. (See p. 128 for directions on how to use these visuals.)

(Project transparency 6C.) **God told Jonah to go to Nineveh and tell the people to stop doing evil things or their city would be torn down. At first, Jonah did not obey God. He tried to run away. Did God know where Jonah was? Yes, and after God gave Jonah time to think, Jonah told God that he was sorry for disobeying. God forgave him and again said, "Go to Nineveh."**

(Jonah enters the scene, walking back and forth as though he is preaching.) **This time Jonah obeyed! He walked around the city for one whole day saying, "In forty days God will tear down your city because you have done many evil things."**

(Add several children to the scene. Have them kneel and pray.) **Everyone heard God's message and believed in Him. They promised to do what was right. This made God very happy, but not Jonah. He was angry with God.** *(Jonah looks angry.)*

Do you know why Jonah was angry? God wanted the people of Nineveh to

do good. That is why God sent Jonah with the special message. God loves all people, but Jonah did not like these people. He did not want God to forgive them. *(Remove transparency 6C and the children. Add transparency 6D.)*

Jonah still thought God would destroy Nineveh, so he sat on a hill where he could see the whole city. *(Jonah sits down on the hill.)* It was sunny and hot, so Jonah made a shelter for some shade. *(Place silhouette 6-a so it appears to be over Jonah's head.)* While Jonah watched the city, God made a plant with big leaves grow around and over the shelter. *(Add silhouettes 6-b and 6-c to silhouette 6-a.)* This made more shade for Jonah. He liked the plant and its shade.

The next day, Jonah was still sitting in the shade of the plant. God knew Jonah needed to learn an important lesson about obeying. He sent a hungry worm to eat all the leaves on the plant. Suddenly, the plant died. *(Remove silhouettes 6-c.)* Jonah was very sad because his shade was gone. It was so hot he felt sick. *(Jonah looks sad and hot.)*

Jonah began complaining, "Why did you let the worm eat the plant?"

The Lord replied, "You were sad the plant died, but you did not make it grow. I did. I also made the people of Nineveh, and they are more important than a plant. I love them, and I want them to live."

God wanted Jonah to know how much He loves everyone. *(Turn off the projector.)*

Story Review: Where Is Jonah?

You will need the words for "Where Is Jonah?" from p. 128.

Let's learn another verse to the song that will help us remember the story of Jonah.

Teach the fourth verse of "Where Is Jonah?" and use the following motions:

Where is Jonah? (Use the same motion suggested for this phrase in verse one, p. 130.)

On a hill! (Make a tent by putting both hands together over your head. This can represent the hill as well as the shelter Jonah was sitting under.)

What is Jonah doing? (Do the *W* motion again for these two phrases.)

Learning to love. (Put both hands over your heart.)

Sing the fourth verse several times; then sing all the verses with motions. In between verses, ask the following questions:

What happened when Jonah disobeyed God and tried to run away?

What happened when Jonah prayed inside the fish?

What happened when Jonah preached to the people of Nineveh?

How did God help Jonah learn a lesson about loving people?

Bible Memory: Who's Saying That?

You will need a tape recorder and a blank tape.

Our Bible words remind us to obey God. We need to have listening ears to know what God wants us to do. Who can say our Bible words?

Individually record each of the children saying the verse. Give help as needed. Finally, record each child telling good things he can do. (It might be helpful to keep a record of the order in which the children speak, in case you can't recognize their voices.) Then rewind the tape.

Let's play the tape. Raise your hand when your listening ears have figured out whose voice you hear talking. Play the first recording. Compliment the children for being good listeners and thinking of good things they can do.

> **Bible Words**
> "Now change your lives and start doing good and obey the LORD your God" (Jeremiah 26:13).

▼ 3. What Does This Mean to Me? ▲

My Songbook of Jonah

You will need the booklet pages from pp. 149 and 150, the Jonah sponge pattern from p. 151, construction paper, a stapler, crayons or markers, glue, and craft sticks.

Before class, photocopy pp. 149 and 150, back-to-back. Fold on the broken line to make a booklet of the story of Jonah. Use the construction paper to make front and back covers for the booklets. On the front covers print, "My Songbook of Jonah." Staple the pages inside the covers.

Let the children color the pages in their books. Provide a photocopy of Jonah for each child. Help each child glue Jonah onto one end of a craft stick.

Sing "Where Is Jonah?" as the children turn to each verse in their songbooks and hold the stick figures of Jonah up to the pictures.

When our song ends, what is Jonah learning?
What can you tell us about love?
What are some ways we can show love to others?

Learning to Love

You will need the words of "Where Is Jonah?" from p. 128.

Have the children form a circle. Choose one child to go to the center and curl up in a ball, hiding his head.

Use the same tune as "Where Is Jonah?" and have the children sing, "Where is (child's name)? Where is (child's name)?" As the child in the center uncurls and stands up, he sings, "Here I am. Here I am." Then the children in the circle sing, "What is (child's name) doing? What is (child's name) doing?" The child answers by singing, "Learning to love. Learning to love." Then ask this child to tell one way he is learning to love. Use the following question to help the children talk about loving:

How can you be loving when your baby brother messes up your toys?
How can you be loving when your sister wants to watch a different TV show than the one you want to watch?

Let each child have a turn being in the center. If a child is too shy to do it alone, have an adult do the motions and sing with him.

▼ 4. What Can I Do to Please God? ▲

I'm Sorry

You will need to provide each child with a large red construction paper heart. Use a dark marker to print, "God Loves You and I Love You," around the edges of the hearts. (Do this once on a large white heart, then make photocopies on red paper.) You will also need a Bible, assorted colored paper scraps, and glue.

Our Bible words remind us that God wants us to do good things. But sometimes we forget to do good and do something unkind.

Have you been unkind to someone in your family or to a friend? Did you say words that hurt their feelings? Did you use your hands or feet in an unkind way? Would you like to tell that person that you are sorry?

Here is a paper heart you can decorate and give to a person to whom you have been unkind. Give each child a heart and read the words aloud. Show the children how to tear the scraps of paper into smaller pieces and glue them all over the heart. Be sure they understand the words are not to be covered up.

On the back of each finished heart, print "To:" and "From:" and fill in the name of the receiver and the giver.

Like Jonah, we are still learning to love others. Let's ask God to help us love others. Pray, thanking God for the children who are choosing to love, and asking God for help to keep doing good things.

I Love You

Repeat one of the children's favorite cleanup activities for this unit. Then gather the children in a circle.

The story of Jonah has taught us how to be good listeners. Today we learned about God's love for all people. When we were learning to be good listeners, we practiced by using our ears to hear directions and sounds. Did you know someone who cannot hear with their ears?

Many deaf people use sign language to communicate with others. Do you think God wants deaf people to hear about His love? Yes! You can tell a deaf person you love him or her by using your fingers and hand. Here's how. Hold your hand up as though you were saying, "Stop." Now fold down your middle finger and ring finger so they touch your palm. Now you are saying, "I love you." It will take a little practice to learn to keep your two fingers down, but you can do it. It pleases God when we tell others we love them.

Ask for volunteers to demonstrate the "I love you" sign and tell how they will choose to love someone this week. Give each child a turn to show and tell; then close with prayer. Thank God for His Word that helps us know how to love people.

▼ Bonus Activity ▲

Snack Attack! Gingerbread Jonahs

You will need a gingerbread man for each child. Provide candy hearts, any color of frosting, and jumbo craft sticks.

Let the children spread frosting over the gingerbread men. Show them where to add the candy heart.

Have a prayer and then eat the gingerbread Jonahs. Use the following questions to review the story of Jonah.

Why was Jonah sitting on a hill?
Why was he angry with God?
What did God grow to provide shade for Jonah?
Did Jonah like the plant?
What ate the plant?
Why was Jonah sad?
What did God teach Jonah about His love?

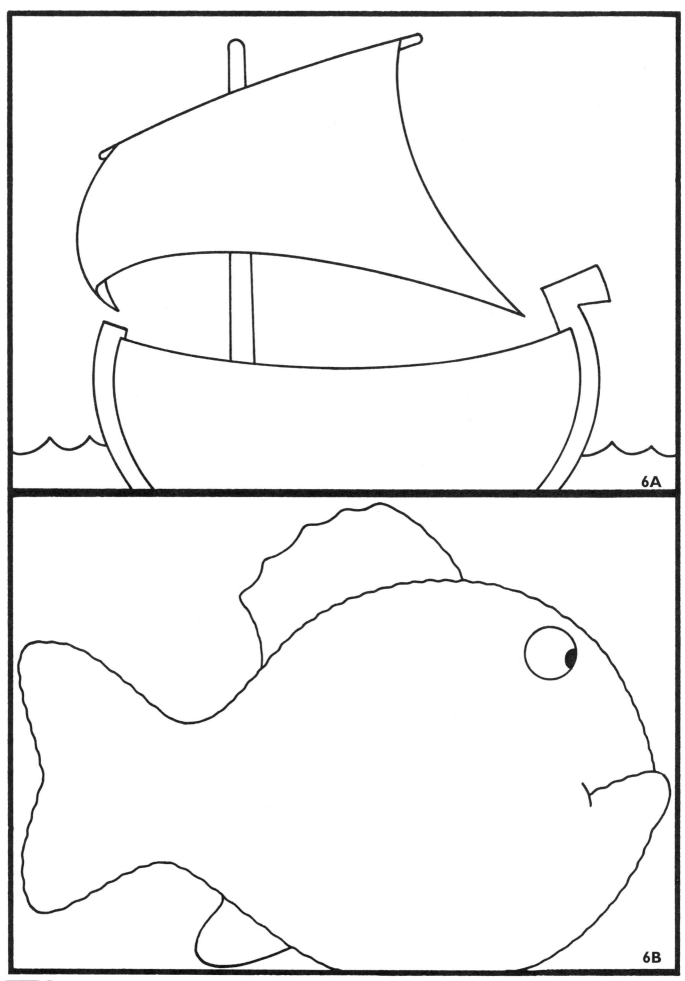

6A

6B

6C

6D

Directions:

You will need an ear book and eight stickers (five on this page and three on p. 151) for each child, card stock, 8 1/2" x 11" paper, scissors, stapler, white glue, vinegar, peppermint extract (optional), and a small paint brush.

Copy this page onto card stock. Cut around the ear book and fold on the broken line. To make the inside pages, fold two half sheets of paper in half. Place these inside the folded ears with all folded edges together. Using the ears as a pattern, cut around the edges of the blank paper so the inside pages are also ear-shaped. Open and staple on the fold.

To make stickers, mix two parts white glue and one part vinegar. Add a few drops of peppermint extract if desired. Lightly "paint" the mixture onto the backs of the uncut stickers. Let dry. Cut out the stickers.

fold

My Ear Book

Choosing to Listen Pictures

Choosing to Disobey Pictures

Danger Cube

Directions: Color and cut out the cube.

Fold on the broken lines to make a cube.

Stuff with tissue to make the cube more durable.

Tuck in tabs and tape or glue.

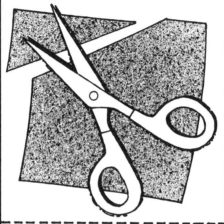

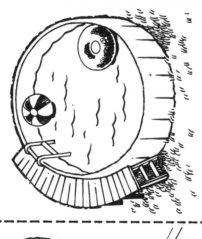

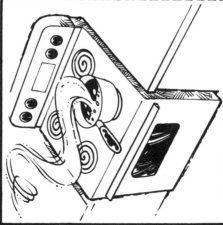

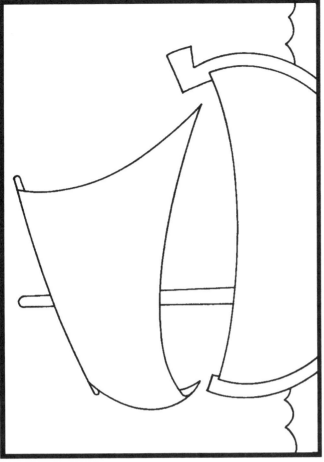

Where Is Jonah?

Sing to the tune of "Where Is Thumbkin?"

Where is Jonah? Where is Jonah?
In a boat! In a boat!
What is Jonah doing?
What is Jonah doing?
Running from God.
Running from God.

1

Where is Jonah? Where is Jonah?
On a hill! On a hill!
What is Jonah doing?
What is Jonah doing?

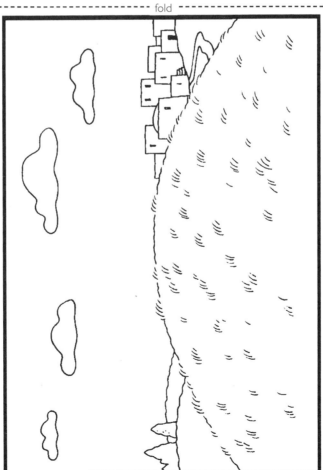

Learning to love.
Learning to love.

4

Where is Jonah? Where is Jonah?
In a fish! In a fish!
What is Jonah doing?
What is Jonah doing?
Praying to God.
Praying to God.

2

--- fold ---

Where is Jonah? Where is Jonah?
Nineveh! Nineveh!
What is Jonah doing?
What is Jonah doing?
Preaching for God.
Preaching for God.

3

Sponge Figures

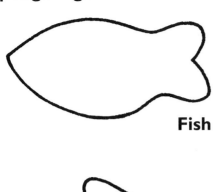

Fish

Jonah

Ear Book Stickers

Directions: You will need sponges in two colors. Cut one color into a fish, using the pattern here. Cut the other color into Jonah. Each child will need one sponge fish and one sponge Jonah.

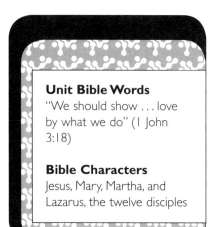

UNIT 7

Learning to Love

Lessons 26-29

Unit Bible Words
"We should show . . . love by what we do" (1 John 3:18)

Bible Characters
Jesus, Mary, Martha, and Lazarus, the twelve disciples

26 Jesus Shows Love to Children

Matthew 19:13-15; Mark 10:13-16; Luke 18:15-17—Jesus' disciples do not want Jesus to be bothered by children. They try sending the children away, but Jesus, who loves all people regardless of age or status, scolds His followers and blesses the children.

27 Jesus Shows Love to a Family

John 11:1-44—Mary, Martha, and Lazarus were among Jesus' special friends. When Lazarus becomes ill, Mary and Martha know Jesus has the power to heal. When Jesus arrives, Lazarus has been buried for four days. Jesus reveals His love for this family when, out of compassion and for God's glory, He raises Lazarus from the dead.

28 Mary Shows Love to Jesus

John 12:1-8—Mary, Martha, and Lazarus invite Jesus to a special dinner. Lazarus serves as the host. Martha serves the food. Mary performs an act of love. She pours very expensive perfume on Jesus' feet. The scent attracts the attention of everyone. She is unashamed of her deep love for Jesus.

29 Jesus Shows Love to His Friends

John 13:1-17—Jesus has very little time left to be with His disciples. This is His last supper with them. Now Jesus must prepare them for His death. He chooses to teach them one more lesson on how to show love by serving others. Using a bowl of water and a towel, He washes each man's feet. Then He tells them to follow His example of love.

By the end of this unit, the children and leaders will

Know: Bible people who learned about love from Jesus.
Feel: Love for Jesus and others.
Do: Choose to show love for Jesus and others.

Why Teach This Unit to Four- to Six-Year-Olds?

The most essential need of young children is love. It has been proven that babies must have love to thrive and grow. Even if well-nourished, a lack of love will cause developmental delays. There is power in love. Its potential cannot be measured.

Four-, five-, and six-year-olds are at an age where they are beginning to be less self-centered. They are developing some independence. They still depend on the love of those around them to thrive, but they are now able to give love to others. Now, while they are still forming their own thoughts and attitudes, is the time to open their hearts to loving and appreciating others.

Use this unit to create an environment in which your students can learn about love from the Master Teacher, Jesus. In each lesson, the children will see Jesus responding with love to the needs of others. His example of showing love in an unselfish way makes Him the perfect role model for children.

Meet Jesus

Jesus is God's gift of love to the world. Jesus came humbly as a baby, totally dependent on human care. While He was growing up, His loving attributes drew approval from His parents and those who knew Him. As an adult, His love made a difference in the lives of people He touched. He is the best example of love.

Meet Mary, Martha, and Lazarus

This family of one brother and two sisters lived in Bethany. Their relationship with Jesus was unique. He frequently visited their home for rest, relaxation, and to enjoy their friendship. Jesus demonstrated His compassion and sympathy for this family when He cried at Lazarus' tomb. Mary's unselfish act of anointing Jesus' feet with very expensive perfume showed her depth of love for Jesus. Jesus accepted this very loving act.

Meet the Twelve Disciples

Jesus chose twelve men from a variety of backgrounds to disciple. For three years they followed Him, listening to His teachings and observing His behavior. They had never met a man more loving and self-sacrificing. Jesus made a profound difference in their lives.

Unit Visuals: A Living Drama

You will need to make a transparency of p. 175 for this unit. Cut the transparency into three sections—7A, 7B, and 7C. Color the figures of Jesus with permanent transparency markers. (Hint: Handle the transparency as little as possible. Colored pens will not mark easily over fingerprints.)

If a plain wall is not available for projection, tack a large white sheet to the wall. Be sure that one edge of the sheet meets the floor.

These three figures of Jesus will be used for Bible story drama with live characters pantomiming and interacting with Jesus as if He were a live person. Ask parents, teenagers, older children, or children from your class to play the Bible characters. Bible-time costumes can be made easily with bathrobes and towels draped over heads. Other props will be suggested when needed.

An alternate idea is to hang a sheet several feet away from a wall, shine a bright light behind the actors and let live actors, including a live Jesus, pantomime their parts behind the sheet. The children will see moving shadows on the sheet and yet will not recognize any of the actors.

Unit Song

The More We Love
(Tune: "Did You Ever See a Lassie?")

Verse 1
"Little children, come to me, to me, to me."
"Little children, come to me. I love you so much."
His friends said, "Go away!" But Jesus said, "Please stay!"
"Little children, come to me. I love you so much."

Verse 2
The more I love my family, my family, my family,
The more I love my family the happier I'll be.
My mom will be happy. And so will my daddy.
The more I love my family the happier I'll be.

Verse 3
The more we all love Jesus, love Jesus, love Jesus,
The more we all love Jesus the happier we'll be.
We give our love to Him 'cause He is our best friend.
The more we all love Jesus the happier we'll be.

Verse 4
The more we love each other, each other, each other,
The more we love each other the happier we'll be.
Be kind and be helpful. Be loving and caring.
The more we love each other the happier we'll be.

Jesus Shows Love to Children

Matthew 19:13-15; Mark 10:13-16; Luke 18:15-17

Know: Bible people who learned about love from Jesus.

Feel: Love for Jesus and others.

Do: Choose to show love for Jesus and others.

Children will accomplish the goals when they
- Explore the differences between children and adults.
- Tell how Jesus showed love to children.
- Begin to memorize 1 John 3:18.
- Name times Jesus loves them.
- Choose to show love to other children.

▼ 1. What Is This Story About? ▲

Did You Ever See?

Let's learn a song about people Jesus loves.

Teach the children the following words to the tune of "Did You Ever See a Lassie?"

Did you ever see a mommy, a mommy, a mommy?
Did you ever see a mommy go this way and that?
Go this way and that way, and this way and that way,
Did you ever see a mommy go this way and that?

Have the children stand in a circle. While the children are singing "this way and that way," have them act out something a mother does. At the end of the verse, discuss all the different things you saw the children do.

Repeat this song replacing "mommy" with "daddy," "grandpa," "grandma," "teacher," and other adults familiar to your students. Each time, act out what that person does.

Finally, repeat the song replacing "mommy" with "a child." Let them act out things they like to do.

We have acted out different things adults and children do. Adults and children do not do the same things. They do things that are right for their ages. Jesus loves adults, and He loves children. He loves everyone!

▼ 2. What Does the Bible Say? ▲

Bible Story: Don't Stop the Children!

You will need the words for verse one of "The More We Love" from p. 153, transparency 7A from p. 175, children and adults dressed in Bible costumes (portraying disciples, Bible-time parents, and children), and an overhead projector. (See p. 153 for directions on how to use the visual.) Or, use a live actor for Jesus also.

(Project transparency 7A.) **Wherever Jesus went, there were crowds of people. People would call to Him from the roadside. They would gather around Him as He walked through the streets of their towns. If He stopped at someone's house, people would squeeze into the rooms to see Him and hear Him teach. Many came to see Jesus because they were sick and wanted to be healed.**

Sometimes, to rest and pray, Jesus would go out on a lake in a boat. *(Disciples enter.)* **His followers always tried to help Him. They knew He needed time to rest and be alone with His Father, God.**

(Enter parents and children walking toward the figure of Jesus.) **One day some mothers and fathers brought their little children to see Jesus. Do you think they were excited about seeing Jesus? Yes, they probably were. Before the children and their parents could see Jesus, His followers stopped them.** *(Disciples walk up to parents and children and stop them. Parents and disciples pantomime the action described as the story is told.)*

"What do you people want?" asked Jesus' followers.

"We want Jesus to touch our children and pray for them," replied the parents.

"Jesus does not have time for little children," the followers said. "He is much too busy healing and teaching the grown-ups."

The parents and children sadly turned to walk away. Jesus saw them looking so sad. He heard what His followers said to them and knew they were wrong. Of course He had time for children!

Jesus called to His followers, "Stop! Do not send the children away. Let the little ones come to me!" *(Everyone turns toward Jesus.)*

Then He said something very important. "I am telling you the truth. You must have the faith of a little child to enter the kingdom of heaven."

Jesus wanted His followers to know children are very special. *(Parents and children stand close to the figure of Jesus and smile.)* He gathered the children around Him. He may have held the babies and hugged the older children. The parents were happy when Jesus prayed and blessed their children. *(Turn off projector.)*

Would you like to have been one of those little children? Close your eyes and imagine you are there with Jesus. What would you like to say to Him? Let the children respond. Then teach the first verse of "The More We Love."

Story Review: Bring the Children to Jesus

You will need pictures of children cut from magazines, card stock, glue, a picture of Jesus, masking tape, and a blindfold.

This game is played like the game "Pin the Tail on the Donkey."

Mount the magazine pictures on card stock and put an inside-out circle of masking tape on the back of each one. Hang the picture of Jesus on a blank wall or door. Blindfold the children one at a time and let them tape the pictures of the children as close to Jesus as they can.

Before you blindfold each child, ask a question to review the story:

Wherever Jesus went, who gathered around Him?

Why did people like to be around Jesus?

What would happen when Jesus was in someone's home?

Why did sick people want to be near Jesus?

Where did Jesus go when He needed to rest?

Why did His followers try to give Jesus time to be alone?

Why did the mothers and fathers want to bring their children to Jesus?

What did the followers say to the parents of the children?

What did Jesus say to His followers when they told the children and their parents to go away?

What did Jesus do with the children who gathered around Him?

Bible Memory: Say It! Do It!

Our Bible words will help us remember to be like Jesus. Let's learn our new words.

Have the children stand in a circle. If there are more than ten children in your class, form more than one circle. Show the children the following motions to the Bible words.

"We should show love *(Hug yourself.)*

by what we do." *(Pat someone on the back.)*

1 John 3:18. *(Open your hands with palms up to form a Bible.)*

Practice this several times in unison. Then go around the circle having the first child say, "We should show love," and hug himself. The second child will say, "by what we do," and pat the third child on the back. The third child will say, "1 John 3:18," and open his hands like a Bible. Continue around the circle several times.

To whom did Jesus show love?

How did Jesus show love?

> **Bible Words**
> "We should show . . . love by what we do" (1 John 3:18).

▼ 3. What Does This Mean to Me? ▲

Jesus Has Time for Children

You will need for each child a paper plate, a paper fastener, and a copy of the clock face and two clock hands from p. 169. You will also need paper, crayons or markers, and glue. Before class, cut out a clock and a pair of hands for each child. Make a sample clock.

In our Bible story, the followers of Jesus learned an important lesson. They learned that Jesus always has time for children. We're going to make a clock to remember that Jesus loves us all the time.

Let the children color the clock faces and the clock hands. Show them how to glue the clock face on a paper plate. Help them attach the clock hands to the paper-plate clock with a paper fastener.

Show your sample clock. **Our clocks say, "Jesus has time for children." Read the pictures and words with me.** Point to each picture and word as you read the sentence. Repeat until all the children can say the sentence.

Place the hands on your clock at seven o'clock. **When your clock says it is time to get up, remember that Jesus loves you.** Ask the children to show times on their clocks when Jesus loves them. Talk about the different times Jesus loves them.

When you are eating breakfast, does Jesus love you? (Yes.)
When you fall and hurt your leg, does Jesus love you? (Yes.)
When you disobey your dad, does Jesus love you? (Yes.)
When you are sad and crying, does Jesus love you? (Yes.)
Is there anytime when Jesus doesn't love you? (No.)

▼ 4. What Can I Do to Please God? ▲

Learning to Love

You will need the words for the song "The More We Love" from p. 153, red construction paper, black marker, glue, tape, and pictures of children cut from magazines and catalogs.

Cut the construction paper to form large hearts. Make a heart for each child. On each heart print, "(Child's name) is learning to love." Use these hearts to decorate the classroom. Hang the pictures at a child's eye level. Each week the children will add pictures to their "Learning to Love Hearts."

In our Bible story today, we learned what Jesus did to show love to children. He wants us to show love to other children, too.

Let each child choose a picture of a child and glue it onto his paper heart, which is hung up in the classroom. Gather the children around one of the hearts and sing the first verse of "The More We Love."

What did Jesus do to show love to children?

What can you do to show love to other children? Give each child a turn to say what she can do to show love.

Boy-Girl Paper Dolls

You will need a copy of the "Boy-Girl Paper Dolls" from p. 170 for each child, the words for "The More We Love" from p. 153, crayons or markers, glue, yarn, and scraps of felt or fabric. Cut out the dolls before class time.

Our Bible words remind us to show love by what we do. We're going to decorate paper children to remind us to show love to others.

Provide crayons or markers, glue, yarn, and felt or fabric scraps for the children to use to decorate the dolls.

When the dolls are finished, help the children form a circle and hold their dolls so they join hands around the circle.

We have many different kinds of paper children in our circle: boys and girls, some wearing different kinds of clothes, and some with different hair and skin. If Jesus were sitting with us, what do you think He would do to show love to these children?

What can you do to show love to other children who you play with?

What can you do to show love to other children at the park? At school? At church?

What are some loving words to say to other children?

How can you show love to another child when he is sad? Lonely? Hurt?

If you want to show love to other children this week, hold your paper children up high. If you want to show love like Jesus did, put your paper children on the floor. Let's fold our hands and pray together. Pray with the children, asking God to help them show love to other children this week.

▼ Bonus Activity ▲

Snack Attack! Cookie Children

You will need waxed paper, a batch of refrigerated sugar cookie dough, raisins, access to an oven, cookie sheets, toothpicks, powdered chocolate, baking utensils.

Wash hands. Give each child a square of wax paper and some cookie dough. Show the children how to roll the dough into balls. They will need one ball for the head and one for the body. Place the ball for the head on the wax paper and flatten it with the palm of your hand. Then place the ball for the body below the head and flatten it. Use the rest of the dough to make arms and legs. Use the raisins for facial features. Let each child use a toothpick to carve his or her initials on the body of the cookie. The initials will be readable after baking if you sprinkle powdered chocolate in the cracks. Let the cookies bake while you do another activity.

Pray, thanking Jesus for His love. Then eat and enjoy!

Jesus Shows Love to a Family

John 11:1-44

Know: Bible people who learned about love from Jesus.

Feel: Love for Jesus and others.

Do: Choose to show love for Jesus and others.

Children will accomplish the goals when they
- Explore what families do.
- Tell how Jesus showed love to a family.
- Memorize 1 John 3:18.
- Name ways to show love to their families.
- Choose to show love to their families.

How to Say It
Lazarus: LAZ-uh-rus

▼ 1. What Is This Story About? ▲

Family Show and Tell

You will need clothing and objects that represent different family members (a purse, tie, cooking utensils, tools, baseball cap, skates, blocks, hair bow, doll, bottle, bib, reading glasses, cane).

God has given each of us a family. Each person in a family likes different things and has different jobs. Let's tell each other about our families. You can use some of the objects I have to tell about your family.

Take your turn first and use the objects to tell about people in your family. You might want to wear the object or pretend to do something with an object and let the children guess who you are pretending to be. Then give each child a turn to tell about the different people in his family.

Everyone's family is different. Some families have many children. Some have a grandpa and grandma. We can thank God for the people in our families.

▼ 2. What Does the Bible Say? ▲

Bible Story: Jesus Loves a Family

You will need two adult women to play Mary and Martha, an adult man to play Lazarus (in Bible costumes), transparency 7A, white toilet paper, and an overhead projector. (See p. 153 for directions on how to use the visual.) You will also need an assistant to wrap Lazarus in toilet paper between scenes.

Instruct the adults to pantomime the actions as you read them.

(Project transparency 7A.) **Jesus had many friends.** *(Enter Mary, Martha, and Lazarus.)* **Three of his friends, Mary, Martha, and Lazarus, were in the same family. These two sisters and one brother loved Jesus, and He loved them. Jesus visited them many times. Martha liked to fix good food for Jesus and His followers. Mary loved to hear Jesus teach about God.** *(Remove figure of Jesus, but leave the projector light on.)*

(Lazarus lies down on the floor. The two women pretend to take care of him.) **One day Lazarus became very sick. Mary and Martha sent someone to tell Jesus.** *(Turn the projector off while Mary, Martha, and Lazarus exit.)* **Several days later Jesus arrived, but Lazarus was already dead. He had been buried in a tomb for four days.**

(Project transparency 7A. Martha runs up to Jesus and pantomimes the action as the story is told.) **When Martha heard Jesus had arrived, she ran out to meet Him. When she saw Him, she said, "Jesus, if you had come sooner, my brother would not have died. I know you could have made him well again."**

Jesus replied, "Your brother will live again. I am the giver of life. Everyone who believes in me will live. Martha, do you believe in me?"

She answered, "Oh, yes! I believe you are the Son of God." *(Martha exits.)*

Martha hurried home to tell Mary. *(Mary enters and bows before the figure of Jesus.)* **Mary was so excited she also ran to see Jesus. She fell down at His**

feet and cried, "Jesus, if you had been here Lazarus would still be alive."

It made Jesus very sad to see Mary and Martha crying. *(Martha enters. Both women are crying.)* Jesus said, "Take me to the place where Lazarus is buried."

"Come, we'll show you," they said. *(Mary and Martha stand on either side of the figure of Jesus and pantomime the action as the story is told.)*

When Jesus came to the place where Lazarus was buried and saw how sad His friends were, He cried, too. Everyone could tell Jesus loved Lazarus.

Then Jesus surprised everyone by saying, "Move the stone away from the tomb."

Some strong men did what Jesus said. Then Jesus called in a loud voice, "Lazarus, come out!"

As the people watched, they saw an amazing thing happen. Lazarus came out of the tomb! *(Enter Lazarus wrapped in strips of toilet paper.)* He was alive! Strips of cloth were wrapped around him from head to toe. Jesus said. "Unwrap Lazarus so he can walk." *(Mary and Martha unwrap Lazarus.)*

Jesus did a wonderful thing for this family. He showed them He loved them very much. *(Turn off projector.)*

Story Review: Who Can Say?

You will need a mixing bowl and spoon, a picture of an ear, a handkerchief, a flat rock, some strips of cloth, and a heart (paper cutout, stuffed, or an old Valentine).

Display the items where the children can easily see them.

These items remind me of someone or something in today's Bible story.

Who or what does the mixing bowl and spoon remind you of? (Martha who fixed food for Jesus.)

Who or what does this ear remind you of? (Mary who liked to listen to Jesus.)

Who or what does the handkerchief remind you of? (The people who cried when Lazarus died.)

Who or what does the rock remind you of? (The stone that covered the entrance to the tomb, Jesus ordered the stone to be moved.)

Who or what do the strips of cloth remind you of? (Lazarus wrapped in cloths.)

Who or what does the heart remind you of? (Jesus; He loved His friends, and they loved Him.)

Bible Memory: Family Talk

You will need the bag of family items used in the "Family Show and Tell" activity.

Our Bible words remind us to show love. Let's take turns saying 1 John 3:18.

Reach in the bag and pull out an item. If you can wear it, put it on. If the item belongs to a dad, then say our Bible words in a dad's tone of voice. Do the same for mother, brother, sister, and baby. Let the children take turns reaching into the bag and saying the verse in the family member's tone of voice.

Our Bible words will help us remember that everyone in our family needs love. When we show love to our families, we are doing what the Bible words say.

> **Bible Words**
> "We should show . . . love by what we do" (1 John 3:18).

▼ 3. What Does This Mean to Me? ▲

Family Finger Puppets

You will need the "Family Finger Puppets" from p. 171, paper, crayons or markers, and clear tape.

Copy the finger puppets so that each child has puppets to represent each member of his family. (You may need to call parents to plan how many copies to make.) Cut out the puppets before class. Be sure to have a supply of puppets on hand for visitors.

Jesus loves all the people in your family. Can you name each person in your family?

Help the children choose the appropriate puppets to represent their family members. Let them color the puppets. Then tape each one to fit around their fingers.

Let the children use their puppets to act out and say things their family members do and say. Then ask the children to name ways they can show love to family members. Encourage each child to participate.

What can you say that shows you love your mother?

What can you do to show your little brother you love him?

When you are with your father at the grocery store, what can you do to show love to him?

What can you do to show your big sister you love her?

What are some ways you show love for your grandparents?

▼ 4. What Can I Do to Please God? ▲

Love Is in the Bag

You will need the items collected for the "Family Show and Tell" and "Family Talk" activities. Put all the items in a large grocery bag.

Jesus showed He loved the family of Mary, Martha, and Lazarus. He spent time with them, He ate with them, He talked with them, He cried with them, and He helped them. Let's choose ways we can show love to our families this week.

Let a child reach into the bag and pull out an item. Ask her to tell one way she can show love to the person in her family who uses that item. For example, if a child pulls out an item that a dad might use, he could say that he will help his dad wash the car. For a mom, the child might say he will help her fold and put away the clean clothes. Give each child a turn to choose an item from the bag.

You have chosen good ways to show love to your families. Let's ask God to help us do these good things this week. Pray, giving each child an opportunity to pray. Then close the prayer time: **Dear God, thank You for Jesus. Help us be like Jesus this week by showing love to our families. In Jesus' name, amen.**

The More I Love My Family

You will need the paper hearts made during Lesson 26, the words for "The More We Love" from p.153, glue, and pictures of families cut from magazines or catalogs.

In our Bible story today, we learned how Jesus showed love to a family. He wants us to show love to our families, too.

Let each child choose a picture of a family and glue it onto his paper heart, which is hung up in the classroom. Gather the children around one of the hearts and sing the first two verses of "The More We Love."

What did Jesus do that showed love to a family?

What can you do to show love to your family? Give each child a turn to say what he can do to show love this week.

Mary Shows Love to Jesus

John 12:1-8

▼ 1. What Is This Story About? ▲

Know: Bible people who learned about love from Jesus.

Feel: Love for Jesus and others.

Do: Choose to show love for Jesus and others.

Children will accomplish the goals when they

- Discover what the Bible says about Jesus.
- Tell how Mary showed love to Jesus.
- Recite 1 John 3:18.
- Name ways to show love to Jesus.
- Choose to show love to Jesus.

"I Love Jesus" Box

You will need a large box with items and pictures that remind you of Jesus: old curriculum pictures, a Bible, Bible storybooks, a toy boat, sandals, a baby doll, a decorative cross. Put the items in the box and print "I Love Jesus" on it.

You will also need the "I Love Jesus" box from p. 172. For each child, copy one box top and bottom on white card stock. Before class, cut out the box tops and bottoms and crease the folds. Make a sample box to show to the children. Tape the corners inside end flaps as illustrated to create a box bottom and a box top. Provide crayons or markers and clear tape.

This is my "I Love Jesus" box. In it are pictures and items that remind me that Jesus is special. Let me show you what is in my box. Bring the items out one at a time and let the children tell you how each item reminds them of Jesus.

After you discuss each item, give the children their own boxes to color. While the children are coloring, talk about what the Bible says about Jesus. Encourage the children to tell Bible stories about Jesus that they remember. Then put their names on their boxes and tape each box together.

My Jesus Book

You will need a copy of "My Jesus Book" from p. 173 for each child, crayons or markers, a stapler, and scissors. Trim the sides off the "My Jesus Book" copies before class.

The Bible tells us many things about Jesus. It is an important book. We're going to make a little book to help us remember what the Bible says about Jesus.

Give each child a copy of the "My Jesus Book" to color. After the pictures are colored, make three folds as indicated. Hold the sheet so that you can read "fold 1." Fold 1 is made so that the pictures are on the outside of the sheet. Fold line 2 away from you, and fold line 3 toward you so that you have an accordion shape, with the title page on top. Ask each child to write his name on the back of his book, and give help as needed.

Gather the children with their completed books away from the work area. Read through the book and talk about each event pictured.

What was special about Jesus' birth? (Angels told about His birth, a special star was in the sky, wise men brought Him gifts.)

What happened when parents brought their children to see Jesus? (Review the first story in the unit.)

What miracles did Jesus do? What miracle is pictured in our books? (Jesus makes Lazarus live again.)

What story tells about the three crosses? (People who didn't love Jesus had Him killed on a cross.)

What happened after Jesus died? (He came back to life, and He went to live in Heaven with God.)

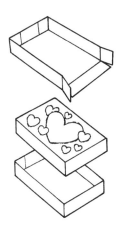

▼ 2. What Does the Bible Say? ▲

Bible Story: Mary's Gift of Love

You will need the transparency 7B, and two women (Mary and Martha) and two men (Lazarus and Judas) dressed in Bible costumes. (See p. 153 for directions on how to use the visual.) You will also need a spray bottle of mild-smelling perfume, a fancy bottle, a large cooking bowl, a wooden spoon, and an overhead projector.

Remember our last Bible story about Mary, Martha, and Lazarus? Remember how sad Jesus was when His friend Lazarus died? *(Briefly review the story of Jesus raising Lazarus from the dead.)* **When Jesus brought Lazarus back to life, everyone was amazed. It was a miracle. Mary and Martha were very happy and thankful.**

(Project transparency 7B.) **The next time Jesus was in Bethany where Lazarus and his family lived, they had a special dinner just for Jesus.** *(Enter Lazarus.)* **Lazarus invited many people to come and eat.** *(Enter Martha with bowl and spoon in her arms.)* **Martha cooked and served delicious food. The family wanted this to be a very special time for Jesus. They were probably trying to say thank-you to Jesus for loving them and bringing Lazarus back to life.** *(Exit Martha.)*

(Enter Mary carrying a fancy bottle.) **Mary also loved Jesus. She always sat right at His feet when He was teaching. She listened carefully to everything Jesus said.**

Mary wanted to show Jesus how much she loved him. *(Mary begins to pantomime the action described as the story is told.)* **While Jesus was eating with Lazarus, Mary got on her knees in front of Jesus and began to pour a very expensive perfume on Jesus' feet. As she poured the perfume, she wiped His feet with her long hair.** *(Spray perfume into the air.)* **Soon the whole house smelled sweet. Everyone could smell the perfume.**

(Enter Judas frowning. He stands beside the figure of Jesus and pantomimes the action described as the story is told.) **Judas, one of Jesus' followers, smelled the sweet odor, and complained to Jesus.**

"This perfume is very expensive. It would take a whole year to save enough money to buy it," grumbled Judas. "This perfume should be sold and the money given to the poor."

Judas did not love Jesus, and he really did not care about the poor.

"Let her alone," replied Jesus. "What she is doing is very good. The poor will always be here, and you can give them money any time. I won't always be here.

Jesus knew He was going to die soon. He was happy Mary loved Him and wanted to show it. *(Turn off the projector.)*

Story Review: Hearts for Jesus

You will need to provide a heart-shaped cookie and napkin for each child. If possible, use icing to print "I love Jesus" on each cookie.

Show one cookie. **While we talk about the Bible story, we can eat these cookies to remember how much Mary loved Jesus. I'll ask a question, and when someone gives the correct answer, you may take one bite of your cookie.** Distribute cookies and napkins. Then review the story using the following questions:

Where did Mary, Martha, and Lazarus live? (Bethany)

Why was Jesus at the house of Mary, Martha, and Lazarus? (He was invited to dinner.)

Where did Mary like to sit when Jesus was teaching? (At His feet.)

What did Mary do to show Jesus how much she loved Him? (Poured perfume on His feet and wiped it off with her hair.)

What did Judas think about what Mary did? (He thought the perfume should have been sold and the money given to the poor.)

Was Jesus pleased with Mary? Why? (Because Mary showed how much she loved Jesus.)

Bible Memory: Bubbling Over With Love

You will need a jar of bubbles with a wand.

Our Bible words remind us to show our love. While I blow the bubbles, you shout out names of people that you love.

Blow the bubbles and let the children name people. Then give each child a turn to say the Bible words.

Who can say the Bible words? After each child says the words, give her a turn blowing the bubbles.

Blowing bubbles is fun. I heard lots of laughter while you were blowing bubbles. Our Bible words can help us bubble over with love!

> **Bible Words**
> "We should show . . . love by what we do" (1 John 3:18).

▼ 3. What Does This Mean to Me? ▲

How Can I Love You?

You will need red paper hearts and Jesus stickers. Before class, make enough paper hearts so that each child in your class can find two or three. Put Jesus stickers on three hearts. Hide the hearts before class or during a previous activity.

Hearts remind us to love. There are hearts scattered all over our room. When I tell you to, collect as many as you can. Some hearts have a picture of Jesus on them. When you find one of these special hearts, shout, "I love Jesus." When all the hearts have been found, gather the children in a circle.

Who found the hearts with the picture of Jesus?

How did Mary show love to Jesus in our story?

What are some ways we can show our love to Jesus today? Give the children time to respond; then suggest these ways if they haven't named them: pray to Him, sing to Him, tell friends about Jesus, tell Jesus "I love You," show love to others, learn more about Him.

Close by giving each child a sticker of Jesus to add to one heart. **These Jesus hearts will help us remember to love Jesus this week.**

Bubbling Over With Love for Jesus

You will need a jar of bubbles with a wand (used earlier in the Bible Memory activity).

Our Bible words remind us to show our love by what we do. While I blow the bubbles, you shout out the Bible words.

Blow the bubbles. Encourage and help the children to shout out the Bible words. Then give each child a turn to blow the bubbles.

How did Mary show love to Jesus in our story?

What are some ways we can show our love to Jesus today? Let each child blow some bubbles for telling how he can show love to Jesus. Include these ways to show love: pray to Him, sing to Him, tell friends about Jesus, tell Jesus "I love You," show love to others, learn more about Him.

We can have lots of fun blowing bubbles. It makes us happy. Showing Jesus how much we love Him makes Him happy, too.

▼ 4. What Can I Do to Please God? ▲

The More I Love Jesus

You will need the paper hearts made during Lesson 26, the words for "The More We Love" from p.153, glue, and pictures or stickers of Jesus.

In our Bible story today, we learned how Mary showed love to Jesus. We can show love to Jesus, too.

Give each child a picture or sticker of Jesus to place on his paper heart that is hung up in the classroom. Gather the children around one of the hearts and sing the first three verses of "The More We Love."

What did Mary do that showed love to Jesus?

What can you do that shows you love Jesus? Give each child a turn to say what he can do or say to love Jesus this week. Then pray together, encouraging each child to tell Jesus, "I love You."

Jesus, I Love You!

You will need the "I Love Jesus" boxes the children made in the first activity, the words for "The More We Love" from p. 153, star stickers (or small stars cut or punched from paper), heart stickers (or small hearts cut from paper or heart-shaped candy), small rocks, chenille wire, cotton balls, and spray perfume. Before class, make a cross for each child using two small chenille wires.

Gather the children around you and distribute the "I Love Jesus" boxes they made earlier.

The box you made today is very special. This box is for holding things that will help you remember to love Jesus.

Read what's on the top of the box. Explain that you will be giving them items to put in their boxes. Talk about the following items as you give each one to the children:

Star sticker: It reminds us of the special star that God put in the sky at Jesus' birth.

Heart sticker: It reminds us of the Bible story when Jesus showed how much He loves children.

Rock: It reminds us of the Bible story when Jesus made Lazarus live again. A rock was rolled in front of the tomb where Lazarus was buried.

Chenille wire cross: A cross reminds us of how Jesus died. It can remind us of the love Jesus has for us.

Cotton ball with perfume sprayed on it: Before Jesus went back to Heaven, He told His followers to tell the whole world about Him. Then He disappeared in a cloud. The cotton ball reminds us of the cloud, and the perfume reminds us of the love Mary showed to Jesus.

Let's show Jesus how much we love Him by singing "The More We Love." Sing the first three verses, and then ask the children to use these words to sing the third verse again:

The more that I love Jesus, love Jesus, love Jesus,
The more that I love Jesus, the happier I'll be.
I love You, dear Jesus, 'cause You are my best friend.
The more that I love Jesus, the happier I'll be.

Jesus Shows Love to His Friends

John 13:1-17

▼ 1. What Is This Story About? ▲

Love Show and Tell

You will need a chalkboard and chalk or large paper and a marker.

Line the children up and, starting at one end of the line, have the children take turns saying, "show," "love," "show," "love," one word at a time. Tell each "show" to find a "love." These two will be partners.

Have the partners sit together as the entire group makes a list of people they love (parents, brother, sister, playmate, grandparents, teachers). Print the list on a chalkboard. Ask a pair to pick someone they love from the list. Ask them to pantomime a loving action they could do for that person (rake leaves for grandparents, play ball with brother, pick up crayons for teacher.) Remind them they must do this without talking. The other children watch and guess what the pairs are doing. Give each pair a turn to pantomime for the group.

In today's Bible story we are going to hear how Jesus taught His followers to show love.

▼ 2. What Does the Bible Say? ▲

Bible Story: Follow Me

You will need transparencies 7A, 7B, and 7C, several men or teenage boys (disciples) dressed in Bible costumes, and an overhead projector. (See p. 153 for directions on how to use the visual.)

(Project transparency 7A.) **Jesus traveled many places, teaching the good news about God's love. Many people came to see and hear Him teach. Some people even followed Him from town to town.** *(Enter disciples.)* **Jesus invited twelve men to go with Him everywhere. These special followers were called His disciples.**

Jesus also had many enemies. These people did not believe He was God's Son. They were also jealous and made plans to kill Him.

Jesus knew He was going to die soon. He still had a few lessons He wanted to teach His disciples. On the night before He was to die, Jesus asked His twelve followers to eat a special supper with Him.

The twelve disciples found a room for the dinner and helped get the food ready. *(Remove transparency 7A and project transparency 7B. Disciples sit on chairs on both sides of the figure of Jesus.)* **When it was time to eat, the men were hot and dusty from walking from place to place. Their feet were especially dirty and dusty. Sandals only helped to keep their feet from being hurt by the rocks on the road.**

In Bible times a servant washed the dirty feet of everyone who came to eat or visit. As you might guess, this was a dirty job, but a good host always provided a servant to wash the feet of his guests.

While Jesus and His disciples were eating, Jesus got up from the table. *(Remove transparency 7B and project transparency 7C.)* **He took off His robe and tied a towel around His waist like an apron. He poured water into a bowl**

Know: Bible people who learned about love from Jesus.
Feel: Love for Jesus and others.
Do: Choose to show love for Jesus and others.

Children will accomplish the goals when they
- Explore actions that are kind and helpful.
- Tell how Jesus taught His followers to show love to others.
- Recite 1 John 3:18.
- Tell how they can show love to others.
- Choose to show love and kindness to others.

and began to go around the table, washing and drying the feet of each of His disciples.

(One of the disciples sitting next to the figure of Jesus pantomimes the part of Peter.) **When He started to wash Peter's feet, Peter said, "No! I don't want you to wash my feet." Peter probably felt Jesus was too special to do the job of a servant.**

Jesus said, "I must wash everyone's feet so that you can be my disciples."

When Jesus had finished washing His followers' feet, he asked, "Do you understand what I just did? I am your Teacher and your Lord, but I just washed your feet like a servant. I want you to do kind things for each other, just as I have done for you."

Jesus wanted His followers to learn an important lesson about love. He wanted them to always do kind things and be helpful to one another. *(Turn off projector.)*

Story Review: A Very Special Supper

You will need a long, narrow folding table. Leave the legs folded and put the table on the floor.

Did you know that in Bible times, people did not sit in chairs at a table the way we do? No, they stretched out on couches, and propped themselves up with their arms while they ate. Let's try that. Encourage each child to stretch out on the floor around the table and pretend that they are lying on couches.

Now, let's have some fun remembering the Bible story. I will tell you something about the Bible story. If it is true, raise a foot; if it is not true, raise a hand. Use these statements:

Jesus had twelve special friends. (true)

Jesus and his twelve friends had a special meal together. (true)

Jesus and his followers probably wore shoes like ours. (false)

At the special meal, a servant washed everyone's feet. (false)

At the special meal, Jesus washed His followers' feet. (true)

Jesus showed His followers that serving others is a way to show love. (true)

Jesus asked His followers to show love to each other. (true)

Bible Memory: Musical Feet

You will need the foot pattern from p. 174, white and red construction paper, scissors, recorded music on cassette or CD, and a tape or CD player.

Cut out multiple white footprints and one red heart. Tape the footprints and the heart on the floor to form a circle. If you have more than ten children, form more circles.

Our Bible words remind us to love as Jesus loved.

Have the children stand on the footprints and the heart. Say the Bible words several times in unison. Then start the music. Lead the children in walking around the circle. Stop the music. Ask the child who is standing on the heart to say the memory verse. Give help as needed. Start the music again. Continue until everyone can say 1 John 3:18 from memory.

Play the music again. Each time you stop the music ask the child standing on the heart to tell how she can show love by what she does.

> **Bible Words**
>
> "We should show . . . love by what we do" (1 John 3:18).

 166

UNIT 7, LESSON 29

▾ 3. What Does This Mean to Me? ▴

The More We Love Each Other

You will need the paper hearts made during Lesson 26, the words for "The More We Love" from p.153, glue or tape, and pictures of children (friends) cut from magazines or catalogs.

In our Bible story today, we learned how Jesus showed love to His friends. We can show love to our friends, too.

Let each child choose a picture of friends to place on his paper heart that is hung up in the classroom. Gather the children around one of the hearts and sing the first three verses of "The More We Love."

What did Jesus do that showed love to His friends?

What are some ways you can show love to your friends? Give each child a turn to say what he can do or say to show love to his friends.

Fixin' Food for Each Other

You will need the heart pattern from p. 174, scissors, an X-Acto knife, crayons, drinking straws, frozen waffles, a toaster or toaster oven, heart-shaped cookie cutters, jumbo craft sticks, paper plates, napkins, margarine, powdered sugar in large-holed shakers, apple juice, and cups.

Before class, copy and cut out a heart for each child, and use an X-Acto knife to cut on the broken lines.

If you prefer, divide the children into two groups. One group will begin with the snack activity, and the other group will begin with the heart straw activity. Then switch groups so that each child participates in both activities.

We're going to make two things that will remind us to show love to others.

To make straw hearts, ask each child to color a heart. Then weave a straw through the openings of each heart.

To make the waffle snack, toast a waffle for each child. Then let the children us the cookie cutters to cut the waffles into heart shapes. Use jumbo craft sticks to spread margarine on the waffle hearts, and then sprinkle them with powdered sugar. Cover to keep warm.

Eat on a table with the legs folded. (See the Story Review activity.) Distribute a heart straw (for apple juice) and a waffle heart to each child. While the children eat, talk about ways to show love to others. Give each child a turn to participate.

What are some ways friends show love to each other?

How did you show love to someone while we were making our straws and waffles?

What kinds of things do you do to show love to your friends at home?

▾ 4. What Can I Do to Please God? ▴

Roll a Kind Deed

You will need the words for "The More We Love" from p. 153 and a beach ball or rubber ball for each group of ten children.

Have the children sit on the floor in a circle. Show the children how to spread their legs so their feet are touching the feet of the children on either side. It will be important for the children to keep their feet touching so the call cannot roll out of the circle. (If you have little girls wearing skirts, adapt the activity so they can sit on their legs.)

Give one child the ball and let him roll it to another child. Continue rolling the ball back and forth inside the ring of legs and feet. Sing "The More We Love" while the ball is rolling. After the children have played for a while, stop the ball. **After Jesus washed His followers' feet, He told them to love each other. Jesus also wants us to show that we love each other. Now when the ball is rolled to you, catch it and say the name of someone you will show love to this week. Also tell how you will show love for that person. For example, you might say, "I will show love to my sister Madison by helping her put her toys away."** Give help with ideas as needed. Continue rolling the ball until everyone has had a turn.

Lead the children in a prayer, asking God to help them show love to others.

Show Love by Doing a Good Deed

You will need the words for "The More We Love," copies of the foot pattern from p. 174, scissors, a black marker, and a big boot.

Before class, prepare the feet. On each one of the feet, print the name of an area or object in your classroom that needs cleaned or straightened. Cut the feet out and put them in a big boot.

Our Bible words remind us to show our love by what we do. Let's show our love by helping.

Let each child reach into the boot and pull out a paper foot. Read the word(s) on the foot and send the child to help clean up.

When the room is straightened, gather the children in a group. Thank them for showing love to all of the leaders by helping to clean up the classroom. Sing "The More We Love." Remind the children to follow Jesus' example and show love to others every day. Close with prayer.

▼ Bonus Activity ▲

Extra Action! Heart and Sole Mix-up

Today our Bible story was about Jesus washing the feet of His followers. He wanted to show He loved them. He told them to go and show their love for others by doing kind deeds, too.

We are going to play a game with our shoes. Explain how to play the game. See next paragraph. **After you are finished, show love to the other children by doing kind deeds, such as helping others find their shoes. If you know how to tie shoelaces, help those who do not know how to tie their shoes.**

Have the children take off their shoes, mix them up, and put the shoes in a line. Have the children stand in a line on the other side of the room, across from their shoes. Give a signal for the children to run to the shoes, find their shoes, carry them back to the starting line, and put them on. Repeat the game as long as time allows.

Clock

has time for

Boy-Girl Paper Dolls

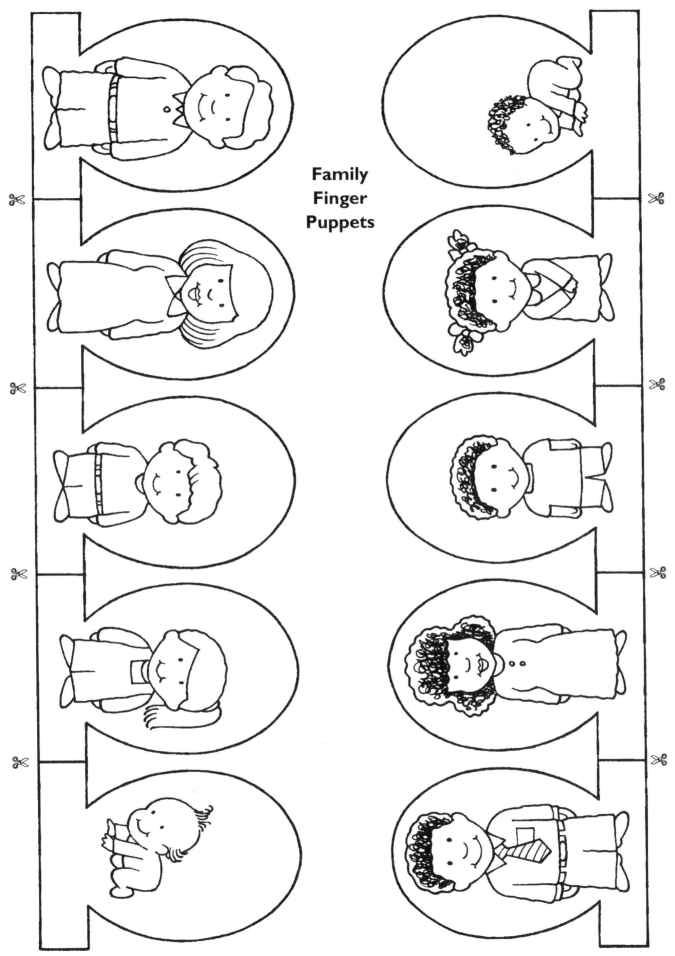

Family
Finger
Puppets

cut · · · fold · · · cut

fold

cut · · · fold · · · cut

Box
Top

cut

cut · · · fold · · · cut

fold

cut · · · fold · · · fold · · · cut

cut · · · fold · · · cut

Box
Bottom

cut

Jesus was born.

My Book

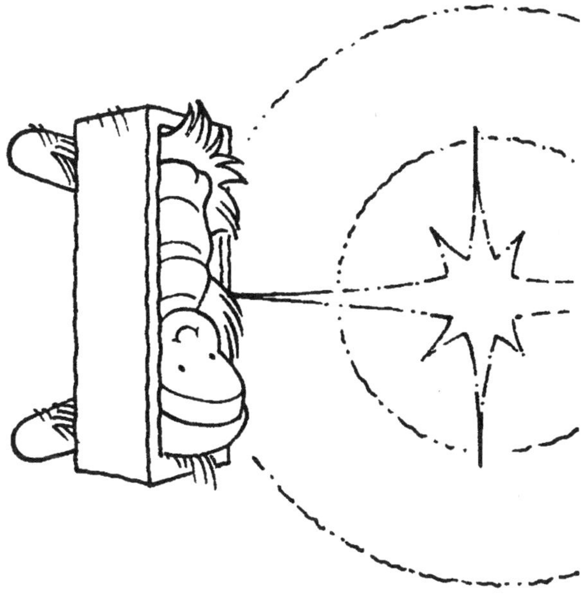

Jesus loves children.

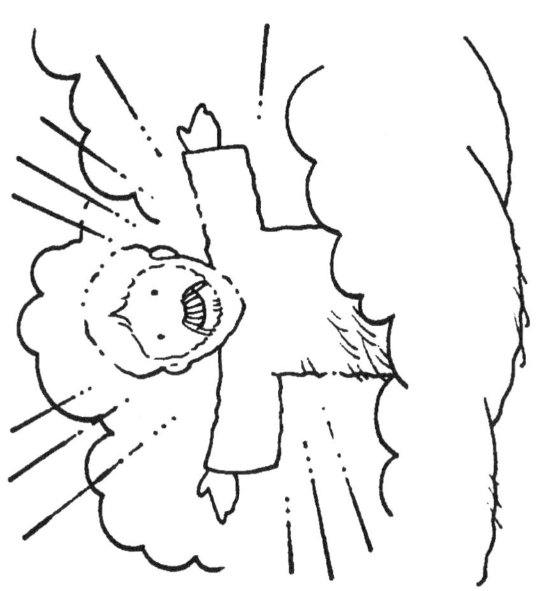

fold 3

Jesus went to Heaven.

fold 1

Jesus did miracles.

fold 2

Jesus died on the cross.

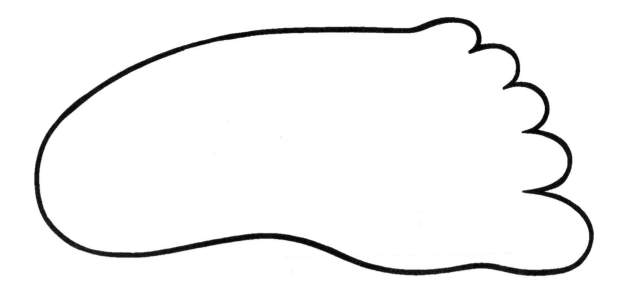

Heart Straw

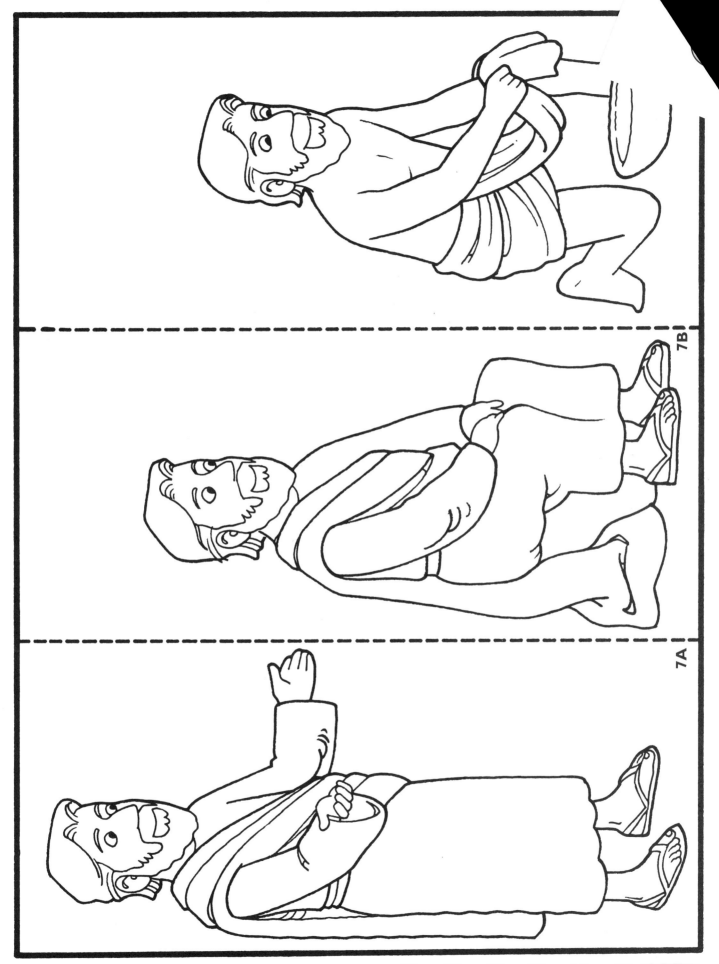

7B

7A

Learning to Be Happy

Lessons 30-33

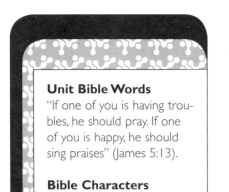

Unit Bible Words
"If one of you is having troubles, he should pray. If one of you is happy, he should sing praises" (James 5:13).

Bible Characters
Jesus, John

30 A Happy Shepherd

Luke 15:4-7; Psalm 23—Jesus tells the parable of the shepherd who searches for one lost sheep even though he has ninety-nine who are safe. Jesus wants everyone to know that God is like the shepherd. He rejoices when one person changes his heart and does what is right.

31 A Happy Woman

Luke 15:8-10—This parable tells about a woman who loses one of her ten coins. She cleans her entire house and finds the lost coin. All of her friends are called to join her in celebrating her happiness. Jesus says there is happiness in Heaven when one lost sinner is found. Go and share happiness with others.

32 A Happy Father

Luke 15:11-24—In this parable a son asks for his inheritance and then wastes it all. Finally, he makes a wise decision. He returns home to his father. The father, who spent his days watching for his son to return home, welcomes the son with open arms and gives a party to share his joy with others. God always forgives and welcomes us with love.

33 Be Happy Forever

John 14:1-4; Revelation 1:9-11; 2:10; 4; 5; 21; 22—John is on an island to keep him from preaching about Jesus. Jesus visits him and tells him to write down everything he sees. John sees the gates of Heaven open and tries to describe the glory and splendor of Heaven.

By the end of this unit, the children and leaders will

Know: Happiness comes from God.
Feel: Eager to say and sing praises for God's goodness.
Do: Tell others about the happiness God has given them.

Why Teach This Unit to Four- to Six-Year-Olds?

Little children, like everyone else, are curious about Heaven. As they grow in their understanding of God and Jesus, they will ask questions like these: "What does Heaven look like? Where is it? Who will go there? How can I go there?" Use this unit to help four, five, and six-year-olds develop a desire to go to Heaven.

During His earthly ministry, Jesus was asked many times about Heaven. This unit teaches three of the stories Jesus told to explain Heaven. These stories also tell about God's love because His love flows through Heaven and makes it such a happy place.

The last story in this unit tells what John saw when he was told to write a description of Heaven. The children will begin to see Heaven is even more wonderful than human words can describe. This unit also encourages children to share happiness with others. The Christian life is one of joy and praise. Begin now to plant the seeds of joy that will grow into mature praise as the children grow. Encourage them to openly share with others the joy that only God can give.

Meet Jesus

In this unit Jesus is the Master Teacher, answering questions about Heaven and God's love. Jesus used parables to relate common events to characteristics of God. He wanted everyone to fully comprehend the power and love of the heavenly Father.

Jesus is also the one who invites us to enter Heaven and live forever in happiness with God. John was given a vision of Heaven so wonderful he declared with excitement, "Come quickly, Lord Jesus."

Meet the Shepherd, the Woman, the Father, and the Son

Were these real people or just characters in a story? The beauty of a parable is that it is a believable story, an event that could have happened. Jesus intended that those who were willing to listen and think would understand His parables. Sometimes, however, His listeners needed Jesus' interpretation. The parables in this unit are ones young children can enjoy and begin to understand when explained. Children and adults of all ages love the characters in these three parables because they help them understand the love God has for them.

Meet John

John was a fisherman called by Jesus to be one of His disciples. John followed Jesus all during His earthly ministry. He was called "the disciple whom Jesus loved." After Jesus returned to Heaven, John was actively involved in spreading the gospel. He was so zealous that he was imprisoned on an island in an attempt to keep him from preaching about Jesus. While on this island, Jesus visited him and instructed him to write a description of Heaven to be sent to seven churches.

Unit Visuals

Transparencies made from pages 195 and 196 will be used in this unit. Cut the transparencies in half, making four scenes. Add color to the transparencies, if desired, with permanent transparency markers. (Hint: Handle the transparencies as little as possible. Colored pens will not mark easily over fingerprints.)

These four transparencies will be used as background scenery for the Bible stories. If a plain wall is not available for projection, tack a large, white sheet to the wall. Silhouettes, found on pp. 106 and 194 will be added to the scenes. Copy the silhouettes onto card stock or light cardboard and cut out.

In each Bible story you will find a list of the transparencies and silhouettes for that lesson. Project the transparency and place the appropriate silhouettes on the transparency according to the directions throughout the story. Sometimes the silhouettes will be projected alone.

Unit Projects

To help develop the theme of happiness, the children will make rhythm instruments. These will be made in each of the four lessons. Decide whether you want the children to take the instruments home each week, or whether you want to collect them and keep them until the unit is finished. If the children do take the instruments home, make several of each kind to keep in the classroom so there will be a variety of sounds to accompany the children as they sing. All of the instruments are simple to make, but they will require some early planning to gather the supplies.

Unit Song

Be Glad, Not Sad
(Tune: "This Old Man")

Verse 1
When troubles make you sad,
Here's good news to make you glad.
With a smile and a giggle,
Say a prayer today!
God will hear and lead the way.

Verse 2
Our dear God and His Son,
They bring joy to everyone.
With a smile and a giggle,
We will not be sad!
Share the news, make someone glad.

Verse 3
If something makes you glad,
Praise the Lord and don't be sad.
With a smile and a giggle,
Sing a praise today!
God will hear. He is the way.

Verse 4
Heaven is a happy place,
God's love shines on every face.
With a smile and a giggle,
Happiness is there!
We'll live forever in God's care.

A Happy Shepherd

Luke 15:4-7; Psalm 23

Know: Happiness comes from God.

Feel: Eager to say and sing praises for God's goodness.

Do: Tell others about the happiness that God has given them.

Children will accomplish the goals when they

- Discover what the Bible says about sheep.
- Tell about a shepherd who finds his lost sheep.
- Begin to memorize James 5:13.
- Name ways God shows His love to them.
- Choose to tell others about God's love.

▼ 1. What Is This Story About? ▲

The Lord Is My Shepherd

You will need the party hat pattern from p. 197, white card stock, scissors, a hole punch, an X-Acto knife, Bible, crayons or markers, glue, cotton balls, and yarn or elastic thread. Optional: children's book about Psalm 23.

Before class, copy the hats onto card stock and cut out. Punch holes where indicated and use an X-Acto knife to cut on the broken lines.

What do you know about sheep? (Let the children respond.) **The Bible tells us that God is like a shepherd and we are like His sheep. He wants to take care of us like a shepherd takes care of his sheep.**

Give each child a party hat. Tell the children to look at the picture of the shepherd on the hat while you read Psalm 23 from a Bible or from a children's book about Psalm 23. Point out things in the picture as you read.

Ask the children to color the hats and glue small pieces of cotton on the sheep. Roll the hats into cones and join the sides by slipping the tabs into the slots. Glue the tabs. Tie yarn or elastic through the hat holes and tie the hats on the children's heads.

What kind of care do sheep need?

How does the shepherd from Psalm 23 take care of his sheep?

Today we are going to hear a story Jesus told about a good shepherd.

Leading Sheep

You will need a large stick or cane to use as a staff.

What do you know about sheep? (Let the children respond.) **Bible people knew a lot about sheep and taking care of sheep. Let's pretend to be sheep and learn what sheep are like.**

Ask the children to get down on their hands and knees and pretend to be quiet sheep. Then tell them about sheep while you lead them around the room, pretending to be the shepherd. Let them practice baa-ing before you begin.

Sheep need a lot of care. A shepherd is very busy. Day and night a shepherd must care for his sheep. During the day, sheep need fresh grass to eat. (Lead children to a place where they can pretend to eat.) **Sheep also need fresh water.** (Lead them to another place.) **Sheep can't see very well, so the shepherd must lead them. The hillsides are full of rocks. The paths are steep and winding.** (Lead the children around a few obstacles in the room.) **The shepherd must lead his sheep on paths that they can follow.**

A shepherd also keeps his sheep safe. He carries a long stick with a hook at the top. He uses his staff to lift sheep that have fallen in a hole or down the side of a hill. There are also wild animals in the hills. The shepherd must watch for bears and wolves. These animals hunt sheep to eat.

If you have time, give several children a turn to be the shepherd.

Today we are going to hear a story Jesus told about a good shepherd.

▼ 2. What Does the Bible Say? ▲

Bible Story: A Shepherd Finds His Lost Sheep

You will need transparency 8A, silhouettes 8-a shepherd, 8-b staff, and 8-c shepherd with sheep, and an overhead projector. (See p. 177 for directions on how to use the visual.)

Jesus wanted all people to know how much God loves them, so He told a story. *(Project transparency 8A. Place silhouette 8-a in the center of the transparency.)* **The story was about a shepherd and his sheep. The people listening to Jesus knew about sheep. There were probably some shepherds in the group.**

What do you know about sheep? *(Encourage the children to tell what they learned.)*

Let's listen to Jesus' story about a good shepherd.

A shepherd had one hundred sheep. One night he counted his sheep "One, two, three . . ." all the way to "ninety-six, ninety-seven, ninety-eight, ninety-nine . . . Ninety-nine?"

"I have one hundred sheep, not ninety-nine! Oh, no! I've lost one of my sheep. It may be in danger. I must find it!"

The shepherd looked and looked for the lost sheep. Finally, he found the sheep. *(Remove transparency 8A and silhouettes 8-a and 8-b. Project silhouette 8c.)* **He picked up the sheep and put it on his shoulders. Happily, he carried the sheep home.** *(Lay transparency 8A on top of silhouette 8-c.)* **He counted his sheep again. This time how many sheep did he count? Yes, he had one hundred sheep. He was so happy! He called his friends and neighbors and told them, "I have found my sheep! I want you to be happy, too!"**

After Jesus told this story, He said, "There is happiness in Heaven when one person on earth is sorry he disobeyed God and chooses to do good." *(Turn off the projector.)*

Story Review: Shepherd, Where's Your Sheep?

You will need a stuffed toy lamb or a sheep beanbag. (To make a sheep beanbag, you will need a white cotton sock, dried beans, and a black permanent marker. Fill the sock with some beans, leaving enough room to tie the opening closed. Draw a sheep's face on the sock.)

Play this game the same way "Doggy, Doggy Where's Your Bone?" is played. Have one child sit in a chair with his back to the rest of the children. His eyes must stay covered with his hands. Put the toy or beanbag sheep under the chair. Silently point to one child to tip toe up to the chair and take the sheep back to where he was sitting. Have him hide the sheep behind his back with his hands. All the children should have their hands behind their backs, too. Lead the children in saying, "Shepherd, Shepherd Where's Your Sheep? He is lost and far from home." This is the signal for the child sitting in the chair to turn around and try to guess who is hiding the sheep behind his back. Give him three guesses. The child who is hiding the sheep becomes the next shepherd.

Between turns, ask the following questions to review the story.

How do you think the shepherd felt who lost a sheep?

How would it feel to find a lost sheep?

Why is God like a shepherd who has found his lost sheep?

Why did Jesus tell this story?

Bible Memory: Say and Do

Our Bible words will help us remember two things we can do anytime.

Teach the words to James 5:13 using the following motions. Say the words and do the motions one line at a time.

If one of you *(Point to someone.)*
is having troubles, *(Make a sad face.)*
he should pray. *(Bow head and fold hands.)*
If one of you *(Point to someone.)*
is happy, *(Smile and clap two times.)*
he should sing praises. *(Raise your hands in the air.)*
James 5:13 *(Hold hands like an open Bible.)*
Repeat several times. Have the children do the motions while you say the words. Then have them say the words while you do the motions. Then do it altogether.

What can we do if we're having troubles?
What can we do when we're happy?

▼ 3. What Does This Mean to Me? ▲

I've Got Rhythm

You will need the words to the unit song, "Be Glad, Not Sad," from p. 177, four-inch blocks of wood cut from a 2" x 4", sheets of medium sandpaper, wood glue, and cotton swabs. Before class time, sand the rough edges on the blocks and cut the sandpaper into 4" x 4" pieces.

The rhythm instrument for this lesson is sandpaper blocks. Give each child two blocks of wood and a small scrap of sandpaper. The rough edges will have been sanded, but show the children how to sand the sides and edges of their blocks. (They will enjoy the process.) Then help the children spread glue with a cotton swab onto the back of the sandpaper and attach it to one side of each block. Let dry.

In our Bible story, we learned about a shepherd who loved his sheep. Let's learn a song that will help us remember one way God shows how much He loves us.

While the blocks are drying, teach verse one of "Be Glad, Not Sad." As you teach the words, use the following motions to help the children learn the new words. Later they will be using the sandpaper blocks to keep the rhythm.

When troubles make you sad, *(Use pointing fingers to make lips frown.)*
Here's good news to make you glad, *(Use pointing fingers to make lips smile.)*
With a smile and a giggle, *(Place palms of hands together and rub back and forth, as if you were holding the sandpaper blocks.)*
Say a prayer today! *(Fold hands in prayer.)*
God will hear and lead the way. *(Cup hands to ears and smile.)*
Help the children name ways God shows His love to us.

What will God do when we pray? (He will hear us.)
What else does God do to show His love for us?
God is like the shepherd. How does He care for us?

God Loves Me

You will need small paper drinking cups, tape, a serving tray, and enough copies of the six pictures from p. 198 so that each child has one picture.

Before class, cut out the pictures and tape them to the bottoms of the cups. (Enlarge or reduce if needed.) Then fill the cups half full of water and put them on a tray.

Gather the children around the tray of cups. **In our Bible story, we learned about a shepherd who loved his sheep. If you were sheep grazing on grass all day, you would get thirsty and need water. Your shepherd would lead you to a stream where the water is calm and cool. You would follow the shepherd because you know he always takes good care of you.**

God is our shepherd, and He loves us very much. He takes good care of us. Water is one way God shows His love. Let's drink the cool water God

created for you. When everyone's cup is empty, ask the children to turn their cups upside down. **Look at the pictures on the bottom of your cup. It shows one way God loves you.** Give each child a turn to tell about the picture on her cup and how it shows God's love. Give help as needed.

▼ 4. What Can I Do to Please God? ▲

Glad/Sad Puppet

You will need the words of the unit song, "Be Glad, Not Sad," from p. 177, copies of the eyes, ears, nose, and mouth from p. 198, crayons, 9" white paper plates, glue, paper fasteners, yarn (hair colors), jumbo craft sticks, and tape. Before class, copy and cut out the face pieces for each child.

Our Bible words remind us what to do when we're sad and when we're happy. Let's make a puppet to tell other people that God loves us all the time.

Ask each child to color the eyes, ears, nose, and mouth for his puppet. Distribute the paper plates and let the children glue all but the mouth in the correct places. Help each child attach the mouth with a paper fastener. Show the child how to make the mouth smile and how to make it frown. Pass out yarn and let the children glue on pieces for hair. Glue or tape the craft stick on the back of the puppet for a handle.

When the children have finished their puppets, talk about times God shows His love to them.

Name a time when you are happy. (Ask the children to make their puppet mouths smile and raise their puppets to be called on.) **Does God love you then? How does God show His love to you? Who will you tell about God's love?**

Name a time when you are sad. (Ask the children to make their puppet mouths frown and raise their puppets to be called on.) **Does God love you then? How does God show His love to you? Who will you tell about God's love?**

Encourage each child to participate. Then sing the first verse of "Be Glad, Not Sad" and let the children use their puppets at the appropriate times in the song.

Be Glad Time

You will need the sandpaper blocks made in "I've Got Rhythm" and the words to "Be Glad, Not Sad" from p. 177.

After the children help you clean and straighten the classroom, gather them for a time of singing with the sandpaper blocks. Sing familiar songs of joy and verse one of "Be Glad, Not Sad."

Let's thank God for His love and for giving us a happy time together. Lead in prayer or ask several children to pray.

▼ Bonus Activity ▲

Snack Attack! Find a Sheep

You will need English muffins (split), cream cheese, raisins, shelled peanuts, jumbo craft sticks, and small paper plates. (Check for peanut allergies. Mandarin orange slices would also make cute ears.)

Be sure the children wash their hands. Place all of the items on a table. **Does anyone see a sheep on this table? No? Let me find a sheep for you!** Demonstrate how to make a sheep's face by spreading the cream cheese on the muffin and then using the raisins for its eyes and nose and peanuts (or orange slices) for its ears. Let the children "find" their own sheep.

A Happy Woman

Luke 15:8-10

▼ 1. What Is This Story About? ▲

Share Your Happiness

You will need a copy of the cube from p. 199 and card stock. Color, cut, and assemble one cube before class. (Stuffing the cube with tissues will make it more durable.)

We learned last time that God loves us very much. That makes me happy and makes me want to share my happiness.

Gather the children around the cube and let them take turns rolling it. After a child rolls the cube, ask him to describe the picture on top. Then ask him to tell how he can share happiness with the person pictured or how he can use the object pictured to share happiness with others. For example, the toy ball can be shared with a friend; a pretty picture can be colored for a mother; a double stick Popsicle can be divided and shared with a friend; a hug can be given to a dad; coins can be put in the missionary offering; a friend can be invited to play with you. Give help with ideas as needed.

When you do something nice for someone else, how do you feel? Yes, being nice to others makes me feel good, too. God is also pleased when you share happiness with others.

I've Got Rhythm

You will need the words to the unit song "Be Glad, Not Sad" from p. 177, a large nail, and a hammer. You will also need the following for each child: a clean, empty soup or vegetable can, one large machine nut, two half-inch metal washers, a twelve-inch piece of string, and stickers.

The rhythm instrument for this lesson is a tin can bell. To assemble the bell:

1. Punch a small hole in the end of the can with a nail and a hammer.

2. Tie the machine nut onto one end of the string. About two and a half inches up from the nut, tie a big nut and slide on one of the washers.

3. Thread the string through the inside of the can to the outside. Pull the string until the washer stops it from coming through the hole. Slide the other washer onto the string until it stops at the hole in the end of the can. Tie another knot securing this washer. (The two washers will keep the string in place so the machine nut can move inside the can as the clapper for the bell.) Use the remaining string to make a loop for holding the tin can bell.

Involve the children in as much of the assembly process as you can. Provide stickers for them to use to decorate the bells.

Review the words to verse one and teach the new words for verse two of "Be Glad, Not Sad." As the children sing, let them keep rhythm with their tin can bells. **Our song says we should share the joy God and Jesus give us. What are some ways to share the news and make someone glad?** Let the children respond. Possible answers: tell someone how much God loves him, tell who Jesus is and what He can do, send a card, help a family member, share toys or food.

Know: Happiness comes from God.
Feel: Eager to say and sing praises for God's goodness.
Do: Tell others about the happiness that God has given them.

Children will accomplish the goals when they

- Explore ways to share happiness.
- Tell about a woman who finds her lost coin.
- Memorize James 5:13.
- Name something about God to tell others.
- Choose to tell others happiness comes from God.

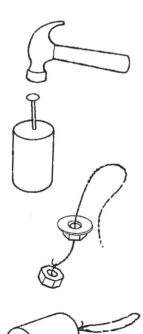

▼ 2. What Does the Bible Say? ▲

Bible Story: A Woman Loses One Coin

You will need transparency 8B, silhouettes 8-d woman and 8-e broom, ten coins, and an overhead projector. (See p. 177 for directions on how to use the visual.)

One time some important men were complaining because Jesus talked to people who did bad things. To teach these men about love, Jesus told them a story. Listen carefully while I tell the same story to you. Once there was a woman who had ten silver coins. *(Project ten coins. Ask the children to help count the coins.)* **These ten silver coins were very valuable. To earn one coin a person would have to work very hard for one whole day.**

The woman wasn't very careful. *(Remove one coin.)* **She lost one of the coins. She now had only nine coins.** *(Remove all coins and project transparency 8B. Add silhouette 8-d, moving it around the room on the transparency.)*

"Oh my!" she cried. "Where did I lose my coin? How will I find it? I guess I'll have to clean my whole house." *(Add silhouette 8-e to 8-d.)*

The woman started cleaning her house. *(Move silhouettes 8-d and 8-e around the room on the transparency.)* **She even used a candle to help her see under the furniture and in the cupboards and closets. She looked carefully for the lost coin as she cleaned everything in her house.**

Suddenly, there it was! She had found her lost coin! What a wonderful surprise! *(Remove transparency 8B and all silhouettes.)*

The woman was so happy she called all of her friends and said, "I had ten silver coins and I lost one. *(Project nine coins.)* **I was very sad. When I cleaned my whole house, I found the lost coin!** *(Add the tenth coin.)* **Be happy because I am happy."**

Jesus said the happiness the woman felt is like the happiness celebrated in Heaven when one person changes his heart and starts loving God. Jesus talked to the people who were doing bad things so they could learn about God's love and change their hearts. *(Turn off the projector.)*

Story Review: Scavenger Hunt

You will need the words to "Be Glad, Not Sad" from p. 177, copies of the Scavenger Hunt Pictures from p. 201, and paper lunch sacks. Glue the pictures onto a sack for each child.

Gather the items pictured and hide one of each for each child (or more than enough).

Lead the children to the room or area where you have hidden the items for the hunt. Pass out the sacks and say, **We are going on a scavenger hunt. Look at the pictures on your sack.** Describe each one and/or show a sample. **You may begin looking for the things pictured on your sack. When you find one, put it in your sack. But be sure to put in only one of each thing. After you have found all of the things, come back to me and I will check your sack. Happy hunting!**

When the children have found the items, ask, **Was it fun looking for the things pictured on your sack? How did it feel when you found something you needed? How did you feel when you could not find one of the things? How did the woman in our Bible story feel when she found her lost coin? What did she do? Let's celebrate by singing "Be Glad, Not Sad."**

Bible Words

"If one of you is having troubles, he should pray. If one of you is happy, he should sing praises" (James 5:13).

Bible Memory: Ring the Bell

You will need a tin can bell made in the "I've Got Rhythm" activity. Hang this bell somewhere in the classroom where it can hang freely and be low enough to be rung by the children, such as in a doorway or from the ceiling.

Our Bible words remind us what to do when we're sad and happy. Let's play a game to learn them better.

Have the children stand in a line about eight to ten feet from the hanging bell. Point to the first child in line and say, "If one of you is having troubles, he should . . ." Tell the child to run up to the bell, say the missing word, "pray," and ring the bell. Ask the child to go to the end of the line. Say to the next child, "If one of you is happy, he should . . ." This child will run up to the bell and say, "sing praises." Continue down the line.

When everyone has had one turn, go through the line again, varying the number of words in each sentence you give. This will require the children to say more from memory.

▼ 3. What Does This Mean to Me? ▲

Praise Coins

You will need several 2" circles cut from cardboard, aluminum foil, heart stickers, a coin purse, and envelopes. For each child, cover a circle with foil to resemble a silver coin. Put a heart sticker on one side of each coin and put the coins in a coin purse. You will also need additional quantities of these supplies so that the children can make their own silver coins.

Gather the children around you and show the coin purse. Count out ten coins from the purse. **When the woman in the Bible story found her lost coin, what did she do? Yes, she shared the good news with her friends. I know some good news that's even better than finding a lost coin. It is the good news about God's love for me and you. When you know something good, you want to share it with others. Do you know some good news about God and Jesus you can share with others?** Let the children respond. Possible responses: Jesus loves me, God made me special, God takes care of me, God is with me all the time, Jesus wants me to follow Him, Jesus died and came back to life, I can live with Jesus in Heaven.

We're going to make coins you can take home with you. You can give your special coins to your family and your friends and tell them good news about God and Jesus.

Help the children make coins. Put each child's coins in an envelope with his name on it. If there's time, have the children practice giving a coin and telling good news about God and Jesus.

▼ 4. What Can I Do to Please God? ▲

Penny Posies

You will need copies of the flower picture from p. 200, the flower petal and easel patterns from p. 201, three pennies for each picture (or foil circles or pompoms), cardboard, and white glue.

Before class, use the flower petal pattern to trace and cut out several petals from gift wrap or wallpaper samples. Use the cardboard to cut a back and an easel for each picture.

Just like the woman who celebrated when she found her lost coin, we

can celebrate by sharing God's happiness with other people.

Give each child a flower picture. Tell the children to color only the stems, leaves, and vase. Demonstrate how to glue the gift wrap or wallpaper petals on the stems and then the pennies in the flower centers. Mount each picture on cardboard and attach to an easel as illustrated.

Do you know someone who is sick or feeling sad? Do you know someone who is lonely and needs a visit from you? Do you know someone who would enjoy your picture and spending time with you? Encourage each child to name someone to whom he will give his picture and share God's happiness.

Let's Be Glad!

You will need the words to "Be Glad, Not Sad" from p. 177, the tin can bells made today, the sandpaper blocks made in Lesson 30, and stickers for each child.

Organize the children into small groups and assign each an area of the classroom to clean and straighten. Provide dust cloths and hand brooms, or whatever the children need. As the children are working, walk around the room and compliment each child on his effort. Pass out stickers, smiles, and hugs!

Gather the children to sing the first two verses of "Be Glad, Not Sad." Pass out the tin can bells and let the children play along as they sing. To add variety, add the sandpaper blocks made during last week's lesson.

Ask the children to name people with whom they will share God's happiness. Use the names instead of singing "someone" in the last line of verse two.

Let's thank God for the happiness that we have shared with each other today. Ask several children to pray.

▼ Bonus Activity ▲

Snack Attack: Fruit and Veggie Coins

You will need bananas, carrots, and cucumbers. Peel them and slice them to make "coins."

Have the children wash their hands and pray before eating.

As the children eat, review the Bible story.

A Happy Father

Luke 15:11-24

Know: Happiness comes from God.

Feel: Eager to say and sing praises for God's goodness.

Do: Tell others about the happiness that God has given them.

Children will accomplish the goals when they
- Talk about how they love their families.
- Tell about a father whose lost son returns home.
- Recite James 5:13 and do what it says.
- Name ways to please God.
- Choose to show God's love by forgiving others.

▼ 1. What Is This Story About? ▲

I Love My Family Because . . .

You will need pictures of your family. Also, during the week before this lesson, call or write each child and ask him to bring pictures of his family to show the rest of the class. If any child forgets the pictures or is new to the class, give him paper and crayons to draw a picture of his family.

Gather the children around your family pictures and share what you love about each member of your family.

One at a time let each child share about his family. As he shows his pictures or drawings, ask questions about each person in his family. Encourage the children to tell something they love about each family member. **Let's say a prayer thanking and praising God for our families.** Pray with the children.

Today our Bible Story is about a father and his two sons. The father loved his sons very much, but one of the sons left home. This made the father sad. During the story, we will find out how the son made his father happy again.

I've Got Rhythm

You will need the words to "Be Glad, Not Sad" from p. 177, a shoe box lid or bottom and six rubber bands for each guitar, and a variety of stickers.

The rhythm instrument for this lesson is a shoe box guitar. Let the children decorate their shoeboxes with stickers. Then stretch the six rubber bands around the entire box length-wise. New rubber bands are less likely to break. Space the bands evenly. Demonstrate how to strum the guitar and sing.

Review the words to the first two verses of "Be Glad, Not Sad." Then teach the words to verse three. After the children have sung the new words several times, let them strum their guitars as they sing all three verses.

Our new song verse says, "If something makes you glad, praise the Lord." What makes you glad? I'm glad about my family. Tell the children something about your family that makes you glad.

What makes you glad about your family? Give each child a turn to share. **Praising God is one way to thank God for His goodness to us.**

Today our Bible story is about a father and two sons. During the story, we will find out why the father is sad and then is happy again.

2. What Does the Bible Say? ▲

Bible Story: A Sad Father Becomes a Happy Father

You will need transparency 8C, silhouette 8-f the son, three silhouettes of 8-g pig, and an overhead projector. (See p. 177 for directions on how to use the visual.)

Do you remember why Jesus told stories? Yes, His stories always taught a lesson. We have heard the stories of the lost sheep and the lost coin. These stories help us learn about God and Heaven. God is happy when one person chooses to do good. He is just like a shepherd who is happy when

a lost sheep is found. In the story of the lost coin, we learned to share happiness with others. We know there is happiness and joy when a person changes his heart and starts doing good.

Today we will hear a story about a sad father who becomes a happy father. Let's listen to this special story that was told by Jesus.

(Project transparency 8C.) A father had two sons. The father owned land and had many servants. He was rich.

(Add silhouette 8-f.) One day the youngest son asked his father for his share of the family land and money. The son took the money and went far away from home. *(Remove transparency 8C, but leave silhouette 8-f.)*

The son did not save any of his money. He wasted it, and one day the money was gone. Without money he couldn't buy food. He was very hungry, so he decided to get a job to earn enough money to buy food.

A man who owned a farm gave the boy a job feeding pigs. *(Add all three 8-g silhouettes.)* While the son was feeding the pigs, he was so hungry he wanted to eat the pig's food. But the farmer did not give him anything to eat. This made the son think about the money he had wasted. He thought about the food his father gave his servants. Right there, while feeding the pigs, the son decided to go back home to his father. *(Remove all the silhouettes. Project transparency 8C.)*

Back home, the father had missed his son. Every day he looked down the road to see whether his son was coming home.

One day when the father was looking down the road for his son, he saw him. *(Add silhouette 8-f.)* He started running to meet him. The father hugged and kissed his son. He was so happy. The son was happy, too.

The son said to his father, "I'm sorry. I wasted all of my money. May I have a job as one of your servants?"

The father replied, "No! You are my son. I want to have a party and celebrate with my friends. I will tell them my son was lost, but now he is found."

The father arranged a big celebration. He gave his son a new coat and a ring. The father wasn't sad any more. He was a happy father and he shared his happiness with his friends. *(Turn off the projector.)*

Story Review: A Family Picture

You will need a copy of the "Father and Son" picture from p. 204 for each child, crayons or markers, plastic drinking straws, and glue or tape. Before class, cut out the pictures and make a sample.

Ask the children to color the robes of the father and son different colors. Glue the father and son back-to-back with a straw sandwiched between. (Optional: Tape the straw to the picture and then add glue.) Let dry.

Using the sample to demonstrate, place the straw between the palms of your hands and roll the straw back and forth very quickly. You will see the father and son together.

Review the story using the following questions. The children can take turns answering the questions using the sample craft.

Who had two sons? (father)
Who asked for his share of the family money? (son)
Who took the money and went far from home? (son)
Who wasted his money and couldn't buy food? (son)
Who finally got tired of feeding pigs and decided to go home? (son)
Who kept looking for his son to come home? (father)
Who ran to meet his son when he saw him coming home? (father)
Who was happy? (father and son—twirl)
Who was sorry? (son)
Who forgave? (father)
Who celebrated together? (father and son—twirl)

Bible Memory: Prayer and Praise

You will need the shoebox guitars made in the "I've Got Rhythm" activity, the words to "Be Glad, Not Sad" from p. 177, and other familiar praise songs.

Let's say James 5:13 together. Repeat the verse several times to help the children review.

Now let's form a circle and pray together. James 5:13 says, "If one of you is having troubles, he should pray." Do you know of any troubles that we can pray about? Give ideas if needed. Let the children pray about these needs.

James 5:13 also says, "If one of you is happy, he should sing praises." Let's sing "Be Glad, Not Sad." Pass out the guitars and encourage children to "play" along. Sing other songs of praise. Lead the children in another prayer, praising God for His love and the happiness He gives.

▼ 3. What Does this Mean to Me? ▲

God's Love Goes Round and Round

You will need a quarter, a Sacagawea dollar, or a silver dollar.

Have the children stand and hold hands to form a circle. **This circle reminds me of God's love. A circle has no beginning and no end. God's love is like that. He will never stop loving you.**

Ask the children to stop holding hands and sit on the floor, but stay in a circle. Show your coin. Describe how it is completely round. It has no beginning and no end. It is like God's love. Describe the two sides of your coin. Explain that one side is called "heads" and the other side is called "tails." Demonstrate how you can spin the coin and how it finally falls down.

Let's think about ways we can show God how much we love Him. If the coin falls heads up, tell something you can do that would please God. If the coin falls tails up, tell something you can say that would please God.

Go around the circle and spin the coin in front of each child.

Just like the son in our Bible story, sometimes we will forget to do what pleases God. And just like the father in our Bible story who never stopped loving his son, God will never stop loving us.

▼ 4. What Can I Do to Please God? ▲

I Forgive You

You will need one copy of the four pictures from p. 202. Enlarge the pictures, if possible, and add color.

Our Bible story reminds us that God wants us to forgive other people.
Who made a bad choice in our Bible story? (son)
Who came home and said he was sorry? (son)
Who was waiting for him, ready to forgive him? (father)
The father in the story is like God. When we tell God we are sorry for doing wrong, He forgives us. He will never stop loving us.

Display one of the four pictures. Ask a volunteer to tell what is happening in the picture. **Who did something wrong? Who needs to say, "I'm sorry"? Who needs to forgive someone?**

Talk about the rest of the pictures and how the children can show forgiveness.

Close with prayer. Model a prayer: **Dear God, thank You for always loving me. Help me forgive when someone does something wrong to me. Help me show them your love.** Ask each child to pray for God's help to forgive others.

Let's Celebrate

You will need the words to "Be Glad, Not Sad" from p. 177, the guitars made during the "I've Got Rhythm" activity, the sand paper blocks made in Lesson 30, the tin can bells made in Lesson 31, and additional praise songs about joy, happiness, and God's love.

Let's pretend we are helping the father get ready for the party to welcome the son who has returned home. First let's clean the house. Assign jobs to all of the children to clean and straighten the classroom. After the room is clean, gather the children. **Now, let's celebrate by singing "Be Glad, Not Sad."** Pass out the shoebox guitars and other instruments made in previous lessons. Sing the first three verses and play the rhythm instruments. Sing other songs about joy, happiness, and God's love.

Close with prayer. Model a prayer: **Dear God, thank You for always loving me. Help me forgive when someone does something wrong to me. Help me show them your love.** Ask each child to pray for God's help to forgive others.

▼ Bonus Activities ▲

Snack Attack! Pig Food

You will need small, frozen corn on the cob, margarine, salt, carrots, toothpicks, vegetable parer, ice water, a bowl, plates, and napkins.

Before class, use the vegetable parer to cut the carrots into thin strips. Roll the strips and secure with toothpicks. Place the rolled strips in ice water to soak until the carrot strips curl like pig tails.

Prepare corn on the cob as directed on the package. Keep warm until served. Serve with margarine and salt.

Have the children wash their hands. Pray with the children before they eat. Thank God for the good food you have to eat and pray for those who are hungry.

As the children eat the corn on the cob, explain that, in North America, cobs are given to pigs for food. Explain that they didn't have corn in Israel, but whatever the pigs were eating was probably some kind of leftover garbage or plants parts that people would never eat.

Have you ever been really hungry? How did you feel? What did you want to eat? How do you think the son felt when he had no food to eat? Do you think he might have eaten the pig's food?

Extra Action! Feed the Pig

You will need the pig face pattern from p. 203, a paper grocery bag, scissors, glue, an X-Acto knife, and a wastepaper basket that the grocery bag will fit over.

Before class time, cut out the pig face. Open the paper bag and set it open side down. Glue the pig face on the bottom of the bag. Cut out the pig's mouth with an X-Acto knife, being sure to cut through the paper bag. Invert the paper bag over a wastepaper basket to play the game.

Line the children up about ten feet away from the grocery bag pig. Give each child something to feed the pig, such as leftover corncobs or banana peels wrapped in plastic wrap. Teach the children these words, "Yuck! I'm going back home to my father." Have the children run to the pig, drop the trash in his mouth and say, "Yuck! I'm going back home to my father." Then return to the end of the line.

After you have finished playing, gather the children around the pig and review the story. **Do you think the son made a good choice when he decided to go home to his father? How do you think he felt when his father gave a party to welcome him home?**

Be Happy Forever

Know: Happiness comes from God

Feel: Eager to say and sing praises for God's goodness.

Do: Tell others about the happiness that God has given them.

Children will accomplish the goals when they

- Discover what the Bible says about Heaven.
- Tell what John wrote about Heaven.
- Recite James 5:13 and praise God for His goodness.
- Name what they can tell someone about Heaven.
- Tell someone how wonderful Heaven is.

▼ 1. What Is This Story About? ▲

I've Got Rhythm

You will need the words to "Be Glad, Not Sad" from p. 177. You will also need to provide each child with a toilet paper cardboard tube, a four-inch square piece of waxed paper, a rubber band, and stickers for decorating the tubes.

Heaven is a very happy place. Everyone will sing praises to God and to His Son, Jesus. We're going to make another instrument to use when we praise God here.

Give each child a tube to decorate with stickers. Then demonstrate how to put the wax paper over one end of the cardboard tube and secure it with a rubber band to make a kazoo. Demonstrate how the kazoo works. Loosely hold the open end up to your mouth and sing.

Review and the first three verses of "Be Glad, Not Sad." Then teach verse four. After the children sing the new verse several times, divide the class into two groups. One will sing with the kazoos and the other will sing with the other instruments. Sing all four verses with the two groups, alternating who sings with kazoos.

What do you know about Heaven?

What does our song tell us about Heaven? (happy place, God is there, we'll live forever)

We'll learn about Heaven when we listen to the Bible story today.

Heaven Is a Rainbow of Color

You will need recorded songs about Heaven and songs of praise, tape or CD player, different colors of construction paper, gold and silver wrapping paper, and glue. Before class, cut the paper into 2" x 9" strips.

The Bible tells us that Heaven is a beautiful place. John, one of Jesus' followers, wrote about Heaven in the Bible. He said every color of the rainbow is there. Let's make something to remind us of how beautiful Heaven is.

Show the children how to make chains with the paper strips by gluing the ends of each strip together and linking strips. Keep the chains colorful by varying the colors of the loops. Make the chains as long as you need to provide a decoration in some area of your classroom (frame a doorway or window, loop from the ceiling, make a rainbow on a bulletin board).

As the children work on the chains, talk about Heaven.

What do you know about Heaven?

How many colors can you name? What is your favorite color?

Won't Heaven be a beautiful place?

We'll learn more about Heaven when we listen to the Bible story today.

▼ 2. What Does the Bible Say? ▲

Bible Story: John Sees Heaven

You will need transparency 8D, silhouettes 8-h, Jesus, 8-i, John, two of 8-j, angel, and an overhead projector. (See p. 177 for directions on how to use the visual. Coloring transparency 8D will help communicate the idea that Heaven is colorful.)

Do you ever wonder what Heaven will be like? I do. When Jesus was on earth, He used stories, such as the lost sheep, the lost coin, and the lost son, to tell people about God and Heaven. People have always wondered about Heaven. The Bible tells us some important things we need to know about Heaven. These things were written in a special book called Revelation by a preacher named John.

Once when John was on an island, Jesus visited him. He told John He wanted to show John Heaven. *(Project silhouettes 8-h and 8-i.)* **Jesus told John to write down what he saw. At first John was afraid, but Jesus told him not to be afraid.** *(Remove silhouette 8-h and move silhouette 8-i to the side.)*

As John watched, he saw the door to Heaven open. *(Project transparency 8D.)* **He could see God's throne. It was the most beautiful place he had ever seen. All the colors of the rainbow were there. It was very bright. Everything looked brand new. John wrote that everything looked like beautiful jewels. Everything sparkled.**

(Add two 8-j silhouettes beside the throne.) **John also saw many angels. They were singing praises about God and Jesus. They sang, "Holy, holy, holy is the Lord God All-Powerful. He was, he is, and he is coming"** (Revelation 4:8).

John wrote down everything he saw and heard. It was exciting to see Heaven.

He saw a beautiful city there. Its walls and gates were made of gold and jewels. Even the street was gold. A river flowed right down the middle of the street. It was clear and very shiny.

John noticed there was no sun or moon in Heaven. What made everything so bright and sunny? God and Jesus did! They are Heaven's light. Because they are there, Heaven never has night.

Everyone John saw was happy. No one was crying or sad. Why? God is living there with His people. Everyone will be happy forever.

As beautiful as the city is, the best part about Heaven is that Jesus is there. *(Add silhouette 8-h.)* **When John heard Jesus say, "I am coming to earth again soon," he was very excited! John replied, "Come quickly, Lord Jesus!"** *(Turn off the projector.)*

Story Review: Rainbow Cups

You will need a clear plastic cup for each child, three or more colors of gelatin, and plastic spoons.

Before class, mix one flavor of gelatin as directed on the package and pour a small amount into each cup. Chill until firm. Then prepare another flavor of gelatin. Let cool and then pour it on top of the first layer in each cup. Continue this until the cups are full.

After everyone washes hands, pray for the snack. Distribute the gelatin cups and spoons.

Our snack today reminds of Heaven and all the bright and shiny colors that are there. While we eat, let's remember what else John said about Heaven.

How many colors are in Heaven?

What are the walls and gates of Heaven made of?

What are the streets of Heaven made of?

Why is it so bright in Heaven?

Is there any sadness or crying in Heaven? Why not?

What is your favorite part of Heaven?

Bible Memory: Pop-up Praises

Our Bible words remind us to pray and praise. Let's say the words with the motions we learned.

Ask the children to stand in a circle. Review the motions taught in Lesson 30. Help the children recite the verse together using the motions.

Then help the children "do" the verse by leading them in a time of "pop-up praise." Tell the children to stoop down. Go around the circle and tap children who, one at a time, will "pop up" and praise God for something.

When all the children are standing, ask for volunteers to say the verse by themselves or with a friend.

Who can say our Bible words?

What should we do when we have troubles?

What should we do when we are happy?

In Heaven everyone will be praising God. We will be happy forever.

Bible Words

"If one of you is having troubles, he should pray. If one of you is happy, he should sing praises" (James 5:13).

▼ 3. What Does This Mean to Me? ▲

Crown of Life

You will need the words to "Be Glad, Not Sad" from p. 177, the crown pattern and instructions from p. 102, cardboard, aluminum foil, a music cassette or CD, a cassette or CD player, and the kazoos made today.

Make a crown using cardboard. Keep in mind that a child's head can be 21" in circumference. Cover the completed crown with aluminum foil.

Gather the children in a circle. **Jesus told John to write in his letter that everyone who believes in Him will be given a crown of life to wear in Heaven.** Show the cardboard crown. **This crown is not anywhere near as pretty as the one Jesus has promised, but we are going to use it to tell the good things we learned about Heaven from John's letter.**

As the music plays, have the children pass the crown around the circle. Stop the music. The child holding the crown puts it on his head and names something he can tell someone about Heaven. Start the music and continue passing the crown around the circle. Give every child a turn to wear the crown and tell about Heaven.

Pass out the kazoos and let the children sing all four verses of "Be Glad, Not Sad."

Heaven is a wonderful place. God and Jesus will be there. We will sing songs of praise, do many wonderful things, and be happy forever.

▼ 4. What Can I Do to Please God? ▲

Heaven's Gates

We're going to play a game to practice telling what we know about how wonderful Heaven is.

Play the following game the same way "London Bridge Is Falling Down" is played and sung.

Have the children form a circle. Designate two of them to be "Heaven's gates." These two children will stand facing each other, holding hands. Ask them to hold their arms up high as the children walk under them and sing the following words.

Heaven's gates are open wide, open wide, open wide.
Heaven's gates are open wide. Come on in.

When the word "in" is sung, have the two children lower their arms and trap the child passing through. The child in the gates will tell something wonderful she has learned about Heaven. Then sing the following words.

We are here to praise the Lord, praise the Lord, praise the Lord.
We are here to praise the Lord, God loves (child's name).

Have the two children lift their arms again and start the song over. Continue until each child has an opportunity to be in the gates and tell about Heaven.

Our Bible words remind us to praise God when we're happy. Heaven is a wonderful place, and we will want to praise God all the time.

Hooray for Heaven!

You will need the musical instruments made in the "I've Got Rhythm" activities of the four lessons in this unit, the words to "Be Glad, Not Sad" from p. 177, and other happy praise songs.

Ask the children to help clean the classroom so it will look "brand-new" like Heaven. Then gather the children for a time of singing praises. Pass out the kazoos and the other instruments made during this unit. Sing "Be Glad, Not Sad" and other happy praise songs. Between the songs, lead the children together in saying, "Hooray for Heaven!" Make this time together a very joyful celebration. Give each child a turn to name someone to tell about Heaven this week. Pray together, thanking God for Heaven.

▼ Bonus Activities ▲

Extra Action! Sun Catcher

You will need the crown stencil pattern from p. 204, white card stock, an X-Acto knife, waxed paper, several small hand-held pencil sharpeners, a variety of brightly colored old crayons with paper removed, a two-inch stack of newspapers, an iron, glue, a hole punch, yarn, and tape.

Copy the crown onto card stock, making two copies for each child. Use an X-Acto knife to cut out the center of the crown. (The outside frame will be used and the center is discarded.) Also, each child will need two pieces of waxed paper slightly larger than the crown cutout.

Let the children use the pencil sharpeners to shave the old crayons. Scatter a small amount of crayon shavings on one piece of the waxed paper. Put the second piece of waxed paper on top of the shavings. Carefully place this on the stack of newspapers and press down with a warm iron (not hot) for a few seconds. (Be sure that an adult stays between the children and the iron.)

Glue the ironed waxed paper between the two crown cutouts. Punch holes in the two top corners and tie on a piece of yarn for hanging the picture. Hang the sun catcher in a window using tape.

When the sun shines through the window, your sun catcher will remind you of the beautiful colors you will see in Heaven.

Be Glad, Not Sad
(Tune: "This Old Man")

Verse 1
When troubles make you sad,
Here's good news to make you glad.
With a smile and a giggle,
Say a prayer today!
God will hear and lead the way.

Verse 2
Our dear God and His Son,
They bring joy to everyone.
With a smile and a giggle,
We will not be sad!
Share the news, make someone glad.

Verse 3
If something makes you glad,
Praise the Lord and don't be sad.
With a smile and a giggle,
Sing a praise today!
God will hear. He is the way.

Verse 4
Heaven is a happy place,
God's love shines on every face.
With a smile and a giggle,
Happiness is there!
We'll live forever in God's care.

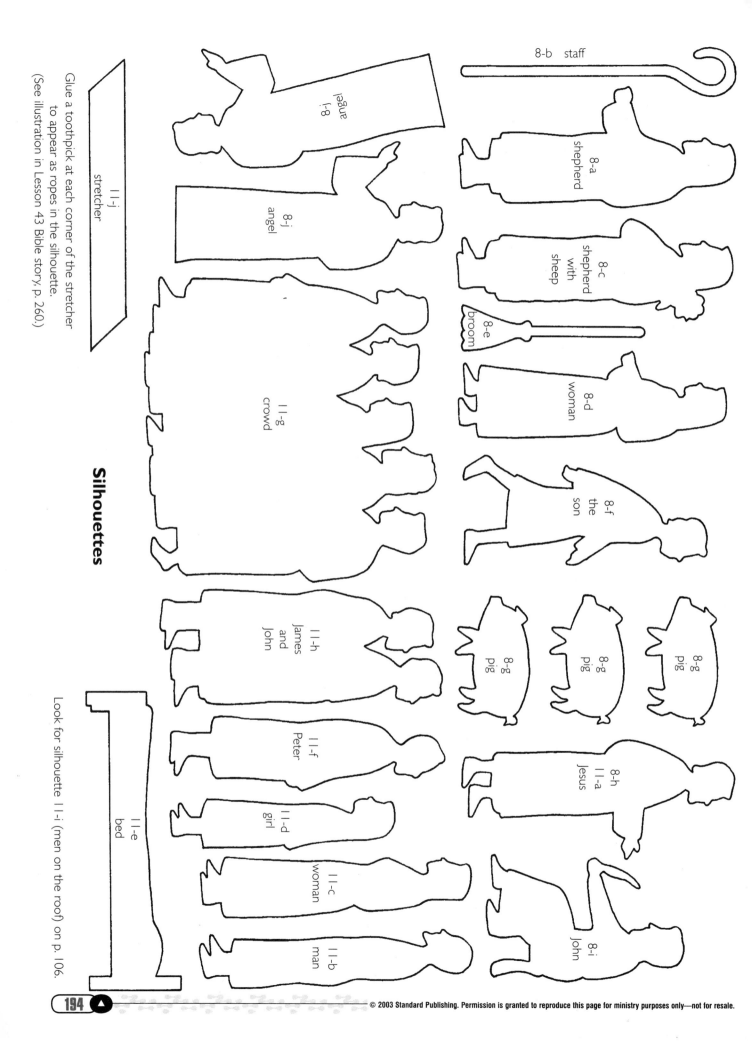

Silhouettes

Glue a toothpick at each corner of the stretcher to appear as ropes in the silhouette.
(See illustration in Lesson 43 Bible story, p. 260.)

11-j
stretcher

8-b   staff

8-a
shepherd

angel
8-i

8-j
angel

8-c
shepherd
with
sheep

8-e
broom

8-d
woman

11-g
crowd

8-f
the
son

11-h
James
and
John

8-g
pig

8-g
pig

8-g
pig

11-f
Peter

8-h
11-a
Jesus

11-d
girl

11-e
bed

11-c
woman

8-i
John

Look for silhouette 11-i (men on the roof) on p. 106.

11-b
man

194

8A

8B

8C

8D

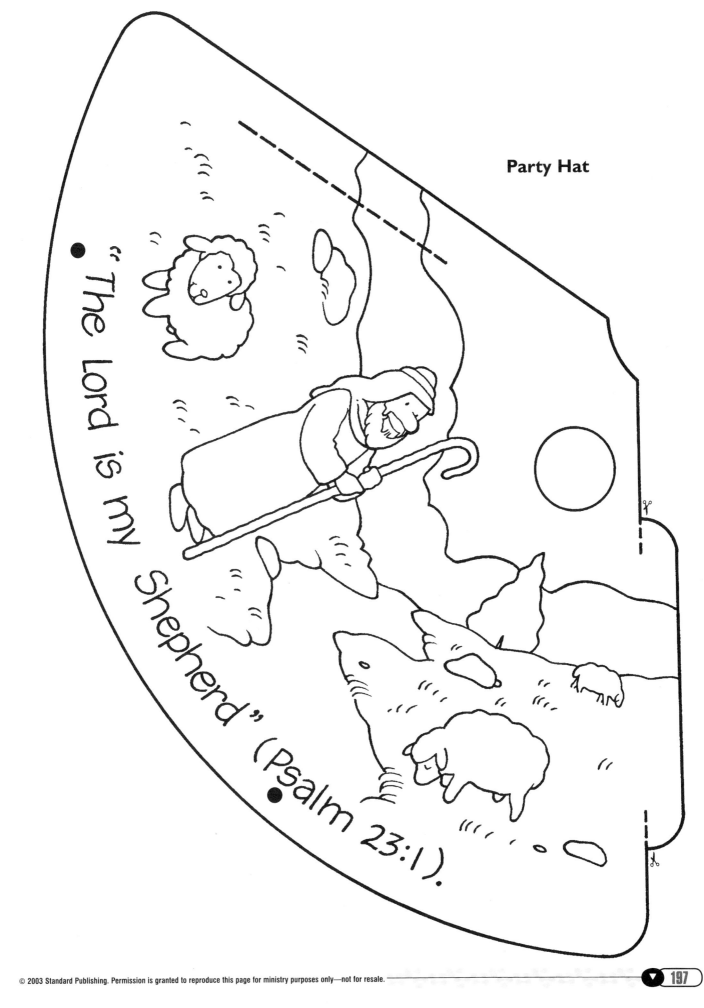

Party Hat

"The Lord is my Shepherd" (Psalm 23:1).

Glad/Sad Puppet

God Loves Me

Cut out and color as desired.
Fold into a cube.
Stuff with tissue to make the
   cube more durable.
Tuck in tabs and tape or glue.

Scavenger Hunt Pictures

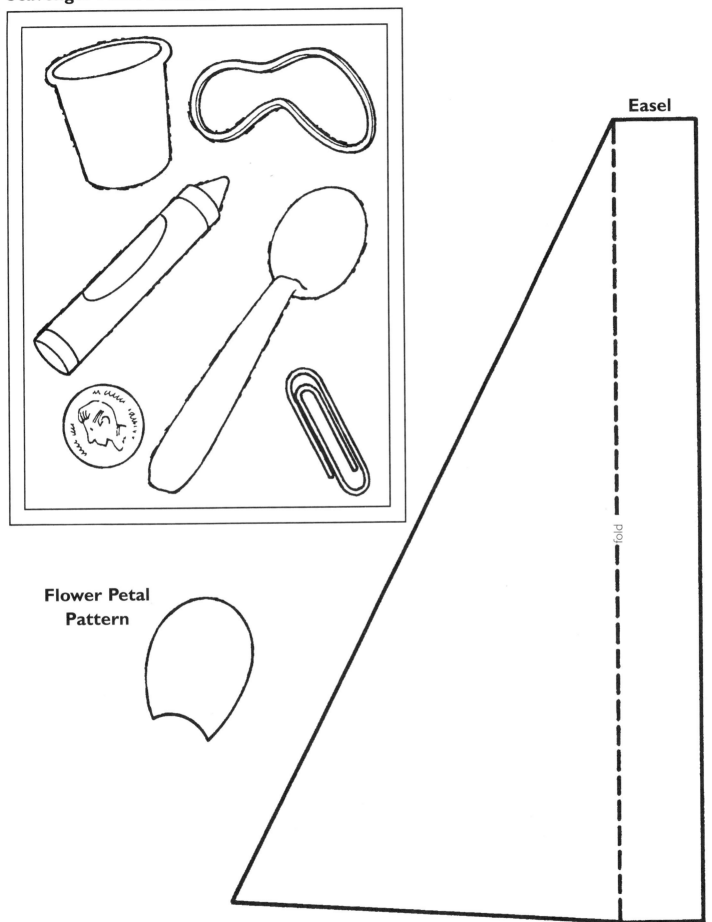

Flower Petal Pattern

Easel

fold

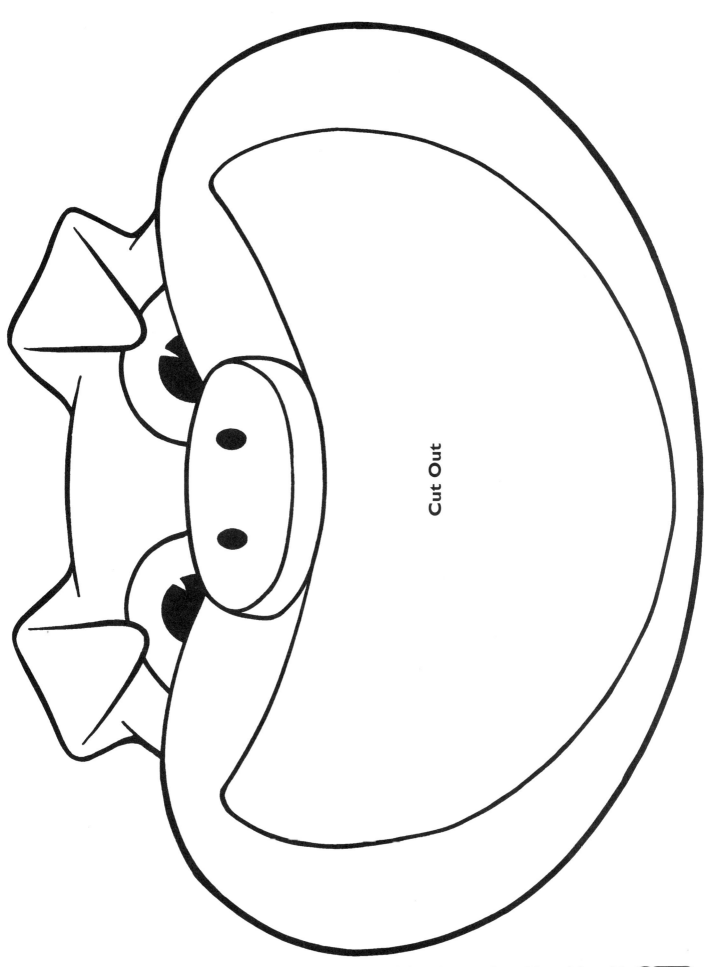

Cut Out

Father and Son

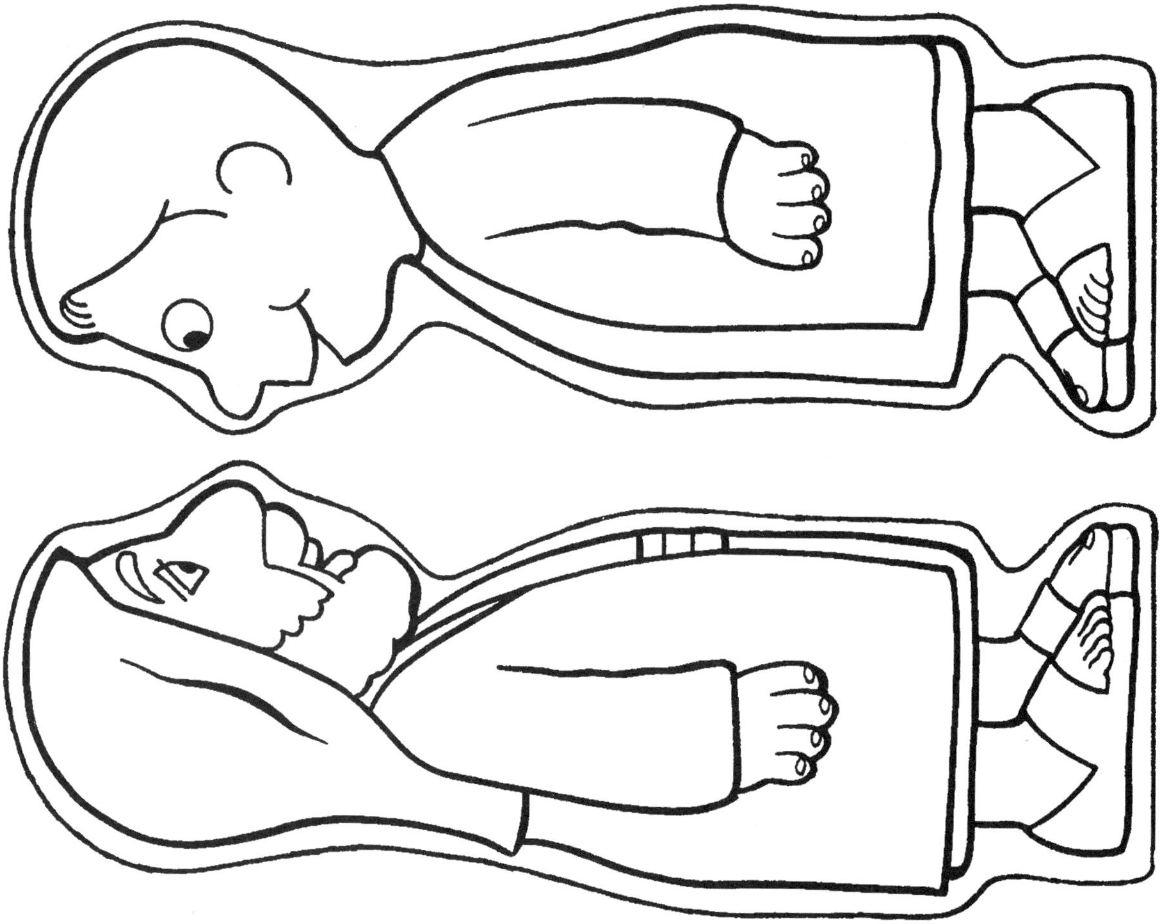

Crown Stencil

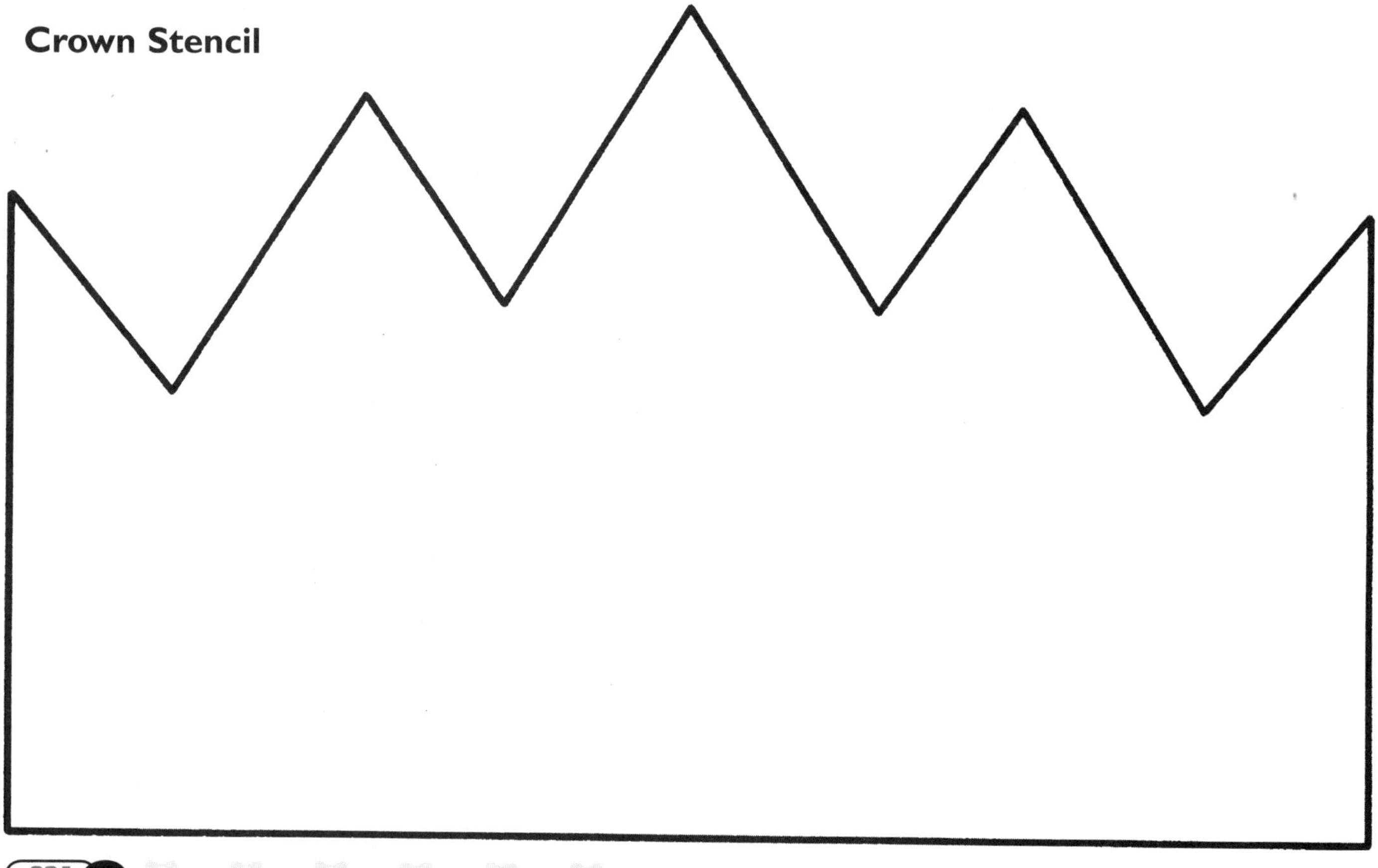

Learning to Be Thankful

Lessons 34-37

Unit Bible Words
"Give thanks to the Lord because he is good. [His love continues forever]" (Psalm 136:1).

(Note: This verse has been divided into two parts. If you are teaching four-year-olds, use only the first part. If you are teaching older children, also include the part of the verse in brackets.)

Bible Characters
Simeon, Anna, Jesus, Peter

34 Thank God for Jesus

Luke 2:22-38—All of the Old Testament prophecies about a Messiah are fulfilled when Jesus is born. Simeon and Anna recognize this fulfillment when they see Mary and Joseph carrying baby Jesus into the temple. Their hearts are filled with thanksgiving.

35 Thank God for Food and Clothes

Matthew 6:25-34; Psalm 136:1, 25—During the Sermon on the Mount Jesus uses birds and flowers to explain how important people are to God. God will always provide for His people. Instead of worrying about food and clothing, we should be thankful and do the things God wants us to do.

36 Thank God for Healthy Bodies

Acts 3:1-16; 4:1, 2, 18-22—Peter and John are passing by the Beautiful Gate on their way to the temple to pray when a disabled man asks them for money. Neither of them has any money, but Peter calls upon the power of Jesus to heal the man. Immediately the man stands up and begins jumping for joy and thanking God for healing him.

37 Always Remember to Thank God

Luke 17:11-19—On His way to Jerusalem, ten men who have leprosy stop Jesus. They ask Him to help them. Jesus sends them to see a priest who will check to see whether the leprosy is gone. As they go, they are healed. When they realize they are healed, only one man returns to say thank-You to Jesus.

By the end of this unit, the children and leaders will

Know: Why it is important to thank God for His goodness.
Feel: Thankful for God's love and care.
Do: Say "thank You" to God.

Why Teach This Unit to Four- to Six-Year-Olds?

Some parents begin training their children in manners at a very young age. Their children are just barely walking when they mutter their first "Sank shoe!" These parents beam with pride at their children's first attempts at good manners. As this training continues, the children are taught to respond to the question, "What's the magic word?" Then, as if by magic, things appear when the children respond with the proper "please" or "thank-you."

This training has its place, but this unit on being thankful is designed to create an environment where four-, five-, and six-year-olds meet people who demonstrate a thankfulness that comes from within. This appreciation is more than training in good manners. It is a heartfelt response to the power of the Lord God Almighty. It reflects an appreciation of God's love and care that overflows from the heart. This is the kind of thankfulness we want to teach in this unit.

Meet Simeon and Anna

Both Simeon and Anna yearned for God to send the promised Messiah. The suffering they endured as Jews under Roman rulers intensified their yearning.

Simeon was a devout man. The Holy Spirit promised him he would see the Messiah before he died. Through divine guidance, Simeon was in the right place at the right time to see Mary and Joseph as they presented baby Jesus in the temple. His heart overflowed with thankfulness.

Anna was also very devout in her worship of God. She never left the temple. Night and day she devoted herself to prayer and fasting. When she saw baby Jesus, she instantly knew He was the promised Messiah and began telling all of the worshipers in the temple the good news.

Meet Jesus

Jesus was present during the creation of the world, so it was natural for Him to use examples from creation in His teaching. When He spoke about the birds and the flowers, He spoke from firsthand knowledge.

Jesus was also the Master Teacher, and often used common things to describe profound truths. During the Sermon on the Mount, Jesus was teaching about internal attitudes. He did not want the daily worries about food and clothing to occupy people's attention. Instead, Jesus directed their energy toward doing God's will.

Meet Peter and the Lame Beggar

The resurrection of Jesus was the final proof Peter needed to become a very aggressive apostle. He boldly proclaimed the power of Jesus, even in the temple, the stronghold of the Jewish leaders. When a man who could not walk asked for money, he responded with more than generosity; Peter called upon the power of Jesus to heal the man.

The beggar had spent over forty years unable to walk. He was totally dependent upon his family, friends, and community for care and financial support. His joy at being released from this humiliating dependency was unrestrained. He jumped up and down with the aid of muscles that had never before worked. His thankfulness drew the attention of all the worshipers and leaders in the temple.

Meet the Ten Lepers

Leprosy was the dreaded disease of Bible times. It not only impaired and disfigured people, but it isolated them from their family and friends. Lepers were banned from any contact with healthy people. This contagious disease had no known cure. Lepers were confined to live and die in colonies outside the villages—poor, alone, and ostracized.

When the opportunity came to ask Jesus for help, these ten men ventured out of their confinement. At great risk of being stoned, they sought the Great Physician. They were not disappointed! But only one man returned to show his gratitude.

Unit Craft Project

The craft project for this unit is a wind chime. You and the children will work on it during each lesson. You need to gather some special items. You will need clear plastic lids from frozen non-dairy whipped topping or margarine (one per child), lids from cans of frozen juice concentrate (four per child), fishing line, and clear polyurethane spray.

Special Note:

The unit project for Unit 10 will require a little advance planning. You will need to send a Parent's Letter home with your students at the end of Unit 9, and you may want to make plans to involve the whole church. Please read about "Unit Project: Sharing With Others" on p. 230, and photocopy the letter from p. 247.

Unit Song

Thank-You Prayer
(Tune: "Three Blind Mice")

Verse 1
Morning prayer. Morning prayer.
Greet the new day. Greet the new day.
Thank You, dear God, for a brand new day.
Help me in all that I do and say.
The best way to start is to sing and pray—a morning prayer.

Verse 2
Noontime prayer. Noontime prayer.
Time for some lunch. Time for some lunch.
Thank You, dear God, for good food to munch.
My mother fixes a healthy lunch.
I like to eat food that has a crunch—a noontime prayer.

Verse 3
Playtime prayer. Playtime prayer.
Fun in the sun. Fun in the sun.
Thank You, dear God, for strong legs to run.
Riding bikes and playing can be great fun.
You're never too busy to hear just one—a playtime prayer.

Verse 4
Bedtime prayer. Bedtime prayer.
Thanks for the day. Thanks for the day.
For keeping my family and friends okay,
For helping me do my jobs and obey.
The best way to end the day is to pray—a bedtime prayer.

Thank God for Jesus

Luke 2:22-38

▼ 1. What Is This Story About? ▲

God's Promises

You will need a Bible, star A and star B from pp. 223 and 224, Plasti-Tak, and a firm surface on which to mount the star pieces (cardboard, bulletin board, wall).

Copy star A onto yellow paper and star B onto blue paper. Glue the stars back-to-back. Cut the stars apart on the solid lines so that you have six puzzle pieces. (Note: Only the yellow side will be used for this activity. The blue side will be used later in "Let's Thank God for Jesus.") Save at least one of these star patterns. You will need it two more times.

As you hold the Bible, display the center of the star so the word "Jesus" shows. **Our Bible tells us what happened when Jesus was born and the things He did on earth. These things are written in the part of the Bible called the New Testament. The Bible also tells what happened before Jesus was born. These things are written in the Old Testament. In this part of the Bible, God began telling His people that Jesus was coming to live on earth. Here are some of the things God promised.** As you add the points of the star, use the following comments to guide the children in discovering what the Old Testament told about Jesus' birth.

Baby: (Isaiah 9:6) Isaiah, God's messenger, told the people God would send His Son, Jesus, to earth as a baby.

Mary: (Isaiah 7:14) Isaiah also told the people that a young girl would have a baby boy.

Crown: (Isaiah 9:7) Isaiah told the people Jesus would be a new king.

Bethlehem: (Micah 5:2) Micah, another one of God's messengers, told the people that the new king would be born in Bethlehem.

Heart: (Isaiah 61:1) Isaiah also said God was sending Jesus to make the sad hearts of the people happy again.

What shape did all these messages make? Yes, it's a star. The Bible said a star would come from a certain family. (See Numbers 24:17.) **It was the family in which Jesus was born. He was the promised star.**

Let's pray and thank God for keeping His promises and sending Jesus to earth.

Sing-a-Long

You will need live or recorded music of songs about Jesus. Select songs that tell about His birth and ministry.

After the children sing a song, ask questions, such as: **Who is this song about? What was Jesus doing in this song? Who did Jesus help? Who was praising Jesus? Why?**

Know: Why it is important to thank God for His goodness.
Feel: Thankful for God's love and care.
Do: Say "thank You" to God.

Children will accomplish the goals when they

- Discover what the Old Testament says about Jesus' birth.
- Tell what Simeon and Anna did when they saw Jesus.
- Begin to memorize Psalm 136:1.
- Give reasons to thank God.
- Demonstrate ways to thank God for Jesus.

How to Say It
Micah: MY-kuh
Simeon: SIM-ee-un

▼ 2. What Does the Bible Say? ▲

Bible Story: Simeon and Anna Thank God for Jesus

You will need a baby doll wrapped in a blanket.

Jesus was born! God had promised He would send His Son to be the new king. God's people had been waiting and waiting.

Two of those people lived in Jerusalem. One was Simeon. He was a very good man who loved God with all of his heart. God promised him he would see Jesus before he died. The other was an old woman named Anna. She never left the temple. She stayed there worshiping God and praying.

Soon after Jesus was born, Mary and Joseph went to the temple in Jerusalem to offer a special prayer for their new baby. (Hold the doll, cradle it, and admire it as you speak.) **Simeon was there. When he saw Mary and Joseph carrying a baby, he walked over to them. When he looked at the baby, he knew in his heart that this was the Savior. He took Jesus in his arms and thanked God for keeping His promise to him. He said many things about Jesus that amazed Mary and Joseph.**

Anna was in the temple, too. She was praying and thanking God when she saw Mary, Joseph, and baby Jesus. She also knew in her heart that Jesus was God's Son. She began telling everyone in the temple the good news. She told them Jesus was the Savior.

Story Review: Star Search

Use the star pattern from "God's Promises" to trace and cut out a plain star for each child. You will also need a dark marker.

Give each child a star. Most children this age can recognize their name when it is printed. To review, print every child's name on a star as they watch. Then collect the stars.

Take the children out of the classroom. Have someone hide the stars. Tell the children they are to search for the star that has their name on it. If they find a star with another child's name, they are to leave it alone and continue looking for theirs.

Some of you found your stars right away. Others had to look and look. Did you want to give up looking? Remember Simeon and Anna in our Bible story? They had to wait and wait to see God's promised star, Jesus. Simeon and Anna did not give up.

What did Simeon do when he saw Mary and Joseph with Jesus?
How do you think he felt?
What did Anna do when she saw Mary and Joseph with Jesus?
How do you think she felt?

Bible Memory: Pass the Star

Before class, use the star pattern from the "God's Promises" activity to cut one star out of cardboard and cover it with aluminum foil for each group of ten children. You will also need a Bible.

Form circles of no more than ten children. Read Psalm 136:1 from the Bible to the children. Give a star to one child in each group and say the first word of the verse. Ask each child to pass the star to the child on his left. Say the second word. Continue passing the stars around the circles as each word of the verse is said. Encourage the children to say the words with you. Continue passing the stars until the children can say the verse with ease.

Our verse tells us to always give thanks to the Lord because He is good. Sending Jesus to earth was the very best thing God did for us. Let's pray and thank Him for sending Jesus.

Bible Words

"Give thanks to the Lord because he is good. [His love continues forever]" (Psalm 136:1).

(Note: This verse has been divided into two parts. If you are teaching four-year-olds, use only the first part. If you are teaching older children, also include the part of the verse in brackets.)

▼ 3. What Does This Mean to Me? ▲

Wind Chime (Part 1)

You will need one clear plastic lid (frozen non-dairy topping lid, margarine lid) and one frozen juice can lid for each child, a black permanent marker, a nail, hammer, fishing line, and scissors. You will also need colored permanent markers, glue, and clear gloss polyurethane spray.

This is a unit craft project. During each lesson a part of the wind chime will be made and attached to a clear plastic lid. You will need four frozen juice can lids (the kind with rounded edges) for each child. One will be used with each lesson to complete the unit craft.

Before class time, print "Thank You, God" on each lid with a permanent marker. Use the nail and hammer to punch a small hole near the top edge of each lid. String a five-inch piece of fishing line into the hole and tie it into a loop for a hanger. Punch four evenly spaced holes opposite the hanger. Label each lid with a child's name. (Or let the children do the printing.)

Make copies of the circles from p. 223. Cut out all of the circles. (Jesus and the star will be used for this lesson. Save the other circles for the following lesson.)

We are making wind chimes to remind us to thank God for all the good things He has given us.

Let each child color a Jesus and a star circle. Glue them back-to-back on the juice can lid.

Have an adult punch a hole in the top of the circles with a nail and hammer. After the children have decorated their lids, spray both sides with polyurethane. (Spraying outdoors is best.) When dry, tie a ten-inch piece of fishing line from the juice can lid to the plastic lid. (Or, so that you don't get the lids mixed up, let each child attach his lid to his circle and then take all the wind chimes outside for spraying.)

Keep these for the next lesson when another juice can lid will be attached. If a child is absent today, set aside the materials he will need. Let him catch up during the next class.

Today we added a chime that will remind us to say thank-You for Jesus.

Why do you want to thank God for Jesus? Let children respond. Possible reasons: Jesus loves me, Jesus heals people, Jesus is powerful, Jesus loves everyone, Jesus helps people.

▼ 4. What Can I Do to Please God? ▲

Let's Thank God for Jesus

You will need the star from the "God's Promises" activity, Plasti-Tak, and a hard surface on which to display the parts of the star.

Display the yellow side of star A first. As you talk about ways to thank God, turn over the center to display the words, "Thank You, God, for Jesus." Then turn over each of the points of the star as they are discussed. When the activity is completed, the entire blue side of the star, star B, will be showing.

Let's take our yellow star and use it to discover how to say, "Thank You, God, for sending Jesus to earth." Turn over the yellow center.

Lips: **Simeon and Anna said words of praise, thanking God for sending His Son Jesus. They also told others what they knew about Jesus. Simeon told Mary and Joseph. Anna told everyone in the temple. You can tell your friends and your family about Jesus. What would you tell them about Jesus?** Encourage the children to respond.

Music notes: **What are these? Yes, they are music notes. These notes**

remind us to sing songs praising God for Jesus. Do you have a favorite song about Jesus? Let's sing some right now.

Praying hands: **What are these? Yes, they are hands. They remind us to pray. Praying is talking to God. What would you like to say to God about His Son, Jesus?** Let the children respond. Then lead them in saying special prayers to God about Jesus.

Heart: **This heart is to remind us to say thank-You to God for Jesus by sharing His love with others. Jesus is God's gift of love. We can say thank-you by loving others the way God and Jesus love us. How can you show love to others?** Encourage the children to respond.

Coins: **What is the picture on this last point? Yes, it is money. When we give our offerings, we are saying thank-You to God. Our offerings are used to tell others the good news about Jesus. Our offerings could be used to buy Bibles, or food for a hungry person.**

When the entire blue star is showing, review the names of each point. Then lead the children in prayer, thanking God for sending Jesus.

A Morning Prayer

You will need the words of the unit song, "Thank-You Prayer," from p. 206 and a copy of the picture for verse 1 from p. 225.

Enlarge the picture if possible. Then color it and mount it on poster board.

Direct the children in helping to clean and straighten the classroom. Then gather them and show the picture for verse 1 of the unit song. Teach the words to the verse. **What can you thank God for when you wake up in the morning?** Allow responses and then ask the children to say thank-you prayers.

All day long we can thank God for His goodness and for Jesus. When you come back to our next class time, we will sing another verse thanking God.

▼ Bonus Activity ▲

Snack Attack! Stars Galore

You will need to bake star-shaped cookies before class time, or order plain ones from a bakery. Provide different colors of tubes of frosting and paper towels.

Have the children wash their hands. Give each child a paper towel section and several star cookies. Let them take turns using the tubes of frosting to squeeze colorful dots on the cookies as decorations.

Lead the children in a thank-you prayer before they eat. While the children are eating, review today's Bible story and who the promised star was.

At night we can see many stars in the sky. When you see the stars, remember to thank God for sending the star He promised, His Son, Jesus.

Thank God for Food and Clothes

LESSON 35

Matthew 6:25-34; Psalm 136:1, 25

▼ 1. What Is This Story About? ▲

Birds and Flowers

Gather some picture books about birds and flowers from your local library, home library, and friends.

Let's think about how God takes care of the birds and flowers.

Let the children look at the books at their own pace. Go from child to child asking questions about the books. Then gather the children around you as you share one of the books with the entire group.

If there is time, play "Flower, Flower, Bird" like "Duck, Duck, Goose." When the tapper taps a child and says, "bird," the "bird" must fly around the circle and try to catch the tapper before the tapper gets back to "bird's" place.

Have you ever seen a bird plant seeds to grow his own food? Have you ever seen a flower sew beautiful designs to wear?

God takes care of the wonderful things He made. In our Bible story we will hear what Jesus said about God's care.

Food and Clothes

You will need two tables; a variety of foods for tasting (foods that are sweet, such as banana slices or apple slices; salty foods, such as crackers or potato chips; and sour foods, such as dill pickle slices); different types of clothing to display (winter clothes, summer clothes, rain gear, and beach wear); the words of "Thank-You Prayer" from p. 206, a copy of the picture for verse two from p. 225, and poster board.

Enlarge the picture if possible. Then color and mount it on poster board. Set up two tables. Use one for clothing and one for food.

Gather the children around the clothing table and let them browse for a few minutes and then lead them in a discussion about the different kinds of clothes they wear. **When your mother or dad or aunt or grandmother buys you new clothes, do you say, "Thank you"? Do you thank God for your new clothes, too? We should be thankful for our clothes. Our winter clothes help keep us warm. Our summer clothes keep us cool. I'm glad we have different kinds of clothes. What kind of clothes do you wear when it rains? When it snows? When you go swimming?**

At the food table, encourage the children to try a bite of each food. Talk about their favorite foods. **Do you remember to thank God for the food you eat at breakfast, lunch, and dinner? It is good to thank God. He is very good to us.**

Show the picture for verse two and teach the words for the second verse of "Thank-You Prayer." Sing it several times.

▼ 2. What Does the Bible Say? ▲

Bible Story: God Cares for Us

You will need a real flower and a real bird in a cage. If a real bird cannot be

---

Know: Why it is important to thank God for His goodness.
Feel: Thankful for God's love and care.
Do: Say "thank You" to God.

Children will accomplish the goals when they
- Explore how God takes care of His creation.
- Tell what Jesus taught about God's care.
- Memorize Psalm 136:1.
- Give reasons to thank God.
- Thank God for His love and care.

obtained, get a feathered one from a craft store, or use the bird picture from p. 223 (wind chime circle). If using the bird picture, enlarge it on a copy machine. Color and cut out the picture and glue a craft stick to the back for a handle.

People followed Jesus everywhere He went. He was a good teacher. He taught people about God's love and care. They liked to hear Him talk about God. When Jesus talked about God, the people could understand. He used things the people understood to describe God's love and care.

One day many people gathered on a hillside. They sat on the soft grass. The birds were flying over their heads and the flowers were blooming. The people listened very carefully to everything Jesus was saying. He told them what they could do to please God. He said it was important to love and worship God. He taught them how to pray. Everything He said was good.

(Show the bird.) **Then Jesus said, "Look at the birds flying up in the sky. Do they plant seeds the way a farmer does to grow their food? Do the birds collect the grain that grows from the seeds? Do they have barns for storing grain?"**

What do you think the answer is to these questions? You are right! Of course, birds do not plant seeds, gather grain, or store it in barns. How do the birds get food to eat? Listen to what Jesus said. He said, "God feeds the birds."

We know that is true. Just think of all the birds that you see every day at your house or at the playground. You might put some birdseed in a bird feeder, but there are too many birds in the world for you to feed! God takes care of them all.

Why did Jesus tell the people not to worry about food? He said, "You are much more important to God than the birds. Do not worry about getting enough food to eat. God will give you all the food you need."

Let's stop and thank God for our food. *(Lead in prayer.)*

Jesus wanted the people to know more about God's care, so He said, "Look at the flowers. *(Show a real flower.)* **Do flowers work to earn money to buy their beautiful colors? Do they sew beautiful designs for their petals?"**

Do you know the answer to those questions? You are right again! Of course, flowers do not work or make clothes to wear. Who do you think makes the flowers look so beautiful? Yes, God does. Jesus told the people that even the richest king in the world does not have clothes as beautiful as a flower.

Why did Jesus tell the people not to worry about clothes to wear? He said, "God knows what you need and will take care of you."

Let's thank God for our clothes. *(Lead the children in prayer.)*

Story Review: Flowers vs. Birds

Divide the class into two even groups. Call one group the "Flowers" and the other group the "Birds." Read Matthew 6:25-29 aloud to the children. When the flower group hears the word "flowers," tell them to stand up and say, "How pretty!" When the bird group hears the word "birds," tell them to stand up and say, "Yummy seeds!" Read the verses slowly so that the children can hear and respond at the appropriate times. Read the verses again and this time have the groups switch. The birds are now the flowers and the flowers are the birds.

Why does Jesus not want us to worry about food? Why does Jesus not want us to worry about clothes? Yes, God is our father and He will take care of us. Can worrying grow food? Can worrying make clothes? Who does God love more than He loves birds? Who does God love more than He loves flowers? Let's pray and thank God for loving us the most.

Bible Memory: Give the Shirt Off Your Back Relay

You will need one adult T-shirt for every ten children. The size will depend on the size of your students.

Review the words to Psalm 136:1 before beginning this relay.

Divide your class into groups of no more than ten students. Subdivide each group

Bible Words

"Give thanks to the Lord because he is good. [His love continues forever]" (Psalm 136:1).

(Note: This verse has been divided into two parts. If you are teaching four-year-olds, use only the first part. If you are teaching older children, also include the part of the verse in brackets.)

into two teams. Keep a space of about ten feet between the teams. Give the first child on one team a T-shirt to put on over his clothes. Give a signal for this child to run to the first child on the opposite team. Have the runner recite Psalm 136:1 and then take off the T-shirt and give it to the child. (This runner then goes to the end of the line.) The receiver puts on the T-shirt and runs to the opposite team and recites the memory verse and removes the T-shirt. Give each child at least two turns. This relay just goes on and on. If a child asks when the game ends say, **This game never ends! It just goes on and on! This game reminds me of God's love. His love for us goes on and on. It never ends.** If no one asks say, **We must stop because we have other things to do, but this game reminds me of God's love. . . .**

▼ 3. What Does This Mean to Me? ▲

Wind Chime (Part 2)

You will need the wind chimes started in last week's lesson, a frozen juice can lid and the two circles (bird on flower, shirt and banana) from p. 223 for each child. You will also need permanent markers, glue, clear polyurethane spray, a nail, hammer, and fishing line.

This is a unit craft project. During this lesson, another part of the wind chime will be made and attached to the clear plastic lid.

We are making wind chimes. They will make a pretty sound when the wind blows and remind us to thank God for all the good things He has given us.

Have the children color the circles and glue them back-to-back on a juice lid. Have an adult punch a hole in the top of the circles with a nail and hammer. Spray both sides of the juice can lids with polyurethane. (Spraying outdoors is best.) When dry, tie a ten-inch piece of fishing line from the juice can lid to the plastic lid. Or, so that you don't get them mixed up, tie each child's circle to his wind chime, and then take them all outside to spray.

Keep the wind chimes for the next lesson when another juice can lid will be attached. If a child is absent today, set aside the materials she will need. Let her catch up during the next class.

Today we added a chime that will remind us to thank God.

What will these pictures remind us to thank God for? (Thank God for birds, flowers, food, clothing, God's love and care for us.)

What are some other reasons to thank God? (Thank God for Jesus.)

▼ 4. What Can I Do to Please God? ▲

What's Happening?

You will need familiar praise songs and a copy of the six pictures on p. 227. Enlarge the pictures. Add color and mount them on construction paper.

Jesus told the people not to worry about food and clothes. Do you know what Jesus told the people to do instead? He told them to obey God.

Here are some pictures showing children obeying God. Let's see what they are doing.

Use the following comments to discuss the action in each picture.

Picture 1: **What are the two children doing? How many pictures are they coloring? How many boxes of crayons do you see? How are these children obeying God? What things can you share to show you want to obey God?**

Picture 2: **What is this child doing? When you hug someone, how does that person feel? How is this child obeying God? How can you show love so God will know you want to obey Him?**

Picture 3: **What are these two children doing? Are they sad or happy? How are they obeying God? With whom can you share happiness?**

Picture 4: **What is this child doing? What do you think the child is saying to God? Is this child obeying God? Name other things for which we can thank God.**

Picture 5: **Why is the baby crying? What is the child doing? How is the child obeying God? How can you help others and show you want to obey God?**

Picture 6: **Why is this child singing? Is this child obeying God? Do you have a favorite song you like to sing to Jesus?** Let the children suggest and sing several songs.

Let's take time to pray to God right now. What are some things we want to tell God today? Ask the children to respond. Include these ideas: **Thank You, God, for loving and caring for us; Thank You, God, for our food and clothes; Thank You, God, for helping us learn to obey You.** Pray a short thank-you prayer; then give each child a turn to pray.

Feathered Friends

You will need the words to "Thank-You Prayer" from p. 206 and the pictures from p. 225 for the first two verses.

Ask the children to pretend they are birds and fly around the room, cleaning up their nests. Then gather the children around you and show the pictures for the first two verses of the unit song. Discuss what is happening in each picture and sing the verses. Ask the children to pray and thank God for His goodness.

▼ Bonus Activities ▲

Snack Attack! A Bird's Nest

You will need the words to "Thank-You Prayer" from p. 206, chow mein noodles, waxed paper, peanut butter, and grapes. (Check for peanut allergies. Melted chocolate may also be used, and jellybeans instead of grapes.)

Arrange the noodles in small circles on waxed paper, one for each child. Heat the peanut butter until runny. Pour it over the chow mein noodles. When this is cool enough to touch, shape the noodles into small cup-shaped nests. Before serving, add three grapes in the center of the nest for the bird eggs.

Prepare the nests ahead of time unless you have a kitchen or microwave available for heating the peanut butter. Then involve the children in shaping the nests and adding the grapes. Make sure everyone washes hands first.

Before eating, have the children sing the second verse of "Thank-You Prayer." Then lead the children in thanking God for the food and for His love and care.

Extra Action! Fruit Basket Upset

Play "Fruit Basket Upset." Have the children sit on chairs in a circle. Ask them to name their favorite fruits. Select four fruits to be used in the game. Go around the circle telling each child what "fruit" he will be in the "basket." Review the names of the different fruit by asking the children to stand as their fruit is called.

Remove one chair from the circle. The child who was sitting on that chair will be the first caller and will stand in the center. The caller shouts the name of a fruit in the basket. The children who are that fruit, plus the caller, must run to a different chair and sit on it. The child left without a chair calls out another fruit and those children exchange chairs. The caller can also say, "Fruit Basket Upset." Then all of the children must change chairs.

Always remember to thank God for creating the fruit trees that give you good food to eat.

Thank God for Healthy Bodies

Acts 3:1-16; 4:1, 2, 18, 22

▼ 1. What Is This Story About? ▲

Watch My Shadow

You will need a copy of the picture for verse 3 from p. 226 and the words to "Thank-You Prayer" from p. 206, poster board, an overhead projector, and a blank wall. If a blank wall is not available, cover a wall with a plain sheet.

Enlarge the picture if possible. Color and mount it on poster board. Shine the light from the overhead projector onto the wall or sheet.

Let the children take turns standing in the light, facing the wall. As they move, they will see their shadows on the wall. Let the children demonstrate what they can do with their bodies.

Let's watch Joseph move his arms. Show us how your shadow can wave, Joseph. Kayla, can you make your shadow's head say no and yes? Good for you. Abigail, can you make the legs of your shadow jump up and down?

All of you can do many things with your bodies. Who made your bodies so strong? Yes, God did.

Show the picture for verse 3. **Here is another verse to our song, "Thank-You Prayer." This verse is a playtime prayer. We should always remember to thank God for our strong bodies that help us play and run.** Teach the third verse. Then lead the children in a thank-you prayer for their bodies.

Kindness in Action

Find a job your students can do. It can be cleaning up your classroom or another area of the building. Look outdoors for jobs, such as picking up litter or watering plants.

God has given us strong bodies for playing. He also has given us strong bodies to help others. We can show God how thankful we are for our strong bodies by helping others.

After the children have completed their kind deed, gather them and lead them in a prayer time. Encourage the children to thank God for their ability to help others.

▼ 2. What Does the Bible Say? ▲

Bible Story: Something Better Than Money

You will need the jointed figure used in Unit 1 and found on p. 25, six paper fasteners, scraps of material, scissors, glue, and markers.

Cut out the figure pieces and join them with paper fasteners as illustrated on p. 25. Add material for clothing and draw in facial features.

Do you know what being disabled means? It means that part of a person's body is not strong, or doesn't work right. A person who is "lame" cannot walk because his legs are not strong. In Bible times, people who were lame, or whose arms did not work, could not work to earn money. Their family and friends took care of them. Disabled people were often very

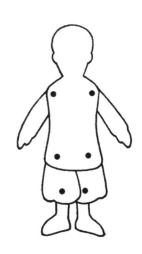

> **Know:** Why it is important to thank God for His goodness.
> **Feel:** Thankful for God's love and care.
> **Do:** Say "thank You" to God.
>
> **Children will accomplish the goals when they**
> - Demonstrate things their bodies can do.
> - Tell how a lame man was healed by God's power.
> - Recite Psalm 136:1.
> - Give reasons to thank God.
> - Thank God for their bodies.

poor. Begging was the only way they could get money for food and clothes. It was a very hard life.

Our story today is about one of these men. *(Show the jointed man.)* **This man could not walk, so every day some of his friends carried him to the temple gate.** *(Set the figure in the open palm of your hand.)* **He would sit by the gate all day, begging for money from the people going into the temple.**

One afternoon Peter and John came to the temple to pray. As usual, the man who could not walk was sitting by the gate. "Please give me some money," begged the man.

"I do not have any money," replied Peter. "But I can give you something better. By the power of Jesus, stand up and walk!"

Peter took the man's hand and helped him stand up. *(Help the jointed figure to stand.)* **Right away the man's legs and feet became strong. Move the figure's legs up and down. The man jumped up! He could stand! He could walk! Never before had his legs been strong enough for him to stand. Now he could walk on them. He could even jump. Yes, being able to walk was better than money!**

The man was very happy! He followed Peter and John into the temple. He could not stop jumping up and down. As he jumped and walked, he praised God. Many people saw him. They knew he was the man who had never before been able to walk who had sat begging at the gate. *(Move the legs of the figure up and down.)* **All of the people were amazed, but they wondered how such a wonderful thing happened.**

Peter started teaching the people about Jesus. Peter told the people that the man was healed by the power of Jesus.

Story Review: Give Thanks for Your Body

You will need a blindfold, a roll of paper towels, and a bag of pretzels.

To help the children understand how important different parts of their bodies are, use the following activities to limit the use of a part of their body. (Be sensitive to children who have physical handicaps.) Set up different centers where they can do these activities. You will need an adult or teen helper at each center. Let the children go from center to center doing the activities. If you have limited help, do the activities one at a time with all of the children.

Eyes: Place a blindfold over a child's eyes. Lead the child around the room. **When you cannot see with your eyes, you need someone to help you walk safely around our classroom. Are you thankful that God gave you eyes so you can see? Who saw the man who could not walk sitting by the temple gate?**

Hands: Place two or three pretzels on a paper tower. Have the child put his hands behind his back and tell him to pick up the pretzel with his mouth and teeth. **When you cannot use your arms and hands, you have to use another part of your body. It might be fun to pick up pretzels with your teeth, but soon you will get tired of not being able to use your arms and hands. Let's always thank God for our arms and hands. In our story, who used his hands to clap for joy?**

Legs: Ask a child to stand with his arms at his side and his left shoulder and leg against a wall. Then tell the child to lift up his right leg. Encourage him to keep trying, even though it is impossible. **How did it feel when you could not pick up your right foot? Did it feel strange not to be able to do something so easy? We walk and run without thinking about what our legs and feet are doing. Let's remember to say thank-you to God for strong legs. How did the man who could not walk show he was thankful when his legs became strong? Yes, he jumped up and down and praised God. Let's jump up and down and show God how strong our legs are, too. Now, let's thank God and praise Him for our healthy bodies.** Ask the children to say prayers of thanks to God for their bodies.

Bible Memory: Clap Your Hands

You will need the words to "Thank-You Prayer" from p. 206.

Say the Bible words several times to review them with the children. Then teach the following rhythm as you recite the words. Do not be concerned about everyone staying in rhythm together. Just have fun!

Give thanks *(Slowly clap as you say each word.)*
to the Lord *(Quickly clap as you say each word.)*
be-cause *(Slowly clap on each syllable.)*
He is good. *(Quickly clap as you say each word.)*
His love *(Slowly clap as you say each word.)*
con-tin-ues *(Quickly clap on each syllable.)*
for-ev-er *(Slowly clap on each syllable.)*
(Psalm 136:1). *(Quickly clap on each syllable.)*

God has given us hands to clap. It is fun to try new things with our hands. At first it might be hard, but the more you do something, the easier it gets. Raise your hand if you can print your name. When you were learning, you had to print the letters over and over. Sometimes your hand got tired, but soon you could print your name without help. Ask the children to give other examples of things they have learned or are learning to do with their bodies. **Let's always give God thanks for helping our bodies learn to do new things.**

Sing the third verse of "Thank-You Prayer."

Bible Words

"Give thanks to the Lord because he is good. [His love continues forever]" (Psalm 136:1).

(Note: This verse has been divided into two parts. If you are teaching four-year-olds, use only the first part. If you are teaching older children, also include the part of the verse in brackets.)

▼ 3. What Does This Mean to Me? ▲

Wind Chime (Part 3)

You will need the wind chimes started in Lesson 34, a frozen fruit juice can lid and two circles from p. 224 (girl, boy) for each child. You will also need permanent markers, glue, clear polyurethane spray, a nail, hammer, and fishing line.

This is a unit craft project. During this lesson, another part of the wind chime will be made and attached to the clear plastic lid.

We are making wind chimes that will make a pretty sound when the wind blows. The sound will remind us to thank God for all the good things He has given us.

Have the children color the circles and glue them back-to-back on one juice lid. Have an adult punch a hole in the top of the circles with a nail and hammer. Spray both sides of the juice can lids with polyurethane. (Spraying outdoors is best.) When dry, tie a ten-inch piece of fishing line from the juice can lid to the plastic lid. Or, so that the circles don't get mixed up, tie them to each child's wind chime first and then take them outside to spray.

Keep these for the next lesson when another juice can lid will be attached. If a child is absent today, set aside the materials he will need. Let him catch up during the next class.

Today we added a chime to remind us to thank God.

What do these new pictures remind us to thank God for? (Thank God for our bodies; thank God for creating us.)

What are some other reasons to thank God? (Thank God for birds and flowers, food and clothing, God's love and care, Jesus.)

▼ 4. What Can I Do to Please God? ▲

Exercise Time

You will need active songs the children know, such as "Head and Shoulders, Knees and Toes."

Have the children form a circle with lots of space for movement. Sing active songs the children know. Then ask a child to stand in the center of the circle and tell what his favorite exercise is. Give each child a turn to lead the group in an exercise.

Exercise is one way we keep the bodies God has given us healthy. You should exercise every day. When you take good care of your body, God knows you are thankful for it.

Let's exercise our legs by kneeling and take some time to pray. What are some things you want to tell God today? Ask the children to respond. Include these ideas: **Thank You, God, for loving and caring for us; Thank You, God, for making us with special bodies; Help us take good care of our bodies.** Pray a short thank-you prayer; then give each child a turn to pray.

Take Time to Pray

You will need the words to "Thank-You Prayer" from p. 206 and the mounted pictures for the first three verses from pp. 225 and 226.

Ask the children to use their strong and healthy bodies to help straighten the classroom. Then gather them around you and show the pictures for the three verses of "Thank-You Prayer." Review what is happening in each picture and sing the verses.

Every day, let's remember to thank God for His love and goodness. Sometimes we get so busy playing, we forget to thank God for our legs and arms. Our bodies help us enjoy fun times with our family and friends.

Let the children take turns giving thanks to God.

▼ Bonus Activity ▲

Snack Attack: Healthy Food for Healthy Bodies

You will need the words to "Thank-You Prayer" from p. 206, slices of fresh fruits and vegetables, and paper plates for the children.

Be sure the children wash their hands. Sing the second verse of "Thank-You Prayer." Then lead the children in a special prayer, thanking God for good food that makes their bodies healthy and strong.

While the children are eating, use the following questions to review the Bible story.

What part of your body is not strong if you are lame?
Where were Peter and John going?
What did the lame man ask for?
What did Peter say to the man?
What did the power of Jesus do for the man?
How did the man show he was thankful?
How can we show God we are thankful for our healthy bodies?

Always Remember to Thank God

Luke 17:11-19

▼ 1. What Is This Story About? ▲

Practice Saying Thank-You

You will need a small white paper plate, a jumbo craft stick, and a rubber band for each child. You will also need glue, a ball of string, a stapler, crayons or markers, and yarn in hair colors.

Twenty-four hours before the class session, glue a craft stick onto the back of each paper plate for a handle. Also tie a twelve-inch piece of string to each rubber band, and staple the rubber band onto each plate to form a mouth. Be sure the string is attached to the lower lip. See the illustration.

Show the children a sample of the talking puppet. Then pass out the paper plates and markers or crayons. Let the children draw the eyes and nose on their puppets. Let them glue on yarn hair. Now the puppet is ready to talk. Just pull the string gently to make the mouth move.

Gather the children and their talking puppets, and ask them to name some people who help them. Select a child to demonstrate with his talking puppet how he would say thank-you to the person he named. Let every child have a turn.

Do you always remember to say thank-you when someone helps you? Does your mother have to remind you? What does she say when you forget?

In today's Bible story, Jesus will help ten men to get well. Do you think they should thank Jesus? We will find out what happened later.

From Me to You

You will need a copy of the thank-you card from p. 228 for each child and crayons or markers. Trim the edges of the photocopies from cards before class time.

Ask each child to think of someone she would like to give a thank-you card to. Pass out the thank-you cards. Read each section aloud and give the children directions for coloring. After the children have colored each section, show them how to fold the page into a card. Gather the children and their cards around you. Let each child tell about the person who is going to receive his card, and let him show it to the class.

God is pleased when we say thank-you to others. He is pleased when we thank Him, too.

Know: Why it is important to thank God for His goodness.
Feel: Thankful for God's love and care.
Do: Say "thank You" to God.

Children will accomplish the goals when they
- Demonstrate ways to thank someone.
- Tell what ten lepers did when they were healed.
- Recite Psalm 136:1 and thank God for His goodness.
- Give reasons to thank God.
- Promise to always thank God for His blessings.

▼ 2. What Does the Bible Say? ▲

Bible Story: Only One Thankful Man

You will need construction paper, a marker, scissors, ten craft sticks, and glue.

Cut out twenty circles, all the same size. (Hint: Trace around a bowl or plastic lid.) On ten circles draw simple smiling faces. On the rest of the circles, draw frowning faces. Glue a smiling face and a frowning face back-to-back with a craft stick in between for a handle.

Do you know what leprosy is? It is a terrible skin disease. People with leprosy are covered with sores. They cannot live with their families anymore; instead they must live with others who have leprosy, too. This makes them very sad. They cannot go near healthy people, because they might give this disease to others.

Jesus was traveling to Jerusalem when He met ten men with leprosy. *(Ask nine children to hold nine sticks. You keep one and tell the children to show the frowning faces and the smiling faces when you do.)* **These ten men were covered with sores. They were not allowed to go near people, so they stood far away and called, "Jesus! Please help us!"**

Do you think Jesus had the power to help these men? Yes, He did! Jesus answered the men saying, "Go to the village and show your skin to a priest." Jesus knew the law about leprosy. A priest must look at a leper's skin. If the sores were gone, the priest would let the person go home to live with his family and friends.

Quickly the ten men left to find a priest in the village. On the way they began to feel better. When they looked at their skin, all of the sores were gone! *(Turn the frowning faces to happy faces.)* **The leprosy was gone! Now they were really in a big hurry to see the priest.**

Suddenly, one of the ten men stopped. He remembered something very important. *(Draw a child without a stick to you.)* **He turned around and ran back to Jesus. He bowed down at His feet.** *(Bow the smiling face down to the child at your side.)* **The man said, "Thank you for healing me."**

Jesus looked at the man, and then He looked down the road. "Where are the other men?" He asked. "There were ten men with leprosy. Where did the other nine men go? Are you the only one who came back to say thank-you?" Then Jesus said something very important to the man. He said, "Stand up and go home. You are healed."

Happily, the man went home to his family.

Story Review: Happy Steps

You will need several colors of crepe paper, live or recorded music with different tempos, and a cassette or CD player.

Cut streamers about three feet long. Give each child a paper streamer. **Pretend that you are one of the men with leprosy. Wave your streamer and call to Jesus. Now Jesus has told you to go to the village to see a priest. Hold your streamer up and start walking. Look at your skin. It is clean! How do you feel? Can you show me with your movements how you feel?** Play the music. Guide the children to move around the room as slow or as fast as the music makes them feel.

How did the slow music make you feel? How did the faster music make you feel? How do you think the men felt when Jesus made them well again? How do you think Jesus felt when only one man remembered to say thank-you?

Bible Memory: A Bag Full of Thanks

You will need a paper bag and an assortment of items for which children might be thankful, such as a picture of a family, a toy, a small Bible, a picture of Jesus, a piece of fruit, a raw vegetable, a leaf, a flower, an adhesive bandage, a sock, and a marker.

Have the children sit in a circle. Recite the Bible words together several times. Give the paper bag full of items to one of the children. The child will reach in the bag and take out an item. Ask the child to tell why he is thankful for that item. Then have all the children say the Bible words together.

▼ 3. What Does This Mean to Me? ▲

Wind Chime (Part 4)

You will need the wind chimes worked on in the previous three lessons, a frozen juice can lid and two circles from p. 224 (family, group of friends) for each child. You will also need permanent markers, glue, clear polyurethane spray, a nail, hammer, and fishing line.

This is a unit craft project. During this lesson, the last part of the wind chime will be made and attached to the clear plastic lid.

We are finishing our wind chimes today to remind us to thank God for all the good things He has given us.

Have the children color the circles and glue them back-to-back on one juice can lid. Have an adult punch a hole in the top of the circles with a nail and hammer. Spray both sides of the juice can lids with polyurethane. (Spraying outdoors is best.) When dry, tie a ten-inch piece of fishing line from the juice can lid to the plastic lid. Or, so that you don't get the circles mixed up, tie them to the plastic lids and then take them all outside to spray.

Our wind chimes are finished today. When you take yours home, ask your parents to help you find a place to hang it. If you can hang it outside, every time the wind blows the sound will remind you to thank God for all the good things He has given you.

What do these new pictures remind us to thank God for? (Family and friends.)

What are some other reasons to thank God? (Thank God for birds and flowers, food and clothing, God's love and care, Jesus, our bodies.)

▼ 4. What Can I Do to Please God? ▲

Sing a Song of Thanks

You will need the words to Thank-You Prayer" from p. 206 and the mounted pictures for all four verses from pp. 225 and 226.

Show the picture for morning prayer (v. 1). Review with the children what they can thank God for when they wake up. Then sing the verse.

Next show the picture for noontime prayer (v. 2). Ask the children whether their families pray before they eat. Encourage the children who answered no to ask their families whether they can start praying at mealtime. Sing the second verse.

Show the picture for playtime prayer (v. 3). Ask the children to stand and then lead them in a couple of simple exercises. Sit down and sing the third verse.

Show the last picture for bedtime prayer (v. 4). Ask the children whether they pray before they go to bed each night. Ask the children who said yes to tell one thing they pray about at bedtime. Teach the words to the fourth verse and sing it several times.

Bible Words

"Give thanks to the Lord because he is good. [His love continues forever]" (Psalm 136:1).

(Note: This verse has been divided into two parts. If you are teaching four-year-olds, use only the first part. If you are teaching older children, also include the part of the verse in brackets.)

Thank-You Prayer
(Tune: "Three Blind Mice")

Verse 1
Morning prayer. Morning prayer.
Greet the new day. Greet the new day.
Thank You, dear God, for a brand new day.
Help me in all that I do and say.
The best way to start is to sing and pray—a morning prayer.

Verse 2
Noontime prayer. Noontime prayer.
Time for some lunch. Time for some lunch.
Thank You, dear God, for good food to munch.
My mother fixes a healthy lunch.
I like to eat food that has a crunch—-a noontime prayer.

Verse 3
Playtime prayer. Playtime prayer.
Fun in the sun. Fun in the sun.
Thank You, dear God, for strong legs to run.
Riding bikes and playing can be great fun.
You're never too busy to hear just one—a playtime prayer.

Verse 4
Bedtime prayer. Bedtime prayer.
Thanks for the day. Thanks for the day.
For keeping my family and friends okay,
For helping me do my jobs and obey,
The best way to end the day is to pray—a bedtime prayer.

Let's be like the man who came back to thank Jesus for making him well. Let's thank God for His goodness and love. Ask several children to pray.

Listen for the Wind Chimes

You will need the words to "Thank-You Prayer" from p. 206, the four verse pictures, and some bags to put the wind chimes in so they can be taken home with ease.

Have the children help clean and straighten the classroom. Put their wind chimes in bags. Then gather the children around you. Show one of the wind chimes. Review each picture. Remind them to listen for the chimes to make sounds in the wind. **When you hear the chimes, stop and say, "Thank You, God."**

Show the pictures as each verse of "Thank-You Prayer" is sung.

All day long remember to thank God for His love and goodness. Be sure to thank Him for Jesus, too.

▼ Bonus Activity ▲

Snack Attack! God's Love Goes On and On

You will need refrigerated breadstick dough or biscuit dough.

Roll each piece into a strip until it is as thin as a pencil. Form each strip into a heart shape. Pinch the ends together. Place the hearts on lightly greased cookie sheets. Brush the tops with milk or melted margarine. Sprinkle with cinnamon and sugar. Bake the hearts ahead of time unless you have access to an oven and would like to involve the children in the process. Bake until lightly browned and serve warm, if possible.

When you are ready to serve the hearts, line them up side by side down the middle of the table. **Look, these hearts just go on and on down the table. They remind me that God's love continues forever. His love just goes on and on. Let's pray and thank God for His love that never stops, and for these yummy hearts that we get to eat.**

For Unit 10

Pass out copies of the Parent's Letter from p. 247. **Next time we meet we are going to begin a very special project. We are going to collect food for families who don't always have enough to eat. We are also going to practice sharing. Next week, I want you to bring one of your favorite toys with you.** Read the letter to the children. **Please take these letters home with you so that your family can help you remember to bring a toy next week, and help you remember to bring food all during the month.**

Wind Chime Part 1

Wind Chime Part 2

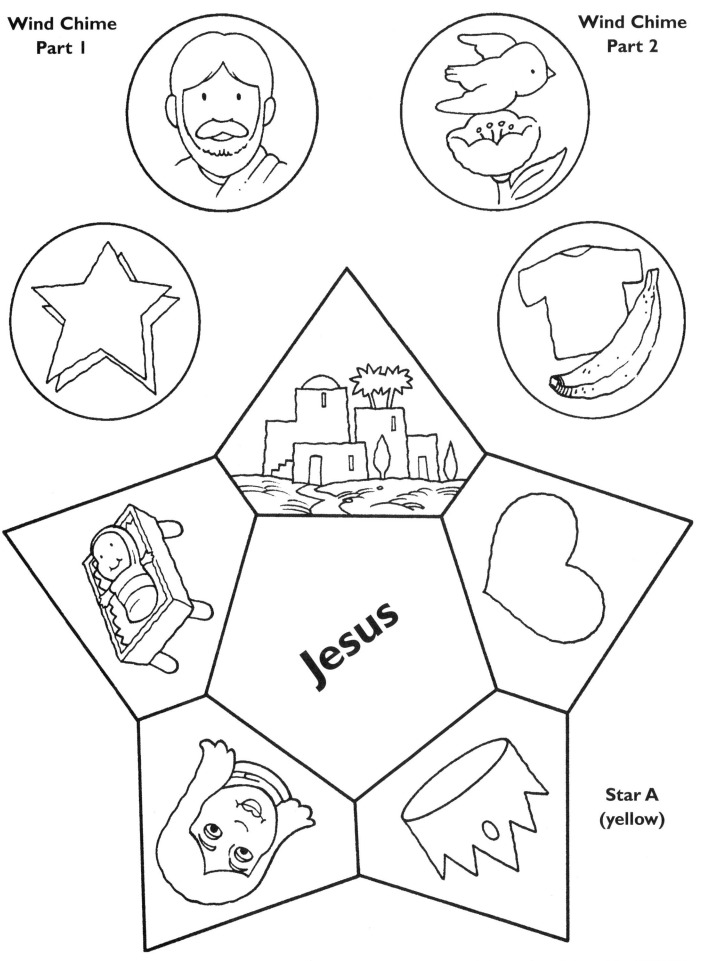

Jesus

Star A (yellow)

**Wind Chime
Part 3**

**Wind Chime
Part 4**

Thank You, God, for Jesus.

**Star B
(blue)**

verse 1

verse 2

verse 3

verse 4

_____

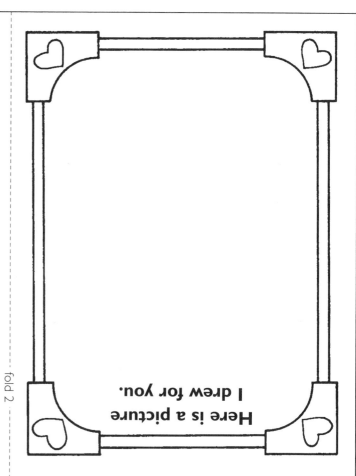

Here is a picture
I drew for you.

Love,

You always understand,
when I need
a helping hand.
So this card
is from me to you,
because I want
to say,
"Thank you!"

fold 2

fold 1

A ♡-made card

Learning to Share

Lessons 38-41

Unit Bible Words

"Do not forget to do good to others, and share with them" (Hebrews 13:16).

(Note: This verse has been divided into two parts. If you are teaching four-year-olds, use only the first part. If you are teaching older children, also include the second part of the verse.)

Bible Characters

Jesus, boy, widow, the church, Aquila and Priscilla

38 A Boy Shares

Matthew 14:15-21; John 6:5-13—The disciples are baffled. How are 5,000 men, plus all the women, and children going to get food? It is late in the day. The surrounding villages are some distance away. Jesus uses a boy's lunch to teach how a little in the eyes of men is much in the hands of God. Sharing even small things can bring great joy to others.

39 A Woman Shares

Luke 20:45-47; 21:1-4—When Jesus sees the rich parading through the temple in their fancy clothes giving huge gifts to the temple treasury, He takes the opportunity to teach His helpers an important truth about sharing. He focuses their attention on a poor widow whose meager gift of two coins is unnoticed by others, but attracts God's attention. A gift shared by a loving heart is priceless.

40 A Church Shares

Matthew 28:18-20; Acts 1:9; 2:44-47; 4:32-37—The first church puts the teachings of Jesus into practice and the results are wonderful. Every believer shares what he has. No one is homeless or hungry. Every need is met. God wants us to share and help others, too.

41 A Man and His Wife Share

Acts 18; Romans 16:3-5—Aquila and Priscilla share their home, their business, and their love for Jesus with Paul and others. They are wonderful role models of how Christians should share.

By the end of this unit, the children and leaders will

Know: God wants them to share what they have with others.

Feel: A desire to share with others.

Do: Share joyfully with others.

Why Teach This Unit to Four- to Six-Year-Olds?

Children are not born with a desire to share. One of the first words uttered by a young child is "Mine!" They are naturally selfish. Tantrums are the result of selfish desires. Parents and teachers must constantly remind children to share. The issue of sharing causes frequent arguments when children are playing. To learn how to share, children need role models, guidance, and practice. This unit is designed to provide this kind of help.

This unit creates an environment that will introduce four-, five-, and six-year-olds to the idea of sharing. They will meet real people who shared with others. They will be guided through activities that give them opportunities to practice sharing. By the end of the unit you will have laid the groundwork for future lessons on sharing that will come from daily interaction with others. Hopefully, each child will experience the joy that sharing can bring to one's heart.

Meet a Boy with a Small Lunch

Can you imagine how an ordinary boy with an ordinary lunch felt when he was asked to share his lunch with more than 5,000 men, women, and children? Only Jesus could take a meager lunch of fish and bread and provide an abundance of food that resulted in twelve baskets of leftovers.

Meet a Poor Woman

We know little about this woman. Her appearance indicated that she was poor and a widow. Jesus knew a lot about her because He sees the heart. Her gift to the temple treasury was totally unselfish. Her love for God made her rich in spirit. God who sees the heart will reward those who lovingly share all they have.

Meet the People of the First Church

Ten days after Jesus ascended into Heaven, the Church began in Jerusalem. This church grew rapidly in numbers. There was power in the message the apostles were preaching. Also, outsiders liked what they saw happening in the lives of the believers. No one was selfish. Everyone shared what they had. Everyone's needs were met physically, emotionally, and spiritually.

Meet Aquila and Priscilla

This husband and wife were Jews who became Christians in Rome. They were forced to leave when the emperor of Rome evicted all Jews from the city. They moved to Corinth and were tentmakers. This man and wife were a real blessing to Paul. He lived with them, worked as a tentmaker with them, worshiped with them, and traveled with them to share the good news with others. They openly shared all they had with others.

Unit Project: Sharing With Others

In this unit, you will organize a food drive for needy people. This food drive can involve your class only, or your class can sponsor and organize it for the entire church. Some planning will be necessary.

Make posters to hang outside your classroom door to inform parents of what you are collecting and the dates. If this will be a church-wide event, make posters to be hung around the church and establish collection sites. Be sure to get permission to do this.

Throughout this unit children will gather, sort, and count food items, make and pack food boxes, and create greeting cards.

Invite a representative receiving the food to visit your class. Let the children present their filled boxes. If your children are mature enough to be sensitive to people less fortunate, take the children to the location where the food boxes will be distributed.

Unit Visuals: A Living Drama

You will need transparencies made out of the following backgrounds: palace/temple 4A from p. 105, town 6C from p. 145, room in house 8B from p. 195, Jesus standing 7A and sitting 7B from p. 175, and the crowd on a hill 10A from p. 247.

Color may be added to the transparencies. Use only permanent overhead projector pens. (Hint: Handle transparencies as little as possible. Colored pens will not mark easily over fingerprints.)

If a plain wall is not available for projection, tack a large, plain sheet to the wall. Be sure that the edge of the sheet meets the floor.

These transparencies will be used as backdrops to the Bible stories. Therefore, project each scene at floor level. When the characters step into the light, they will come to life.

Use children and/or adults to play the parts of the Bible characters. Keep costuming simple, such as bath robes and colored T-shirts. If special costuming is required, it will be described at the beginning of the story. There are no speaking parts. All of the action will be pantomimed in front of the projected scenes, and the storyteller will give the directions.

Unit Song

Share What You Have
(Tune: "Skip to My Lou")

Verse 1
Do, do, do good to others.
Do, do, do good to others.
Do, do, do good to others.
Do not forget to do good.

Verse 2
Share, share, share what you have.
Share, share, share what you have.
Share, share, share what you have.
Share what you have with others.

Verse 3
Give, give, give from your heart.
Give, give, give from your heart.
Give, give, give from your heart.
Give from your heart to others.

A Boy Shares

Matthew 14:15-21; John 6:5-13

▼ 1. What Is This Story About? ▲

Be Fair! Share!

You will need building blocks, a bag of pretzels, a blanket, and some adults and/or teens to role-play the situations.

Who knows what it means to share? Let's watch to see who shares in these little skits.

Ask the adult/teen volunteers to role-play the following situations:

1. Two children are playing with some blocks. Another child joins them, but the two children ignore the new child and refuse to share any of the blocks.

2. One child has a bag full of pretzels. He is sitting alone eating from the bag. After a while, he looks up at the class staring at him. He looks down at the bag and keeps eating. Then he looks up again and back down at the bag. Finally, he walks among the children and offers each child a pretzel.

3. Two people are camping. It is a cold morning and there is no fire to keep them warm. One is wrapped up in a blanket. The other one does not have a blanket and is shivering. The one with the blanket ignores the one shivering.

After each role play, ask the following questions:

Who had something to share?

Who chose to share with someone else?

Who did not share what they had?

Sharing Time

You will need the toys the children brought from home. Have extra toys available in case a child does not bring a toy.

Gather the children with their toys in a circle. **Thank you for bringing a toy to share today.** Let them show and tell about the toys they brought. Help the children set up any games and teach others how to play them.

Encourage any child who is having difficulty sharing. Take the child aside and talk quietly with him about sharing. Try to resolve the conflict. If it can not be resolved, then ask the child to put the toy away. Get the child involved with children who are enjoying sharing. They can be good role models for him.

I am glad you shared your toys with one another. Today we are going to hear about a boy who shared his lunch. God is pleased when we share with others.

▼ 2. What Does the Bible Say? ▲

Bible Story: Little Is Much

You will need transparencies 7B and 10A, an overhead projector, twelve baskets of various sizes and shapes, and a sample pouch from the Story Review activity, "Pack a Lunch." (Optional: Dress the children in simple Bible costumes.)

Project transparency 7B and have the children sit at the feet of Jesus, facing him. (See p. 230 for directions on how to use the visual.)

Know: God wants them to share what they have with others.

Feel: A desire to share with others.

Do: Share joyfully with others.

Children will accomplish these goals when they

- Explore what it means to share.
- Tell about a boy who shared his lunch.
- Begin to learn Hebrews 13:16.
- Name ways to share.
- Participate in a sharing project.

Wherever Jesus went, people followed Him. Jesus would take time to teach people and heal those who were sick. One day, a very large group of people stayed all day to hear Him teach. Late in the afternoon Jesus' helpers told Him it was time for supper. They wanted Jesus to tell the people to go into the villages and buy food.

Jesus said, "They do not need to go and buy food. You can give them food to eat."

When He said this, His helpers were very surprised. *(Have one of the boys stand next to the figure of Jesus.)* A helper named Philip replied, "There are many, many people here. We would all have to work for one month to buy enough food to give everyone just a bite."

(Have another boy stand on the other side of the figure of Jesus.) **Andrew, another one of Jesus' helpers, said, "The only food I have found is a boy's lunch.** *(Have another boy stand, holding the "Pack a Lunch" pouch with the bread and fish in it.)* **He only has five small loaves of bread and two small fish. That is not enough to feed so many people."** *(Ask the boy playing Andrew to take out the bread and fish from the pouch and count them.)*

Jesus said, "Bring the boy's lunch to me."

Then Jesus told the people to sit down on the grassy hillside. *(Ask all the children to sit down.)* **He picked up the bread and looked up to Heaven. He prayed and thanked God for the bread. Then he held the two fish and thanked God for them.**

After Jesus prayed for the food, His helpers passed the bread and fish to all the people. *(Remove transparency 7B and project 10A. Ask several boys to pretend to pass out the food to the children. Ask the children to pretend to eat.)* **Everyone ate and ate. All of the men and women ate until they were full. The children ate until they could not eat another bite.**

Jesus asked His helpers to pick up the leftover bread and fish. *(Pass out the bread baskets to the same boys and ask them to pretend to collect the leftover food.)* **There was so much food left over the helpers filled twelve baskets.** *(Count the twelve baskets.)*

Jesus blessed a little lunch shared by a boy and fed more than 5,000 people. *(Draw attention to the number of people projected on the wall.)* **There were even leftovers! This was a miracle! Do you know what a miracle is? It is something only God can do. Let's thank God for this miracle and for the boy who shared his lunch.** *(Turn off the projector. Pray.)*

Story Review: Pack a Lunch

You will need a copy of "Loaves and Fish" from p. 248 for each child, scissors, brown construction paper, crayons, glue, a hole punch, and yarn.

Let each child color and cut out the two fish and the five loaves of bread. This project is simple enough for beginning scissor skills, but young four-year-olds will get tired of cutting. Give help as needed.

Show the children how to fold a piece of brown construction paper in half and glue the side edges together to make a pouch. Punch a hole in the top left- and right-hand corners of the pouch. Attach a piece of yarn for a handle.

Help the children count the fish and bread as they put them in their pouches.

How many fish did the boy have in his lunch?

How many loaves of bread did he have?

How many did he share with Jesus?

What did Jesus do before He gave the bread and the fish to the people? Then what happened?

Did everyone have enough to eat? Was there any food left over?

How do you think the boy felt when his little lunch fed so many people?

Bible Memory: Don't Forget!

You will need the words of the unit song, "Share What You have," from p. 230, string, scissors, and a Bible.

Before you teach the verse, tie a string in a bow around one of your fingers. Act as if you do not know it is there. Explain what it means only when a child asks about it. Say, **Some people think tying a string around their finger will help them remember something important. I put this string around my finger to remind me to do good.**

Open the Bible to Hebrews 13:16 and read the verse. **The first part of our Bible verse says, "Do not forget to do good." Here is a song to help us remember the first part of our Bible words.** Sing the verse several times. Then divide the class into three groups. Point to each group when it is their turn to sing.

Group 1: Do, do,
Group 2: do good
Group 3: to others.
(Repeat two more times.)
All: Do not forget to do good.

Sometimes we forget to do good. Let's ask God to help us remember to do good. Lead the children in prayer. (Optional: Tie string around each child's finger.)

> ### Bible Words
> "Do not forget to do good to others, and share with them" (Hebrews 13:16).
>
> (Note: This verse has been divided into two parts. If you are teaching four-year-olds, use only the first part. If you are teaching older children, also include the part of the verse in brackets.)

▼ 3. What Does This Mean to Me? ▲

Let's Share, Too

You will need a copy of the note to parents from p. 247, poster board, a dark marker, butcher paper or shelf paper, magazine pictures of food, scissors, glue, one large corrugated box (large enough to hold several grocery bags full of food), and assorted labels from food cans and boxes.

Cover the large box with plain paper. Clearly print the information about the food drive onto the poster board. Leave space for the children to glue on pictures of food.

Introduce the food drive project by gathering the children around the empty box. **God is pleased when children share. Every day your parents remind you to share with others. What are some ways that you share? With whom do you share your things?**

Today we are going to plan a way to share food with hungry people. We will work on this project during the next three lessons. On the day of the last lesson we will give the food we collected to (the group or organization of your choice). Let the children decorate the large box with the labels from food cans and boxes.

If you did not send the note to parents home last week, you will need to do that this week and highlight the information about the food drive.

We are also going to make some posters to hang up outside our classroom to remind you and your parents to bring food each time you come to our class.

Set out the poster board and pictures of food. Let the children glue the pictures on the posters. When the posters are completed, take the children with you to hang the posters. Gather the children around one of the hanging posters. Lead a prayer asking God's help for this project.

▼ 4. What Can I Do to Please God? ▲

Extra Action!
Catch Your Lunch

Play a simple game of tag. Select one child to be the boy in the Bible story. The rest of the children will be fish in a pond. Set boundaries for the pond. The fish are to run around within those boundaries trying not to get caught. Give a signal for the boy to go fishing. The child will run around trying to catch a fish. When one fish is caught, the boy must hold the hand of the fish and continue trying to catch another fish. When the child has caught two fish, he has caught his lunch. Select another child to be the boy and continue playing. Be sure everyone gets to go fishing.

How many fish did the boy in our Bible story have in his lunch? How many loaves of bread did he have? When Jesus prayed and thanked God for this boy's lunch, what happened? What is a miracle?

Our Class Shares

You will need the words to "Share What You Have" from p. 230, copies of the note to parents about the food drive from p. 247.

Note: Before copying the note about the food drive, fill in the blanks with the last day the food can be brought, the name of the group or organization to whom the food will be given, and your name and telephone number. Parents may have questions about this project and want to call you.

Ask the children to pretend they are Jesus' helpers, cleaning up after the huge crowd of people in today's Bible story. Place a wastebasket in the center of the room. Send the children to collect the trash in the classroom and put it in the basket. Then gather them around your classroom food collection box.

Our Bible words remind us to do good to others and share with them what we have.

What are we going to do that will be good for others?

What do you want to bring to share with others?

When you bring canned or boxed food from home to share, remember to put it in this box. Thank you for helping with this project. Let's ask God to help us remember to bring food to share. Model a prayer: Thank You, God, for all the good things You give me. Help me remember to share what I have with others. Then give each child a turn to pray.

Sing the first verse of "Share What You Have."

▼ Bonus Activity ▲

Snack Attack! Fish Food

You will need cream cheese, large crackers, tiny fish-shaped crackers, jumbo craft sticks, and paper plates.

Be sure the children wash their hands. Let them spread the softened cream cheese on the large crackers. Then put fish-shaped crackers on top.

What did Jesus do before He gave the bread and the fish to the people? Yes, He prayed. He thanked God for the food the boy had shared. Let's thank God for our food, too.

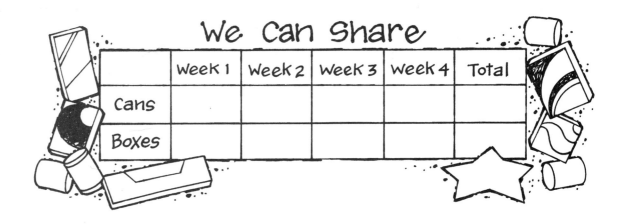

We Can Share

	Week 1	Week 2	Week 3	Week 4	Total
Cans					
Boxes					

A Woman Shares

Luke 20:45-47; 21:1-4

▼ 1. What Is This Story About? ▲

Happy Hearts vs. Grumbling Hearts

You will need red construction paper, scissors, a dark marker, glue, a hole punch, yarn, and a variety of fun books and puzzles.

Cut out two 3" hearts for each child. Draw a smiling face on one and a frowning face on the other. Have each child glue his two hearts (one happy and one sad) back-to-back so the faces show. Make a necklace by punching a hole in the middle of the hearts and threading a piece of yarn through the hole. Tie the ends of the yarn and place it around the child's neck.

Give half of the children books or puzzles. Tell these children to find someone who did not get one and share. Give the children some time to look at the books or work the puzzles. **If you did not get a book or puzzle when I passed them out, how did you feel? Show me by turning your heart to a smile or a frown. I see lots of frowns. Were you grumbling when you didn't get one? If I gave you a book or puzzle how did you feel? Show me a smiling or frowning heart. Yes, you were smiling inside. Maybe you were even glad you got one and your friend did not. How did you feel when you had to share your book or puzzle with someone? Show me a smile or a frown. Sometimes it is hard to share. We do it because the teacher says to do it, but we really don't want to share. Do you think God knows whether our hearts are smiling or frowning when we share? Yes, He does! What kind of a heart do you think He wants us to have when we share? Yes, He wants us to be happy about sharing.**

Let's pray and ask God to help us have happy hearts when we share and not grumbling hearts. Lead the children in prayer. Then remove the necklaces and keep them for use in Lesson 40.

Share What You Have

You will need the words to "Share What You Have" from p. 230.

Review the first verse taught in last week's lesson. Then teach the second verse. Have the children form a circle and hold hands. As the children sing the first verse, walk to the right. Then sing the second verse and walk to the left. Repeat the verses several times.

How do you feel when someone shares a toy or a cookie with you? How do you feel when someone does not want to share with you? How does sharing with others make you feel?

▼ 2. What Does the Bible Say? ▲

Bible Story: A Poor Woman with a Rich Heart

You will need transparency 7A, an overhead projector, large moneybags, two pennies, a large foil-covered box without a lid, and a small table. Dress two or three boys and one girl in colorful Bible time clothes. Add a lot of jewelry. They

Know: God wants them to share what they have with others.

Feel: A desire to share with others.

Do: Share joyfully with others.

Children will accomplish these goals when they
- Explore attitudes about sharing.
- Tell about a woman who shared all that she had.
- Recite Hebrews 13:16.
- Name ways to share.
- Share with others.

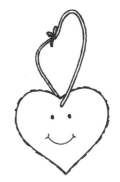

will be the rich people. Dress one girl in a dark robe and put a long dark shawl or blanket over her head. She will be the poor woman.

Project transparency 7A. Place the box on a table opposite Jesus. (See p. 230 for directions on how to use the visual.)

In our last story, Jesus taught a huge crowd of people on a grassy hillside. In today's story Jesus is teaching in the temple. Wherever Jesus went, He told people about God and what they should do to please Him.

(Have one rich boy and one rich girl stand next to the figure of Jesus.) **On this day, people came up to Jesus and asked Him questions as He walked around the temple. He answered each question truthfully. This made the temple leaders and teachers angry.** *(Have another rich boy enter and look very mad.)* **The temple leaders did not want the people to hear the truth. They wanted the people to believe only what they said. These men were proud of their important jobs.** *(Have all the rich boys walk around looking important.)* **They wore expensive clothes and walked around the temple looking important. When they prayed, they said very long, very loud prayers. They wanted others to think they were very good.** *(Exit all the rich people.)*

Jesus told His helpers not to be like these men. Pretending to be important is wrong. God was not pleased with the way these men acted.

While Jesus was talking, some rich people came into the temple. *(All the rich people enter again carrying the moneybags and acting important. Have them walk over to the collection box.)* **They were wearing beautiful clothes. Everyone watched as they walked by. They had come to put gifts in the temple collection boxes. These were large open boxes where worshipers put their money. When the rich people put their money in the box, they wanted everyone to see how much they gave.** *(Have them put the bags in the collection box.)* **They liked others to think they were important.** *(The rich people exit.)*

After the rich people left, a very poor woman walked up quietly to the collection box. *(Have the poor woman enter and walk up to the box and put her two pennies in the box quietly.)* **She quickly put in two tiny coins and left.** *(Poor woman exits.)* **No one noticed her except Jesus.**

Jesus said to His helpers, "Listen to me. This is the truth. When this poor woman put two coins in the box, she gave more than the rich people gave."

His helpers were confused. They saw all the money the rich had given. How could two tiny coins be more valuable?

Jesus explained, "The rich people gave a lot of money, but they did not need the money they put in the box. They have money left to buy more expensive clothes and food. This woman is very poor. She had only two coins, and she put them in the offering box. She gave all she had. Now she has nothing left for food or clothes."

Finally, Jesus' helpers understood. God sees a person's heart. When a person shares because of the love in his heart, this pleases God. Do you think a person who shares but grumbles about it pleases God? No! God wants us to share and have a loving heart. *(Turn off the projector.)*

Story Review: Big Steps, Little Steps

You will need an empty space to play this game.

Have the children stand in a row. Ten or more feet away, have a teacher stand opposite the children with her back to them. The children will take a big step when the teacher says something that reminds them of the poor woman with a rich heart. They will take a small step when the teacher says something that reminds them of the people who thought they were important. Use the following statements and make up your own.

God is pleased when our prayers come from our hearts.
God loves only people who wear expensive clothes.
God likes loud and long prayers the best.
God is pleased when we quietly help others.

God loves only people who give a lot of money to the church.
God loves the person who gives all she has to help others.
God loves a selfish heart.
God is pleased with a person who grumbles about having to share.
God loves a person who gives because of a heart filled with love.

Bible Memory: Drop the Coin

You will need a coin to play this version of the game "Drop the Handkerchief."
Say Hebrews 13:16 in small phrases several times with the children repeating each phrase after you.

Our Bible words remind us to share like the woman who shared her coins. Let's play a game to learn our Bible words.

Have the children form a circle and put their hands behind their backs. Walk around the outside of the circle. Pretend to put the coin in each child's hands; then put a coin in one child's hand. Ask the child to recite Hebrews 13:16. Give help as needed. Trade places with the child. He will walk around the circle and put the coin in another child's hand. This child will recite the verse and continue the game.

> **Bible Words**
> "Do not forget to do good to others, and share with them" (Hebrews 13:16).
>
> (Note: This verse has been divided into two parts. If you are teaching four-year-olds, use only the first part. If you are teaching older children, also include the part of the verse in brackets.)

▼ 3. What Does This Mean to Me? ▲

Sharing Hands

You will need the words to "Share What You Have" from p. 230, newspaper, tempera paint, paper plates, large plain white paper or newsprint, and paint shirts.

Begin now to collect cardboard boxes without lids (the size that reams of paper come in would be good) for use in Lesson 41. The wrapping paper made during this activity will be saved and used to wrap the boxes for use in Lesson 41, "Wrap It Up!"

Cover the work area with newspaper. Pour a thin layer of tempera paint in the paper plates. Have the children place the open palm of their hands in the paint and then on the paper. Cover the paper with different colors of handprints. Explain how this decorated paper will wrap the boxes used to deliver the food to the needy people (this unit's special project). Sing verses one and two of "Share What You Have" while you work.

Your handprints remind me of the kind hands of the woman in our Bible story. She probably worked with her hands to earn the money she gave to God. Sharing money is one way to share with others. What are some other ways we can share?

My Sharing Bank

You will need the bank pattern and Bank Wrapper from p. 249, cardboard, an X-Acto knife, an empty toilet paper roll for each child, crayons or markers, white glue, paper plate, and two pennies for each child.

Copy and cut out a bank wrapper from p. 249 for each child. Use the square pattern to trace and cut out two cardboard squares for each child. In the center of one square, cut a 1" slit with an X-Acto knife.

Give each child a bank wrapper to color. Let the children glue the wrapper onto the tube.

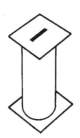

Place white glue on a paper plate. Dip one open end of the covered paper tube into the glue, and then place the glued end in the center of one of the squares. Repeat this process with the other end. Let dry.

Use this bank to save money for sharing with God. When the bank is full, bring it to church and put it in the offering basket. I would like to share

some pennies with you so you can start saving today. Put two pennies in each child's bank. **These pennies will remind you of the two coins the woman in our Bible story put in the temple money box.**

What are some other ways we can share what we have? (Share food, share toys, invite someone to eat with you, share time by helping.)

▼ 4. What Can I Do to Please God? ▲

Share Your Heart

You will need the words to "Share What You Have" from p. 230, three 3" hearts for each child, and crayons. (A jumbo heart punch from a craft store will make quick work of this task.)

Pass out three hearts to each child. Ask each child to print his name on one side of each heart and decorate the other side. Explain that they are going to give the hearts away, and that they should make them as nice as possible. Give help as needed.

Collect the hearts. Then lead the children out of the classroom. Ask another leader to hide the hearts around the classroom. While you are waiting with the children, sing "Share What You Have." When the hearts are hidden, tell the children to look until they have found three hearts. If they find one with their name on it, they are to leave it for someone else to find.

When all the hearts have been found, gather the children together and read the names on the hearts found by each child. Compliment the children on making such pretty hearts to share with their friends. Also compliment children who remember to thank the children who decorated the hearts they found.

When you do your best to decorate a heart, it can be hard to give it away. If you feel like grumbling, remember how a happy, sharing heart pleases God. It can be fun to share with others. It makes me feel good to see something I made make my friend happy.

We Can Share!

You will need the words to "Share What You Have" from p. 230, "We Can Share" art from page 234, poster board, markers, magazine pictures of food, scissors, and glue.

Before class time, make a poster titled "We Can Share" using the art from page 234. Let the children decorate it with pictures of food.

When the room is clean, gather the children around the collected food. Help the children count the number of items brought today. Write the number on the poster. Compliment the children on their efforts.

Sing "Share What You Have." Ask the children to pray and ask God to help them share with others.

Bonus Activity

Snack Attack!
Preparing and Sharing
You will need bread, peanut butter, jelly, jumbo craft sticks, and paper plates. (Check for peanut allergies. Instead of PB & J, these children can have J & J sandwiches!)

Be sure the children wash their hands before beginning this project. Let each child make a half of a sandwich and put it on a paper plate. Ask each child to give his sandwich to the person on his left. Compliment the children who remember to say thank you. Ask several children to thank God for the snack and for friends who share. **Sharing is fun! It makes our hearts happy.**

A Church Shares

Matthew 28:18-20; Acts 1:9; 2:44-47; 4:32-37

▼ 1. What Is this Story About? ▲

"I Will Share" Headbands

You will need 1 1/2" wide strips of paper 22"–24" long to make headbands for each child. Print "I Will Share" on them. You will also need paper clips, assorted stickers, two pictures from a coloring book, four crayons, four cookies, and building blocks.

Fit a headband to each child's head and paper clip it. **Sharing is a very kind thing to do. Your headband says, "I Will Share." Before we hear our story about sharing, we are going to act out some problems that could happen here at church.** Help the children role-play the following scenes.

1. Give two children pictures to color and two crayons each. Ask both children to give ideas on how they can share.

2. Have two children sit at a table and give each two cookies. Then ask another child to sit at the same table. Ask the children with cookies to show a way to share.

3. Have three children sit on the floor, playing with some blocks. Then ask another child to join the group. Ask the children with the blocks how they share.

I want you to wear your headbands during the rest of our class time. When I see you sharing, I will put a sticker on your headband. Give each child a sticker now.

How High Can You Build?

You will need two clothes baskets or boxes and as many empty and clean vegetable and fruit cans as you can gather. Leave the labels on the cans.

The object of this relay game is to see how high each group can build its tower of cans before it falls down. Divide the children into groups of no more than ten. Line each group up about ten feet away from where the cans are to be stacked. Place a basket filled with cans next to each stacking area. Let the children take turns going to the stacking area, taking a can from the basket, and adding the can to the tower. When a tower falls down, count how many cans high it was. Put the cans back in the basket and start building again. Encourage the members of each team to cheer for one another. Do not compare scores with the other team(s). Encourage each team to keep bettering its own record.

As I watched you play this game, I saw children sharing by taking turns. You waited for the children in front of you to stack their cans. You were happy when the children on your team did a good job of stacking their cans so the tower did not fall down. When the tower fell down, you helped pick up the cans and tried again. You worked together to build the tower. It can be fun to work together.

In our story time, we will learn that the first church worked together, too. People liked the way the believers shared. I liked the way you shared as you played this game, too.

I Will Share

Know: God wants them to share what they have with others.

Feel: A desire to share with others.

Do: Share joyfully with others.

Children will accomplish these goals when they

- Explore ways to share with others.
- Tell how the church shared.
- Recite Hebrews 13:16 and do what it says.
- Make something to share.
- Choose to share this week.

▼ 2. What Does the Bible Say? ▲

Bible Story: The First Church Shares

You will need transparencies 7A and 8B, an overhead projector, several baskets of various sizes and shapes, and a moneybag. (Optional: Dress the children in simple Bible costumes.)

Project transparency 7A and have the children sit at the feet of Jesus, facing him. (See p. 230 for directions on how to use the visual.)

After Jesus rose from the dead, He spent forty more days with His disciples. When He was ready to go home to God, He gathered His followers and told them to tell everyone about Him. He said that His Spirit would be with them forever. Then He went up into Heaven. (*Move transparency 7A so that Jesus appears to be going up into Heaven. Turn off the projector.*)

The disciples did what Jesus said to do. They started by telling everyone in Jerusalem the good news about Jesus. Many people heard and became believers in Jesus. They became the very first church.

The believers did everything together. Every day they met at the temple. They also met for Bible study and prayer meetings in people's homes. (*Project transparency 8B. Have four children act out sharing food. Use the bread baskets as props.*) **If one family had a dinner, everyone was invited to eat at their house. Their hearts were filled with joy every time they were together. They were always praising God.**

None of the believers was selfish. Everyone shared what he had. Some of the people sold their land and some sold their houses. (*Have some children pretend to give money to other children.*) **They shared the money with other believers who needed it.** (*Give a moneybag to one boy who will pretend to be Barnabas.*) **One man named Barnabas came from a far away country. He sold some land and gave the money to the disciples.** (*Have Barnabas give the moneybag to another boy.*) **This made everyone very happy.** (*Have all the children walk up to Barnabas and shake his hand and say, "Thank you!"*)

Everyone in the new church shared. No one was ever hungry. Everyone had the clothes he needed. Everyone had a place to live. Each person was given the things he needed.

This pleased God, and He blessed the people in the church. Many other people liked the believers. They liked the way they shared. Every day more and more people believed in Jesus and became a part of this very first church. (*Turn off the projector.*)

Our church shares with others, too. We want to do good and always share. (*Tell how your church shares with others, such as providing food or clothing, sharing the building with various groups, supporting missionaries.*)

Story Review: Give from Your Heart

You will need the words to "Share What You Have" from p. 230, the heart necklaces made and used in Lesson 39, another red paper heart with a smile on it for each child, and glue. (Be sure new hearts are the same size as the necklace hearts.)

Review and sing verses one and two of "Share What You Have." Then teach verse three of the song. Sing it several times.

Pass out the heart necklaces. **Look at your necklace. Show me the kind of heart Jesus saw when the little boy shared his lunch and more than 5,000 people were fed. Right! Jesus saw a happy heart. When the rich people put their offerings in the temple money box, what kind of heart did Jesus see? Yes, He saw grumbling hearts. They really did not care about giving to God. They just wanted other people to see how much they gave. What kind of hearts did the people in the first church have? Yes, they shared everything they had with happy hearts.**

Now, show me what kind of heart God wants you to have when you share with others. Yes, He wants us to always have happy hearts. Raise your hand if you will try to have a happy heart when you share. Here is a smiling heart for each of you. Let's glue it over the grumbling heart on your necklace so that we will always have a happy heart.

Bible Memory: Fruit Share-a-Thon

You will need a Bible, a banana, an apple, an orange, and several cutting knives to be used by adults only. (More fruit may be needed if your group is large.)

Open the Bible to Hebrews 13:16. Read the verse. Read the verse again by breaking it down into two- or three-word phrases. Have the children repeat each phrase several times.

Show the fruit. **I have only three pieces of fruit. Do I have enough for each child to have a whole piece of fruit? What can I do so everyone will get a piece? Yes, I can cut the fruit in small pieces for everyone. God is pleased when we share. The Bible tells us not to forget to do good and share.**

As the fruit is passed out, ask each child to recite the words of the verse and tell something good he can do for others, such as help mother set the table, help dad take out the trash, or play with baby brother or sister.

▼ 3. What Does This Mean to Me? ▲

Sharing Hearts

You will need the "We Can Share" poster made during Lesson 39, the "hand printed" wrapping paper made during Lesson 39, several large boxes (the kind you get from grocery stores when moving), the items brought in today for the food drive, the card from p. 250 copied onto white card stock, and crayons or markers.

Before class, wrap the large boxes in the "hand-printed" wrapping paper. If possible, have one box for each family that will be receiving food. Help the children count the number of items brought in for the food drive and divide the items among the boxes. Tally the number of food items on the "We Can Share" poster. Compliment the efforts made by the children. Be sensitive to the children who have not brought anything yet.

Tell the children when the last day will be for the food drive. **Here are some cards we will deliver with the food boxes. While you are decorating a card, I want each of you to think of something you would like to tell these people. I will write your message on the card for you.** Give help as needed.

▼ 4. What Can I Do to Please God? ▲

Mini Banner

You will need a copy of the mini banner from p. 249 for each child, crayons, markers, or watercolors for coloring the banner, two craft sticks for each child, scissors, and yarn.

Here is a mini banner for you to make and take home to help you remember our Bible words. What are the children doing in the picture? God wants us to do good and share like the children in the picture.

Let the children color their pictures. Show them how to glue a craft stick to the back at the top and bottom of the banner. Tie an 8" piece of yarn to the ends of the top craft stick for hanging the banner.

"Do not forget to do good to others, and share with them."
(Hebrews 13:16)

Who can say our Bible words?
What is something good you can do this week?
What is one way you will share this week?
Close with prayer, asking God to help each child remember to share with a happy heart.

Share a Good Word

You will need copies of the reminder to parents from p. 250. Fill in the date the food drive will end, the group or organization to receive the food, and your name and telephone number before copying the letter. Fill in a variety of trail mix ingredients, such as cereal, nuts, pretzels, or dried fruit on the letters after they are copied, so that each child brings something different. If you have children with nut allergies in your classroom, don't ask for nuts for your trail mix.

Carefully observe the children as they help clean up the room. Give a complimentary word to each child while she is helping. Compliment each child on the number of stickers on his "I Will Share" headband.

Remember! The next time you come will be the last day to bring something for our food drive. We are going to share our food boxes with (name of organization). This note asks your parents to help you remember the food and a special snack.

Our Bible words remind us to do good and share with others.
Who can say our Bible words?
What is something good you can do this week?
What is one way you will share this week?
Close with prayer, asking God to help each child remember to share with a happy heart.

▼ Bonus Activity ▲

Snack Attack! Banana Buddies

You will need a loaf of banana bread, softened cream cheese, a jumbo craft stick for every two children, paper plates, and a knife for an adult to cut the bread.

Wash the children's hands and then gather them around the loaf of bread. **Here is our snack. How can we share it with everyone who is here today? Yes, we can count the number of children and adults. Then we can cut enough pieces for everyone to have one. When we share with others, God is pleased. It makes us feel good, too. Let's pray and thank God for our snack and all the friends who are here to share it.**

Place a dollop of cream cheese on each slice of bread and serve. **I'm going to let you spread your own cream cheese on the bread—what? You don't all have spreaders? But the person next to you has a spreader, doesn't he? What do you think you should do? Yes, taking turns would be a good idea. That way, everyone can spread the cream cheese. Sharing is a good idea, isn't it?**

A Man and His Wife Share

Acts 18; Romans 16:3-5

▼ 1. What Is This Story About? ▲

The Bible Teaches Me

You will need the pictures of a shirt, food, and a bed from p. 251, plain white paper, a white crayon, newspapers, paint shirts, a Bible, paintbrushes, watercolors or thinned tempera paints, and water.

Before class, trace the three pictures with a white crayon onto white paper. Cut the pictures apart so that each child has three separate pictures.

Cover the working area with newspaper and have the children wear paint shirts. Give each child a traced copy of the T-shirt. Open your Bible to Luke 3:11 and tell them to listen to what John the Baptist said about sharing. Read the first sentence only. **On your paper is something John said to share. Take a paintbrush and cover the paper with paint. What do you see? John the Baptist said that if you have two shirts you should share one of them with a person who does not have one.**

Read the last sentence of Luke 3:11. Let the children paint the food. **What else does John tell us to share? If you cannot remember from the verse I read, paint your paper to find out. Yes, we are to share our food, too.**

Pass out the last traced picture and tell the story of a family who built a room for Elisha to stay in whenever he visited them (2 Kings 4:8-10). **Cover this paper with paint and you will see what this family shared with Elisha.**

There are many stories in the Bible about sharing. Today we will learn about a man, Aquila, and his wife, Priscilla, who shared with many people.

Know: God wants them to share what they have with others.

Feel: A desire to share with others.

Do: Share joyfully with others.

Children will accomplish these goals when they

- Discover what the Bible says about sharing.
- Tell about a man and his wife who shared their home.
- Recite Hebrews 13:16 and give examples of doing good.
- Name things to share with others.
- Share food with others.

▼ 2. What Does the Bible Say? ▲

Bible Story: Aquila and Priscilla Share

You will need transparencies 4A, 6C, and 8B, an overhead projector, one breadbasket, and a dark blanket. (See p. 230 for directions on how to use the visual.) Dress three boys in Bible costumes to play the parts of Aquila, Paul, and Apollos. Dress one girl to play the part of Priscilla. (Optional: Dress the rest of the children in simple Bible costumes to be the people at the synagogue.

(Project transparency 6C. Paul enters.) **A man named Paul was a missionary during Bible times. He traveled from city to city telling people Jesus was the Son of God.**

While Paul was teaching in the city of Corinth, he became friends with a man named Aquila and his wife, Priscilla. *(Enter Aquila and Priscilla.)* **They invited Paul to live with them.** *(Remove transparency 6C and project transparency 8B.)* **They were glad they could share their home with Paul.**

Aquila and Priscilla were tent makers and so was Paul. *(Have Paul, Aquila, and Priscilla pretend to be making a tent out of the blanket.)* **Paul earned money to pay for trips to other cities, so he could teach even more people the good news about Jesus.**

(Remove blanket and transparency 8B. Project transparency 4A.) **Every Sabbath, Paul, Aquila, and Priscilla went to the synagogue to worship. Paul was**

How to Say It

Apollos: uh-PAHL-uhs
Aquila: ACK-wih-luh
Corinth: KOR-inth
Elisha: e-LYE-shuh
Ephesus: EF-uh-sus
Priscilla: prih-SIL-uh

often asked to preach. *(Have all the children sit and look at Paul. Have Paul pretend to be preaching.)* **He told the people Jesus was the Son of God. Many people listened and many believed. Even the ruler of the synagogue and his family became Christians. Aquila and Priscilla were happy they could share their home with Paul so he could preach. Paul was happy, too. This husband and wife were his very special friends.**

(Remove transparency 4A and project transparency 8B. Have Paul, Aquila, and Priscilla pretend to be talking.) **When it was time for Paul to go to another city, Aquila and Priscilla asked whether they could go with him as his helpers. Paul was glad they wanted to go. He could use good helpers and teachers, such as Aquila and Priscilla.** *(Remove transparency 8B.)*

They traveled by boat across the sea to a city called Ephesus. *(Project transparency 6C.)* **The people in Ephesus liked Paul's teaching. They wanted him to stay. Paul knew he needed to go to other cities, so left his special friends, Aquila and Priscilla, to teach the people more about Jesus.** *(Paul exits. Aquila and Priscilla stay standing.)* **This man and his wife were good teachers. They loved sharing the good news.**

(Remove transparency 6C and project transparency 4A.) **While Paul was gone, Aquila and Priscilla met a man named Apollos.** *(Enter Apollos.)* **Apollos was a preacher, but he did not understand everything Jesus had taught. Aquila and Priscilla told him more about Jesus and His teachings. Apollos was glad to learn more about Jesus. He was glad Aquila and Priscilla had shared more of the good news with him.**

Apollos wanted to tell people what he had learned from Aquila and Priscilla, so he left Ephesus and went to another city to spread the good news. *(Have Apollos wave to Aquila and Priscilla as he exits.)*

(Remove transparency 4A and project 8B. Have Paul enter.) **When Paul came back to Ephesus, Aquila and Priscilla told him about Apollos.** *(Have the three children pretend to be talking and smiling.)* **Paul was glad they had taught Apollos more about Jesus. His friends were good workers and teachers.** *(Turn off the projector.)*

You can be like Aquila and Priscilla. Our preacher and teachers need your help, too. Do you know how you can help? You can pray for them. You can always be friendly to them. You can thank them for telling you about Jesus. They are glad you are here and want to learn more about Jesus. They want you to share the good news about Jesus with others, too.

Story Review: Remember to Share

You will need for each child a small plastic snack bag, copy of one fish from p. 248, two pennies, a red paper heart, and the words "Good News" printed on a small slip of paper. Before class, collect all of the items. Each item should be small enough to fit in the plastic bag.

Our Bible stories have taught us how to share. Let's remember each story and who shared with other people.

Give each child a fish picture. **What story does this fish remind you of? Who shared in this story? What did he share?**

Give each child two pennies. **What story do these pennies remind you of? Who shared in this story? What did she share?**

Give each child a red heart. **What story does this red heart remind you of? Who shared in this story? What did hhe share?**

Give each child the words "Good News." Read the words. **What story do these words remind you of? Who shared in this story? What did they share?**

Our Bible stories remind us to share our food, our money, our love, and the Good News of Jesus.

Bible Memory: Share and Tell

You will need magazines, catalogs, newspaper ads, a large sheet of paper, and glue.

Review the Bible memory words. Have the children say them several times.

Our Bible words remind us to share. Let's look through these pictures for things that we can share with others.

Gather the children around the magazines, catalogs, and newspaper ads to find the pictures. As they find one, ask them to tear it out and glue it onto the paper.

When everyone has found a couple of pictures, gather the children around the poster. Let each child point to a picture that he put on the poster. Then ask the child to tell with whom he can share that item. Also encourage each child to say the Bible words alone. Give help as needed. Compliment each child's efforts.

Bible Words

"Do not forget to do good to others, and share with them" (Hebrews 13:16).

(Note: This verse has been divided into two parts. If you are teaching four-year-olds, use only the first part. If you are teaching older children, also include the part of the verse in brackets.)

▼ 3. What Does This Mean to Me? ▲

House Puzzle to Share

You will need the house puzzle pieces from p. 252. Copy the pieces onto card stock. If this cannot be done, glue the copies onto cardboard. You will also need crayons or markers, scissors, and envelopes for storage and carrying the puzzles.

Give each child a copy of the puzzle to color. If your children have scissor skills, let them cut out their own puzzles. If not, do this for them.

Demonstrate how the puzzle goes together. Let the children work on their own puzzles. Then let them trade and share their puzzles with their classmates.

When you take your house puzzle home, find someone with whom you can share it. It is fun to work on puzzles with someone else.

Look at the words above the door of the house. They say, "Welcome Home." This house reminds me of the way Aquila and Priscilla shared their house with Paul.

What do you share when someone sleeps over at your house?

What are you sharing when people eat dinner with you?

What other things at your house can you share?

Share the Good News

Play this game the way the game of "Telephone" is played. Have the children sit side by side in a circle.

It is fun to share good news with our friends. The best news we can share with others is about Jesus. What good news do you know about Jesus? Here is some good news I want to share. Whisper a message in the ear of one child. Ask the child to whisper the same message into the ear of the child on his right. Give help as needed to keep the message going around the circle. When the last child receives the message, have him whisper it in your ear. Is it the same message? Let the children take turns starting messages.

▼ 4. What Can I Do to Please God? ▲

Wrap It Up!

You will need the words to "Share What You Have" from p. 230, the "We Can Share" poster, the wrapped boxes and cards made in Lesson 40, and extra food items for children who have not contributed. (Be sensitive to children who have not contributed.)

Help the children count the new items brought today. Add the total on the "We Can Share" poster. Say a special prayer thanking God for helping them collect the food.

Set out the boxes wrapped in the hand-printed paper. Lead the children in deciding how many items can go in each box. Also, talk about the variety of items in each box. This will be a good opportunity for the children to sort and compare. Give help as needed to fill the boxes. While the children are working, sing all the verses to "Share What You Have."

Pass out the cards made last week and let the children put their cards in the filled boxes.

If you have invited a guest to tell the children about the people who will receive the food, ask that person to talk now.

You have done a good job of collecting food to share with others. Just think now happy the people will be when they eat the good food you have shared. God is pleased when we share with others.

Share a Hug

You will need the words to "Share What You Have" from p. 230.

Ask the children to help clean up the classroom. Remind them that helping others pleases God.

Gather the children in one circle. Sing all the verses to "Share What You Have." Have the children wrap their arms around their neighbors on each side. Then take a big step together toward the center of the circle and carefully hug their friends.

We have shared many good things today—food, toys, good news about Jesus, and love. Lead the children in prayer.

▼ Bonus Activity ▲

Snack Attack! Friendship Mix

(Note: To do this activity you will need to send the letter to parents on p. 250 home with the children the week before this lesson is scheduled. See Lesson 40.)

You will need a large mixing bowl, large wooden spoon, a long-handled cup for dipping, and individual sandwich bags.

Have the children hold the ingredients they brought. One at a time, let them pour their ingredients into the mixing bowl. Let the children take turns stirring the mix with a wooden spoon. Let several children take turns filling a sandwich bag for others. Take the children to a special place to eat their snack, such as outdoors.

Sharing our food can be fun. Look at all the different kinds of cereal, nuts, and dried fruit we have in our Friendship Mix. Sharing is fun! Let's thank God for our friends and our snack. Lead the children in prayer.

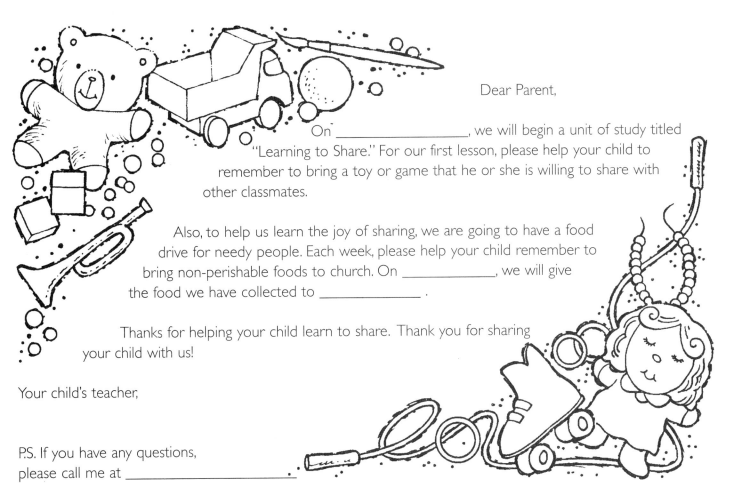

Dear Parent,

On _____, we will begin a unit of study titled "Learning to Share." For our first lesson, please help your child to remember to bring a toy or game that he or she is willing to share with other classmates.

Also, to help us learn the joy of sharing, we are going to have a food drive for needy people. Each week, please help your child remember to bring non-perishable foods to church. On _____, we will give the food we have collected to _____ .

Thanks for helping your child learn to share. Thank you for sharing your child with us!

Your child's teacher,

P.S. If you have any questions, please call me at _____ .

10A

Loaves
and
Fish

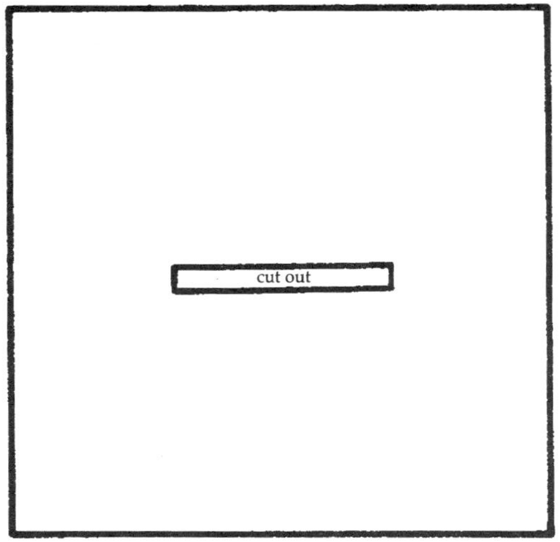

Mini Banner

"Do not forget
to do good to others,
and share with them."
(Hebrews 13:16)

Bank Wrapper

cut out

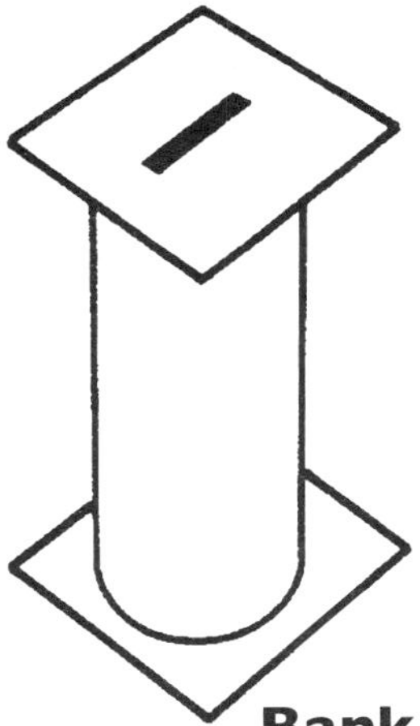

MY SHARING BANK

Dear Parent,

Our non-perishable food drive ends
_____ . These foods are being
gathered so that we may share them with
_____ .

We will celebrate the end of our food drive by
making Friendship Mix to share with each other.
So that each child may contribute to the Friendship
Mix, please let your child bring a package of
_____ to our class next week.

Your child's teacher,

P.S. Please call me at _____
if you have any questions.

Don't Forget

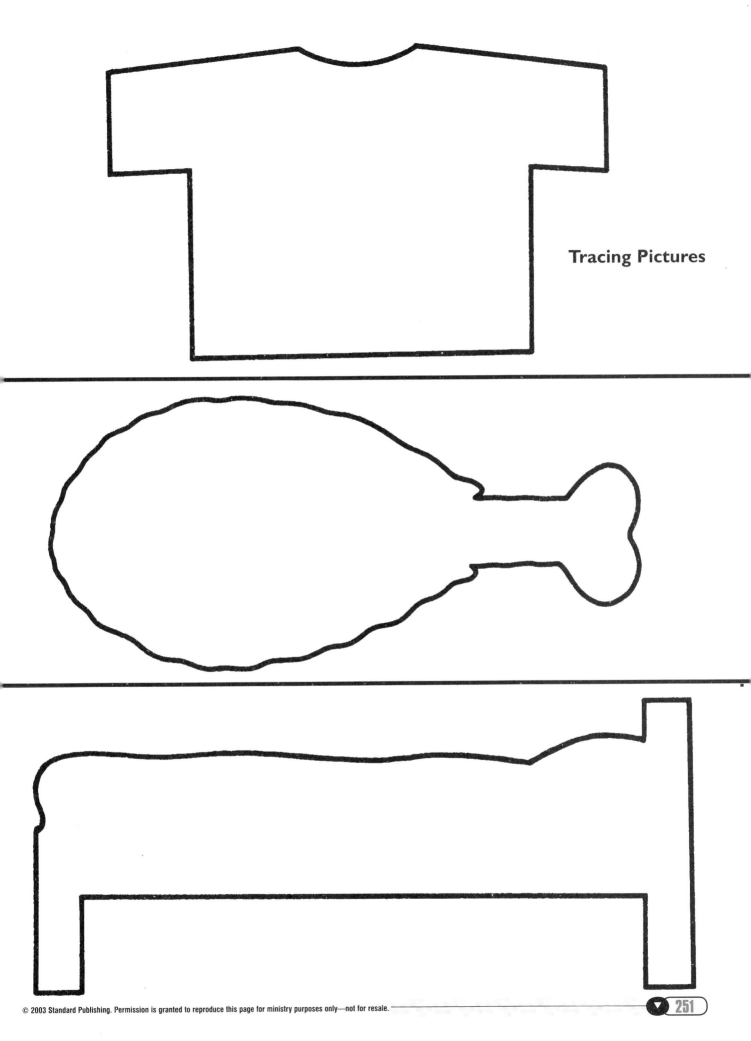

Tracing Pictures

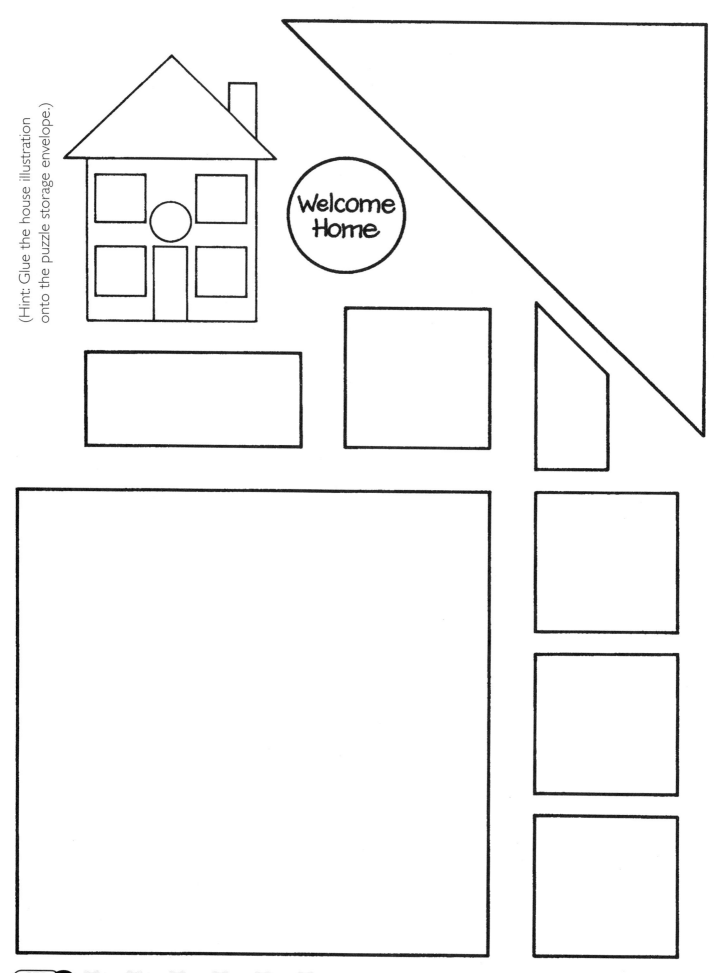

Learning to Help Others

Unit Bible Words
"Do for other people what you want them to do for you" (Luke 6:31).

Bible Characters
Jesus, four friends, Good Samaritan, Dorcas

42 A Father Helps His Child

Mark 5:21-24, 35-43—A young girl is very sick. Her father wants to help her. He asks Jesus to come and heal her. Before Jesus arrives, the girl dies. The power of Jesus' touch brings her back to life.

43 Four Friends Help a Sick Man

Mark 2:1-12—Four friends carry their crippled friend to a house where Jesus is preaching. They will do anything to help their friend. They remove part of the roof and lower their friend on his bed down through the crowd. Jesus heals their friend. Thank God for friends who help us.

44 Jesus Helps His Friends

Mark 4:35-41—Jesus and the disciples travel by boat to the other side of a lake. On the way Jesus falls asleep. His frightened disciples, pleading for His help, awaken Him. Jesus speaks to the wind and waves and they become calm. We can always depend on Jesus to help us.

45 A Samaritan Helps a Traveler

Luke 10:25-37—Jesus uses a Samaritan to teach a lesson about neighborly love. In the story, a Jewish traveler is robbed and beaten. Two Jewish leaders pass right by him. The only one who stopped to help was a lowly Samaritan. Jesus wants us to help everyone.

46 Dorcas Helps Others

Acts 9:36-42—Dorcas is a very willing helper. She uses her talent of sewing to provide clothing for the poor. When she dies, her friends send for Peter. He prays and asks God to bring Dorcas back to life. God's power brings Dorcas back to continue helping others.

By the end of this unit, the children and leaders will

Know: God wants them to help others.
Feel: Joyful when helping others.
Do: Be helpful to families, friends, and others.

Why Teach This Unit to Four- to Six-Year-Olds?

Most four-, five-, and six-year-olds cannot wait to be "big enough" to help. Use this unit to create an environment that encourages helping skills and deepens the desire to be helpful. Encourage your students to ask, "May I help?" and approach the task with the outlook, "I can do that!"

This unit provides these young children with role models of different ages and gender. They will meet a father who helps his sick daughter, four men who help a sick friend, a traveler who helps a stranger, and a woman who helps the poor. The best role model of all is Jesus, who is always ready to help when asked.

Meet a Father

Jairus was a ruler of a synagogue in Galilee. His 12-year-old daughter was very sick. When he heard Jesus was in town, he immediately went to find Him and ask Him to come and heal his daughter. This father wanted to help his daughter. He knew Jesus could provide the help she needed.

Meet Four Friends

The familiar saying "a friend in need is a friend indeed" applies to these four men. They had a friend with a tremendous need. He was paralyzed. They took their friend to Jesus to be healed. These men did not allow any obstacle to get in their way. A huge crowd surrounding Jesus did not stop them. A tile roof did not stop them either. They made a way through the crowd and the roof. Jesus said their faith healed their friend!

Meet Jesus

Jesus has authority in Heaven and on earth (Matthew 28:18). While on earth, He used His authority to help others. His mission on earth was to minister love. He never used His authority and power for His own benefit, but He freely used it to raise the dead, heal the sick, and calm the fearful. He willingly helped others without any thought of how they could help him in return. We need to follow His self-giving attributes.

Meet a Samaritan

The Jews in the Bible were prejudiced against the Samaritans. Every Jew could trace his bloodline back to Abraham. As a result, they felt superior. The Samaritans were only part Jewish. They had intermarried with pagans and no longer had pure bloodlines. The Jews felt the Samaritans had forsaken their heritage, and no longer deserved the rights and privileges Jews enjoyed.

Meet Dorcas

Dorcas was a devoted Christian woman living in Joppa. She spent her life helping the poor. Her talent of sewing clothing had touched the hearts of many of Joppa's poor. When she died, many grieved. Through Peter, God brought Dorcas back to life. There was great joy among her friends and many people in Joppa became believers.

Unit Project: Invite Fathers, Friends, and Mothers

Invite guests to participate in these lessons about helping others. Lesson 42 suggests inviting fathers or other male caregivers as you teach about a father who helps his child. Lesson 43 is a study of friends who helped a sick man and includes activities for pairs of friends. Mothers or other female caregivers are invited for Lesson 46 to hear about Dorcas, a helpful woman.

Provide other options if mothers and fathers cannot attend. Suggest other relatives or people in the church. Ask senior citizens or other adults to fill in for missing parents.

On the day when children bring friends, ask parents to choose guests ages four to six. Or invite another class or department to come as guests.

You will need to plan ahead in order to extend these invitations.

Unit Visuals

A variety of visuals will be used to illustrate the Bible stories in this unit. Each lesson will use a transparency and overhead projector. You will need a blank wall or a plain sheet tacked to a wall to project the scenes and/or silhouettes.

This unit will be illustrated with transparencies made from pp. 144, 145, and 195, illustrations 6A, 6C, 6D, and 8B. Color may be added to the transparencies. Use only permanent overhead projector pens. (Hint: Handle transparencies as little as possible. Colored pens will not mark easily over fingerprints.)

Silhouettes will be used in some lessons and are found on pp. 106 and 194. Copy the silhouettes onto card stock and cut out, or glue onto light cardboard and cut out.

At the beginning of each Bible story you will find a list of the transparencies and silhouettes (if needed) for that lesson. Project the transparency and place the appropriate silhouettes on the transparency according to the directions throughout the story. Sometimes the silhouettes will be projected alone.

Some stories will use children and/or adults to play the parts of the Bible characters. Keep costuming simple, such as bathrobes and colored T-shirts. All of the action will be pantomimed in front of the projected scene and the storyteller will give the directions. There are no speaking parts.

A Father Helps His Child

Mark 5:21-24, 35-43

▼ 1. What Is This Story About? ▲

My Family Helps Me

You will need the "Family Finger Puppets" used in Unit 7 and found on p. 171, and the "Grandparent Puppets" from p. 276. You will also need cardboard tubes to support the puppets. (You can make your own tubes from rolled up cardboard.)

Copy, color, and cut out the puppets. Instead of using them as finger puppets as was suggested in Unit 7, provide cardboard tubes to help them stand up.

Glue a puppet around each tube (toilet paper or paper towel tube cut to size). This will make it easier for the children to manipulate the puppets.

Set up the puppets so the children can see them all. Point to each puppet, asking the children to name each family member represented. Ask the children to tell how each of these family members helps them. For example, mom cooks, dad fixes things, brother finds my lost shoe, grandmother reads to me. Select a child to stand in front of the class and demonstrate how one of these family members helps her. Before the child begins an action, have the child whisper in your ear the name of the person she is pantomiming. Ask the class to guess what the child is demonstrating. Point to the puppet who would help in that way. Give every child (and guest) a turn.

Our family helps us in many ways. Let's thank God for giving us families. Lead in prayer. **Today in our Bible story we will hear about a father who helped his sick daughter.**

Help, Help Your Neighbors

You will need the words to "Help, Help Your Neighbors" from p. 257 and play dough. (To make play dough, see p. 16.)

Give each child and guest some play dough. Tell the children to make a play dough figure of someone in their family they helped today. While the children are working, begin singing the song, "Help, Help Your Neighbors." Ask the children to sing along.

When they have finished making their figures, ask each person to tell whom he made and how he helped.

What did your family member say to you when you helped? How did helping make you feel? How do you think the person felt?

Our new song says "All love and kindness comes from above." That means God gives you the love and kindness you need to help your family. Let's thank God right now for love and kindness.

▼ 2. What Does the Bible Say? ▲

Bible Story: Jesus Helps a Dad

You will need silhouettes 11-a Jesus, 11-b man, 11-c woman, 11-d girl, 11-e bed, 11-f Peter, 11-g crowd, 11-h James and John, and an overhead projector. (See p. 254 for directions on how to use the visual.)

Know: God wants them to help others.
Feel: Joyful when helping others.
Do: Be helpful to families, friends, and others.

Children will accomplish the goals when they
- Explore how people in families help each other.
- Tell about a father who needed Jesus' help.
- Begin to memorize Luke 6:31.
- Name ways to help in their family.
- Choose to help someone in their family.

Special Guests

Invite your students' fathers to attend and participate in this lesson. If a child's father is not able to attend, ask another relative or man in your church to come in his place. Involve the guests in all the activities. Ask them to sit with their children during the story time.

(Project silhouettes 11-a and 11-g.) **Everywhere Jesus went, crowds of people followed Him. They listened to Him teach. He was a good teacher. He told them about God. He also healed sick people. People were amazed by what He said and did.**

One day a big group of people was around Jesus. *(Add silhouette 11-b. Tilt it to look as though the man is bowing and then place the man upright.)* **A very important man from the synagogue came and bowed in front of Him. The man said, "My daughter is very, very sick. Please come and touch her so she will get well."**

(Turn silhouettes 11-a, 11-b, 11-g so they are going in the same direction.) **Jesus started walking with the father to his house. His helpers went with Him. All of the people followed Him, too.**

Before they arrived at the house, some men came looking for the girl's father and said, "Do not bother Jesus. Your daughter is dead."

The father was very sad. He wanted his little girl to be touched by Jesus so she could walk and talk and play again. Jesus looked at the sad father and said, "Do not be sad, just believe in me. She will come back to life."

When Jesus arrived at the father's house, many friends of the girl's family were there. They were crying. There was a lot of noise and a lot of people.

Jesus looked at all the people and said, "Do not cry. The girl is not dead. She is sleeping." The people laughed at Jesus. They did not believe in His power.

Jesus told all the people to leave. *(Remove silhouette 11-g. Add silhouette 11-c.)* **Jesus followed the father and mother into the bedroom.** *(Add silhouettes 11-f and 11-h.)* **Peter, James, and John, Jesus' helpers, were there, too.**

(Add silhouettes 11-d and 11-e.) **The girl was lying on a bed. Her eyes were closed and she did not move.** *(Move silhouette 11-a close to the girl on the bed.)* **Jesus walked over to the bed and picked up the little girl's hand. He said to her, "Little girl, get up!"** *(Place silhouette 11-d in a standing position.)* **Right then, the little girl stood up and started walking.**

The father and mother were very surprised. Peter, James, and John were surprised, too. Everyone was very happy. Jesus brought the little girl back to life. Now she could walk and talk and play again. She could eat, too. Jesus told the parents to give her some food. *(Turn off the projector.)*

Story Review: Teamwork

You will need one beanbag for each adult guest. (Fill socks with dried beans or rice. Tie the neck in a knot.)

Line up the guests with their children facing them (a few steps away). Give each adult a beanbag. Call out the review question. The guest tosses the beanbag to the child. The child catches it and answers the question. Then the child tosses it back and the guest answers the next question.

How did this father help his child? (He went looking for Jesus.) **How did he know that Jesus could help his daughter?** (He had heard about what Jesus had done for others.) **When Jesus and the little girl's father got to the house, some men told them something. What did these men say?** (They said not to bother Jesus anymore because the little girl was already dead.) **Why didn't these people think Jesus could help the little girl?** (They did not believe in His power.) **What did Jesus do when He went into the girl's bedroom.** (He took her by the hand and said, "Little girl, get up!") **What happened then?** (The little girl got up and began walking.) **Who else was in the room?** (The girl's mother and father, and Peter, James and John.) **How did these people feel when the little girl got up?** (Surprised and very happy.) **Why is Jesus able to make people live again after they have died?** (He is the Son of God.)

When you are sick, your family cares about you, too. Let's thank God for our families who take care of us. Lead in prayer.

Bible Memory: Let's Learn the Golden Rule

Recite Luke 6:31 and ask an adult to explain why this verse is called the "Golden Rule." (Prearrange with someone or ask for a volunteer, rather than putting someone on the spot.)

Line up the children and guests, alternating adult, child, adult, child. Say to the first child in the line **"Do for other people."** Have the child turn to the guest behind him and repeat, "Do for other people." Each person in the line repeats the phrase to the person behind him. Give help as needed until the last person in line repeats the words to the leader. Listen and make corrections as the phrases are repeated down the line. Now start the next phrase, **"what you want them"** down the line. When the last person says it to the leader, start the last phrase, **"to do for you."** If the guests are helping you, try sending the phrases down the line one right after the other. (There will be several people talking at the same time.) Without the guests to keep it going, this will be too difficult for the children to do alone. The children and the guests will enjoy working on the challenge together.

> **Bible Words**
> "Do for other people what you want them to do for you" (Luke 6:31).

▼ 3. What Does This Mean to Me? ▲

How Can I Help My Family?

You will need the following items or pictures of these items: trash bag, broom, rake, dust cloth, a toy, a rolled up newspaper, a potted plant or flower, a plastic cup, a grocery bag filled with non-perishable groceries, a bucket and a sponge, and a jacket.

Have the guests and children form a half circle in front of a wall where the collected items are lined up. Have the children name each item. Ask a guest to stand in front of the group and pantomime using one of the items in a helpful way. He may use his child to help him. The rest of the group must look at the items and guess how the guest is helping his family or his child. The person who guesses correctly is the next to pantomime a helpful action.

In a happy family, members are always helping each other. Dads help the family with big and small jobs. Children can help, too. When everyone in the family works together, they are pleasing God. Another way that we can help our families is by praying for them. Have the guests and children form a prayer circle. Ask the children to pray for their guests.

▼ 4. What Can I Do to Please God? ▲

I Will Help My Family

You will need the words to "Help, Help Your Neighbors," the tube puppets from the "My Family Helps Me" activity, and a paper sack.

Place the puppets in the sack ahead of time. Sing the first verse of "Help, Help Your Neighbors." Let the children take turns choosing a puppet from the sack without looking. Ask each child to show the puppet and tell how he can help this member of his family. If the child selects a person not in his family, let him choose again.

You have chosen to do many good things for your family members. How do you think they will feel when you help them? I know they will be glad to have the help. I also know it will make you feel good because you were able to give help. It pleases God to see you helping your family.

Ask the guests how they feel when their children help them. Ask if a guest would like to tell about a time when his child helped him.

> **Help, Help Your Neighbors**
> (Tune: "Rock-a-bye Baby")
>
> **Verse 1**
> Help, help your neighbors.
>   Treat them with love.
> All love and kindness comes
>   from above.
> Help, help your friends and
>   family, too.
> You can be helpful in all that
>   you do.
>
> **Verse 2**
> I'll not be afraid 'cause Jesus
>   is near.
> We know during storms
>   that Jesus is here.
> He calmed the waves one
>   stormy day.
> He hears and He helps us
>   when we pray.

Thanks for Coming

Ask the guests and children to form teams to clean up the classroom. Then gather everyone together to talk about the time they have just spent together.

What did you like best about having your guest come to class with you? How did your guest help you during class?

Ask the adults the following questions. **What did you like best about our class today? How did your child help you during class? Would you like to come and help us again?** Take note of who responds and invite them to help again!

Form a circle and have a group hug. Have the children wrap their arms around their neighbors on each side. Then instruct the everyone to take a big step together toward the center of the circle and carefully hug their friends.

Ask a guest to volunteer to close with prayer.

Remind the children to bring a friend next week. (See the Unit Project on p. 254.)

▼ Bonus Activity ▲

Snack Attack! A Dad-Size Sundae

You will need bowls, spoons, and the fixings to make ice cream sundaes. Be aware of any special dietary restrictions.

Have a prayer with everyone before they begin. Then let the guests and children enjoy making their own sundaes. Allow enough time for the guests and the children to visit with each other while they eat. Gently encourage guests to spend this time with their children, not visiting with each other.

(Optional: Give awards for the creativity that went into making the sundaes. If you do this, be sure each person gets an award. These can be made by cutting ribbons into 3" lengths and attaching a motivational sticker to the top.)

Four Friends Help a Sick Man

Mark 2:1-12

▼ 1. What Is This Story About? ▲

My Friend Helps Me (Part 1)

You will need three or four centers, depending on the size of your group. Each center will need a teen or adult leader.

This is a two-part activity. Part one will be done now and part two will be done in Step 3. You may already have some of the following centers set up in your room. Use only as many centers as you have leaders:

Block Center with building blocks, cars, and trucks

Home Living Center with dolls, kitchen equipment, and a table with chairs

Art Center with washable ink pads, paper, and colored pencils. Two friends make one picture using their thumb and finger prints. Use colored pencils to turn their prints into bugs, flowers, critters, and so on.

Puzzle Center with the picture of two friends playing from p. 226 of Unit 9. Enlarge and copy onto card stock. Have the two friends color the picture. When the coloring is finished, the adult leader can cut the picture into eight puzzle pieces. Provide a plastic bag for the pieces.

Play Dough Center with 2-3 colors of play dough. Let the friends work together to make one item for one of them to take home.

As the children arrive with their guests, greet each new child and tell him how glad you are he came. Ask each friend to show his guest around the classroom. Then ask the friend to select one center for him and his guest to visit. At the center, encourage each friend to invite his guest to help him with the activity.

It is fun to do things with our friends. How did your guest help you? Let the children share their experiences.

Meet My Friend

Gather the children in a circle. Ask each friend to introduce his guest. **Sometimes people become friends because they like to do the same things. Some friends meet each other at the park because they both like to play on the swings and slides. Some friends meet at church because they both love Jesus. Some people become friends because they live near each other. Where did you meet your friend? What do you like to do with your friend?**

After all the introductions have been made, teach the following song to the tune of "Mary Had a Little Lamb."

(Child's name) is a friend of mine,
friend of mine, friend of mine,
(Child's name) is a friend of mine,
And I am his (her) friend, too.

Have the children take turns standing in the center of the circle. Sing the song several times to include each child's name.

Know: God wants them to help others.
Feel: Joyful about helping others.
Do: Be helpful to families, friends, and others.

Children will accomplish the goals when they
- Explore what friends do.
- Tell how four friends helped their sick friend.
- Memorize Luke 6:31.
- Name ways to help friends.
- Choose to help a friend.

Special Guests

Have the children invite a friend to come with them today. Ask them to choose a friend close to their age. Send a note home several weeks in advance telling parents about the special day for guests. Provide name tags as the guests arrive and make them feel welcome.

▼ 2. What Does the Bible Say? ▲

Bible Story: Four Friends Help

You will need transparency 8B, silhouettes 11-a Jesus, 11-b man, 11-g crowd, 11-i men on the roof, 11-j stretcher, and an overhead projector. (See p. 254 for directions on how to use the visual.)

People followed Jesus everywhere He went. They followed Him as he walked on the roads between towns. When He arrived in a town, the news spread quickly from person to person. Many people wanted to hear Him teach. Many sick people wanted Him to make them well again.

(Project 8B. Add silhouettes 11-a and 11-g.) **One day while Jesus was preaching in a house, a large group of people came to listen to Him. The house was so full, the people had to stand. All of the rooms in the house were filled with people. There were even people standing in the doorways. There was not room for one more person.**

Four men heard the news that Jesus was in town. One of their friends could not walk. They knew Jesus could help their friend walk again. The four men carried their sick friend on a small bed to the house where Jesus was.

"Oh, no!" said the men when they saw the people standing around the outside of the house. "Our friend must see Jesus. How can we get him inside the house?"

"Look," said one of the men pointing to the roof of the house. "Here are some stairs going up to the roof."

Many houses in Bible times had stairs to the roof because people liked to sit on their roofs and enjoy the cool evening breeze. So the men carried the bed with their sick friend on it up the stairs. Now, how were they going to get the man inside the house? Do roofs have windows or doors that open? No, of course not! What were they going to do now?

(Add Silhouette 11-i.) **One of the men decided to take the roof apart. First, he removed a small part of the roof tiles. Could he see Jesus? Maybe, but he needed a bigger hole. The four men worked together making the hole in the roof bigger. Finally they could see Jesus. The hole was even big enough for their sick friend's bed to fit down inside. Using some ropes, they carefully lowered their friend and his bed right down in front of Jesus.** *(Add silhouettes 11-b and 11-j in front of Jesus.)*

Jesus stopped teaching and looked up. He saw the four men looking down at him. He knew they believed He could heal their sick friend. Then Jesus said to the man on the bed, "Stand up! Pick up your bed and go home." *(Place silhouette 11-b in a standing position.)* **Right then, the man did what Jesus said. He walked out of the crowded house, carrying his own bed.** *(Remove silhouettes 11-b and 11-j.)*

Wow! The people who had filled the house were amazed. Many of them said, "I have never seen anything like this!" *(Turn off the projector.)*

Story Review: Who Am I?

Pantomime the actions of different people in the Bible story to help the children review.

I am going to pretend to be someone in today's Bible story. Who am I? Pantomime the man who was lame. **Yes, I am the man who the four friends carried to see Jesus. How do you think this man felt when his friends started lowering his bed through the roof?** Encourage discussion.

Now, who am I? Pantomime the man making the hole in the roof. **Yes, I am one of the friends who made the hole in the roof. Why did he choose to make a hole in the roof?**

Now, who am I? Pantomime Jesus. **Yes, I am Jesus. What do you think Jesus thought when the man's bed started to come through the roof?**

Continue to pantomime others in the story such as the owner of the house and someone in the crowd. Ask questions about what these people might have been thinking.

The sick man had wonderful friends. His friends must have loved him a lot. They had to work very hard to get their friend to Jesus so he could be healed. Would you like to have friends that love you that much? Would you like to be a friend like that? Let's pray and ask God to give us good friends and to help us be good friends.

Bible Memory: Clap Your Hands

Our Bible words teach us the best way to help our friends. Say the Bible words several times with the children. Have each friend and guest stand and face each other. Teach the following rhythm. Clap your hands and slap your partner's hands, palm to palm as noted here.

"Do	(clap)
for	(slap)
other	(clap)
people	(slap)
what	(clap)
you	(slap)
want	(clap)
them	(slap)
to	(clap)
do	(slap)
for	(clap)
you"	(slap)
Luke	(clap)
6:	(slap)
31).	(clap)

Have the partners say the verse and do the rhythm several times.

This verse tells you to be the first one to be a friend to others. Do not wait for someone else to be friendly. When you help your friends, you are showing them you would like their help, too. When you are friendly to others, you are showing them you would like them to be friendly to you.

> **Bible Words**
> "Do for other people what you want them to do for you" (Luke 6:31).

▼ 3. What Does This Mean to Me? ▲

I Help My Friend (Part 2)

You will need the words to "Help, Help Your Neighbors" from p. 263, and the centers used in the "My Friend Helps Me" activity.

When you arrived today, you each took your guest to a center you chose. Your guest helped you do the activities. Now your guest will choose a center and you will help him.

Give the children time to do another center and then gather them together to discuss how they helped.

How did you help your guest at the center? Let the friends share.

Was your friend a good helper? Encourage the guests to share.

Working together and helping each other can be fun. Comment on what you observed as the children worked together. Sing together the first verse of "Help, Help Your Neighbors." Lead the children in a prayer, thanking God for the guests who are visiting your class today.

Watching for Ways to Help

Before class, photocopy or write each of the following five situations on a slip of paper.

Let the children take turns pulling a piece of paper from a bowl. Read the scenario out loud and let the children tell you what they could do to help. Then have volunteers act out the answers.

1. Your mother has said that if everyone's room is straightened up by the time Dad gets home, you will go out for pizza. If not, you will have to stay home and eat leftovers. You have cleaned your room and now it is time for your favorite TV show. Your brother is having trouble getting his room clean. **What can you do to help?**

2. Your best friend broke his leg. He has asked you to come over and play games with him, but the rest of the neighborhood kids are playing on a friend's brand new jungle gym swing set. **What can you do to help?**

3. There's a new child at your preschool. He's from another country and it's hard to understand him when he talks. The other kids just leave him alone. **What can you do to be helpful?**

4. It's the day after Valentine's Day. You got a whole bag full of cards and candy. Your sister (or brother) is too little to go to school, so she (he) didn't get anything. **What can you do to help?**

5. Your little sister made a big mess in the kitchen. You know your mom is going to be upset when she sees it. **What can you do to help?**

▼ 4. What Can I Do to Please God? ▲

Friendship Necklace

You will need the "Friendship Necklace" pattern from p. 276, colored card stock, scissors, yarn, clear tape, crayons or markers, paper cups, and Fruit Loops.

Before class time, copy the pattern onto colored card stock for each pair of children. Cut out the circles and punch two holes in each as indicated. Cut yarn into two-foot strips (one for each child), and wrap the yarn ends with tape.

Team each friend with his guest and pair friends together who did not bring guests. Show the circle to the pairs and read the caption, "We are friends." Cut on the black line to divide the circle into two pieces. Give each child one half circle to color. While the children are coloring, insert a yarn strip in each hole. Give each pair of children a small cup of Fruit Loops and have them work together to string the cereal on one of the necklaces. Have them do the other one together also. Tie the ends of each necklace together and let the children wear them. Show the children how to hold their halves together to make a whole circle. (If you have an uneven number of children, have one of the adult leaders share a necklace with a child.)

What are some ways friends help each other?
What do you like best about having a friend?
What will you do to help your friend this week?
Whenever you wear your necklace, remember to pray and thank God for your friend.

Let's Be Friends

You will need the words to "Help, Help Your Neighbors" from p. 263.

Ask the friends and guests to work in pairs to help clean up the classroom. When the room is straightened, thank the children for being your friend and helping you.

Gather the children in a circle. Sing the first verse of "Help, Help Your

Neighbors." Close with a prayer, thanking God for friends.

Lead the children in a group hug. Standing in a circle, have the children wrap their arms around their neighbors on each side. Then instruct the children to take a big step together toward the center of the circle and carefully hug their friends.

Be sure to tell each guest you were glad he came today and invite each one to come back next time.

▼ Bonus Activities ▲

Snack Attack! P. B. and J. Friends

You will need bread, peanut butter, jelly, plastic knives, and paper plates. (Be aware of any peanut allergies. Substitute cream cheese or another kind of jelly.)

Help the children wash their hands. Have the children work in pairs to make sandwiches. Ask one child to spread peanut butter on one slice of bread. Have the other child spread jelly on the other slice. Then help the children put the slices together and cut them in half. Each child will eat one of the halves.

It was fun to make sandwiches with our friends. I like the way everyone worked together. God is pleased when friends help each other. Let's pray and thank God for our snack and our friends who helped us make it.

Extra Action! Me and My Shadow

Ask all of the guests to stand in a line facing you. Then ask each friend to stand behind his guest. (If two children who attend regularly are paired together, for this activity, pretend one is the guest.) Tell them you are going to call out some actions and the friends should be the shadows of the guests. When you call out an action, such as jump up and down, the guests will jump and the friends will try to jump at the same time like a shadow. (Additional actions: march, nod head, salute, hands on hips, touch your toes, put arms above your head and sway like a tree, twirl around, sit down.) Half way through the actions, switch the children. Have the guests become the shadows.

It was fun to try to copy the way your friend moved. When you are playing with your friend, sometimes you do what she wants to do and sometimes your friend does what you want to do. When you take turns, you are showing love and kindness to each other.

Help, Help Your Neighbors
(Tune: "Rock-a-bye Baby")

Verse 1
Help, help your neighbors.
    Treat them with love.
All love and kindness comes
    from above.
Help, help your friends and
    family, too.
You can be helpful in all that
    you do.

Verse 2
I'll not be afraid 'cause Jesus
    is near.
We know during storms
    that Jesus is here.
He calmed the waves one
    stormy day.
He hears and He helps us
    when we pray.

Jesus Helps His Friends

Mark 4:35-41

Know: God wants them to help others.

Feel: Joyful when helping others.

Do: Be helpful to families, friends, and others.

Children will accomplish the goals when they

- Explore ways Jesus can help them.
- Tell how Jesus helped His friends when they were afraid.
- Recite Luke 6:31.
- Name times and places Jesus can help.
- Praise Jesus for helping them.

▼ 1. What Is This Story About? ▲

Jesus Helps Me Every Day

You will need a copy of the "Jesus Is My Helper" book from p. 277 for each child, the "Jesus Stickers" from p. 276, a stapler, and crayons or markers.

To prepare the Jesus stickers, you will need white glue, vinegar, peppermint extract (optional), a small paintbrush, and scissors. Before class time, mix two parts white glue and one part vinegar. Add a few drops of peppermint extract, if desired. Lightly paint the mixture onto the backs of the uncut stickers. Let them dry. Cut out.

The Bible tells us many things about Jesus. It tells us He is our helper.

Give each child a "Jesus Is My Helper" book to color. After the pictures are colored, fold the pages into a book. Be sure each child's name is on his book.

Gather the children with their completed booklets and the supply of Jesus stickers in your story area.

Let's look at each picture and talk about how Jesus can help each child pictured. Tell some of your own experiences in these situations to give examples of how Jesus has helped you. This will encourage the children to share their experiences. As you do this, give each child a Jesus sticker to lick and place on the circle outline on each page.

Jesus Helps When I'm Afraid

You will need clear plastic bottles with lids (shampoo-size bottles work best), water, liquid blue food coloring, liquid vegetable oil, glue, a dark permanent marker, and paint shirts for protection from the food coloring. You will also need the words to "Help, Help Your Neighbors" from p. 267.

Involve the children in the following process as much as possible. Fill each bottle half full of water. Add several drops of blue coloring. Fill the rest of the bottle with oil. Glue the lid on the bottle and shake. Watch the waves! Make several bottles for classroom play or make one for each child.

The waves in this bottle remind me of the waves in our Bible story. We are going to hear a story about Jesus helping His friends. They were in a boat during a terrible storm. The wind blew the waves into their boat. They were very afraid. When have you been afraid? Encourage responses. **Jesus promises to always be with us and help us when we are afraid. We're going to write "Jesus is my helper" on each bottle to remind us.**

Teach verse two of "Help, Help Your Neighbors." Sing the verse several times as the children make waves with the bottles.

▼ 2. What Does the Bible Say? ▲

Bible Story: Jesus, Help Us!

You will need transparency 6A and children dressed in simple Bible costumes. You will need actors to play the parts of Jesus and several disciples. (See p. 254 for directions on how to use the visual.)

Remember how crowds of people followed Jesus everywhere He went? There was a big crowd around Jesus when the father of the sick girl came to ask Jesus to go home with him and make his daughter well. Another time, the people crowded into a house where Jesus was preaching. How did the four men get their sick friend to see Jesus so he could be healed? Yes, they made a hole in the roof and lowered his bed through the hole with ropes. Do you think Jesus ever got tired? Listen to what happened after Jesus taught all day.

(Project 6A. Have Jesus get in the boat and motion to the group of disciples to come.) **It was evening and Jesus needed to rest. He said to His helpers, "Come and go across the lake with me."** *(Have the disciples get into the boat and sit down.)* **His helpers got in the boat where Jesus sat teaching and started sailing across the lake. The waves gently rocked the boat back and forth and up and down. Jesus and the disciples rocked back and forth gently. Jesus was very tired from teaching all day. He found a pillow in the back of the boat and went to sleep.** *(Have Jesus put His head down as if sleeping.)*

While Jesus was sleeping, the waves grew bigger and bigger. The boat went up on top of the waves, and then down between the tall waves. *(Have the disciples rock faster and faster.)* **A terrible storm was all around the boat. The wind blew harder and harder, making the boat rock faster and faster.** *(Have the disciples huddle together and look frightened.)* **The water spilled over and into the boat. Jesus' helpers were very frightened, but Jesus did not wake up. He was still sound asleep in the back of the boat.** *(Jesus remains asleep.)*

(The disciples gather around Jesus and shake Him.) **Finally, the helpers woke Jesus up saying, "Teacher, Teacher, help us! How can You sleep? We are going to drown!"**

(Jesus wakes up, stretches, and stands up.) **Jesus woke up and saw the terrible storm.** *(Have Jesus stretch out his arms.)* **He stood up in the boat and said, "Be quiet! Be still!"**

Suddenly, the wind stopped howling. The waves became smooth. *(Jesus and the disciples rock gently.)* **The boat rocked gently on the calm water. Jesus' friends were so surprised!**

Jesus asked the helpers, "Why were you so afraid? Don't you believe in my power to help you?" The helpers just looked at one another and said, "Even the wind obeys Jesus and so do the waves!" *(Turn off the projector.)*

Story Review: Jesus Is Near

You will need the words to "Help, Help Your Neighbors" from p. 267, copies of the boat from p. 276, 9" white paper plates, crayons or markers, and glue.

Before class, fold each paper plate in half and cut waves into the top fold, leaving the two ends uncut. Print "Jesus is near" around the edge of the paper plate with a black marker. Also cut out the boats.

Give the children paper plates and tell them to color the water blue. Then give them boats to color brown. (Optional: Copy the boats onto brown paper.) Help the children assemble the rocking boats. Read the words printed on the plates. Sing the second verse of "Help, Help Your Neighbors" several times as the children rock their boats.

Jesus helped his friends during the terrible storm. The boat rocked back and forth like yours. When the storm came, the boat rocked faster and faster. Jesus' friends were very afraid. But Jesus helped them by calming the storm. He promises to always be with us, too and help us when we are afraid.

Bible Memory: Who Needs My Help?

You will need a large poster board, a dark marker, magazines and/or newspaper ads for a variety of pictures of faces, and glue. On the poster board print, "Who Needs My Help?"

Gather the children around the magazines and newspaper ads. Show them how to look for faces and tear them out. Put the faces in a pile. When you think you have enough to cover the poster, stop. Have the children help glue the pictures on the poster to make a big collage.

While the children are working on this project, review the Bible words. Work with individual children, helping them to recite the verse from memory. Talk about how Jesus has helped them and how He wants them to help others. Then ask the children to tell how they could help people like those on the poster. For example, older people need help picking up things from the floor; babies need help learning to walk; moms need help clearing the table after supper.

Jesus is the best helper. He wants us to be a helper like He is. You are big enough to help others. Always remember Jesus will help you, too.

▼ 3. What Does This Mean to Me? ▲

The Best Helper

You will need a beach ball and an open area for playing with the ball.

Have you ever been in a boat on a lake, a river, or the ocean? Was it a rainy day or was it a sunny day? When you visit a lake, a river, or the ocean on a sunny day, there are many things you can do. You can swim in the water and play on the shore. You can fish from a dock or a boat. Let's pretend we are on a sandy beach at the edge of the water. Let's play with this beach ball. Bring out the ball and toss it in the air and catch it. **I am going to toss this beach ball into the air. If you catch it, tell about a time when Jesus can help you. Then toss the ball up into the air and let another person catch it.** Continue playing until everyone has a turn.

Which Friend Is This?

You will need a large paper grocery sack. Cut out holes for eyes.

Have the children sit in a circle. Ask them to cover their eyes with their hands. Walk around the outside of the circle. Tap a child on the shoulder and motion for him to go to the center of the circle. Place the sack over his head, so he can see out. When ready, ask the rest of the class to uncover their eyes and guess which friend is under the sack. When the child hears his name, tell him to remove the sack and name one place where Jesus is with him. Play until everyone has a turn.

Sometimes we needed help to guess the right name of the person under the sack, but Jesus always knows. He sees us wherever we are, and He is always ready to help us. We just need to ask Him.

▼ 4. What Can I Do to Please God? ▲

Heavenly Hugs

You will need a large soft blanket. Larger classes may need more than one blanket.

If Jesus were here, what would He do to help clean and straighten this classroom? Listen to the children's responses and send them to clean up the areas they suggest.

Then gather the children as close as possible. Have other leaders help you wrap a blanket around the children.

When you are afraid at night or just feeling lonely, do you hide under your blankets? How does the blanket make you feel? I know someone who can help you when you're afraid. This person is better than the biggest and softest blanket. Do you know who this person is? Yes, He is Jesus. Jesus is better than a blanket when you are afraid or lonely. Let's praise Jesus for helping us.

Lead the children in a time of prayer and praise. Begin with a short prayer of your own: **Thank You, Jesus, for helping me when I'm afraid,** or **I praise You, Jesus, because You are with me all the time.** Then encourage each child to pray. Give hugs to the children as they leave.

▼ Bonus Activity ▲

Snack Attack! Edible Waves

You will need blue gelatin, clear plastic cups, an electric mixer, brown paper, scissors, clear tape, and plastic spoons.

Prepare the gelatin in a deep bowl as directed on the box. After adding the cold water, beat the gelatin with a mixer for several minutes or until it is foamy. Pour it into the cups and chill until firm. The gelatin will form layers as it settles. The foamy layer will be on top.

Cut out small boats with sails from brown paper. (Optional: Reduce the sailboat on p. 276.) Tape the boats onto the spoon handle tips. When the gelatin is firm, stick a spoon in the center of each cup.

Pray before serving the children. As you pass out the cups, review the Bible story.

(Optional: Reduce the sailboat on p. 276.)

Help, Help Your Neighbors
(Tune: "Rock-a-bye Baby")

Verse 1
Help, help your neighbors.
  Treat them with love.
All love and kindness comes
  from above.
Help, help your friends and
  family, too.
You can be helpful in all that
  you do.

Verse 2
I'll not be afraid 'cause Jesus
  is near.
We know during storms
  that Jesus is here.
He calmed the waves one
  stormy day.
He hears and He helps us
  when we pray.

A Samaritan Helps a Traveler

Luke 10:25-37

Know: God wants them to help others.
Feel: Joyful when helping others.
Do: Be helpful to families, friends, and others.

Children will accomplish the goals when they
- Show how they can be kind and help others.
- Tell how a man helped a traveler.
- Recite Luke 6:31 and talk about times to do it.
- Name ways to help people they know.
- Choose to help others.

▼ 1. What Is This Story About? ▲

Be Kind! Be Helpful!

Let's have some fun acting out ways to be helpful.
Choose pairs of children to pantomime kind actions, such as raking leaves for a grandparent, playing ball with brother, picking up crayons for a teacher. Ask the rest of the class to watch and guess what they are doing. Give everyone a turn.

In today's Bible story we are going to hear a story Jesus told to help us be kind and helpful to others.

Why Me?

You will need an adult or teen to help you role-play these three situations. After each role play, discuss why it was difficult for the person to help.

1. Sarah pushes Emily. Then, as Sarah walks away, she trips and scrapes her knee. She cries for help. Emily has to decide whether she wants to help Sarah. Finally, she helps.

Think of someone who has been unkind to you. Would it be hard to help this person if she was hurt? What would Jesus tell you to do?

2. Create a mess in one area of the classroom. Take the children to see the mess. Complain about the "mystery" mess-maker. Finally, you decide you will help and clean up the mess.

Have you ever cleaned up a mess at home or school you did not make? Did you grumble? What would Jesus want you to do?

3. Jeff is playing with a toy. Mother asks Jeff to help her by sweeping the patio. At first Jeff complains and says he would rather play. Finally, he helps sweep the patio.

Do you like to stop playing so you can help your mom or dad? This can be hard to do. What does Jesus want you to do?

Jesus told a story about a man who helped his enemy. Do you think this would be hard to do? We're going to hear that story today.

▼ 2. What Does the Bible Say? ▲

Bible Story: A Helpful Traveler

How to Say It
Levite: LEE-vite
Samaria: Suh-MARE-ee-uh

You will need transparencies of backgrounds 6D and 8B, an overhead projector, and Bible costumes. (See p. 254 for directions on how to use the visual.) Dress children in Bible costumes to play the parts of the traveler, robbers, priest, Levite, Samaritan, and hotelkeeper.

In Bible times many people called Jesus "Teacher." They did this because Jesus taught them about God and His laws. One day a man said to Jesus, "God's law says, 'Love your neighbor as much as you love yourself.' Who is my neighbor? Can you tell me?"

Boys and girls, do you know the answer? Listen and I'll tell you the same story Jesus told. Then we will talk about the right answer to the man's question.

(Project transparency 6D. Enter the traveler.) **One day a man was traveling alone. Step by step he walked down the road. It was a very long and hard trip.**

(Enter the robbers. Pretend to take the traveler's clothes and money.) **Some robbers, who were hiding on this road, saw the man. They jumped out and took the traveler's clothes and beat him. Then they ran away, leaving the hurt man all alone.** *(The robbers exit. The traveler lies down on the floor.)*

(Enter the priest.) **After a while, another traveler came walking down the road. He was a priest from the temple. He had a very important job. He said prayers to God for the people. Sometimes he even taught about God's law.**

Do you think the priest helped the hurt man? No! *(The priest walks past the hurt man.)* **He saw him, but he decided to walk on the other side of the road. Maybe he was in a hurry and did not want to be late.**

(Enter the Levite.) **Later, another man came walking down this road. He was a Levite. He was also a very important man. Some Levites were teachers and some took care of the temple. Do you think the Levite stopped when he saw the hurt man?** *(Have the Levite bend over and look at the man.)* **Yes, he did stop, but he only looked at the man and then decided not to help. Maybe he thought he was too important. Maybe he did not want to get his clothes dirty.** *(The Levite exits.)* **After he looked at the man, he crossed over to the other side of the road and went away.**

(Enter the Samaritan.) **Finally, another man came walking down the road. This man was not important like the priest and the Levite. He was from Samaria. The beaten traveler was Jewish and Jews did not like Samaritans. They were enemies. Do you think this man stopped and helped? Yes, he did!** *(Have the Samaritan stop and help the hurt man.)* **When the Samaritan saw the hurt man, he felt sorry for the man. He cleaned the man's cuts and bruises. He put medicine and bandages on them.** *(The Samaritan and traveler exit.)* **Then he put the traveler on his donkey and took him to a hotel.** *(Remove transparency 6D and project 8B. Enter the Samaritan and the hurt traveler. Have the Samaritan help the traveler lie down on the floor.)* **At the hotel, the Samaritan took care of the man.**

The next day, the Samaritan left to continue his trip. *(Enter the hotelkeeper.)* **Before he left, he gave the owner of the hotel some money.** *(The Samaritan hands the hotelkeeper some money.)* **He said, "Take care of this man until he is well. If this is not enough money, I will give you more when I come back."** *(Turn off the projector.)*

When Jesus finished telling the story, He asked, "Who was a neighbor to the hurt man?" Do you know the answer? Yes, the kind traveler who helped him. We call this man the Good Samaritan. The man who had asked Jesus who his neighbor was knew the answer, too.

Jesus told the man to go and do the same thing—show love to others. Our Bible words tell us to do this, too. Let's say the words together. *(Recite Luke 6:31.)*

Story Review: Going on a Trip

Gather four bags of any kind: a medium-sized brown grocery bag, a little shopping bag with handles, a plastic grocery bag, a small carry-on, a briefcase—whatever you have handy. Cut a large letter out of cardboard or card stock for each bag: "T" for traveler, "P" for priest, "L" for Levite, and "S" for Samaritan. Put a washcloth and an empty medicine bottle in the Samaritan's bag.

Line the bags up and choose four volunteers to each take a bag and stand in front of the rest of the class.

"T" stands for "traveler." Ask the traveler to step forward. **Who can tell me what happened to the traveler in today's story?** When the children answer that he was beaten and robbed, take his bag away and have that child lie down on the floor.

"P" stands for "priest." Who can tell me what the priest did when he saw the hurt man? As the children answer, guide the priest past the traveler, take his bag away, and have him rejoin the class.

"L" stands for "Levite." Who can tell me what the Levite did when he saw the hurt man? As the children answer, guide the Levite past the traveler, take his bag away, and have him rejoin the class.

Who can tell me what the "S" stands for? Who can tell me what the Samaritan did when he saw the hurt man? Guide the Samaritan to kneel down beside the traveler. Tell him to look in his bag and see what he can do to help. When he is finished and the children are finished retelling the story, have the children applaud the actors. Have the traveler and Samaritan rejoin the class.

Bible Memory: Be a Helper Everywhere You Go

You will need a copy of the three "Be a Helper Pictures" from p. 279. If possible, enlarge the pictures. Color and mount them on card stock.

Gather the children around you and show the pictures one at a time. Discuss each situation.

Picture 1: **What happened in this picture? What could you do to help the workers in this grocery store? Have you ever helped put things back on the shelves? What do our Bible words tell us to do?** Ask the children to say the words in unison.

Picture 2: **What do you see all over the park? Yes, there is litter. Have you ever picked up litter left by someone else and put it in the wastebasket? What do our Bible words tell us to do?** Say the words in unison again.

Picture 3: **It is very crowded in this mall. How can children help these people enjoy shopping? Yes, children shouldn't run or yell while shopping in the stores. What do our Bible words tell us to do?** Say the words together and then ask for volunteers to say the Bible words by themselves or with a friend.

Bible Words

"Do for other people what you want them to do for you" (Luke 6:31).

▼ 3. What Does This Mean to Me? ▲

Give Kind-Aid

You will need copies of p. 278, and crayons or markers.

Before class time, follow the directions on the page to assemble the pouches, ready the picture stickers, and cut out the bandages.

Jesus wants each of us to be a neighbor to people we meet. He wants us to help others. Maybe the person is someone you know very well, like someone in your family. Hold up the sticker of a family. **Maybe the person is a playmate you play with at the park.** Show the sticker of playmates at the park. **The person who needs your help may be old.** Show the person in a wheelchair. **Or he may be just a baby.** Show the baby. **Or maybe she's a teenager, such as a teenage baby-sitter.** Show a teenager.

Let's think of ways we can be kind and helpful to these people. How can we do what Jesus said and be a neighbor to them? Give each child copies of the picture stickers and bandages. Allow the children to lick the picture stickers and apply them to the bandages. Then color the bandages and picture stickers. Discuss ways they can help the people represented in the pictures. When finished, give each child a Kind-Aid pouch in which to store his bandages.

▼ 4. What Can I Do to Please God? ▲

First Aid Kit

You will need copies of the "First Aid Kit" label from p. 280, scissors, crayons or markers, a zipper-locking plastic sandwich bag for each child, clear tape, cotton balls, and adhesive strips. Cut out the labels before class time.

Give each child a label to color. Be sure each child's name is printed on the label. Then pass out the plastic bags and help the children tape their labels on their bags. Next, pass out the first aid supplies. Fill the bags and zip them shut. **Where will you keep your first aid kit? Who will need the bandages in it? When you use your supplies, you will be showing love and kindness by helping someone who is hurt. You will be like the Good Samaritan. It is good to listen to Jesus and then do what He says.**

Be a Good Samaritan

You will need the words to "Help, Help Your Neighbors," the armband from p. 280 copied onto red paper, scissors, and tape. Cut out the armbands before class.

Explain how Red Cross workers wear armbands when they help others. Tape an armband on each child. **When you wear this around your arm, people will know they can ask you for help. They will know you are like the Good Samaritan.**

Sing the first verse of "Help, Help Your Neighbors." **Now, let's each be a Good Samaritan and clean up our classroom.**

Gather the children in a circle for prayer. Before you pray, ask each child to name someone she can help this week or something he can do to help at home this week. Then pray together. Ask God to help all the children be Good Samaritans wherever they go this week.

▼ Bonus Activity ▲

Snack Attack! Get-Well Food

You will need pretzels served in paper cups.

Divide the children into two groups. One group will be the Good Samaritans. The other will be injured travelers. Have the Good Samaritans help the injured travelers find a comfortable place in the classroom to lie down. Have the Samaritans serve the snack to the injured first and then to themselves. Ask one Samaritan and one traveler to pray for the snack.

While the children are eating, review the Bible story. Use the following questions. **Who hurt the man? Who was not a good friend? Who helped the hurt man? How did the Samaritan help? Who is your neighbor? Who told this story?**

Help, Help Your Neighbors
(Tune: "Rock-a-bye Baby")

Verse 1
Help, help your neighbors.
  Treat them with love.
All love and kindness comes
  from above.
Help, help your friends and
  family, too.
You can be helpful in all that
  you do.

Verse 2
I'll not be afraid 'cause Jesus
  is near.
We know during storms
  that Jesus is here.
He calmed the waves one
  stormy day.
He hears and He helps us
  when we pray.

Dorcas Helps Others

Acts 9:36-42

Know: God wants them to help others.

Feel: Joyful when helping others.

Do: Be helpful to families, friends, and others.

Children will accomplish the goals when they:

- Explore how mothers help their children.
- Tell how Dorcas helped her friends.
- Recite Luke 6:31.
- Practice helping others.
- Ask Jesus to help you be a good helper.

Special Guests

Invite your students' mothers to attend and participate in this lesson. If a child's mother is not able to attend, ask another relative or woman in your church to come in her place. Involve the guests in all the activities. Ask them to sit with their children during the story time.

▼ 1. What Is This Story About? ▲

Bible Mothers

You will need a Bible, the "Paper Dolls" from p. 279 enlarged if possible and printed on card stock, crayons or markers, X-Acto knives, and scissors.

Read the following Scriptures ahead of time: Exodus 1:1–2:10; 6:20; 1 Samuel 1; 2:18-21; and Luke 2. Be prepared to tell these three stories in your own words.

Have the guests (mothers) and children work together coloring and cutting out the paper dolls. Ask the adults to cut the slits for inserting the extra pieces in the hands of the paper dolls.

When all of the paper dolls are finished, gather the children and guests with their dolls. **Mothers are very special to their children. In the Bible there are many mothers. You have made paper dolls of three of those mothers. Let's see how each mother helped her child.**

First, let's talk about a mother named Jochebed. Show the Jochebed paper doll. Have the mothers and children hold theirs, too. As you tell the story, slip Moses into Jochebed's arms. **How did Moses' mother help him? Yes, she hid him and saved him from being killed by the mean king's soldiers.**

The second mother is Hannah. Slip Samuel's hand into his mother's hand. **How did Samuel's mother help him? Yes, she made him a new coat every year.**

The third mother is Mary. Whose mother was she? Yes, she was Jesus' mother. Slip Jesus into Mary's arms. **How did Mary help Jesus? Yes, she took good care of him when He was born.**

Mothers help their children in any ways. How does your mother help you? Encourage responses.

This Is the Way I Can Help

Form a circle with all the guests and children. Teach these new words to the tune: "Did You Ever See a Lassie?"

Did you ever see a mommy, a mommy, a mommy?
Did you ever see a mommy go this way and that?
Go this way and that way. Go this way and that way.
Did you ever see a mommy go this way and that?

Ask one of the guests to stand in the circle while the group sings and act out something a mother would do to help her family (cook, wash the car, go to work). At the end of the song, ask the group to describe what the mother was doing.

Repeat the song using "daughter," "son," and "teacher." Give everyone a turn to be in the middle.

God is pleased when we choose to help our family and friends. He knows that when you help others, it makes you happy, too.

▼ 2. What Does the Bible Say? ▲

Bible Story: Dorcas Sews Clothes

You will need transparency 6C, silhouettes 11-c woman (Dorcas), 11-e bed, 11-f Peter, 11-g crowd, and 11-h James and John, and an overhead projector. (See p. 254 for directions on how to use the visual.)

(Project transparency 6C and silhouette 11-c.) **In the town of Joppa there was a woman named Dorcas. She was kind and spent a lot of her time helping others. The poor people in Joppa loved Dorcas because she did so many good things for them.**

Dorcas was very good at sewing. She made clothes for poor people. If a poor woman needed a dress, she knew Dorcas would sew one for her. If a poor man needed a new shirt, Dorcas lovingly made one for him. When poor children out grew their clothes, Dorcas would sew bigger ones for them. Everyone loved Dorcas. They needed her help.

One day Dorcas became very sick. *(Remove transparency 6C and silhouette 11-c.)* **She was so sick that she died.** *(Project silhouettes 11-c, 11-e, and 11-g. Lay 11-c on 11-e.)* **When the poor women heard Dorcas was dead, they rushed to her house. They sadly took her body to a room upstairs and began planning to bury her.** *(Remove all the silhouettes.)*

(Project transparency 6C and silhouette 11-f.) **Some people in the church at Joppa heard that Peter was preaching in a nearby town. Peter had been one of Jesus' followers. After Jesus went back to Heaven, Peter traveled from town to town telling everyone the good news about Jesus.**

(Add silhouette 11-h.) **Two men left Joppa and went to get Peter. When the men found him, they said, "Hurry and come to Joppa. Everyone is very sad because Dorcas is dead." Peter left right away and went to Joppa with the two men.** *(Remove the transparency and silhouettes.)*

(Project silhouettes 11-c, 11-e, 11-f. and 11-g. Lay 11-c on 11-e.) **The men took Peter to the upstairs room where Dorcas was lying on a bed. All of the women gathered around Peter and cried. They showed him the beautiful clothes Dorcas made. They told Peter how kind she was to everyone. Peter saw how sad the women were. He saw the beautiful clothes Dorcas had make when she was alive.**

(Remove silhouette 11-g.) **Then Peter said, "Everyone leave the room." Peter got on his knees beside Dorcas' bed and prayed. He wanted to help the people who loved Dorcas, so he asked God to show him what to do. After he prayed, Peter looked at Dorcas and said, "Dorcas, stand up!"** *(Bring silhouette 11-c to a standing position.)* **Peter took her by the hand and she stood up. She was alive! God had answered Peter's prayer and brought Dorcas back to life.**

Peter called to the people who were waiting outside, "You can come in now." *(Add silhouette 11-g.)* **When the people stepped into the room, they were very surprised and very happy. Dorcas was not dead. She was alive!**

Everyone in the town of Joppa heard the good news about Dorcas. Many of them believed that Jesus was the Son of God because the power of God had brought Dorcas back to life. *(Turn off the projector.)*

Story Review: Sew Like Dorcas

You will need the "Sew Like Dorcas" coat pattern from p. 281, card stock, scissors, hole punch, yarn, clear tape, and crayons or markers. Before class, copy a coat pattern onto card stock for each child.

Before class, cut out the coats and punch holes around the edges as indicated. Prepare the yarn by cutting it into one-yard lengths and wrapping the cut ends with tape (to make a sewing point).

> **How to Say It**
> Jochebed: JOCK-eh-bed
> Joppa: JOP-uh

Have the children color and decorate their coats. Ask the guests to show their children how to weave the yarn around the sewing card.

How did Dorcas help other people? What did she sew?
What happened to Dorcas?
Who was sad that Dorcas died?
Who was preaching in a nearby town?
What did Peter do to help Dorcas?
What happened because Dorcas came back to life?

Bible Memory: Hands Up!

Bible Words
"Do for other people what you want them to do for you" (Luke 6:31).

You will need a plastic latex glove for each child. (A local doctor, dentist, or hospital may donate these.)

Inflate the gloves by mouth and tie each one securely. Do this ahead of time, but save one to inflate while you are explaining the game. The children will enjoy watching the hand expand.

Ask each guest and child to stand facing each other. Teach the following motions for Luke 6:31.

"Do for other people *(Point to the person opposite you.)*
what you want *(Point to yourself.)*
them to do *(Point to the person opposite you.)*
for you." *(Point to yourself.)*

Have pairs say the words and do the motions several times. When everyone knows the verse fairly well, try this:

Give one inflated glove to each child. As the children recite the Bible words, have them bat the inflated hands, trying to keep them up in the air, while they shout out the words (in unison might help). Encourage the guests to help. The object is for everyone to help keep all the hands up. After the children have recited the words several times, stop the activity. **We are having a lot of fun keeping the hands up in the air and saying the Bible words at the same time. Our Bible words and these hands remind us to help others.**

▼ 3. What Does This Mean to Me? ▲

Big Enough to Help

You will need copies of the "Helping Hand Badge" from p. 280, scissors, a hole punch, and yarn.

Before class, copy the hand onto colored paper and cut it out. Punch a hole where indicated and attach an 18" piece of yarn. Tie the yarn ends together.

Before this lesson, look around the building where you meet. Are there jobs your students can do to help keep the building looking nice? Can they sweep the sidewalks, pick up litter outside, empty wastebaskets in other classrooms, or polish wooden furniture or door knobs? Find simple jobs that will give your students an opportunity to be helpful. When the jobs are completed, put a helping hand badge around each child's neck.

Did you enjoy helping to clean up our building? How did it make you feel to be helpful? You are big enough to help. God is pleased when we help others. When we help, we are showing others love.

▼ 4. What Can I Do to Please God? ▲

My Hands Belong to God

You will need copies of the "Folding Hands" from p. 281, crayons or markers, scissors, and pencils.

Dorcas used her hands to sew the clothes she gave to the poor people. We can use our hands to help others, too. Here is a pair of hands for you to color. After you color the hands, you are going to do something special on the inside.

Give each child a pair of hands to color. Ask the guests to print their children's names above the wrist and then cut out the hands. Fold the hands so they appear to be praying.

Now, open the hands. Think of someone who could use your help. Draw their picture on the palm of one of the hands. Ask the guests to make sure the children draw only on one palm. Give each adult a pencil. **Now, tell your guest how you will help this person. Guests, please write what your child says on the blank palm.**

Gather everyone in a circle. **The hands you colored are praying hands. To be a good helper, you need to have Jesus helping you. We are going to go around our circle and let each of you tell whom you want to help. You can show us their picture, too. Then we will pray that Jesus will help you do a good job.**

Go around the circle and give every child a turn to tell about the picture he drew. Then pray together, asking God to help everyone be good helpers this week.

Thanks for Coming!

Ask the guests and children to form teams to clean up the classroom. Then gather everyone together to talk about the time they have just spent together.

What did you like best about having your guest come to class with you? How did she help you during class?

Ask the adults: **What did you like best about our class today? How did your child help you during class? Would you like to come and help us again?** Take note of who responds and invite them to help with the class again!

Form a circle and have a group hug. Have everyone wrap their arms around their neighbors on each side. Then instruct everyone to take a big step together toward the center of the circle and carefully hug their friends.

Ask if an adult will volunteer to close with prayer.

▼ Bonus Activity ▲

Snack Attack! Handy Snack

You will need clear plastic (not latex) disposable gloves (food vendors may donate these), popcorn, twist ties, and toy rings (available at Christian book stores).

Before class time, fill the gloves with popcorn. Secure the openings with twist ties. Put a ring on the ring finger.

Ask the guests and children to tell what they can do with their hands (draw, cut, hold, catch, pick up things). Ask the children to take turns thanking God for the things they like to do with their hands. Then pass out the snack and let them eat. If possible, make two "handy snacks" for each child, one to eat now with his guest and one to take home and share with the rest of the family.

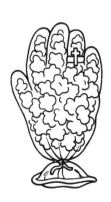

> **Help, Help Your Neighbors**
> *(Tune: "Rock-a-bye Baby")*
>
> **Verse 1**
> Help, help your neighbors.
>   Treat them with love.
> All love and kindness comes
>   from above.
> Help, help your friends and
>   family, too.
> You can be helpful in all that
>   you do.
>
> **Verse 2**
> I'll not be afraid 'cause Jesus
>   is near.
> We know during storms
>   that Jesus is here.
> He calmed the waves one
>   stormy day.
> He hears and He helps us
>   when we pray.

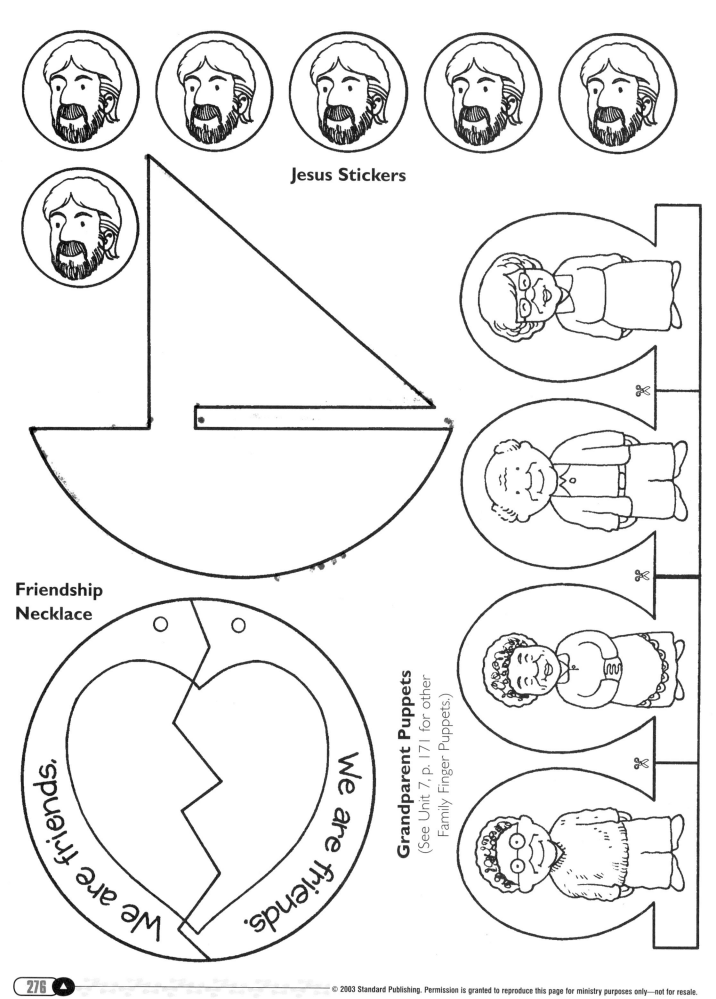

Jesus Stickers

Friendship Necklace

We are friends.

We are friends.

Grandparent Puppets
(See Unit 7, p. 171 for other Family Finger Puppets.)

Jesus helps me when I am alone and afraid.

Jesus sticker

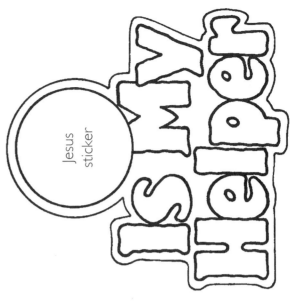

IS MY Helper

Jesus sticker

fold 3

Jesus helps me when I hurt.

Jesus sticker

fold 1

Jesus sticker

Thank you, Jesus, for helping me.

fold 2

Jesus helps me do what is right.

Jesus sticker

Jesus sticker

Jesus helps me love others.

Kind Aid

fold 3

fold 1

fold 2

Stickers

To make stickers, you will need card stock, white glue, vinegar, peppermint extract (optional), a small paintbrush, and scissors.

Copy this page onto card stock. Cut out the pouch. Fold in half on the broken line so that "Kind-Aid" appears on the front. Fold the front side-tabs to the back and glue.

Mix two parts white glue and one part vinegar. Add a few drops of peppermint extract, if desired. Lightly "paint" the mixture onto the back of the uncut stickers. Let dry. Cut out the stickers. Cut out the bandages, too.

Be a Helper Pictures

Jochebed

Hannah

Samuel

Moses

Jesus

Mary

Paper Dolls

**Helping
Hand
Badge**

Label

Armband

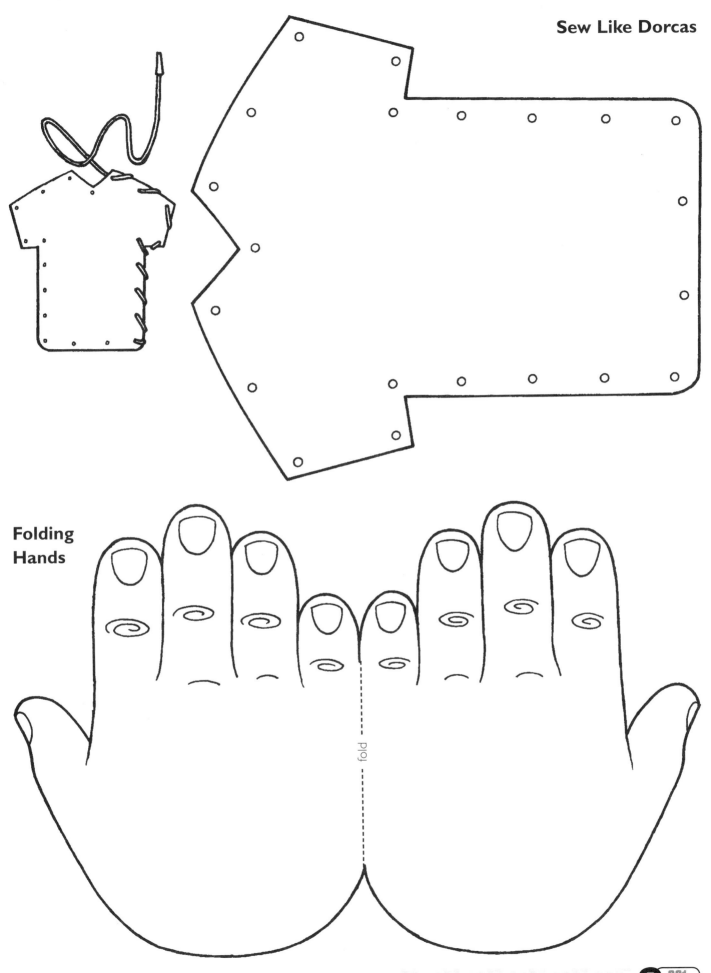

**Folding
Hands**

fold

Learning to Follow Jesus

Unit Bible Words

"Christ ... gave you an example to follow. [So you should do as he did.]" (1 Peter 2:21).

(Note: This verse has been divided into two parts. If you are teaching four-year-olds, use only the first part. If you are teaching older children, also include the part of the verse in brackets.)

Bible Characters

Zacchaeus, Peter, Jailer, Onesimus

47 Zacchaeus Gives Generously

Luke 19:1-9—Zacchaeus, a chief tax collector, meets Jesus. Jesus shows him love and kindness. Zacchaeus responds by giving half of all he has to the poor. We can follow Jesus by treating others with love and kindness.

48 Peter Is Sorry

Luke 22:33, 34, 54-62; John 21:15-17—Peter believes in Jesus; but when Jesus is arrested, he is afraid. He denies knowing Jesus. When the rooster crows, he realizes what he has done and is very sorry. Later, he tells Jesus he really does love Him. We can follow Jesus by always telling the truth. If we do not, we can say we are sorry.

49 A Jailer Is Kind

Acts 16:23-34—Following orders, a jailer puts Paul and Silas in chains. When God uses an earthquake to release their chains, the jailer is thankful that they did not run away. He is kind to Paul and Silas and listens as they tell about Jesus. That very night, the jailer and his family repent and experience God's forgiveness. We can follow Jesus by pleasing God.

50 Onesimus Does What Is Right

Philemon—Onesimus runs away from his Christian owner, Philemon. He meets Paul and becomes a Christian. Onesimus does what is right and goes back to Philemon. Paul sends a letter asking Philemon to forgive Onesimus. When someone says, "I'm sorry," we can forgive him. That's following Jesus!

By the end of this unit, the children and leaders will

Know: Following Jesus means choosing to do what is good.
Feel: Eager to follow Jesus.
Do: Make right choices.

Why Teach This Unit to Four- to Six-Year-Olds?

For the first time in their lives these children are being held responsible for the choices they make. They are learning that their choices effect themselves and others. They are beginning to understand that they can do things that help and please others. They also are more aware of the results of doing and saying things that hurt people. They have experienced some consequences for both right and wrong choices. Now is the time to give them some good examples to follow and imitate. The Bible is the best source for those examples and Jesus is the best example of all.

In these lessons the children will meet people whose lives were changed by their decisions to follow in Christ's footsteps. Their situations were unique to their time, but the lessons to be learned are timeless. Use this unit to create a caring and nurturing environment for your students to observe biblical role models who will help your students learn how to be generous, say "I'm sorry," offer kindness, and make good choices. All of these qualities come from a heart that has decided to follow Jesus.

"Generous," "apologize," "forgive," and "repent," are new words as well as new concepts that will be introduced in this unit. Every Christian spends a lifetime working on these concepts. The purpose of this unit is to begin laying a foundation upon which these concepts can be built.

Meet Zacchaeus

Zacchaeus was a wealthy Jew who worked for Rome as a chief tax collector. He was placed over other tax collectors. Many of these men made their living by cheating people. They were regarded as traitors and put in the same class as sinners. We don't know if Zacchaeus was dishonest, but we do know that he was very generous when Jesus showed kindness to him and became a follower of the Son of God.

Meet Peter

Peter was a fisherman whom Jesus called to help Him "fish for men." Peter is known as the most outspoken and impulsive of the twelve disciples. He loved Jesus with all of his heart and wanted desperately to be a loyal follower, but his humanness often got in the way.

Meet the Philippian Jailer

Philippi was a Roman military colony in Macedonia. Paul visited there several times. The Philippian church was always very helpful to him. The position of jailer carries with it great responsibility. He was to guard the prisoners with his life. If he allowed one to escape, he would be executed. Paul and Silas introduced him to Jesus, and he and his family became followers.

Meet Onesimus

Onesimus was a slave. His owner was Philemon, a Christian man, living in the city of Colosse. Onesimus probably heard Paul preach in Philemon's home where a church met. Onesimus ran away from Philemon. He went to Rome and became "like a son" to Paul. Onesimus became a Christian and returned to his owner, Philemon. According to the law of that day, Onesimus could have been punished severely for running away. He could have even been put to death, but Paul wrote a letter to Philemon asking him to forgive Onesimus.

Unit Visuals

Patterns for four paper sack puppets are provided on pp. 301 and 302. Add fabric, felt, and yarn to dress them up. The patterns can also be used as extra crafts during the unit.

Make a transparency or poster of 1 Peter 2:21 in sign language. See page 300. Not all words are signed, only key words. However, as you sign, say all the words, even those not signed. If a plain wall is not available for projection, tack a large, plain white sheet to the wall.

Unit Song

"If You're a Follower of Jesus"
(Tune: "If You're Happy and You Know It")

Verse 1
If you're a follower of Jesus, clap your hands.
If you're a follower of Jesus, clap your hands.
If you're a follower of Jesus,
then you'll try to do what pleases.
If you're a follower of Jesus, clap your hands.

Verse 2
If your words are sweet as honey, praise the Lord.
If your words are sweet as honey, praise the Lord.
If your words are sweet as honey,
those around you will be sunny.
If your words are sweet as honey, praise the Lord.

Verse 3
If you're a follower of Jesus, tell the truth.
If you're a follower of Jesus, tell the truth.
If you're truthful and you know it,
then your mouth will surely show it.
If you're a follower of Jesus, tell the truth.

Verse 4
If you're forgiven and you know it, say "Thank you."
If you're forgiven and you know it, say "Thank you."
If you're forgiven and you know it,
then your face will surely show it.
If you're forgiven and you know it, say "Thank you."

Zacchaeus Gives Generously

Luke 19:1-9

Know: Following Jesus means choosing to do what is good.
Feel: Eager to follow Jesus.
Do: Make right choices.

Children will accomplish the goals when they
- Explore using kind words.
- Tell why Zacchaeus was so generous.
- Begin to memorize 1 Peter 2:21.
- Identify ways to be kind to others.
- Follow Jesus by being kind.

▼ 1. What Is This Story About? ▲

Sweet and Sour Words

You will need a Bible, a jar of honey, crackers, jumbo craft sticks, a jar of sliced dill pickles, and the words to the unit song, "If You're a Follower of Jesus" from p. 283.

Gather the children around the Bible. Open the Bible to Proverbs 16:24. **A long time before Jesus was born, there was a king named Solomon. God made Solomon the smartest, wisest man on earth. Let's read something that wise King Solomon said.** Read Proverbs 16:24.

Show the jar of honey. **The words we say to others can make them happy or make them sad. King Solomon said that pleasant (nice) words are sweet like this honey. Do you like food that tastes sweet? Pretend you are eating something sweet. I see lots of smiles. Listen to these words and use your face to show me how they make you feel.** (Say: "I love you." "You are a good helper." "I like the way you share your toys.") **King Solomon was right! Kind words are sweet like honey! Let's taste some honey and see what happens to our friend's faces.** Let each child spread some honey on a cracker and eat it.

The opposites of kind words are unkind words. These words don't make us smile. They hurt our feelings. Show the jar of dill pickles. **Have you ever tasted a dill pickle? It is very sour. When I eat dill pickles, my face frowns.** Offer a slice of dill pickle to any child who wants try one. **Watch the faces of the children eating pickles. Unkind words make us frown, too. They are like dill pickles. Listen to these words and use your face to show me how they make you feel.** (Say: "I don't like you." "You can't play with us." "I'm not your friend anymore.") **How do these words make you feel?**

Teach the second verse of the unit song, "If You're a Follower of Jesus."

Today we will meet a man from the Bible named Zacchaeus. Jesus was very kind to Zacchaeus.

What Would You Do?

You will need a broken toy and some blocks.

Show the broken toy. **Let's pretend I invited (name one of the children) to my house to play.** Call the child you named to come up and hold the toy. **Pretend he (she) broke this toy.** Ask the child to tell the class what the child should say to you. Give help if needed. Encourage the child to say, "I'm sorry I broke your toy." **I like the way (child's name) apologized. When you apologize you are saying you are sorry. Sometimes it is hard to apologize, but it is a good thing to do. It pleases God. If you do something unkind on purpose or by accident, you need to say, "I'm sorry."**

Place some blocks on the floor. Ask a child to build a tall tower. **Have you ever built a tower like this one? What if someone comes too close and knocks it down?** Bump into the tower and knock it down. **What should I do? Yes, I should apologize. I should say I am sorry. Is there anything else I should do? That's right! I should help rebuild the tower.**

It pleases God when we apologize and say that we are sorry. Children who are kind to their friends, and who say they are sorry when they make

a mistake, will have friends who will want to play with them.

Today's Bible story is about a man named Zacchaeus who was treated kindly by Jesus. To show how happy this made him feel, he did some kind things for others.

▼ 2. What Does the Bible Say? ▲

Bible Story: A Little Man in a Tree

You will need the completed Zacchaeus puppet from p. 301, or use a real person dressed as Zacchaeus. Use the puppet or the person to tell the story from Zacchaeus' point of view.

Hello, boys and girls. My name is Zacchaeus. I am a rich man from Jericho, and I have a very important job. I collect tax money from other tax collectors and give it to the king. Most people do not like tax collectors, because many tax collectors are not honest. Sometimes they take more money for taxes than the king said was necessary.

One day, people started running through the streets of Jericho shouting, "Jesus is coming! Jesus is coming!" Everyone stopped working and ran down the road to see Jesus. Crowds of people lined the road. Everyone in town wanted to see Jesus. We knew about the sick people He had healed, and we wanted to hear His wonderful stories.

I wanted to see Him, too. I started running down the road with the crowd, but I had a problem. I am short! Everyone was taller than I. Even when I jumped up and down, I could not jump high enough to see Jesus. I tried to squeeze between some people. At first they were going to let me through, but when they saw it was I, Zacchaeus, the chief tax collector, they would not budge.

I started looking around for a way to see Jesus. That is when I saw the sycamore tree by the road. I quickly climbed it and found a branch that was just right for sitting on, so I sat and waited.

Finally, I could see Jesus coming down the road. Everyone was excited! I was, too! I wanted to see this man called Jesus. Jesus came closer and closer to my tree. Suddenly, as I was looking down at Him, He looked up at me! Then He said a very surprising thing. He said, "Zacchaeus, hurry and come down. I am going home with you." Wow! Was I surprised! He knew my name! The people around me were surprised, too! Jesus was going home with the chief tax collector!

Quickly I climbed down and took Jesus to my house. Many people were watching. They started grumbling. "Why does Jesus want to go home with Zacchaeus? Doesn't He know that tax collectors cheat people and steal their money?"

As soon as Jesus entered my house, I took Him to the best room and gave Him the best food to eat. Remember, I was very rich and could buy the best of everything.

While we ate dinner, Jesus talked with me. No one had ever said such nice words to me. His gentle voice and His kind words made me feel good. I just had to tell Jesus how I felt. I said, "Jesus, I am giving half of all my riches to the poor people, and if I have taken too much money from anyone, I will give it all back plus even more."

Jesus was pleased that I wanted to be generous and give so much to the poor. He was also pleased that I wanted to do what was right. He said to me, "You will live in Heaven with God. This is why God sent me to earth." Those kind words made me smile.

Now, I'm a very happy man. I am a follower of Jesus.

Story Review: A Special Dinner Party

You will need a tablecloth, plates, silverware, clear plastic cups, pieces of raw vegetables and fruits, a variety of dips, and fancy serving bowls.

Let the children pretend they are Zacchaeus, preparing dinner for Jesus. Have the children set the table. Pray before the party begins. While you eat, review the story with the following questions:

What was Zacchaeus' job?

Why was Zacchaeus in a tree?

What did Jesus do when He looked up at Zacchaeus?

Do you think Zacchaeus was surprised Jesus wanted to come to his house for dinner?

What kind of food do you think he served Jesus?

What would you serve Jesus if He came to your house?

What did Zacchaeus decide to do after he talked with Jesus?

Bible Memory: Signing Is Fun

You will need an overhead projector and a transparency of p. 300 showing 1 Peter 2:21 in sign language. Option: Photocopy and enlarge this page to make a poster to teach the signs.

Our Bible words remind us to follow Jesus. We're going to learn sign language for some of the words.

Use the transparency or poster and your own demonstration to show the children how to form the key words of the Bible words. Repeat several times.

What are some ways we can follow Christ's example?

Bible Words

"Christ . . . gave you an example to follow. [So you should do as he did.]" (1 Peter 2:21).

(Note: This verse has been divided into two parts. If you are teaching four-year-olds, use only the first part. If you are teaching older children, also include the part of the verse in brackets.)

▼ 3. What Does This Mean to Me? ▲

I Will Be Kind and Generous

You will need a copy of the spinner game from p. 304. Follow the directions for assembling it. If your group is large, make several to use with small groups.

Zacchaeus gave to the poor. We call this being "generous." We can show we are followers of Jesus by being kind and generous like Zacchaeus.

Gather the children around the spinner. Let the children take turns spinning. When the paper clip points to a picture, ask the "spinner" to tell how Zacchaeus used this part of his body in ways that were good and/or generous. For example, he used his mouth to tell Jesus he was giving half of all he had to the poor. In his heart there was love for poor people. He used his feet to lead Jesus to his house. He used his hands to give his things to the poor.

Let each child spin again. Ask the child to tell how a follower of Jesus would use that body part in a kind way. For example, our mouths can use kind words, our hands and feet can help, and our hearts can love.

Following Jesus means doing what Jesus did or doing what He said to do. Jesus was kind, and we can follow Jesus by being kind.

I Must Play Fair

Let's learn a rhyme to help us remember another way to be kind.

Form circles of five to eight children. Each child will need a chair. Teach the following rhyme and motions to the rhythm of "Five Little Monkeys" (jumpin' on the bed). Number each child in each circle. Begin with the highest number and recite the rhyme. Count backwards. When all of the children are sitting down, start over.

(Number) little children playing hide and seek,
(Cover eyes with both hands.)
One turned around and took a peek.
(Turn completely around and spread fingers apart over eyes.)
The other children said, "You must play fair!"
(Shake pointing finger.)
He had to go and sit on his chair."
(One child sits down, but remains in the circle.)
When we play games with our friends, we must play fair. Followers of Jesus can have fun and play fair. This will please Jesus and will show kindness to others.

▼ 4. What Can I Do to Please God? ▲

"Jesus Loves You" Sachets

You will need cotton balls, lightly scented spray perfume, 3" squares of colorful construction paper, a stapler, a hole punch, 4" pieces of yarn, and prepared "Jesus Loves You" stickers from p. 305.

Let each child spray a cotton ball with perfume. Place the cotton ball between two paper squares and help the child staple the square edges together to make the sachet. Punch a hole in one corner of the sachet. Thread the yarn through the hole and tie. Attach a "Jesus Loves You" sticker to one side of the sachet.

When you give this sachet to someone, you will be like Zacchaeus. Remember what he did? Yes, he was happy to meet Jesus and learn about following Jesus. He gave half of all he owned away.

Give each child an opportunity to talk about following Jesus this week. **Our Bible words remind us to follow Jesus. How will you follow Jesus this week? How can you use your sachet to be kind? To whom will you give your sachet?**

Pray together. Thank God for Jesus' example of kindness to Zacchaeus.

I Want to Be Generous

You will need the words to "If You're a Follower of Jesus" from p. 283.

Ask the children to help clean up the classroom. Then gather them in a circle and teach the unit song, "If You're a Follower of Jesus."

Let's pray and ask God to help us be generous and give to others. He is pleased when you choose to follow Jesus.

Peter Is Sorry

Luke 22:33, 34, 54-62; John 21:15-17

Know: Following Jesus means choosing to do what is good.
Feel: Eager to follow Jesus.
Do: Make right choices.

Children will accomplish the goals when they

• Discover what the Bible says about telling lies.
• Tell why Peter said he was sorry.
• Memorize 1 Peter 2:21.
• Name times to tell the truth.
• Follow Jesus by telling the truth.

▼ 1. What Is This Story About? ▲

You Must Speak the Truth

You will need copies of the stone tablets from p. 303 for each child, and crayons or markers.

Before class time, cut out the tablets. Make one sample by coloring the blank side gray (like stone tablets) and also coloring the picture side.

Read Exodus 24:12-18. In your own words, briefly tell the story of God giving the Ten Commandments to Moses. Show the plain side of your sample. **One of the commandments says, "You must not tell lies." Do you know what lying is? Yes, it is telling something that is not true. God says this is wrong.**

Turn the sample over to the picture side. **Let me tell you about two children who chose to lie.** Point to the mother and daughter. **Ashley and her mother were shopping. Ashley saw a pretty pink bow. She said, "Mommy, look at this bow. It is my favorite color. Can we buy it?" Her mother answered, "No, not this time." Ashley really wanted the bow. When Ashley's mother went around the corner, Ashley put the pretty pink bow in her pocket. When her mother came back to the bow aisle, she noticed the pink bow was gone. "Where did the pink bow go?" Ashley knew that she had made a wrong choice, but she was afraid to tell the truth to her mother. Instead she replied, "I don't know. Maybe someone bought it."**

Discuss why it was wrong for Ashley to put the bow in her pocket and why it was wrong to lie to her mother.

Point to the two boys playing with toy cars. **Jared invited Christopher to come over and play with his toy cars. While they were playing, Jared's mother called, "Jared, come and get some cookies." Jared jumped up and ran to the kitchen. While he was gone, Christopher played too rough with a shiny silver car. One of the wheels came off. He was scared, so he hid the car and the wheel in the bottom of Jared's toy box. When Jared came back with the cookies, he told Christopher he wanted to show him his new silver car. He looked and looked, but he couldn't find the silver car. "Did you see a silver car in the toy box while I was getting the cookies?" asked Jared. "No, I didn't see it," replied Christopher.**

Discuss why it was wrong for Christopher to lie about not knowing where Jared's silver car was. What should Christopher have done even though he was scared?

Both of these children were too scared to tell the truth. God's Word says it is wrong to tell lies. Jesus had a friend named Peter. In our Bible story, we'll learn about a time Peter was so scared that he didn't tell the truth.

Let the children color the stone tablets and pictures.

▼ 2. What Does the Bible Say? ▲

Bible Story: Peter Tells a Lie

You will need the completed Peter puppet from p. 301 or a real person dressed as Peter. Use the puppet or the person to tell the story from Peter's point of view.

Hello, boys and girls. I am Peter. I am one of Jesus' helpers. Jesus had a lot of work to do when He came to earth, so He chose twelve men to help Him.

I will never forget the day Jesus chose me to follow Him. I was a fisherman and I had been fishing all night, but I hadn't caught any fish. Jesus came along and said, "Put your nets in the water." I did and my nets were so full of fish they started to rip. It was amazing!

Then Jesus said to my brother, Andrew, and me, "Come and follow me." Quickly, we left our boats, our nets, all the fish, and followed Him. We went everywhere He went. We listened carefully as He told us about God and why God had sent Him to earth. We spent three years traveling with Jesus. We saw Him make sick people well, and provide food for the hungry. We knew He was the Son of God.

Late one night, a terrible thing happened. Judas, another one of Jesus' helpers, did a very bad thing. He helped the temple leaders find Jesus. They brought soldiers to arrest Jesus, like police officers do when someone has done something really bad. The soldiers took Jesus away. The rest of Jesus' helpers were afraid and ran away when this happened, but I followed the soldiers. They took Jesus to a house where the temple leaders were waiting to ask Him questions. They wanted to know if He really was God's Son.

The soldiers waited in a big yard outside the house. It was very early in the morning. The sun had not come up yet, so it was very cold. Some soldiers made a fire. I was cold, too, so I walked over to the fire to warm my hands. A young servant girl was there. She looked at me and said, "This is one of Jesus' helpers."

I was afraid, so I said, "I do not know Him." That was not true. I was lying. I was afraid the soldiers would arrest me, too.

Not long after that, another person looked at me and said, "You are one of the helpers!"

I was really getting scared and I yelled back at the man, "I am not!" Now I had told two lies.

After a while, another man looked at me and said, "He really is one of the men who was with Jesus." They could tell by the way that I talked that I was from the same place as Jesus.

I was really mad now and really frightened, so I yelled, "I do not know this man Jesus." Just then Jesus turned and looked right at me. I had lied three times. I had said I did not know Jesus. The truth is Jesus is my best friend. I love Him. I felt awful. My heart hurt, and I cried. I was very sorry I had told those lies.

Later that same day, the soldiers put Jesus on a cross and He died. Wait—don't be sad. I have good news for you. Jesus did not stay dead. He came back to life three days later. I saw Him and I talked to Him many times after that. Jesus forgave me for telling those lies, and He asked me to tell others about Him. I told Jesus I would always love and obey Him, and I spent the rest of my life telling people about Him!

Story Review: Peter Is Sorry

Show the children how to sign "I'm sorry." Make a soft fist with your right hand, thumb on top. Place your fist over your heart and move it in a circular motion, moving it first toward your left shoulder, then down and around. Practice the sign with the children. Then review the story.

Peter was a follower of Jesus. How much time had Peter spent with Jesus?

What kinds of things had Peter seen Jesus do?

How do you think Peter felt when Jesus was arrested and taken away?

What did Peter do because he was afraid? How do you think he felt?

After Jesus came back to life, what did Peter tell Jesus?

What can we tell God when we choose to do something wrong? (Use the sign.)

Bible Memory: Say It With Your Hands

You will need the Bible verse transparency and an overhead projector, or the Bible verse poster.

Review each sign for 1 Peter 2:21. Give help as needed, especially to the children who were absent during Lesson 47. (Be sure the children understand what it means to be deaf.) Repeat the verse several times. When the children are able to sign the verse fairly well, turn off the projector or remove the poster. Recite and sign the verse together.

Our Bible words remind us to follow Jesus' example. What did Jesus do when Peter lied? Yes, He forgave him. How can we follow Jesus' example this week?

Bible Words

"Christ . . . gave you an example to follow. [So you should do as he did.]" (1 Peter 2:21).

(Note: This verse has been divided into two parts. If you are teaching four-year-olds, use only the first part. If you are teaching older children, also include the part of the verse in brackets.)

▼ 3. What Does This Mean to Me? ▲

A Big Decision

You will need the words to "If You're a Follower of Jesus" from p. 283, the "Big Decision Pictures" from p. 305 (enlarged, if possible), construction paper, crayons or markers, and glue. Color, and mount the two pictures on construction paper.

Show the picture of the birthday cake with icing missing. **It was Dad's birthday. Mother bought a beautiful cake at the bakery. After dinner she was going to surprise Dad with cake and ice cream. Before dinner, Michael came inside from playing. He was hungry. He found the box from the bakery and opened it. The icing looked delicious. He had to have a taste, so he stuck his finger in the icing and licked it. Wow! It was so sweet. Michael had to have more. Soon there were large holes in the icing. Finally he closed the box and put it back in the cupboard.**

Ask for volunteers to act out the rest of the story the way they think it ended. Encourage one child to act out Michael telling the truth. You play the part of the mother or father, and forgive Michael because he told the truth.

Show the picture of the spilled jar of paint. **Mrs. Porter's class was painting pictures for a special project. During the clean-up time, Gregory accidentally spilled a whole jar of paint on the floor. He left it and walked quickly to the sink and began washing his hands.**

Ask for volunteers to act out the rest of the story the way they think it ended. Encourage one child to act out the part of Gregory telling the truth. You play the part of the teacher, and forgive Gregory because he told the truth.

What can we learn from these two stories? (Tell the truth.)

When is a good time to tell the truth? (Let children suggest times; also include "all the time.")

Why is it best to always tell the truth? (God wants us to tell the truth, it pleases Him, it pleases our parents.)

Sour Lemons

You will need a knife, lemons, a fruit juicer, a large pitcher, sugar, water, a spoon for stirring, plastic spoons, ice cubes, paper cups, honey, and crackers.

Cut the lemons in half and let the children help you juice them. Ask if any of the children would like a taste. (Have plastic spoons available for tasting.) They will discover lemon juice is very sour. Review Proverbs 16:24.

Use two tablespoons of lemon juice and two tablespoons of sugar for each cup of water to make lemonade. Make enough for the whole class. Also serve crackers spread with honey.

Which tastes better, lemon juice or lemonade? Yes, of course, the lemonade tastes better because it is sweet.

Do you think it is sweeter to tell the truth or tell a lie?

When is a good time to tell the truth? (All the time.)

Why is it best to always tell the truth? (God wants us to tell the truth, it pleases Him, it pleases our parents.)

Even when it is hard or we think we'll be in trouble, God is pleased when we tell the truth.

▼ 4. What Can I Do to Please God? ▲

Tell the Truth

You will need a piece of poster board, crayons or markers, a copy of the "Tell the Truth Mouth" from p. 305 for each child, scissors, and glue. On the poster board, print "I Will Tell the Truth." Before class time, cut out a mouth for each child.

Why was Peter so sad when Jesus looked at him? (Peter had lied three times about knowing Jesus.)

How do we know Peter was sorry for telling the lies? (He cried; later, he told Jesus he really did love Him.)

After Jesus went back to Heaven, Peter became a very brave preacher. He traveled to many cities and told everyone about Jesus. He really did love Jesus. He was telling the truth!

God wants us to tell the truth, too. Here is a paper mouth for each of you. Color the lips and then print your name inside. Give help as needed.

Show the poster and read the title. Ask each child to come up, one at a time, and glue his mouth on the poster. Ask each child to say, "I will tell the truth." When all the children have had a turn, join hands and pray. Ask God to help them tell the truth even when they are afraid.

Happy Mouth Puppet

You will need copies of the "Happy Mouth Puppet" from p. 305, crayons or markers, scissors, paper lunch sacks, glue, and the words to "If You're a Follower of Jesus" from p. 283. Before class, cut out a mouth for each child.

When we tell the truth, we are saying words that please God.

Give each child a mouth to color. Cut between the teeth and bottom lip to separate the lips, and help the children glue the top half of the mouth onto the part of a paper sack that will move up and down. Let the children use their puppets to say words that are true. For example, each child can tell his name or a favorite food or something he knows about Jesus.

Then give each child a turn to choose to tell the truth this week.

Who will choose to tell the truth this week? (Each child can respond using his happy mouth puppet.)

What Bible words can remind us to follow Jesus by telling the truth? (Recite the Bible words from 1 Peter together.)

Let's sing a song to help us remember to follow Jesus this week. (Children can sing using their puppets. Sing the first three verses of the unit song.)

A Jailer Is Kind

Acts 16:23-34

what is good.
Feel: Eager to follow Jesus.
Do: Make right choices.

Children will accomplish the goals when they
- Explore actions to copy.
- Tell why a jailer became a follower of Jesus.
- Recite 1 Peter 2:21 and tell one way to follow Jesus' example.
- Name ways to follow Jesus.
- Follow Jesus.

▼ 1. What Is This Story About? ▲

Copycats

Explain to the children that they are going to be copycats. Ask another adult to help you demonstrate several actions.

If you have a younger brother or sister, you know what a copycat is. Your little brother or sister probably likes to do everything you do. If you have an older brother or sister, you probably like doing what they do. They might even call you a copycat if what you are doing bugs them. Are there any copycats in your house? Encourage the children to give personal examples.

When you are playing with your friends, you might copy the things they are doing. It can be fun to do the same things if what you are doing is something good. What might happen if you copy a friend who is doing something wrong? Yes, your parents will not be happy with you or your friend. You must learn to think about your actions. Are you doing something safe? Are you hurting someone or something? Are you obeying your parents or teachers?

Sometimes it is OK to copy what someone else is doing—in fact, that's how we learn to do new things. Your mom might show you how to set the table, and then you copy her. Your brother might show you how to ride a skateboard, and then you copy him. When we make things here in class, I show you how to do it, and then you copy me. That is OK, isn't it? That is good copying.

But if your friend starts to run out into the street to get a ball, should you copy him? What might happen if you don't stop to think first?

Stand up and let's be copycats. I will say "Copycats" before I do the action. You think about what I've done and decide whether it is a good thing to do or a bad thing to do. Be a copycat only if the action is good.

Use these actions or make up your own:

Negative actions—mad face, stomp feet, beg, whine, make a fist, pretend to kick something, pretend to push someone, say "I don't like you."

Positive actions—smile, skip, say "I'm sorry," hug your neighbor, pretend to pick up something and put it on a shelf, pretend to dust, say "Please," say "I love you."

At the end of the game, compliment the children on being good copycats. **In our Bible story, we are going to hear about a jailer who saw Paul and Silas do something good. He decided to be like them and become a follower of Jesus.**

▼ 2. What Does the Bible Say? ▲

Bible Story: A Jailer Becomes a Follower of Jesus

You will need the completed Jailer puppet from p. 302, or use a real person dressed as the jailer. Use the puppet or person to tell the story from the jailer's point of view.

Hello, boys and girls. I am another person from the Bible. You met Zacchaeus and Peter during the last two classes. Do you remember what

Jesus said and did for Zacchaeus? Do you remember why Peter was sorry?

Let me tell you how I became a follower of Jesus. I am the guard of a jail. My job is to keep people who have broken the laws locked up so they can't run away and break more laws.

Late one night, two men were brought to my jail. Their names were Paul and Silas. A lot of people were angry with these men. They were mad because Paul and Silas were teaching about God and Jesus. The angry people wanted them punished. The judge told some soldiers to beat Paul and Silas and put them in jail. That is when I first saw them. Their bodies were covered with bruises and cuts. Usually the men who come here have done very bad things. No one expects to be treated nicely. My job was to put wooden blocks around their feet so they couldn't run away.

Most prisoners complain about the tight chains and wooden blocks. They complain about their cuts and bruises. Well, Paul and Silas were not like the other prisoners. Instead of complaining, they prayed and sang songs about God. They prayed and sang for a long time, but no one asked them to stop singing. Do you think the other prisoners liked the songs, too?

Suddenly, while Paul and Silas were singing, the earth began to shake. It was an earthquake! The walls and floor of the jail jerked up and down. Everything started falling. The locks on the doors of the jail broke and the doors flew open. Even the chains and the wooden blocks fell off the arms and legs of all the prisoners. Paul and Silas and the rest of the prisoners were free. If they wanted to, they could walk right out of that jail.

I was asleep when the earthquake started, but my shaking bed woke me up. I ran to the place where the prisoners were kept. When I saw the jail doors open, I was very afraid. I thought the prisoners had run away. If they were gone, I would be in trouble. Then I heard a loud voice call to me, "Don't be afraid. We are all still here." It was Paul. I grabbed a light and ran into the jail to see if it was true. It was! I was so surprised. I was shaking, but I got on my knees and bowed before Paul and Silas. Bowing is a way to say "thank you." I was very thankful that all the prisoners had not run away.

I helped Paul and Silas find their way out of the broken down jail. Then I asked them a very important question. I asked, "What do I have to do to be saved?" I wanted God to forgive me for all the wrong choices I had made. This is what Paul and Silas told me, "Believe in the Lord Jesus and you will be saved." They told me the good news about Jesus and God's love and forgiveness. That's why they were singing in jail!

I was so happy to know that God would forgive me that I did something that might have gotten me in trouble with my bosses—I took Paul and Silas home with me, fed them, and washed their sores. I also wanted them to tell me and my family more about Jesus. The good news about Jesus made me so happy. That very night, everyone in my family believed in Jesus and was baptized.

> **How to Say It**
> Silas: SIGH-luss

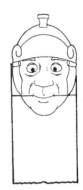

Story Review: Edible Chains

You will need an eighteen-ounce jar of creamy peanut butter, six tablespoons of honey, a box of non-fat powered milk, flour, and a roll of waxed paper.

Mix the peanut butter and honey together. Add the dry milk until it is play dough consistency. A little flour may be added to make the dough easier to handle.

Ask the children to wash their hands and wash the tables. Give each child a ball of dough and a sheet of waxed paper. Show the children how to make chains (links) out of the dough. Review the Bible story while they are making the chains.

Why were Paul and Silas put in jail?

What was the jailer's job?

What happened when the earthquake came?
Did Paul and Silas run away?
Why was the jailer so happy to see that Paul and Silas were still there?
What did the jailer do then?
What did Paul and Silas tell the jailer about Jesus?
What did the jailer do that shows he wanted to follow Jesus?
Let the children eat their creations after praying.

Bible Memory: Jesus Is a Good Example for Me

You will need an overhead projector to show the transparency of 1 Peter 2:21 in sign language (or use the poster).

There are many deaf people in the world. They need to know about Jesus just as people who can hear need to know about Jesus. People who cannot hear can learn about Jesus if someone signs the words. When you learn to sign, you are doing something that can help others. Signing is a good thing to copy and do.

Review each sign of 1 Peter 2:21. Give help as needed. By this lesson, the children should be able to copy the signs fairly well. Turn off the projector or turn the poster over. Recite and sign the verse together.

Our Bible words remind us to follow Jesus—copy Him.

What is something Jesus did or said that you want to copy/follow?

▼ 3. What Does this Mean to Me? ▲

I Will Follow Jesus

You will need the list of positive actions from the "Copycats" activity.

When the jailer chose to be kind to Paul and Silas, he pleased God. When he chose to believe and follow Jesus, he pleased God. When you are kind and follow Jesus, you please God, too. Let's make a circle and sing a song about following Jesus.

Teach the following words to the tune of "Here We Go 'Round the Mulberry Bush."
Jesus is pleased when I follow Him, follow Him, follow Him.
Jesus is pleased when I follow Him. I'll follow every day.

Select one child to stand in the center and act out a way to follow Jesus (being kind, helping, signing Bible words, showing love). Give help as needed, using the positive actions from the "Copycats" activity.

I Am Sorry

Teach the following words to the tune of "Ring Around the Rosy."
I made someone sad today.
Now he doesn't want to play.
I am sorry.
Please forgive me!
When the children know the words, sing the song as everyone walks in a circle. When the children say, "Please forgive me!" have them fall down, just as in the traditional song.

Then sing these words:
I made someone glad today.
Now he always wants to play.
I am happy.
I'm following Jesus!
When we are unkind to our friends, they become sad and do not want to play. Remember to say you are sorry and ask your friends to forgive you.

Bible Words
"Christ . . . gave you an example to follow. [So you should do as he did.]" (1 Peter 2:21).

(Note: This verse has been divided into two parts. If you are teaching four-year-olds, use only the first part. If you are teaching older children, also include the part of the verse in brackets.)

We are following Jesus when we ask others to forgive us. We are following Jesus when we forgive others, too.

What are some other ways to follow Jesus?

▼ 4. What Can I Do to Please God? ▲

A Change of Heart

You will need the heart-shaped card from p. 304, white card stock, and crayons or markers. Copy and cut out one heart card for each child.

When you choose to follow Jesus, your heart changes. Instead of wanting to do wrong, you want to do what is right. Instead of disobeying, you obey. Instead of saying unkind words, you say kind words.

Show the heart card and read what it says on the inside. Ask the children to think of someone they need to tell they are sorry. Pass out the cards and let the children color them. Help each child print the name of the person on the front flaps.

The jailer had a change of heart, too. When he saw that Paul and Silas did not run away when their chains fell off, he took them home and washed their sores. God is pleased when we want to follow Jesus. The person who receives your card will be glad that you want to do what is right. Let's pray and ask God to help us follow Jesus this week. Model a short prayer: **Dear God, thank You for Jesus. Help me follow Him this week.** Then give each child an opportunity to pray.

You Are Forgiven

You will need the words to "If You're a Follower of Jesus" from p. 283.

Review the words to the first three verses of this song. Review the importance of telling the truth and saying kind words. Ask the children to name some words that are "sweet as honey."

The Bible tells us God will forgive us for the things we have done wrong. When we are sorry and really mean it in our hearts, God will forgive us. Think about what happened the last time you disobeyed your mom or dad. Did you tell them you were sorry? Did you tell God you were sorry for disobeying your parent?

Show me what your face looks like before you say you are sorry. Now show me what your face looks like after you say you are sorry. Wow! You have a big smile on your face.

Teach verse four of "If You're a Follower of Jesus." Then sing all four verses again.

How did Paul and Silas follow Jesus in the jail? (Sang, prayed, helped the jailer, told the jailer about Jesus.)

How did the jailer follow Jesus? (Believed in Jesus, was kind to Paul and Silas.)

How will you follow Jesus this week? (Give each child an opportunity to respond.)

Let's pray together. Pray, asking God to help each child follow Jesus this week by being kind.

Onesimus Does What Is Right

Philemon

Know: Following Jesus means choosing to do what is good.
Feel: Eager to follow Jesus.
Do: Make right choices.

Children will accomplish the goals when they

- Explore times to do right.
- Tell what Onesimus did that was right.
- Recite and explain 1 Peter 2:21.
- Talk about a way to follow Jesus.
- Follow Jesus by forgiving others.

▼ 1. What Is This Story About? ▲

Choosing to Do Right

You will need a copy of p. 306 for each child, crayons or markers, scissors, and a stapler. Before class, copy and cut apart p. 306 for each child. Trim the borders so each section of the page is the same size. Staple the four sections together in order to make a booklet.

Give each child a booklet. Before you ask them to color the pages, talk about each picture.

What is the little girl doing in the first picture?
Is she choosing to do something right or something wrong?
What is happening in the second picture?
Why do you think she is crying?
What do you think her mother said?
What would you tell your mother? What would you do?
What is the little boy doing with the cat?
Is he choosing to do something right or something wrong?
What is happening in the next picture?
Why do you think he is crying?
What do you thing his father said?
What would you tell your father? What would you do?

Distribute crayons and ask the children to color their booklets. **Our books will help us remember to do what is right and be sorry when we do what is wrong.**

Let's Be Friends

You will need two adults or teens to do the following role plays, building blocks, and some cookies in a paper lunch sack.

1. Two people are playing with blocks. One person takes a block away from the other. They argue over the block. Finally, they turn their backs to each other and say, "Let's be enemies!" Ask the children to tell how to solve the problem. Invite them to coach the actors in what to do and say.

2. Two people have one sack of cookies. They argue over who gets the biggest cookie in the sack. They both grab the paper sack and pull. They say, "Let's be enemies." Suddenly the sack rips and the cookies fall on the floor. Invite the children to coach the actors in what to do and say to settle the argument.

You have learned a lot about being kind and saying, "I'm sorry." You gave our actors some very good ideas. God is pleased when we choose to do what is right. He does not want us to be enemies. He wants us to be kind to everyone—even people who are mean to us. He wants us to forgive those who have been unkind to us.

▼ 2. What Does the Bible Say? ▲

Bible Story: Paul Says, "Please Forgive Him"

You will need the completed Onesimus puppet from p. 302 or a real person dressed as Onesimus. Use the puppet or the person to tell the story from Onesimus' point of view.

Hello, boys and girls, my name is Onesimus. I am a slave. A slave is a person who belongs to another person and must do whatever that person says. My name, Onesimus, means "useful," but I was not very useful to my owner. I ran away.

I do not want you to think my owner is a bad person, because he isn't. His name is Philemon. He is a good man who loves Jesus. He even has a church meeting in his house. That is where I first saw a man named Paul. This is the same Paul the jailer told you about in the last lesson. He is a traveling preacher who goes from town to town telling people about Jesus.

Well, I heard Paul preach in Philemon's home, but I did not become a believer then. I was too angry. I did not want to be a slave, so I ran away. I went all the way to the big city of Rome. It took me a long time to get there, because in Bible times most travelers walked.

When I got to Rome, I saw Paul again. This time, he was in prison. There was a soldier chained to him so he couldn't get away. He was locked in these chains because he preached about Jesus. Some people who did not believe in Jesus thought this would stop Paul from preaching. It did not work. Paul kept on preaching, and I am glad he did. This time I wanted to hear what Paul said about Jesus, His love, and forgiveness.

One day I decided to become a follower of Jesus. This made Paul very happy. Every day he told me more and more about Jesus. I was happy, too, but there was a part of me that was sad. It was wrong of me to run away from Philemon, so Paul wrote Philemon a letter. He told Philemon that I was now a follower of Jesus. I was now very useful—just as my name says. Paul asked Philemon to let me be useful to him, too. Paul loved me so much that he called me his son. He even told Philemon that he would pay him if I owed him money. Paul was a very good friend to me. Paul and I hope Philemon will forgive me.

Story Review: Traveling Bag

You will need a small suitcase or a backpack and eight items that a person would take on a trip (things like a pair of pants, socks, shirt, toothbrush, comb).

Copy the following questions onto white paper. Cut the questions into strips and pin or tape one question strip on each of the eight items and put them in the travel bag you have selected.

What does the name "Onesimus" mean?
What was Onesimus' job title?
What had Onesimus done to his owner?
Where did Onesimus meet Paul?
What did Paul think about Onesimus?
What did Paul teach Onesimus?
Why did Paul send Onesimus back to Philemon?
What did Paul want Philemon to do for Onesimus?

Ask the children what they use to carry their things in when they go on a trip. If someone names the kind of bag you have say, **"Do you mean a bag like this one?"** Let's see what's in my bag. Rummage around in the bag as if you are looking for something. Look frustrated and ask a child to help you pull any item out of your bag. When the child pulls out the item, act surprised to see the question strip. Read it and encourage the children to answer the question. Continue until all the items have been pulled out and all the questions answered. Let the children help repack the bag. **I'm glad that Onesimus chose to do the right thing and go back to Philemon.**

Bible Memory: I Will Follow

You will need the transparency of 1 Peter 2:21 and an overhead projector, or use the poster.

Our Bible words remind us to follow Jesus. Let's say them together.

Review each sign. Give help as needed. By this lesson, the children may not need the projected signs or poster. Recite and sign the verse together. Encourage individual children to say the verse alone.

What example did Christ give us? (Let children respond. Include the things Jesus did that we can do: loved people, helped, was kind, did what was right, prayed to God, and so on.)

If Jesus was kind, should we be kind?

If Jesus was helpful, should we be helpful?

If Jesus forgave people, should we forgive people?

What are some other ways to follow Jesus' example?

Forgiveness

You will need a shoebox, colorful wrapping paper, scissors, an X-Acto knife, bright bow, colorful yarn, 6" squares of colored tissue paper, one broken used crayon, and a brand new crayon for each child.

Wrap the box with wrapping paper. Use an X-Acto knife to cut a 3" by 4" opening in the top. Add the bow. Tie the new crayons onto one continuous piece of yarn, one about every five inches. Insert the yarn into the box, one crayon at a time. Stuff a square of tissue paper between each crayon to hide one crayon from the other. Leave one end of the yarn hanging out the hole. Attach a card on the end of the yarn that says, "Pull."

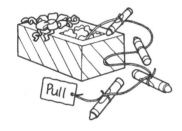

Gather the children around the brightly decorated box. Gently shake the box. **Do you like getting gifts? Of course, we all do! Sometimes I shake the box to see whether I can guess what's inside. Let the children listen as you shake the box again. Would you like to know what's inside this box?**

First, let me tell you about a special gift God has for you called forgiveness.

When you do something wrong and you tell God you are sorry, He will forgive you. Do you know why God's forgiveness is such a wonderful gift? When you have done something wrong, it makes you feel sad inside. Show a broken crayon with a ripped cover. **You are like this broken crayon. It is hard to color with a broken crayon. When you do something wrong, it is hard for you to stop thinking about the wrong thing you did. That's when you need to ask God to forgive you. He is always there to hear you say you are sorry. Then He will give you a wonderful gift called forgiveness.**

Now, would you like to see what is in this gift box? Invite the children, one at a time, to pull the string and remove a crayon. **This brand-new crayon reminds us of God's forgiveness. When God forgives us, we no longer feel like broken crayons that don't work very well. We are like brand-new crayons. We can try again to do what is right. We can feel happy like Onesimus did when he went back to Philemon.** Let each child keep the new crayon to take home.

The new crayons can remind us to forgive others just as God forgives us. This is another way to follow Jesus.

Bible Words

"Christ . . . gave you an example to follow. [So you should do as he did.]" (1 Peter 2:21).

(Note: This verse has been divided into two parts. If you are teaching four-year-olds, use only the first part. If you are teaching older children, also include the part of the verse in brackets.)

▼ 4. What Can I Do to Please God? ▲

A Gift of Forgiveness

You will need construction paper in a variety of colors, tape or stapler, hole punch, chenille wires, hole reinforcements, large mixing bowl, spoon, two small zipper-locking bags for each child, the words to the song "If You're a Follower of Jesus" from p. 283, and ingredients for trail mix: raisins, dried fruit, nuts, pretzels, small crackers, cereals, and sunflower seeds. You will need five cups of ingredients for every ten children.

We are going to make a gift you can give to a person who says to you, "I'm sorry." We can follow Jesus by forgiving people.

Let the children help add and mix the ingredients for the trail mix. Give each child two bags to fill with one-fourth cup of mix. One is for the gift; the other is to snack on while they complete the gift.

Help the children roll the paper into cones and tape or staple them securely. Punch two holes opposite each other near the top edge in the cones and attach chenille wire handles. Let the children insert their trail mix bags into their cones.

When you take this gift home today, save it in a very special place. The next time someone makes you sad and then says he is sorry, you can give him this gift when you say, "It's OK. I forgive you."

Gather the children in a circle. Sing all the verses of "If You're a Follower of Jesus." Then pray together, asking God to help each person follow Jesus this week.

Christ

Place the right "C" at the left shoulder and move to the right waist.

gave

Both hands are closed, fingertips together, facing the floor. Move them in (towards body), up, and forward, ending with palms open and facing up.

you

Point the index finger out.

example

The tip of the index finger is placed against the palm and both are moved outward.

to

Direct the right index finger toward, and then touch, the left index fingertip, which is pointing up.

follow

On both hands, fold the four fingers against the palm. Leave the thumb sticking up. Place the right hand behind the left hand and move them both forward.

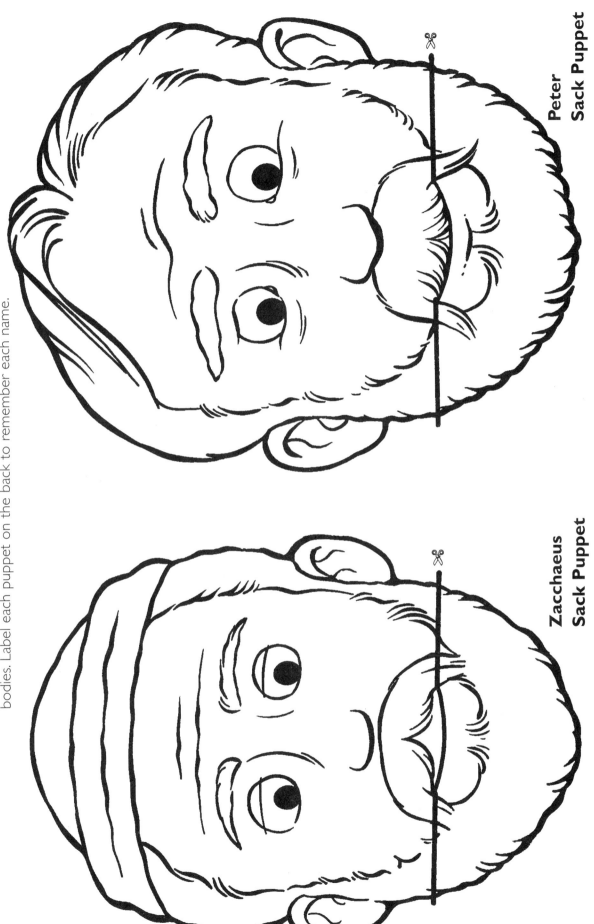

Directions

You will need a copy of the puppet faces, two sacks, scissors, crayons or markers, assorted fabric and yarn, and glue.

Cut out the two puppet faces. Color and glue the faces onto lunch sacks to make puppets. Glue on yarn for hair and fabric to make the bodies. Label each puppet on the back to remember each name.

Peter Sack Puppet

Zacchaeus Sack Puppet

Onesimus
Sack Puppet

Jailer
Sack Puppet

Directions
You will need a copy of the puppet faces, two sacks, scissors, crayons or markers, assorted fabric and yarn, and glue.
Cut out the two puppet faces. Color and glue the faces onto lunch sacks to make puppets. Glue on yarn for hair and fabric to make the bodies. Label each puppet on the back to remember each name.

"You must tell the truth." Exodus 20:16

Spinner Game

Enlarge if possible. Copy onto card stock or mount on cardboard. Color as desired and cut out. Attach a paper clip spinner in the center of the square with a paper fastener.

Fold in.   Fold in.

I'm sorry I was
unkind to you.
Please forgive me.
Thank you.
Love,

_____

Big Decision Pictures

Sachet Stickers

Tell the Truth Mouth

Directions

You will need white glue, vinegar, peppermint extract (optional), a small paintbrush, and scissors.

Mix two parts white glue and one part vinegar. Add a few drops of peppermint extract, if desired. Lightly "paint" the mixture onto the backs of the uncut stickers. Let dry. Cut out the stickers.

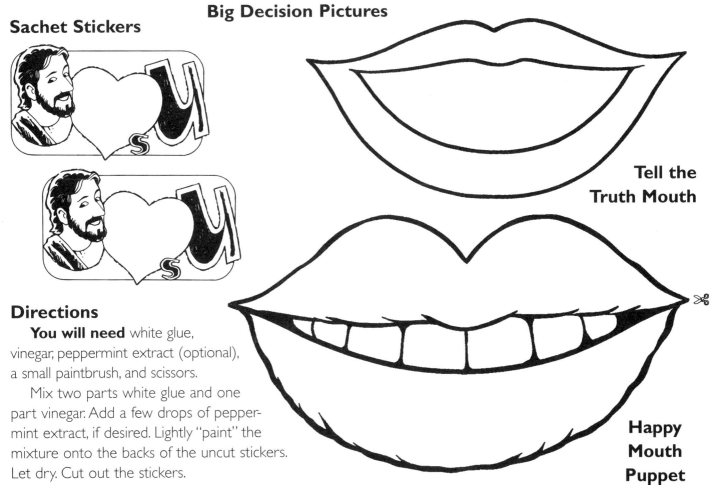

Happy Mouth Puppet

1

2

3

4

Learning to Worship Jesus

Lessons 51, 52

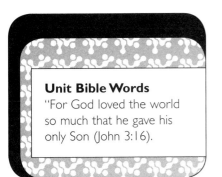

Unit Bible Words
"For God loved the world so much that he gave his only Son (John 3:16).

51 Let's Worship Jesus; He is Born!

Genesis 3; Luke 2:1-20; Matthew 2:1-12—The story of Christmas begins in the Garden of Eden. Adam and Eve disobey God and are banished. God does not leave them without hope. He promises to send a Savior. This promise is fulfilled when Jesus is born. Everyone who sees baby Jesus is happy and worships Him. Let's worship the Savior, too!

52 Let's Worship Jesus; He is Alive!

Matthew 28:1-10; Mark 16:1-11—Jesus, God's Son, grows to be a man. Everywhere He goes people come to hear Him speak about God and heal the sick. Many people believe in Him. However, some Jewish leaders do not. They are angry because He claims to be the promised Savior. They crucify Him. But the good news is Jesus does not stay dead in the tomb. He is alive!

By the end of this unit, the children and leaders will

Know: Jesus is the Son of God.
Feel: a sense of awe because of who Jesus is.
Do: Worship Jesus and tell others about Him.

Why Teach This Unit to Four- to Six-Year-Olds?

This unit contains only two lessons. One is for Christmas; the other is for Easter. Even though they will be taught four months apart, they have a common theme—Worship Jesus. The lessons also share a common memory verse—John 3:16. The focus of each lesson will be around a worship center where the children will give Jesus the honor and praise they know He deserves.

Use these lessons to create a worshipful environment in the midst of rowdy seasonal festivities that can draw attention away from the true meaning of Christian celebrations. Children the age of your students are ready to be taught the true meanings of Christmas and Easter.

Four-, five-, and six-year-olds can worship. Their tender hearts and receptive spirits embrace Jesus. Their sincere faith in Him is something many adults would like to recapture.

Meet Mary and Joseph

Mary and Joseph lived in the town of Nazareth in Galilee. They were engaged to be married when an angel told Mary that she was going to be the mother of God's Son. Joseph, a carpenter and a descendant of King David, was also told about this miraculous birth. Mary and Joseph willingly accepted this awesome responsibility. Mary responded to the news by worshiping God with a song of praise.

Meet the Shepherds

Bible-time shepherds made a humble living. Their life was usually quite peaceful. Sheep are mild and obedient animals, but they do require constant supervision and protection. An occasional wolf or bear brought excitement to the sheepfold.

During these times it could be quite dangerous to be a shepherd. God chose to announce the birth of the Savior of the world to common shepherds, taking care of their sheep outside of Bethlehem. They immediately went to Bethlehem and worshiped baby Jesus.

Meet the Wise Men

Often referred to as Magi or astrologers, some wise men from the east recognized a new star in the sky. Being familiar with Old Testament prophecies, they followed it, looking for the new king of the Jews. The star guided them to a house where they worshiped Jesus with gifts of gold, frankincense, and myrrh.

Meet Jesus

God made a promise in the garden to Adam and Eve. He promised to send a Savior who would punish Satan for deceiving them. After many years of waiting, the promise was fulfilled. God sent His only Son to be born of a virgin in Bethlehem. He was named Jesus, which means Savior. Jesus was born in a humble stable. His birth was announced to some shepherds and wise men. They came looking for the Savior and King. When they saw Him, they bowed in honor and adoration. They were in the presence of God.

Christmas Bell Pictures

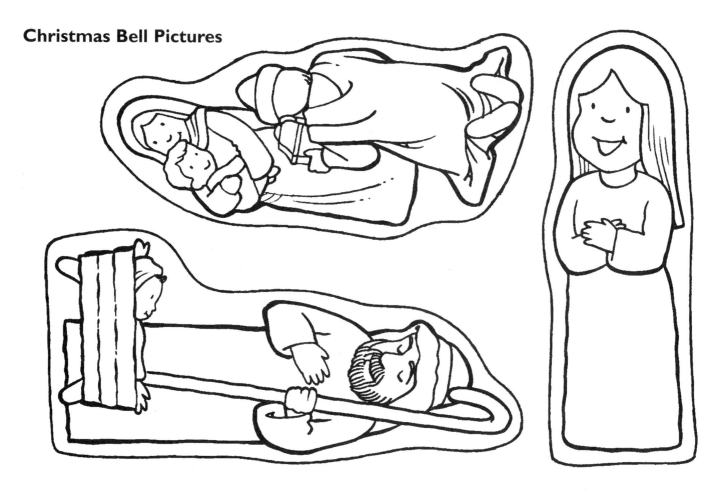

Let's Worship Jesus; He Is Born!

Genesis 3; Luke 2:1-20; Matthew 2:1-12

▼ 1. What Is This Story About? ▲

A Christmas Worship Center

You will need a small area for a worship center, and include in it a table, Bible, string of Christmas lights, small doll wrapped in a plain white blanket, and a manger with hay. The manger can be a plain brown cardboard box filled with shredded brown paper.

Gather the children around the collected items. **We celebrate Christmas to remember the day Jesus was born. We have some items here that will help us worship Jesus. How can these things help us worship Jesus?** (Let the children respond. Suggest these ideas: the Bible tells us how special Jesus is; He was given a special name; angels announced His birth; people came to worship Him; He was given special gifts; there was a special star in the sky; the Christmas lights remind us of the star in the sky; the baby and manger remind us where Jesus was born.)

How do you and your families celebrate and worship Jesus at Christmas?

There are many ways to worship Jesus and tell Him how much we love Him. After our story today, we will use this worship center to sing and praise God for sending Jesus.

Worship Jesus With Praise

You will need the words to "Our Savior's Born" from p. 312 and other familiar songs about Jesus' birth.

We can worship Jesus in many ways. What are some ways you know to worship Jesus? (Sing, pray, praise, give.)

Let's learn a song that tells about Jesus' birth. We will sing it later to worship Jesus at the worship center.

Teach the new song, "Our Savior's Born," and sing other songs about Jesus' birth.

▼ 2. What Does the Bible Say? ▲

Bible Story: God Keeps His Promise

Use figures from a crèche to tell the story. If possible, use figures that the children can handle. Most fabric stores carry a cloth Christmas story panel that can be cut out, machine sewn, and stuffed with polyester filler. This makes a wonderful crèche for children. As the story is told, add the figures.

When God made the earth and filled it with trees, flowers, and animals, He had a plan. He wanted a special place for His people to live. When everything was ready, God made a man and a woman. Their names were Adam and Eve. He loved them very much. He gave them everything they needed and a beautiful garden in which to live.

Then something terrible happened. Adam and Eve disobeyed God. They sinned. God said they could not live in the beautiful garden anymore. He

---

Sidebar

Know: Jesus is the Son of God.

Feel: A sense of awe because of who Jesus is.

Do: Worship Jesus and tell others about Him.

Children will accomplish the goals when they
- Explore ways to worship Jesus.
- Tell about Jesus' birth.
- Memorize John 3:16.
- Tell what is special about Jesus.
- Worship Jesus, God's Son.

also said they would grow old and die. It was a very sad day when Adam and Eve left the garden, but God gave them a promise. He said He would send someone, a Savior, to take away sin.

After many years, the Savior came. God sent an angel to tell a young woman named Mary she was to have a baby boy. The angel told her to name the baby Jesus. He would be the Savior God had promised. This baby would be the Son of God. Mary was so happy that she sang a beautiful song worshiping God for keeping His promise to send a Savior.

Mary was going to marry a man named Joseph. The angel also visited Joseph and told him the good news about the special baby. Mary and Joseph were happy God had kept His promise to send the Savior.

Mary and Joseph had to go on a long trip to Bethlehem. While they were there, Jesus was born. God's promise came true. He sent His only Son to be the Savior.

Mary and Joseph stayed in a stable and used an animal's feeding box, called a manger, for Jesus' crib. They only had strips of cloth to wrap around Him. Still they were happy the Savior was born.

The same night Jesus was born, God sent His angels to tell the good news to some shepherds. The shepherds were taking care of their sheep when an angel visited them and said, "Do not be afraid! I have good news for you. The Savior has been born in Bethlehem. You will find Him wrapped in a blanket and lying in a manger."

The shepherds were happy God had kept His promise to send the Savior. They left their sheep and ran to Bethlehem looking for the special baby. When they found Mary and Joseph, they saw the baby wrapped in cloths and lying in a manger. What the angel had said was true. They were so happy! On the way back to their sheep, the shepherds praised and thanked God for their Savior.

(Remove the shepherds and the stable, if you've used one.)

When Jesus was born, a special star appeared in the sky. Some wise men were studying the night sky when they saw this new star shining brightly. They knew the star was part of God's promise to send a Savior, so they followed it. It took them many months to get from their home to Bethlehem, and by that time Mary and Joseph had found a house to live in. The star led the wise men to the house where Jesus lived with his mother and father. When the wise men saw Jesus, they bowed down, gave Him their gifts, and worshiped Him. They were happy that God had kept His promise.

Story Review: Let's Tell About Jesus

You will need the crèche figures from the Bible story.

Distribute the crèche figures to the children, one figure per child. Ask the children with the figures to tell about that part of the Bible story. Ask the children without a figure to be good listeners so they can tell the story next. When the first group of children are finished telling the story, ask them to give the figures to someone who did not have one. Then ask the second group of children to tell about the story again. Challenge them to include details that were missed the first time. Continue telling the story with the crèche figures until each child has a turn to participate.

What is your favorite part of the story of Jesus' birth? Why?

Bible Memory: Ring Out the Good News

You will need a large jingle bell or several small bells tied together with ribbon, and a Bible.

Have the children form a circle. Read John 3:16 from the Bible. Repeat the verse several times. Add these motions to help the children remember the words.

For God *(Point up.)*
loved *(Hug yourself.)*

Bible Words
"For God loved the world so much that he gave his only Son" (John 3:16).

the world (*Make a large circle with both arms.*)
so much (*Spread arms wide.*)
that he gave (*Pretend to give.*)
his only son." (*Pretend to hold a baby.*)
John 3:16
This verse tells us how much God loves us. He loves us so much that He sent Jesus to earth to be our Savior.

Give one child the jingle bell. Ask the child to say the first word of the verse and ring the bell. The child then passes the bell to the person on his right. This child says the next word and rings the bell. Continue passing the bell around the circle, ringing it, and saying the words until the entire verse is recited.

▼ 3. What Does This Mean to Me? ▲

Christmas Bell

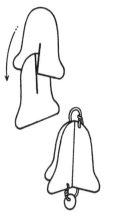

You will need the bell pattern from p. 317, green or red card stock, the bell pictures from p. 308, white paper, scissors, hole punch, yarn, crayons, small jingle bells and the words to "Our Savior's Born" from p. 312.

Before class, copy a bell for each child onto colored card stock. Cut out the bells and cut the slit in each bell piece. Punch holes where indicated.

Copy a set of pictures for each child and cut them out. Cut the yarn into 4" strips, making two for each child.

We're going to make a Christmas bell to remind us of the good news about Jesus.

Show the children how to join the two bell pieces by slipping the slits together. Let them color the pictures and glue them on where indicated with broken lines. While the children are coloring, tie one piece of yarn onto the top of each bell for a hanger. String a jingle bell onto the other piece of yarn and tie it onto the bottom of the bell. Involve the children as much as possible.

When you hear a Christmas bell, what does it remind you of?
What is the good news about Jesus?
What are some things you know about Jesus that you can tell someone?
(Give the children time to respond. Include these ideas: Jesus is God's Son; Jesus was a special baby; Jesus came to be our Savior; wise men worshiped Jesus; wise men gave Him special gifts; the angel told Mary Jesus would have a special name; angels announced Jesus' birth to the shepherds.)

Let's move our bells while we sing a song about Jesus' birth. Sing "Our Savior's Born."

Ring the Bell, Tell the Good News

You will need jingle bells strung on yarn for each group.

Divide the class into teams of no more than five children. Provide yarn with jingle bells for each team. Line up the teams. Place the bells opposite each team, about ten feet away. At the signal, send the first child on each team to his team's jingle bells. Each child will pick up the bells and shake them, saying, **"Our Savior's born. Come and see!"**

Continue until everyone has had a turn. Then repeat the relay, changing the sentence when the bell is rung. Use sentences that tell something special about Jesus, such as "Jesus has a special name," "An angel told about Jesus' birth," "Wise men worshiped Jesus," "Jesus is God's Son!"

Do you know someone who needs to hear the good news about Jesus' birth?
What can you tell this person about Jesus?

▼ 4. What Can I Do to Please God? ▲

Let's Worship Jesus

You will need a white construction paper heart for each child, crayons, the worship center with baby and manger used during "A Christmas Worship Center," the words to "Our Savior's Born" from p. 312, and other familiar songs about Jesus' birth.

When God sent His Son to earth, the first people to know about the birth of Jesus and see Him were very happy. They showed their happiness by worshiping. Mary worshiped by singing. The shepherds worshiped by saying words of praise and thanksgiving. The wise men worshiped by giving gifts.

Let's worship too. We can sing. We can say words of praise and pray. We can give gifts. Did you know that you have a gift you can give Jesus right now? You do not need to go to the store and buy it or get a present from under your Christmas tree. This gift is with you wherever you go. It is your heart. Pass out the white paper hearts and crayons. Let the children decorate their hearts and print their names on them.

Let's take our hearts and go to our special worship center. Let's worship Jesus together. (You may want to collect the hearts and pass them out later.)

First, let's worship by singing songs as Mary did. Sing "Our Savior's Born" and any other familiar songs about Jesus' birth.

Now, let's worship the way the shepherds did. Let's praise and thank God for what He gives us. We can praise Him for His Son. What else can we praise God for? Let the children respond with words of praise for families, legs that can run, and so on.

How did the wise men worship baby Jesus? Yes, they brought Him gifts. Here is our baby Jesus in a manger, and here are our hearts. (Pass out the paper hearts if they were collected.) **Let's put our hearts in this manger. Our hearts are the best gifts we can give to Jesus.** Line the children up and let them walk by the manger, placing their hearts in the manger as their gift to Jesus. Sing about Jesus' birth while the children do this. Then gather the children around the manger and pray.

Our Savior's Born
(Tune: "Twinkle, Twinkle, Little Star")

Listen, listen, sing along
with the bells a happy song.
Hear them ringing joyfully.
Christ is born. Come and
see.
Listen, listen, sing along
with the bells a happy song.

▼ Bonus Activity ▲

Snack Attack! Christmas Cookies

You will need to prepare and bake sugar cookies in the shape of bells, or order plain bell cookies from a bakery. You will also need frosting, candy sprinkles, plastic sandwich bags, and jumbo craft sticks.

Be sure the children wash their hands before beginning this project. Let them spread the frosting on the cookies and decorate with sprinkles. Put some of the decorated cookies in sandwich bags for the children to take home to their families.

Pray before the children eat their cookies.

Christmas is a special time to give gifts to others. Your family will enjoy the Christmas cookies you decorated.

Who gave us the best gift at Christmas time? Yes, God did, because He gave us His only Son to be our Savior.

Let's Worship Jesus; He Is Alive!

LESSON 52

Matthew 28:1-10; Mark 16:1-11

▼ 1. What Is This Story About? ▲

An Easter Worship Center

You will need a small area for a worship center, and include in it a table, Bible, real or silk flowers, plastic vase, two small tree limbs, and twine.

Gather the children around the collected items. Show the tree limbs and twine. Guide the children in using the items to make a cross.

We celebrate Easter to remember the day Jesus came back to life. We have some items here that will help us worship Jesus. How can these things help us worship Jesus? (Let the children respond. Suggest these ideas: the Bible tells us how special Jesus is; He died and came back to life; the flowers remind of new life in the spring; the limbs and twine cross remind us where Jesus died.)

How do you and your families celebrate and worship Jesus at Easter?

There are many ways to worship Jesus and tell Him how much we love Him. After our story today, we will use this worship center to sing and praise God for sending Jesus.

Sing Songs of Praise

You will need the words to "Jesus Lives, O Come and See" from p. 316 and other familiar songs about Jesus' love and resurrection.

We can worship Jesus in many ways. What are some ways you know to worship Jesus? (Sing, pray, praise, give.)

Let's learn a song that tells about the most special thing Jesus ever did. We will sing it later to worship Jesus at the worship center.

Teach the new song, "Jesus Lives, O Come and See," and sing other songs about Jesus' resurrection and love.

▼ 2. What Does the Bible Say? ▲

Bible Story: Jesus Is Alive!

You will need a plastic produce basket (such as for strawberries or mushrooms), a Bible, six small plastic Easter eggs, a permanent marker, a small plastic baby (found at party or craft stores), a small red paper heart or heart sticker, a small leaf, a small cross made from chenille wire, and a small stone. The last five items need to be small enough to fit inside the plastic eggs. (Optional: Provide a basket and eggs with enclosed items for each child.)

Use a permanent marker to write the numerals 1-6 on each egg. Place these items in numbered eggs as follows: 1-baby, 2-heart, 3-leaf, 4-cross, 5-stone, 6-empty

Today is a special day. We are celebrating Easter. Families have different ways of celebrating Easter. Many children wear new clothes on Easter and hunt for eggs. Those things can be a lot of fun.

Today, let's talk about the true meaning of Easter. The Bible tells us why Easter is important. (Open your Bible. Choose a child to open egg 1 with a baby inside.) **What is in your egg? Yes, it is a baby. This baby reminds us the**

Know: Jesus is the Son of God.

Feel: A sense of awe because of who Jesus is.

Do: Worship Jesus and tell others about Him.

Children will accomplish the goals when they

- Explore ways to worship Jesus.
- Tell about the time Jesus came back to life.
- Memorize John 3:16.
- Tell what is special about Jesus.
- Worship Jesus, God's Son.

Easter story begins at Christmas. God sent His only Son, Jesus, to be our Savior. Jesus came as a tiny baby. He grew up to be a man. He was a good teacher. He taught people how to live so they would please God. (*Place egg 1 with the baby inside in the berry basket.*)

As a man, Jesus did many wonderful things. Let's open another egg. (*Select another child to open egg 2 with a heart inside.*) This heart reminds us that Jesus loves every person. He made sick people well. He helped bad people change and start doing good. He told people about God's love. (*Place egg 2 with the heart inside in the basket.*)

Many people loved Jesus. (*Ask a child to open egg 3 with a leaf inside.*) On a special day we call Palm Sunday, Jesus rode a donkey into Jerusalem. The men, women, and children gathered along the road and waved palm leaves. They were happy He had come to be their king. People spread their coats and leaves on the ground so His donkey could walk on a special carpet. Everyone shouted, "God bless the king who comes in the name of the Lord!" It was a very happy day for everyone. (*Place egg 3 with the leaf inside in the basket.*)

This happy day was soon followed by a very sad day. (*Ask a child to open egg 4 with a cross inside.*) Some men who did not love Jesus put Him on a cross. They did not believe He was God's Son. They wanted Him to die. This was part of God's plan to save all people from their sins. (*Place egg 4 with the cross inside in the basket.*)

When Jesus died, one of His followers placed His body in a tomb that was like a small cave. (*Let a child open egg 5 with a stone inside.*) A large stone covered the door to the tomb. Some soldiers stood in front of the stone. No one was allowed to move the stone.

Jesus' body was in the tomb for three days. On Sunday, the day we call Easter, some women went to Jesus' tomb. They loved Jesus very much. Suddenly, the earth shook and the big stone rolled away from the tomb. The women were very frightened. An angel sat on the big stone. He said, "Do not be afraid. I know you are looking for Jesus. He is not here. He has come back to life just as He said He would. Come and see where His body was." (*Place egg 5 with the stone inside in the basket.*)

When the women looked in the tomb, this is what they saw. (*Ask a child to open the last egg, which is empty.*) What is in this egg? It is empty, just as the tomb was. Jesus did not stay dead. He came back to life. What a happy day! The women ran to tell their friends the good news. Jesus is alive! (*Place egg 6 in the basket.*)

Story Review: Hear the Easter Bell!

You will need a playing area with a wall at one end and a sample set of the Easter bells the children will make later.

Put the children in a straight line facing the wall. They should be about ten to fifteen feet away. The leader will stand next to the wall, facing it with his back to the children. When the leader says, "Listen, listen! Hear the Easter bells!" the children sneak toward the wall. When the leader rings the bell, he quickly turns around and the children must freeze. The leader repeats this over and over until all the children have touched the wall.

As each child touches the wall, ask one of the following questions to review the Bible story.

What does the baby remind us of? (Jesus came as a baby.)

What does the heart remind us of? (Jesus loves us very much.)

What event does the leaf help us remember? (When the people welcomed and praised Jesus entering Jerusalem, laying clothing and leaves on the ground.)

What does the cross remind us of? (How Jesus died.)

What does the stone help us remember? (Where Jesus was buried, what covered the entrance to the tomb, what rolled away!)

What does the empty egg help us remember? (The tomb is empty, and Jesus is alive!)

Bible Memory: Is There an Echo Here?

Our Bible words remind us how much God loves us and how special Jesus is.

Ask the children whether they have ever heard an echo. If not, explain what an echo is. Also explain that an echo is not louder than the original sound. Remind the children to be good listeners and repeat what you say. Speak in soft, loud, fast, and slow tones with the children echoing each phrase.

Teacher: For God
Children: For God
Teacher: loved the world
Children: loved the world
Teacher: so much
Children: so much
Teacher: that he gave
Children: that he gave
Teacher: his only Son
Children: his only Son
Teacher: John 3:16.
Children: John 3:16.

You were good listeners. Now it is your turn to start an echo. Ask for volunteers to say phrases of the Bible words for the rest of the children to echo. Give help as needed.

Bible Words
"For God loved the world so much that he gave his only Son" (John 3:16).

▼ 3. What Does This Mean to Me? ▲

Easter Bells

You will need three 8 oz. plastic cups in pastel colors, three jingle bells, and three chenille wires for each child. You will also need a medium nail, a hammer, Easter stickers, and the words to "Jesus Lives, O Come and See" from p. 316.

Step 1: Use a nail and the hammer to punch two holes in the bottom of each cup.

Step 2: Slide a jingle bell onto a chenille wire. Place the bell in the middle of the wire and fold the wire in half.

Step 3: Twist the two chenille wire halves together about 2" from the jingle bell.

Step 4: Reaching inside the cup, insert the chenille wire ends through the holes. Pull through the holes until the chenille wires stop. Twist the two wires on the outside to lock the clapper into place.

Step 5: Make three bells for each child. Join the top wires from all three to make a handle so the bells can be rung.

Involve the children as much as possible in assembling the bells. Let the children decorate their bells with stickers.

When you hear bells ringing at Easter, what does it remind you of?

What is the good news about Jesus?

What are some things you know about Jesus that you can tell someone? (Give the children time to respond. Include these ideas: Jesus is God's Son; Jesus came to be our Savior; Jesus died and came back to life; Jesus loves us; Jesus wants us to live with Him in Heaven someday.)

Let's ring our bells while we sing a song about Jesus. Sing "Jesus Lives, O Come and See."

▼ 4. What Can I Do to Please God? ▲

Come and Worship!

You will need the worship center made earlier, the words to "Jesus Lives, O Come and See" from p. 316, and the other songs about Jesus' love and resurrection.

This is a happy day because Jesus is alive! Let's go to our worship center for a special celebration. Take the children to the worship center.

Why do we have a cross in our Easter worship center? (It reminds us that Jesus died.) **Did Jesus stay dead?** (No, He came back to life.)

Why do we have flowers at our worship center? (Yes, God made them.) **In spring, the new flowers remind us that because Jesus came back to life, we are promised a new life in Heaven, too.**

There is one more thing at our worship center. It is a Bible. Why is the Bible such a special book? (Yes, it is God's Word.) **It tells us about God's love. It tells us about Jesus, too. It also tells us about Heaven. When we read the Bible, we learn many things that help us to love and please God.**

The cross, the Bible, and the spring flowers remind us Easter is a very wonderful day. Let's worship Jesus by singing about this wonderful day. Sing a variety of songs, including "Jesus Lives, O Come and See." Have a special time of prayer, thanking God for sending His Son, Jesus, to be our Savior.

Remembering Stone

You will need a smooth, fist-size rock and a sticker with a picture of Jesus on it for each child. You will also need the words to "Jesus Lives, O Come and See."

After the children have helped clean and straighten the room, gather them in the worship center around the rocks in a pile. **In today's Easter story, we learned that a big stone was put in front of Jesus' tomb. When the earth shook and the stone rolled away, who was inside the tomb? No one! Jesus came back to life. He did not stay dead. Jesus' followers were very happy. They told everyone the good news that Jesus is alive. Here is a stone for each of you. It will remind you that the tomb was empty. Let's put a sticker of Jesus on each stone, too. Now, let's sing our song, "Jesus Lives, O Come and See."**

Close with prayer. Thank God for bringing Jesus back to life.

▼ Bonus Activity ▲

Snack Attack! Cross Cake

You will need heavy cardboard or a tray 15" x 20", aluminum foil, a cutting knife, a 9" x 13" cake, frosting, sprinkles, paper plates, plastic forks, and recorded music.

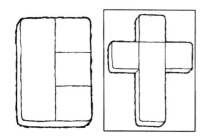

Cover the cardboard with foil. Cut the cooled cake in half lengthwise. Place one half on the foil covered cardboard. Cut the other half into three equal pieces. Add the three pieces to the cardboard, as illustrated, to make a cross. Frost the cake before class time. (Hint: To make frosting easier, freeze the cake first.)

Let the children help decorate the cake with sprinkles. Pray with the children and then cut and serve the cake. Talk with the children about the joy you have because Jesus lives. Play recorded music to add to the celebration.

Christmas Bell

cut

cut

Route 52 Road Map

Ages 3, 4

DISCOVER GOD'S LOVE (42071)

- God Is Great
- God Is Love
- God Is Good
- God Sends His Son, Jesus
- God's Son, Jesus, Grows Up
- God's Son, Jesus
- We Can Know Jesus Is Our Friend
- We Can Know Jesus Is Close to Us
- We Can Be Jesus' Helpers
- We Can Learn to Help
- We Can Learn to Share
- We Can Learn to Love God

DISCOVER GOD'S WORD (42075)

- God Made the World
- God Made People
- God Cares for Me
- Jesus Is Born
- Jesus Is God's Son
- Jesus Loves Us
- Be Thankful
- Help Jesus
- Discover About Myself
- Learn from the Bible
- Talk to God
- Help Others

Ages 4-6

EXPLORE BIBLE PEOPLE (42072)

- Learning That I Am Special (Joseph)
- Learning to Trust God (Gideon)
- Learning to Do What Is Right (Nehemiah)
- Learning to Be Brave (Esther)
- Learning to Pray Always (Daniel)
- Learning to Obey God (Jonah)
- Learning to Love People
- Learning to Be Happy
- Learning to Be Thankful
- Learning to Share
- Learning to Help Others
- Learning to Follow Jesus

EXPLORE BIBLE STORIES (42076)

- Learning About God's Creation
- Learning That God Keeps His Promises
- Learning About God's Care
- Learning About Baby Jesus
- Learning to Be a Friend Like Jesus
- Learning to Follow Jesus
- Learning About Jesus' Power
- Learning That Jesus Is the Son of God
- Learning About the Church
- Learning to Do Right
- Learning That God Is Powerful
- Learning That God Hears My Prayers

Ages 6-8

FOLLOW THE BIBLE (42073)

- The Bible Helps Me Worship God
- The Bible Teaches That God Helps People
- The Bible Helps Me Obey God
- The Bible Teaches That God Answers Prayer
- The Bible Teaches That Jesus Is the Son of God
- The Bible Teaches That Jesus Does Great Things
- The Bible Helps Me Obey Jesus
- The Bible Tells How Jesus Helped People
- The Bible Teaches Me to Tell About Jesus
- The Bible Tells How Jesus' Church Helps People

FOLLOW JESUS (42077)

- Jesus' Birth Helps Me Worship
- Jesus Was a Child Just Like Me
- Jesus Wants Me to Follow Him
- Jesus Teaches Me to Have His Attitude
- Jesus' Stories Help Me Follow Him
- Jesus Helps Me Worship
- Jesus Helps Me Be a Friend
- Jesus Helps Me Bring Friends to Him
- Jesus Helps Me Love My Family
- Jesus' Power Helps Me Worship Him
- Jesus' Miracles Help Me Tell About Him
- Jesus' Resurrection Is Good News for Me to Tell

Ages 8-12

GROW THROUGH THE BIBLE (42074)

- God's Word
- God's World
- God's Chosen People
- God's Great Nation
- The Promised Land
- The Kings of Israel
- The Kingdom Divided, Conquered
- From Jesus' Birth to His Baptism
- Jesus, the Lord
- Jesus, the Savior
- The Church Begins
- The Church Grows
- Reviewing God's Plan for His People

STUDY GOD'S PLAN (42078)

- The Bible Teaches Us How to Please God
- Books of Law Tell Us How God's People Were Led
- History and Poetry Tell About Choices God's People Made
- Prophets Reveal That God Does What He Says
- God Planned, Promised, and Provided Salvation
- Gospels Teach Us What Jesus Did
- Gospels Teach Us What Jesus Said
- Gospels Teach Us That Jesus Is Our Savior
- Acts Records How the Church Began and Grew
- Letters Instruct the Church in Right Living
- OT People and Events Prepare for God's Plan
- NT People and Events Spread God's Plan

Ages 8-12

GROW UP IN CHRIST (42080)

- Growing in Faith
- Growing in Obedience
- Growing in Attitude
- Growing in Worship
- Growing in Discipleship
- Growing in Prayer
- Growing in Goodness
- Growing in Love for Christ
- Growing in Devotion to the Church
- Growing in Grace
- Growing in Confidence
- Growing in Hope

STUDY JESUS' TEACHINGS (42079)

- Jesus Teaches Us About Who God Is
- Jesus Teaches Us That God Loves Us
- Jesus Teaches Us How to Love God
- Jesus Teaches Us About Himself
- Jesus Teaches Us to Do God's Will
- Jesus Teaches Us to Love Others
- Jesus Teaches Us About God's Kingdom
- Jesus Teaches Us How to Live Right
- Jesus Teaches Us the Truth
- Jesus Teaches Us About Forgiveness
- Jesus Teaches Us About God's Power
- Jesus Teaches Us About God's Word

A 52-Week Bible Journey . . . Just for Kids!

Ages 3 to 4

Discover God's Love

Help young children discover what God has done, thank Him for what He made, celebrate Jesus, begin to follow Jesus, and practice doing what God's Word says.

Product code: 42071

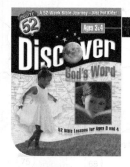

Discover God's Word

Help young children discover what God's Word says about the world, who God is, what He wants them to do, and Bible people who loved God.

Product code: 42075

Ages 4 to 6

Explore Bible People

Stories of Bible people will help children learn that they are special, how to trust God and choose to do right, how to love and obey Jesus, and how to help and share with others.

Product code: 42072

Explore Bible Stories

Bible stories will help children learn about creation, God's promises, power and care, who Jesus is and what He did, and how to follow Jesus' example and teaching.

Product code: 42076

Ages 6 to 8

Follow the Bible

Young readers will learn to follow Bible teachings as they look up Bible verses, experience basic Bible stories, and practice beginning Bible study skills.

Product code: 42073

Follow Jesus

Young learners will learn to follow Jesus as they experience stories from the Gospels. Through a variety of activities, children will worship, follow, and tell about Jesus.

Product code: 42077

Ages 8 to 12

Grow Through the Bible

Kids will grow in their understanding of God's Word as they investigate the Bible from Genesis through Paul's journeys and letters.

Product code: 42074

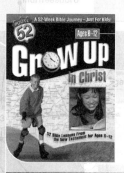

Grow Up in Christ

Kids will grow up in Christ as they explore New Testament truths about growing in faith, obedience, worship, goodness, prayer, love, devotion, grace, confidence, and hope.

Product code: 42080

Study God's Plan

Kids will study God's plan for salvation by exploring Bible people and events, Bible divisions and eras, and Bible themes and content, all while practicing Bible study skills.

Product code: 42078

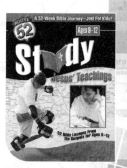

Study Jesus' Teachings

Kids will study what Jesus teaches about who God is, His love, how to love God and others, about God's kingdom, truth, forgiveness, power, God's Word, and doing His will.

Product code: 42079